A Primer of
Ecclesiastical Latin

C.R. Chapter 15

A Primer of Ecclesiastical Latin

John F. Collins

The Catholic University of America Press
Washington, D.C.

Originally published in hard cover
Reprinted with corrections in paper covers 1988

LIBRARY OF CONGRESS CATALOGING IN PUBLICATION DATA

Collins, John F., 1937–
A primer of ecclesiastical Latin.

Bibliography: p.   Includes index.
1. Latin language—Church Latin—Grammar.
2. Liturgical language—Latin.   3. Latin language,
Medieval and modern—Grammar.   4. Latin language,
Postclassical—Grammar.   5. Bible—language, style.
6. Catholic Church—Liturgy.   I. Title.
PA2823.C55   1985   477   84-22957
ISBN 0-8132-0610-3
    0-8132-0667-7 (pbk.)

Preface

Ecclesiastical Latin is a house of many mansions: in it are found the Latin of Jerome's Bible and that of canon law, the Latin of the liturgy and of the scholastic philosophers, the Latin of Ambrosian hymns and papal bulls. The list may be extended. As a sure foundation for the study of any particular form of Latin used by the Church, this text concentrates on the language of the Vulgate Bible and that of such major liturgical texts as the Mass and the Exsultet. Since in the study of Biblical and liturgical Latin the student encounters every major grammatical structure, he will feel confident of his preparation to read other kinds of ecclesiastical Latin.

The chief aim of this text is to give the student—within a year of study—the ability to read ecclesiastical Latin. Although Latin is no longer the universal language of the Church, it continues to shape our thinking about theological matters in the form of vocabulary drawn from Latin texts. Further, while the vernacular has permanently come in, it is still true that anyone wishing to study Augustine or Aquinas must know Latin.

Learning ecclesiastical Latin has two bonuses for the student. Recent studies have shown that the formal analysis of a highly structured language such as Latin gives the student an improved understanding of the purposes and possibilities of language and greatly advances his ability to write and speak effectively. For the student planning to study the Greek of the New Testament, Latin introduces him to a sister-language which shares many of the same methods of expression. Thus the study of ecclesiastical Latin, while an enjoyable and profitable study in itself, looks back to the improvement of English and forward to the mastery of the original language of the Gospels.

The ecclesiastical Latin of this text is largely that of Jerome (c. 340–420) and Ambrose (340–397). Both men were masters of classical Latin (the language of Cicero and Vergil, writers of the first century B.C.), but both were men of their own times who wrote to be understood by their contemporaries. EL and classical Latin share the same vocabulary, the same forms, the same syntax. But EL has informal elements—an enduring part of Latin throughout its history—which were excluded by the literary practitioners of classical Latin. Some EL may be aggressively slangy (e.g., **mandūcāre** 'to gulp down' in place of **edere** 'to eat'). EL, as a form of Latin later by four centuries than the classical, shows expected evolutionary change, approximating the span between Shakespeare and today. But what especially marks EL as different from classical Latin is its use as a language of translation: it borrows or assimilates constructions from *koine* Greek; it borrows vocabulary from *koine* Greek; it adapts some Latin words to meanings and connotations found in the *koine* Greek originals. In some instances the Greek is itself a rendering of the Hebrew. These calques and loan translations are so frequent—particularly in the Vulgate—that some critics go so far as to recognize EL as a separate dialect spoken and understood only by Christians.

Of the thirty-five units of instruction in this text, perhaps twenty may be covered in one semester and fifteen in the next; this leaves approximately three to four weeks for continuous reading of selected original texts (such as Mark's Gospel). In the exercises actual quotations from the New Testament and major liturgical texts occur modestly at first, but by the middle units about half the exercises already are direct quotations; some later units even illustrate their points of syntax and their vocabulary entirely by unadapted citations. The last fifteen units conclude with extended original passages, carefully graded to match the students' growing knowledge of grammar and supplemented only by the necessary glosses; thus, in the second semester, what begins as a partial devotion of time, after Unit 35, ends as an entire devotion to reading.

Drills are included for each unit; they are intended for use during and after each grammar presentation to engage the students immediately in the new material and so make their private study more efficient. Not all exercises need be assigned for homework; there is much for the instructor to choose from to suit the needs of the class. But student recitations of exercises must include translation, precise syntactical explanations, and frequent transformations (such as changes from singular to plural, active to passive, imperfect to perfect, etc.). In addition, students need a quiz each period and frequent examinations to assure them of their progress.

Vocabulary lists give verbs first, then nouns, then adjectives, then all others; the conventional listing of vocabulary alphabetically has been abandoned as artificial and potentially confusing to the students. In general, the meanings given are those most often encountered in EL. With few exceptions, compound verbs are listed under the primitive (i.e., unprefixed) form; this is intended to give students a systematic grasp of compounding, and invite them to analyze any word as far as possible into its constituents.

Also appended to each unit are vocabulary notes of various kinds—on usage or of morphological interest—and English derivatives from Latin (in the interest of conserving space obvious derivations, such as innocence from **innocentia**, have been omitted).

Finally, students from the first are instructed to learn the correct quantities of vowels. There are three lasting benefits to be gained from this practice: students avoid the abuse of anachronism (which the use of an American form of the Italian pronunciation entails); they prepare themselves to appreciate the quantitative prosody of an Ambrosian hymn; they understand the system behind the accent-marks in Latin missals and breviaries still to be found in some libraries.

Table of Contents

Unit 1

1. Pronunciation of Ecclesiastical Latin

The alphabet used to record ecclesiastical Latin is the same as that used for English, except for the absence of k and w.

Aa, Bb, Cc, Dd, Ee, Ff, Gg, Hh, Ii, Jj, Ll, Mm,
Nn, Oo, Pp, Qq, Rr, Ss, Tt, Uu, Vv, Xx, Yy, Zz.

a. Vowels The vowels are a, e, i, o, u, and sometimes y. While English has several different ways to pronounce each vowel, Latin has only two, called long and short. In a strict sense, these terms—long and short—refer to quantity, i.e., the time taken to say them.

ā, as in *father*: **grātia, pāpa, ā**
a, as in *carouse*: **aqua, ad, ab**

ē, as in *they*: **cēna, ecclēsia, ē**
e, as in *get*: **terra, ex, sine, bene**

ī, as in *machine*: **doctrīna, famīlia, vīta**
i, as in *fit*: **missa, in, sine, ibi**

ō, as in *no*: **glōria, nōn, hōra, prō**
o, as in *soft*: **doctrīna, apostolus, dominus**

ū, as in *tuba*: **nātūra, futūrus, Jūdaea**
u, as in *put*: **culpa, cum, super**

N.B.: For **y**, see note 4.

Notes: 1. Long vowels are indicated with a superscribed bar, called a macron (or, simply, a long mark). In this text long vowels will always be thus indicated.
2. Note that short **e**, **i**, **o**, and **u** differ from their long

Notes continued:

forms in quality of sound as well as in quantity. But when ecclesiastical Latin is sung, the short vowels, when in open positions, tend to take on the same quality as the long vowels; since the English speaker's ear is not good at detecting the quantity of a vowel, this in practice goes a long way toward blurring the distinction between long and short vowels. Close short vowels, however, tend in song to retain their own quality. Compare short **e** in **terra** and in **Deō** when sung: terra, but 'day-oh.'

3. There are no silent vowels in Latin: e.g., **confines** is two syllables in English, but three in Latin (**cōn/fī/nēs**).

4. The letter **y** occurs only as a vowel (never as a consonant), in words borrowed from Greek. It came to be pronounced like the short form of **i**: **mystērium, hymnus**.

5. A vowel followed by another vowel, or separated from it by **h**, is usually short: **scīre**, but **sciat**; **nihil**.

b. Diphthongs A diphthong is a sequence of two vowels pronounced together in one syllable. Here are the more frequently encountered diphthongs:

ae, like **ē**: **aeternus, saeculum**
au like *ou-* in *out*: **aurum, laudō**
oe, like **ē**: **oecumenicus, coepī**
ui like *-wi-* in *dwindle*: **huic, cui**

c. Consonants The consonants are pronounced as follows:

b, as in English (but more like **p** before **s** or **t**).
c, like *k* in all positions, except before **e**, **i**, **ae**, or **oe**; then, like *ch* in *church*: **cēna, circā, caelum, coenobium**.
d, f, as in English.
g, like *g* in *gut* in all positions (but see note 1), except before **e**, **i**, or **y**; then, like *j* in *jut*: **angelus, rēgīna, Aegyptius**.
h, as in *hat* (not as in *honor* or *hour*): **honōrēs, hōra**.

j, this is in reality **i** used as a consonant, pronounced like *y* in *yet*: **jam, Jēsūs, jūstus.**

l, m, n, p, as in English.

q, always followed by a (semiconsonantal) **u** + another vowel, pronounced in all positions *kw*, as in *quick*: **quod, antīquus.**

r, like English **r**, but lightly trilled.

s, unvoiced, as in *set* and *loose*: **ecclēsia, missa.**

t, v, x, as in English.

z, like *dz* in *adze*: **baptizō.**

---

discipulus

Notes: 1. The combination **gn** is like *ny* in *canyon*: **agnus, rēgnum.**

  2. **Sc** followed by **e** or **i** is like *sh*: **scelus, scīvī.**

  3. **U** has the character of a consonant in **qu, gu,** and (often) **su. Gu** + a vowel is like *gw*: **sanguis;** **su** + a vowel, like *sw*: **suāvis.**

  4. **X** and **z** count as two consonants (x = ks; z = dz).

  5. **Ti** followed by a vowel is pronounced *tsi* (except when preceded by **s, t,** or **x**): **laetitia, pretiōsus, vitium** (but **hostia**).

  6. **Ph** is like *f*; **ch** and **th** are pronounced as in *character* and *thyme.*

  7. Doubled consonants are doubly pronounced: **ancil/la, mis/sa, pec/cātum, sab/batum, com/mit/tō.**

  8. There are no silent consonants in Latin.

---

d. Syllabication   A Latin word has as many syllables as it has vowels or diphthongs. Division into syllables is made after open vowels—i.e., those not followed by a consonant—(**pi/us, De/us**) or those followed by a single consonant (**vī/ta, hō/ra**). Division is made after the first consonant when two or more consonants follow a vowel—consequently called an enclosed vowel—(**mis/sa, minis/ter, sān/ctus**). But in compounds the parts are separated (**dē/scrībō**).

Note: The sequence of a mute consonant (**b, c, d, g, p, t**) or **f** and a liquid consonant (**l, r**) is taken with the succeeding vowel: **la/crima, pa/tris.**

e. Syllabic Quantity; Accent   The length of a syllable is instrumental in establishing the accent of a word of three or more syllables. A syllable is long (by nature) if it contains a long vowel or a diphthong, or long (by position) if a short vowel is followed by two or more consonants or by a double consonant, x or z; a short vowel made long by position is still pronounced short: **missa**, not **mīssa**.

Accent in Latin is determined by the quantity of the next to last syllable (called the penult); if the penult is long, it bears the accent: **doc/trí/na**, **an/cíl/la**. If the penult is short, then the third syllable from the end (called the antepenult) gets the accent: **ec/clé/si/a**, **án/ge/lus**, **im/pé/ri/um**. Words of two syllables are accented on the penult: **cé/na**, **sí/ne**.

> *Notes:* 1. In prose, the combination of a mute (**b, c, d, g, p, t**) or **f** and a liquid (**l, r**) does not make for length by position: **ce/le/brō**, **te/ne/brae**.
> 2. Traditional Latin missals and breviaries do not use macrons as guides to pronunciation; instead, accent marks (') are used in words of three or more syllables: **cōnfessióne**, **vírgine**.
> 3. The sequences **-nf-**, **-ns-**, **-nx-**, **-nct-**, and (often) **-gn-** cause a preceding vowel to lengthen: **īnferus**, **cōnsecrō**, **conjūnx**, **sānctus**, **dīgnus** (but **mǎgnus**).

2. Nouns: An Overview

In both English and Latin, a noun is a word which indicates a person, place, thing, act, or quality. In either language, nouns have the attributes of gender, number, case, and declension.

a. Gender   The gender of an English noun is revealed by the personal pronoun used in its stead: *he*, *she*, or *it*. Nouns referring to males have masculine gender; to females, feminine gender; to inanimate objects, nearly always neuter (= 'neither') gender. But the gender of a Latin noun is less closely tied to sex; while nouns denoting males are masculine and those denoting females are feminine, other Latin nouns denoting places, things, acts, or qualities may have any gender. Since the gender of such nouns cannot be guessed, it must be carefully memorized. In English, *psalm, water,* and *heaven* are neuter nouns (each may be referred to as 'it'); but in Latin they are masculine (**psalmus** 'psalm'), feminine (**aqua** 'water'), and neuter (**caelum** 'heaven'). These Latin nouns are proof of purely grammatical gender; any pronominal reference to them would have to use the appropriate grammatical gender.

b. Number   Nouns may be singular or plural in their number. Both English and Latin alter the spelling of a noun to change its number: *boy*—singular, *boys*—plural; **puer**—singular, **puerī**—plural.

c. Case   The grammatical task performed by a noun in a sentence is called its case. In English today, there are three cases: a noun used as the subject of a sentence is said to be in the nominative case; a noun used to indicate possession alters its spelling to make the possessive case; a noun receiving the action or following a preposition is in the objective case. These cases may occur in the singular or in the plural.

	SINGULAR	PLURAL
Nominative	*boy*	*boys*
Possessive	*boy's*	*boys'*
Objective	*boy*	*boys*

Knowledge of these six noun forms—called the declension of a noun—is indispensable for correct English. In Latin, too, knowledge of the case system is all important for correct Latin.

d. The Latin Case System   Anglo-Saxon, the earliest form of English, had five cases; today English makes do with only three cases because of its very great dependence on prepositions and on word order. Latin, conversely, has less dependence on such features because of its fuller case system. Of the eight original cases in Proto-Indo-European, Latin has retained seven of them, five major cases (nominative, genitive, dative, accusative, and ablative) and two minor ones (vocative and locative); the functions of the one missing case (the instrumental) are absorbed into the ablative case.

1. Nominative Case   As in English, the nominative case in Latin is used to express the subject of a sentence. Further, any noun used to agree with the subject, whether by predication or apposition, is put into the nominative case. In the sentence, '*John* went for a walk,' *John* is in the nominative case because it is the subject of the sentence. In the sentence, 'The *winner* is *Kathleen*,' *Kathleen* is in the nominative case because it predicates something of the subject; this use is called the predicate nominative. In the sentence, 'My *brother James* is coming to dinner,' *James* is in the nominative case because it directly explains the subject; *James* is said to be in apposition to *brother*.

2. *Genitive Case*   A word used to limit or qualify the meaning of another word (in any case) is put into the genitive case. This delimitation may embrace several ideas, such as association or connection, composition, contents, subjective or objective relationship, origin, possession, authorship, description or characterization, and total or group. Such ideas are all conveyed in English by the preposition *of*: a man of the cloth; feet of clay; cup of water; the redemption of Jesus, the worship of God; man of La Mancha; the home of the brave; the Gospel of Mark; men of good will; half of the proceeds; five members of the team.

3. *Dative Case*   The dative case is used to express reference, benefit or detriment, possession, and the indirect object. These ideas are expressed in English by the prepositions *for* or *to*, or by the word order: who did this *for* you? who did this *to* you? who gave *you* this? (= who gave this *to* you?) *to* whom does this belong?

4. *Accusative Case*   The case of the direct object, that which receives the action, is the accusative case: I saw that *movie*. He broke his *leg*. Bill has no *money*. Certain prepositions require the accusative case.

5. *Ablative Case*   The ablative case is used to express separation, motion away from, manner, location, agency, and instrumentality. It occurs by itself or with a preposition which reinforces one of the basic meanings of the case. The English prepositions used most frequently to translate the ablative case are *from, with, in,* and *by*: from slavery, from the city, with ease, in town, by the student, by the sword.

6. Two Minor Cases (Vocative and Locative)   The case of direct address is the vocative. Although there are some exclusively vocative forms, the nominative case is used to express most instances of direct address. The locative case survives in certain restricted uses; it has largely been absorbed by the ablative case.

e. Declension of Nouns   To perform the various syntactical functions attended to by the case system, a noun must have two components, a base (to indicate the fundamental meaning) and an ending (to indicate the syntactical function). Any noun, therefore, will have one base, but several endings. The listing of the various resultant spellings of a noun—differing as the case differs, for both the singular and the plural—is called its declension; thus a noun is said to be declined. It is standard practice to list the five major cases in two columns (one for each number) in this order: nominative, genitive, dative, accusative, ablative.

There are five declensions in Latin. Each declension has its own set of endings to express the various cases. Thus the spelling of the ending for a case will vary from declension to declension, but the meaning for a case will remain constant. (In English, for example, the endings *-s'* and *-ren's* are quite different in spelling, but are identical in function; both indicate the possessive plural: boys' bikes, children's toys.) The vocabulary lists will provide three data for each noun: its nominative singular form, its genitive singular form, and its gender. These data are indispensable for the proper use of a noun.

3. First Declension Nouns

Nouns of the first declension have **-ae** as the genitive singular ending. To decline a first declension noun, first isolate the base by removing the ending from the genitive singular form; then to the base add the following endings:

	SINGULAR	PLURAL
Nominative	**-a**	**-ae**
Genitive	**-ae**	**-ārum**
Dative	**-ae**	**-īs**
Accusative	**-am**	**-ās**
Ablative	**-ā**	**-īs**

> *Notes:* 1. Since these endings cannot be guessed, the student must commit them firmly to memory.
> 2. Macrons are part of the spelling of these endings; be sure to maintain the distinction between the nominative singular (**-a**) and the ablative singular (**-ā**).
> 3. Context will help to distinguish between case endings which are identical in spelling.

vīta, vītae, f. 'life'; base: **vīt-**

	SINGULAR	PLURAL
Nominative	**vīta** ('life')	**vītae** ('lives')
Genitive	**vītae** ('of life')	**vītārum** ('of lives')
Dative	**vītae** ('for/to life')	**vītīs** ('for/to lives')
Accusative	**vītam** ('life')	**vītās** ('lives')
Ablative	**vītā** ('from/with/in/ by life')	**vītīs** ('from/with/in/by lives')

> *Notes:* 1. This is the paradigm for all first declension nouns; use it as a model when generating any form for any first declension noun. Observe how the base (**vīt-**) recurs in each form, while the case endings keep changing. Learn to associate each form with the meaning indicated in the parentheses; this is crucial for the mastery of the case system.
> 2. Since Latin does not have articles, these forms may be translated with or without an article—'life, a life, the life'—as context demands. Latin is quite different from English in this respect: 'the' is far and away the most frequently used word in English prose.
> 3. **Vīta** is a feminine noun. The great majority of first declension nouns are feminine.

4. Prepositions: An Overview

A distinctive feature of ecclesiastical Latin is its more extensive use of prepositions than that exhibited by its predecessor, classical Latin. For example, while ecclesiastical Latin still uses the dative case for the indirect object, it may also use an equivalent prepositional phrase.

Prepositions in Latin are always used in phrases, consisting of a preposition and a substantive (i.e., a noun, a pronoun, or an adjective used as a noun). Substantives used with prepositions are said to be governed by them; prepositions govern only two cases, the accusative or the ablative. Some prepositions may govern either case, depending on the specific use.

a. Governing the Accusative Case   Prepositions governing the accusative case often involve motion toward or the idea of object. For example, **ad** (preposition + accusative) means 'to, toward; for (the purpose of).' It may also mean 'at,' as in 'look at him.' By extension, it may mean 'at,' as in 'at the right hand of the Father.'

b. Governing the Ablative Case   Prepositions governing the ablative case help to indicate clearly the specific use of the ablative intended by the speaker. Without a preposition (and aside from context), the ablative may mean several different things; but with a preposition, the ablative has only one of its potential uses activated. The translation of the preposition with an ablative always overrides the abstract translation of this case.

c. Ablative of Accompaniment   The prepositions **cum** 'with' and **sine** 'without' govern the ablative case of (most often) a personal noun. For example, **familia, familiae**, f. 'family': **cum familiā** 'with (the/a) family'; **sine familiā** 'without (the/a) family.' Such a use is termed the ablative of accompaniment. Since these prepositions mean 'with' and 'without' in the sense 'in the company of' and 'not in the company of,' it is clear that they will most frequently govern substantives referring to persons. (By analogy, however, the ablative of accompaniment is sometimes extended to apply to inanimate objects.)

Vocabulary

nom.   gen

aqua, aquae, f. water
cēna, cēnae, f. supper, dinner
culpa, culpae, f. blame, fault
doctrīna, doctrīnae, f. teaching, doctrine

ecclēsia, ecclēsiae, f. church;
 assembly
familia, familiae, f. household,
 family
glōria, glōriae, f. glory

grātia, grātiae, f. grace; favor, credit; *pl.*, thanks
hōra, hōrae, f. hour
missa, missae, f. Mass
nātūra, nātūrae, f. nature
pāpa, pāpae, m. pope
terra, terrae, f. earth, land, ground
vīta, vītae, f. life
ā (ab, abs) (*prep.* + *abl.*) from, away from
ad (*prep.* + *acc.*) to, toward; for (the purpose of); at
cōram (*prep.* + *abl.*) in the presence of
cum (*prep.* + *abl.*) with
dē (*prep.* + *abl.*) from, down from; about, concerning

ē (ex) (*prep.* + *abl.*) from, out of
et (1. *coord. conj.*; 2. *intensifying adv.*) 1. and 2. even, too
et . . . et both . . . and
in (*prep.*: 1. + *acc.*; 2. + *abl.*) 1. into, onto; against; for (the purpose of) 2. in, on; among; by means of, with
prō (*prep.* + *abl.*) in front of; in behalf of, for; instead of, on behalf of
-que (*enclitic coord. conj.*) and
sine (*prep.* + *abl.*) without
super (*prep.* 1. + *acc.*; 2. + *abl.*) 1. above, upon; over 2. about, concerning

almost always acc

Vocabulary Notes

Doctrīna 'teaching, doctrine' is a noun derived from the verb **doceō** 'teach' (Unit 19).

Ecclēsia 'church; assembly' has been borrowed from the Greek; it may be used of either the people or the building.

Glōria 'glory' may carry with it the attendant ideas of praise, honor, thanksgiving, splendor, or magnificence.

The preposition **ā** 'from, away from' has three forms: **ā, ab, abs**; **ā** is used before consonants, **ab** before vowels (or **h**), **abs** only before **t** (if at all).

Distinguish between 'to,' a translation of the dative case which indicates relationship, and 'to,' the translation of the preposition **ad**, indicating motion toward.

The prepositions **cum** 'with' and **sine** 'without,' used in the ablative of accompaniment, may also be used more loosely with other, non-personal, nouns: e.g., **sine aquā** 'without water.'

The preposition **ē** has two forms: **ē** or **ex**. **Ē** is used only before consonants; **ex** may be used before either vowels or consonants (especially **p**).

Note that, depending on its use, **et** may be either a conjunction ('and'), connecting words, clauses, and sentences, or an adverb ('even, too'), emphasizing the word it precedes.

The enclitic **-que** 'and' is attached to the second of two terms to be linked: **aqua cēnaque** 'water and supper.' Its addition may cause a shift in the accent of a word: e.g., **térram**, but **terrámque**; **vítā**, but **vītáque**.

Derivatives:	LATIN	ENGLISH
	aqua	aqueous, aquatic, aquarium
	culpa	culpable, culprit, exculpate
	ecclēsia	ecclesiastical, ecclesiology
	famīlia	familiar
	missa	missal
	grātia	gracious, gratitude, gratis
	pāpa	papal, papist
	terra	terrace, terrier, inter
	vīta	vita, vital, aquavit, vitamin
	ā, ab, abs	avert, abrupt, abstain
	ad	admit
	cum	commit
	dē	detour
	ē, ex	eject, exit
	in	inject
	prō	promote, progress
	sine	sinecure
	super	supervise, supersede

- VERY rare

Drills

I. PRONUNCIATION EXERCISE

Pater noster, quī es in caelīs, sānctificētur nōmen tuum; adveniat rēgnum tuum; fīat voluntās tua, sīcut in caelō et in terrā. Pānem nostrum cotīdiānum dā nōbīs hodiē; et dīmitte nōbīs dēbita nostra, sīcut et nōs dīmittimus dēbitōribus nostrīs; et nē nōs indūcās in tentātiōnem; sed līberā nōs ā malō.

→ exception accent

II. Give the case and number of each; give all possibilities; translate (both case meaning and lexical meaning):

a. hōrae	f. aquās	k. cēnae
b. terram	g. glōria	l. doctrīnam
c. pāpā	h. grātiā	m. famīliīs
d. ecclēsiīs	i. missīs	n. nātūrā
e. vītārum	j. culpae	o. terra

III. Complete each phrase with the proper ending in the singular; translate; change to the plural:

a. sine pāp___   d. dē culp___
b. ad glōri___   e. ad ecclēsi___
c. ā miss___

Exercises

I.
1. cōram famīliā
2. ad missam
3. ā missā
4. cum pāpā
5. prō ecclēsiā
6. ab ecclēsiā
7. ad glōriam
8. pāpae ad glōriam; ad glōriam pāpae
9. dē vītā; dē famīliae vītā
10. nātūrā; in nātūrā
11. ē terrīs
12. in ecclēsiārum terrīs
13. in terrās
14. sine famīliā et ecclēsiā
15. et vīta et aqua
16. vīta aquaque
17. super terram; super terrā
18. cum glōriā
19. sine culpā
20. ecclēsiae prō doctrīnīs

II.
1. in behalf of the family of the pope
2. in the presence of the pope
3. without life
4. at the hour
5. for the purpose of the glory of the church

Unit 2

5. Second Declension Masculine Nouns

All nouns of the second declension have **-ī** as the genitive singular ending. Masculine nouns of this declension are of two types, those with a nominative ending (**-us**) and those without a nominative ending; this latter type has a nominative identical with its base (or slightly respelled, ending in **-er**).

To decline a masculine noun of the second declension, determine the base by removing the ending from the genitive singular; then add the following endings:

	SINGULAR	PLURAL
Nominative	**-us** (—)	**-ī**
Genitive	**-ī**	**-ōrum**
Dative	**-ō**	**-īs**
Accusative	**-um**	**-ōs**
Ablative	**-ō**	**-īs**

> *Notes:* 1. Since all nouns are listed with the nominative singular form as well as the genitive singular, there is never any doubt whether the nominative singular ending is to be used or not.
> 2. Although some endings are identically spelled, context will help to distinguish between them.

servus, servī, m. 'servant, slave'; base: **serv-**

	SINGULAR	PLURAL
Nom.	**servus** ('the servant')	**servī** ('servants')
Gen.	**servī** ('of the servant')	**servōrum** ('of servants')
Dat.	**servō** ('for/to the servant')	**servīs** ('for/to servants')

	SINGULAR	PLURAL
Acc.	**servum** ('the servant')	**servōs** ('servants')
Abl.	**servō** ('from/with/in/by the servant')	**servīs** ('from/with/in/by the servants')

puer, puerī, m. 'boy, child'; base: **puer-**

	SINGULAR	PLURAL
Nom.	**puer** ('the boy')	**puerī** ('the boys')
Gen.	**puerī** ('of the boy')	**puerōrum** ('of the boys')
Dat.	**puerō** ('for/to the boy')	**puerīs** ('for/to the boys')
Acc.	**puerum** ('the boy')	**puerōs** ('the boys')
Abl.	**puerō** ('from/with/in/by the boy')	**puerīs** ('from/with/in/by the boys')

> *Notes:* 1. An article (*a, an, the*) may be supplied as needed by the context.
> 2. **Servus** and **puer** are masculine nouns. All second declension nouns in **-er** or **-ir** are masculine; the great majority of those in **-us** are masculine.

6. Present Tense of the Copulative Verb sum 'to be'

The singular and plural forms in the first, second, and third persons for the present tense of **sum, esse, fuī, futūrus** 'to be, exist' are as follows:

	SINGULAR	PLURAL
1st person:	**sum** ('I am')	**sumus** ('we are')
2nd person:	**es** ('you are')	**estis** ('you are')
3rd person:	**est** ('he/she/it is')	**sunt** ('they are')

> *Notes:* 1. A Latin verb form contains both the equivalent of a pronoun ('I, you, he,' etc.) and the basic meaning. Thus Latin does in one word what English does in two: **sum** is a complete statement, *am* is not.
> 2. While **sum** may simply indicate existence (**est** 'he exists'), it is chiefly used to link a subject to a predi-

Notes continued:
> cate nominative or adjective: e.g., Michael *is* the
> captain.
> 3. An overview of the verb will be presented in Section 20.

7. Kinds of Sentences

In Latin, as in English, all discourse takes the form of three kinds of independent clauses, or sentences: statements, questions, and commands (or requests). Further, each of these independent clauses has an indirect, or dependent, form. Thus there are direct and indirect statements, direct and indirect questions, and direct and indirect commands (or requests).

Direct statement: I visited my brother.
Indirect statement: He said that he had visited his brother.

Direct question: Why is the sky blue?
Indirect question: The child asked why the sky is blue.

Direct command (or request):   Get your feet off the sofa!
Indirect command (or request):   His mother told him to get his feet off the sofa.

N.B.: The so-called exclamatory sentence is a special form of the direct statement.

In Latin, as in English, there are seven basic sentence-patterns, each capable of taking the form of a statement, a question, or a command (or request). From these basic patterns the more complicated ones (such as compound and complex sentences) are made:

I.	**(Subject)**	**Intransitive Verb**	
	(—)	a) **Sum.**	
	(I)	am.	
	(—)	b) **Videō.**	
	(I)	see.	
2.	**(Subject)**	**Intransitive Verb**	**Adverb**
	(—)	a) **Sum**	**ibi.**
	(I)	am	here.
	(—)	b) **Videō**	**bene.**
	(I)	see	well.

3.	(Subject)	Transitive Verb	Direct Object
	(—)	**Videō**	**Petrum.**
	(I)	see	Peter.
4.	(Subject)	Transitive Verb	Indirect Obj.	Direct Object
	(—)	**Dō**	**Petrō**	**librum.**
	(I)	give	Peter	the book.

5.	(Subject)	Transitive Verb	Direct Object	Predicate Acc.
	(—)	**Faciō**	**Petrum**	**pāpam/ salvum.**
	(I)	make	Peter	pope/safe.
6.	(Subject)	Copulative Verb	Pred. Nom. or Adj.	
	(—)	**Sum**	**Petrus/bonus.**	
	(I)	am	Peter/good.	
7.	(Subject)	Passive Verb	by + Agent	
	(—)	**Laudor**	**ā Petrō.**	
	(I)	am praised	by Peter.	

Note that Latin need not have an expressed subject, since the person and number of the subject are always indicated by the ending of the verb.

8. Direct Statements

A direct statement is a sentence which expresses a fact or makes an assertion. In Latin it makes complete sense by itself if it contains a finite verb (usually in the indicative mood; see Section 20d).

The forms of **sum** presented in Section 6 are finite forms in the indicative mood.

Sum.
'I am.'   'I exist.'

Pāpa est.
'A pope is.'   'There is a pope.'   'He is the pope.'

Pāpa est minister.
'The pope is a servant.'
[**minister, ministrī**, m. 'servant, minister']

Note the three translations of the second example. 'A pope is' is a literal translation, but it is not idiomatic English. 'There is a pope' entails the use of the expletive 'there'; this is the English idiom for expressing a nominative subject and a finite form of the verb 'to be.' The third translation, 'He is a pope,' construes **pāpa** as the predicate nominative. Either of these last two translations may be correct, depending on the context.

9. Agreement of Subject and Verb

As in English, verbs agree in number with their subjects (whether expressed or not).

Deus est.
'There is a God.'   'God exists.'
[**Deus, Deī**, m. 'God']

> *Note:*   **Deus** is a nominative *singular*; **est** is a third person *singular*.

Puerī sunt servī.
'The boys are servants.'

> *Note:*   **Puerī** is a nominative *plural*; **sunt** is a third person *plural*.

Puer est servus.
'The boy is a servant.'

> *Note:*   **Puer** is a nominative *singular*; **est** is a third person *singular*. It would be as incorrect in Latin to say **puerī est** as it would be in English to say 'the boys is.'

10. Genitive of Possession

The genitive case may be used to indicate the one who owns, possesses, or belongs to someone or something. These three related ideas may be thus illustrated: Amy's book was left in Amy's locker in

Amy's school. Amy owns the book; she possesses the locker; she belongs to the school. The genitive of possession, as this use is called, may be translated with *of* or with the ending of the English possessive case (-'s, -s').

> **Pāpa est minister *Chrīstī*.**
> 'The pope is the minister *of Christ*.'
> 'The pope is *Christ's* minister.'
> [**Chrīstus, Chrīstī,** m. 'Anointed One, Messiah, Christ']

Vocabulary

know all four

sum, esse, fuī, futūrus be, exist
ancilla, ancillae, f. maid, (female) servant
Jūdaea, Jūdaeae, f. Judea
jūstitia, jūstitiae, f. righteousness, justice
Marīa, Marīae, f. Mary
potentia, potentiae, f. power
ager, agrī, m. field; *pl.,* country
agnus, agnī, m. lamb
angelus, angelī, m. messenger, angel
　　archangelus, archangelī, m. archangel
apostolus, apostolī, m. apostle
Chrīstus, Chrīstī, m. Anointed One, Messiah, Christ
Deus, Deī, m. (*nom. pl.,* **diī**) God

discipulus, discipulī, m. disciple, student
dominus, dominī, m. lord, master
episcopus, episcopī, m. overseer, bishop
fīlius, fīliī, m. son
minister, ministrī, m. servant, minister
Petrus, Petrī, m. Peter
populus, populī, m. people
puer, puerī, m. boy, child; servant
psalmus, psalmī, m. psalm
servus, servī, m. servant, slave
hodiē (*adv.*) today
nam (*coord. conj.*) for
nōn (*adv.*) not
trāns (*prep. + acc.*) across

Vocabulary Notes

Sum, esse, fuī, futūrus 'be, exist' is somewhat irregular, as the verb 'to be' is in most Indo-European languages. The present, the imperfect, and the future tenses cannot be reduced to rule: they must be observed and memorized. The fourth principal part is the future participle; since **sum** does not have a regular fourth principal part (i.e., a perfect passive participle) it is customary to give in its stead the future (active) participle—**futūrus**—which cannot be guessed. When used without predication, **sum** means 'exist'; with some form of predication it means 'be,' and is called a copulative verb because it links subject to predicate in the nominative case.

Jūdaea is a noun formed from an adjective, originally modifying the noun **terra**: **Jūdaea terra** 'the Judean/Jewish land.'

Jūstitia is an abstract noun made from the adjective **jūstus** (Unit 5).

Marīa is the Latin from the Hebrew *Miriam*. Originally the **-i-** of **Marīa** was short, but in ecclesiastical Latin it came to be pronounced long.

The base of **ager**, **agrī** is revealed by the genitive case: **agr-**; the nominative is the base alone, but lengthened for convenience of pronunciation: **ager**; the plural also means 'country(side).'

Angelus, **archangelus**, **apostolus**, **Chrīstus**, **episcopus**, and **psalmus** have been borrowed from Greek, the original language of the Church. **Chrīstus** literally means 'the anointed one,' referring to the practice of using precious oils to anoint a king. **Apostolus** in the Greek means 'the one sent out.'

Discipulus is an agent noun derived from the verb **discō** 'learn' (Unit 35). Thus a **discipulus** is a 'student.'

The name **Petrus** is derived from the Greek for 'rock.'

Hodiē literally means 'on this day,' hence 'today.'

Nam 'for' introduces an independent clause, explaining a prior statement; it always stands first in its clause.

The negative adverb **nōn** 'not' immediately precedes the word it negates.

Derivatives:	LATIN	ENGLISH
	sum	essence, essential, future
	ancilla	ancillary
	potentia	potency
	ager	agriculture
	deus	deity, deist
	dominus	domino, dominie, dom, dominate, don, domain
	episcopus	episcopal, bishop
	fīlius	filial
	populus	popular
	puer	puerile
	nōn	nonaligned nations
	trāns	transmit, traverse

Drills

I.   Second declension masculine nouns. Give the case and number of each; give all possibilities; translate.

a. agrī   f. Chrīstī   k. fīlius
b. agnōrum   g. Deō   l. minister
c. angelō   h. discipulīs   m. Petrō
d. archangelīs i. dominum   n. puerum
e. apostolōs   j. episcopī   o. psalmōrum

II. Translate; change the number of the italicized; retranslate.

a. *Agrī sunt* in Jūdaeā.
b. *Ancillae sumus.*
c. *Apostolus est* in Jūdaeā.
d. *Discipulī estis.*
e. *Minister* nōn *est* in Jūdaeā.

Exercises

I.   1. Aqua est in terrā.
     2. Ecclēsia est in terrā.
     3. Discipulī Chrīstī sunt in Jūdaeā.
     4. Nam Agnus Deī est.
     5. Et potentia et jūstitia sunt in terrā.
     6. Petrus nōn est in agrīs.
     7. Hodiē puerī nōn sunt in ecclēsiā.
     8. Marīa est ancilla Dominī.
     9. Dē terrā nōn sunt angelī archangelīque.
     10. Ministrī Deī sumus.
     11. In psalmīs; trāns agrōs; ab apostolīs; cōram servō; dē puerīs; ad fīlium; cum episcopō; sine populō Deī; in glōriā et potentiā.

II. 1. The boy is not in the field.
     2. For we are the people of God.
     3. Peter is the pope.
     4. There are both apostles and disciples.
     5. The bishop is the minister of the people.
     6. The pope is the Servant of the Servants.

Unit 3

11. Second Declension Neuter Nouns

Neuter nouns of the second declension have a nominative and accusative singular in **-um**, and a nominative and accusative plural in **-a**. To decline a second declension neuter noun, derive the base by removing the **-ī** ending from the genitive singular form; then add the following endings:

	SINGULAR	PLURAL
Nominative	**-um**	**-a**
Genitive	**-ī**	**-ōrum**
Dative	**-ō**	**-īs**
Accusative	**-um**	**-a**
Ablative	**-ō**	**-īs**

> *Notes:* 1. Except for the nominative and accusative endings, these neuter noun endings are identical with those used for masculine nouns of the second declension.
> 2. Neuter nouns of whatever declension will duplicate the nominative form, singular or plural, in the accusative.
> 3. Neuter nouns of whatever declension will end in **-a** in the nominative and accusative plural forms.

verbum, verbī, n. 'word'; base: **verb-**

	SINGULAR	PLURAL
Nom.	**verbum** ('the word')	**verba** ('the words')
Gen.	**verbī** ('of the word')	**verbōrum** ('of the words')
Dat.	**verbō** ('for/to the word')	**verbīs** ('for/to the words')

	SINGULAR	PLURAL
Acc.	**verbum** ('the word')	**verba** ('the words')
Abl.	**verbō** ('from/with/in/by the word')	**verbīs** ('from/with/in/by the words')

12. *Imperfect Tense of* sum *'to be'*

The imperfect is a past continuous tense. The imperfect tense of **sum**, **esse**, **fuī**, **futūrus** 'to be, exist' is as follows:

	SINGULAR	PLURAL
1st person:	**eram** ('I was')	**erāmus** ('we were')
2nd person:	**erās** ('you were')	**erātis** ('you were')
3rd person:	**erat** ('he/she/it was')	**erant** ('they were')

> *Notes:* 1. The imperfect of **sum** is compounded of the base **erā-** + the personal endings **-m, -s, -t; -mus, -tis, -nt.** The **-ā-** of the base shortens before **-m, -t, -nt.**
> 2. Literally translated, these forms mean 'I was being, you were being,' etc. English idiom prefers simply 'I was, you were,' etc.

13. *Future Tense of* sum *'to be'*

The future tense of **sum**, **esse**, **fuī**, **futūrus** 'to be, exist' is as follows:

	SINGULAR	PLURAL
1st person:	**erō** ('I will be')	**erimus** (we will be')
2nd person:	**eris** ('you will be')	**eritis** ('you will be')
3rd person:	**erit** ('he/she/it will be')	**erunt** ('they will be')

> *Notes:* 1. The future of **sum** is compounded of the base **eri-** + the personal endings **-ō, -s, -t; -mus, -tis, -nt.** The **-i-** of the base is absorbed by the ending **-ō** in the first person singular (**erō**) and is replaced in the third person plural by **-u-** (**erunt**).

Notes continued:

2. Formerly, a distinction was made between 'shall' in the first person and 'will' in the second and third persons. Since this distinction has largely died out in American English, even in the most formal contexts, this text translates all future forms with the auxiliary 'will.'

14. Dative of the Possessor

The dative of the possessor is used to make a statement concerning ownership or possession. In this construction, the thing possessed is in the nominative case, the possessor in the dative case, and the verb used is **sum** 'to be.'

Liber est *puerō*.
['A book is *to the boy*.']
'The boy has a book.'
[**liber, librī**, m. 'book']

Agrī erant *Petrō*.
['The fields were *to Peter*.']
'Peter owned the fields.'

Note: The very point of these sample sentences is the dative of the possessor. In contrast, the genitive of possession, where it occurs, almost always is no more than an ancillary idea in the sentence.

Vocabulary

rēgīna, rēgīnae, f. queen
chorus, chorī, m. choir
hymnus, hymnī, m. hymn
liber, librī, m. book
vir, virī, m. man, husband
caelum, caelī, n. (*nom. pl.*, **caelī**) heaven, sky

canticum, canticī, n. song, canticle
dōnum, dōnī, n. gift
Evangelium, Evangeliī, n. Good News, Gospel
fēstum, fēstī, n. feast, feast-day

gaudium, gaudiī, n. joy
mystērium, mystēriī, n.
   mystery
odium, odiī, n. hatred
peccātum, peccātī, n. sin
praeceptum, praeceptī, n.
   lesson, precept; command
praemium, praemiī, n. reward
rēgnum, rēgnī, n. kingdom,
   rule
sabbatum, sabbatī, n. Sabbath
sacrificium, sacrificiī, n.
   sacrifice
saeculum, saeculī, n. age,
   world

in saecula (saeculōrum)
   forever (and ever)
testāmentum, testāmentī, n.
   covenant, testament
ūniversum, ūniversī, n.
   universe
verbum, verbī, n. word
vīnum, vīnī, n. wine
vitium, vitiī, n. fault, sin, vice
hīc (adv.) here, in this place
ibi (adv.) there, in that place;
   then

Vocabulary Notes

Chorus, hymnus, Evangelium, and **mystērium** are derived from the Greek. The ch- of **chorus** is pronounced like k- or kh-.

Caelum in the singular is a neuter noun; in the plural, it is a masculine noun. The singular and the plural are used interchangeably, with no difference in meaning: **angelus caelī/caelōrum** 'angel of heaven.'

Fēstum may be used in either number, with no difference in meaning: **hodiē est fēstum/sunt fēsta** 'today is the feast.'

Gaudium means 'joy' as an inner feeling rather than as an outward expression.

Sabbatum 'Sabbath' is derived from Hebrew; the singular or the plural is used indifferently: **hodiē est sabbatum/sunt sabbata** 'today is the Sabbath.'

The prepositional phrase **in saecula saeculōrum** 'forever and ever' is used with adverbial force. The use of the genitive of a word to limit another case of itself is a Hebraic idiom which intensifies the meaning.

Derivatives:	LATIN	ENGLISH
	rēgīna	Regina
	chorus	chorus, choral
	liber	library
	vir	virile

Derivatives:

LATIN	ENGLISH
dōnum	donor
Evangelium	evangelist
fēstum	festival
gaudium	gaudy, joy
odium	odium, odious, annoy
peccātum	peccadillo
praemium	premium
rēgnum	reign
saeculum	secular
verbum	verbal, verbose
vīnum	viniculture, vinyl
vitium	vicious

Drills

I. Second declension neuter nouns. Give the case and number of each; give all possibilities; translate.

a. caelum
b. canticō
c. dōna
d. Evangeliīs
e. fēstī
f. gaudiōrum
g. mystērium
h. odia
i. caelī
j. sabbatīs
k. praecepta
l. sacrificiō
m. testāmentī
n. vīnōrum
o. vitiīs

II. Translate; change the number of the italicized; retranslate.

a. *Librī erant* hīc.
b. In Jūdaeā *apostolus erat*.
c. *Servī* Dominī *erimus*.
d. *Ministrī eritis*.
e. *Liber est* apostolō.

[handwritten: A vowel b/f another vowel is short]

Exercises

I. 1. Potentia et glōria sunt Chrīstō.
   2. Mystērium aquae et vīnī est.
   3. Rēgnum Deī erit in saecula saeculōrum.
   4. Apostolī erant ministrī Chrīstī.
   5. Erit gaudium in caelīs.

[handwritten: Erunt]

neuter

6. Sabbatum est fēstum Dominī.
7. In librō sunt et hymnī et cantica.
8. In saeculō sunt odium et peccātum.
9. Evangelium est populō dōnum Deī.
10. Marīa est Rēgīna Caelī.
11. Hīc est verbum Deī. *Here*
12. Praemium ibi erit virō.
13. Gaudium est chorō angelōrum.
14. Deō et populō est testāmentum.
15. Puerī erunt discipulī Dominī. *man (genitive)*
16. Fīliī virī erant verbī ministrī.
17. Sacrificium Chrīstī erat dōnum Deī.
18. Chrīstus erat et est et erit Dominus ūniversī.
19. Odium peccātī nōn est vitium. *sin vice Hatred*
20. Pāpae est grātia Deī.
21. Populus jūstitiae sumus in terrā.

II.   1. The Church has a pope.
2. There is life and joy both in heaven and on earth.
3. In life we are the servants of the Lord.
4. The people did not have a bishop.
5. For the kingdom of heaven is here.

Unit 4

15. Adjectives: An Overview

As in English, an adjective in Latin is used to qualify or limit a noun
or noun equivalent. An adjective may constitute an integral part of
the structure of its sentence: 1) as a predicate adjective (the man is
old) 2) as a predicate accusative (you make me *happy*). See Section
7.5–6. But more frequently an adjective is used attributively; i.e., it
adds an ancillary idea by directly modifying a noun, and consequently
does not affect the basic structure of its sentence: the *old* man visited his son. In addition, any adjective may be used as a substantive:
the young learn from *the old*.

Adjectives in Latin are inflected: they change their endings to re-
flect precisely the gender, the number, and the case of the words
which they modify. There are two types of adjectives: those which
use the endings of the first and second declensions, and those which
use the endings of the third declension.

16. First/Second Declension Adjectives

Adjectives of the first and second declensions draw their masculine
endings from the second declension, their feminine endings from the
first declension, and their neuter endings from the second declension.

	SINGULAR			PLURAL		
	Masc.	*Fem.*	*Neuter*	*Masc.*	*Fem.*	*Neuter*
Nom.	-us (—)	-a	-um	-ī	-ae	-a
Gen.	-ī	-ae	-ī	-ōrum	-ārum	-ōrum
Dat.	-ō	-ae	-ō	-īs	-īs	-īs
Acc.	-um	-am	-um	-ōs	-ās	-a
Abl.	-ō	-ā	-ō	-īs	-īs	-īs

First/second declension adjectives are listed in the vocabularies by
their nominative singular forms: **bonus, -a, -um; sacer, sacra, sa-**

crum. This manner of listing makes three things clear: the adjective type [first/second declension], the form of the nominative masculine singular [with or without **-us**], and the spelling of the base [**bonus** > **bon-**; **sacra** (fem.) > **sacr-**].

bonus, -a, -um 'good'; base: **bon-**

SINGULAR

	Masc.	Fem.	Neuter
Nom.	bonus	bona	bonum
Gen.	bonī	bonae	bonī
Dat.	bonō	bonae	bonō
Acc.	bonum	bonam	bonum
Abl.	bonō	bonā	bonō

PLURAL

	Masc.	Fem.	Neuter
Nom.	bonī	bonae	bona
Gen.	bonōrum	bonārum	bonōrum
Dat.	bonīs	bonīs	bonīs
Acc.	bonōs	bonās	bona
Abl.	bonīs	bonīs	bonīs

The declension of the adjective **sacer, sacra, sacrum** 'holy, sacred' is exactly like that of **bonus, -a, -um**, except for the fact that it does not use the ending **-us** in the masculine nominative singular. Adjectives of this kind show their base clearly in the feminine nominative singular.

sacer	sacra	sacrum
sacrī	sacrae	sacrī
.	.	.
.	.	.
.	.	.

17. Agreement of Adjective and Noun

Adjectives agree exactly in gender, number, and case with the nouns (or noun equivalents) which they modify. For example, an adjective which modifies an accusative masculine singular noun must have an accusative masculine singular ending: **bonum pāpam; apostolum**

bon*um*. Note that agreement does not mean mere duplication of the ending of the noun: **bon*um* pāpam** is correct because the adjective ending fulfills the three requirements for agreement; likewise, **apostolum bon*um***. The similarity of the endings in this latter phrase is an accidental feature of agreement, not an essential one. Note, too, that these two phrases illustrate the fact that a Latin adjective may either precede or follow its noun (with no difference in meaning).

Petrus erat bonus.
'Peter was good.'

Petrus erat bonus pāpa (pāpa bonus).
'Peter was a good pope.'

> *Notes:* 1. In the first example, **bonus** is a predicate adjective, agreeing in gender, number, and case with the subject of the sentence (**Petrus**).
> 2. In the second example, the noun **pāpa** is a predicate nominative, agreeing in case with the subject of the sentence (**Petrus**); the adjective **bonus** is an attributive, agreeing in gender, number, and case with **pāpa**.

18. Nominal Sentences

In a short sentence the present tense of **sum** 'to be' may be omitted, if there is an expressed subject. Such a sentence lacking a verb is called a nominal sentence.

Apostolī ministrī Chrīstī.
'The apostles [are] the ministers of Christ.'

Verba Dominī bona.
'The words of the Lord [are] good.'

19. How to Answer Syntax Questions (1)

The mastery of Latin is made easier by the careful analysis of the grammatical structure, or syntax, of sentences. Though all aspects of grammar are important, the student is advised to concentrate in particular on two tasks: the identification of the case of any given noun or adjective in a sentence, and the determination of the reason for the case.

Verba Dominī bona.

verba: case? nominative; reason? subject of the sentence.
Dominī: case? genitive; reason? genitive of possession.
bona: case? nominative; reason? predicate adjective, agreeing
  with the subject of the sentence.

Vocabulary

animus, animī, m. heart,
  mind, spirit
gladius, gladiī, m. sword
magister, magistrī, m. teacher,
  master, rabbi
modus, modī, m. manner, way
mundus, mundī, m. world
numerus, numerī, m. number,
  multitude
aurum, aurī, n. gold
cēnāculum, cēnāculī, n.
  dining room, upper room,
  upstairs room
sacrāmentum, sacrāmentī, n.
  sacrament
aeternus, -a, -um eternal
  in aeternum forever
antīquus, -a, -um old, ancient;
  subst., pl.: ancients,
  forefathers
beātus, -a, -um blessed, happy
bonus, -a, -um good
clārus, -a, -um clear, bright;
  glorious, famous

magnus, -a, -um great, large,
  big
malus, -a, -um bad, evil,
  wicked
meus, -a, -um my, mine
mortuus, -a, -um dead
multus, -a, -um much, many
noster, nostra, nostrum our,
  ours
novus, -a, -um new, recent
pius, -a, -um holy; loving,
  tender
  impius, -a, -um wicked,
    godless
sacer, sacra, sacrum holy,
  sacred
tuus, -a, -um your, yours (*sing.*)
vērus, -a, -um true
vīvus, -a, -um living, alive
Sabaōth (*Hebrew: indecl. pl.
  noun*) armies, hosts
ubi (*interrog. adv.*) where?

Vocabulary Notes
Cēnāculum is related to **cēna** (Unit 1); the 'upstairs room' is where 'dinner' was eaten.

Note that the prepositional phrase **in aeternum** idiomatically means 'forever.'

Meus 'my' is translated 'mine' when used substantively ('Mine is not here.') or predicatively ('This is mine.'). Similar observations apply to **noster** and **tuus**: 'our > ours; your > yours.'

In general, **multus** means 'much' in the singular and 'many' in the plural; sometimes, in the singular, 'many a' is the more appropriate translation: **multus vir** 'many a man.'

Note that **impius** is the negative form of **pius**. It has the prefix **in-** 'not' assimilated to **im-** before **p-**.

Sacer 'holy, sacred' is the adjective from which the noun **sacrāmentum** has been formed.

Sabaōth, taken from the Hebrew, is an indeclinable noun, i.e., its form does not change. Since its use is extremely limited in ecclesiastical Latin, its meaning is usually quite clear: e.g., in the phrase **Deus Sabaōth** it is used as a genitive ('God of hosts').

Derivatives:	LATIN	ENGLISH
	animus	animus, animosity
	gladius	gladiator, gladiolus
	magister	magisterial, maestro
	modus	mode, indicative mood
	mundus	mundane
	numerus	numeral
	aurum	ore, aureole, siglo de oro
	cēnāculum	cenacle
	beātus	beatify
	bonus	bonus, bonbon, bounty
	clārus	clear, clarity, clarinet, clarion
	antīquus	antique
	magnus	magnify
	malus	malady, maladjusted
	mortuus	mortuary
	multus	multiply
	noster	nostrum
	novus	nova, novel, novice
	pius	pious, impious
	sacer	sacrum, sacral
	vērus	veracity, aver, Veracruz
	vīvus	viva voce, vivacious

Drills

I. First/second declension adjectives. Translate; give all possibilities; change the number and retranslate.

a. bonā aquā

b. antīquīs ministrīs

c. multus angelus

d. pāpae novō

e. vērum Deum

f. tuae culpae

g. apostolō beātō

h. magna glōria

i. discipulī sacrī

j. aeterna testāmenta

k. impiārum vītārum

l. sacrae rēgīnae

Exercises

I. 1. Ubi sunt multī discipulī?

2. Mea ecclēsia est tua ecclēsia; mea ecclēsia tua ecclēsia; mea ecclēsia tua. →adj alone =substantive

3. Beātī servī Dominī. Blessed are the slaves of Lord

4. Dominus Deus Sabaōth est sacer.   Hebrew

5. Multum gaudium est sacrō populō Deī.

6. Modus mundī est et bonus et malus; modī mundī sunt bonī et malī.

7. Magnus est numerus angelōrum.

8. Novum testāmentum est Deī verbum.

9. Chrīstus est Dominus et vīvōrum et mortuōrum.

10. Deī mystēria sunt aeterna.   living + dead (pl. adj)   neuter

11. Clārum in terrā et in caelō Dominī verbum.   Famous/Bright

12. Deō est pius fīlius in aeternum.

13. Animus virī est beātus et bonus.   mind

14. Chrīstus erat Petrī et apostolōrum magister.

15. In cēnāculō aurum erit puerō.

16. Gladius Petrī érat impius.   sword

17. Hīc est nostrum sacrāmentum.

18. Nostra nātūra dōnum Deī.

19. Cēna Dominī est nostrō populō.

20. Multī in Jūdaeā érant discipulī Chrīstī.

21. Dē novō testāmentō; in magnīs caelīs; sine multīs culpīs nostrīs; cōram Deō.

22. Aurum nōn est apostolō. Acts iii, 6, adapted.

23. Mea doctrīna nōn est mea. Jn. vii, 16.

24. Nōn est discipulus super magistrum nec ('nor') servus super dominum. Mt. x, 24.

II.   1. The living God is holy.
2. The living will be dead, the dead alive.
3. Our forefathers were servants of the Lord.
4. Your word is our command.
5. The kingdom of God is forever.

Unit 5

20. Verbs: An Overview

In both Latin and English, a verb signals existence, or action, or occurrence in time. A typical verb-form has five characteristics: person, number, tense, mood, and voice.

I see	we see
you see	you see
he/she/it sees	they see

a. Person   A verb-form may have one of three persons: the first person, that of the speaker(s) (*I* see; *we* see), the second person, that of the one(s) spoken to (*you* see; *you* [pl.] see), or the third person, that of the one(s) spoken about (*he/she/it* sees; *they* see).

b. Number   A verb-form may have one of two numbers, the singular (I see; you see; he/she/it sees) or the plural (we see; you [pl.] see; they see).

c. Tense: Time and Aspect   A verb-form places its action in time, whether in the past, the present, or the future. It also places its action in relation to the passage of time; this is called its aspect.

The several tenses of English and Latin indicate both time and aspect. In English there are three tenses: present, past, future. Each tense has three aspects: simple, progressive, completed.

		ASPECT		
		SIMPLE	PROGRESSIVE	COMPLETED
TIME	PRESENT:	I see	I am seeing	I have seen
	PAST:	I saw	I was seeing	I had seen
	FUTURE:	I will see	I will be seeing	I will have seen

> *Notes:* 1. In English the present completed, past completed, and future completed tenses are also called the present perfect, past perfect, and future perfect.
> 2. In addition, English has three extended completed tense-forms, for which Latin has no equivalent: *I have been seeing, I had been seeing, I will have been seeing.*

In Latin, these nine categories are filled by only six tense-forms (each called a 'tense'): present, imperfect, future, perfect, pluperfect, future-perfect.

		ASPECT		
		SIMPLE	PROGRESSIVE	COMPLETED
TIME	PRESENT:	**videō** 'I see' [present]	**videō** 'I am seeing' [present]	**vīdī** 'I have seen' [perfect]
	PAST:	**vīdī** 'I saw' [perfect]	**vidēbam** 'I was seeing' [imperfect]	**vīderam** 'I had seen' [pluperfect]
	FUTURE:	**vidēbō** 'I will see' [future]	**vidēbō** 'I will be seeing' [future]	**vīderō** 'I will have seen' [future-perfect]

Thus three Latin tenses each do the work of two categories:

present tense = present simple *and* present progressive
perfect tense = present completed *and* past simple
future tense = future simple *and* future progressive

and three Latin tenses each do the work of one category:

imperfect tense = past progressive
pluperfect tense = past completed
future-perfect tense = future completed

> *Notes:* 1. The perfect, pluperfect, and the future-perfect are accurately named, since **perfectum** in Latin means

Notes continued:

'completed' (pluperfect is from **plūs quam perfectum** 'more than completed'; hence, 'past completed').

2. The imperfect is likewise aptly named, since **imperfectum** means 'not completed'; hence, '(past) progressive.' The progressive aspect also includes repeated or habitual action: I used to see, I kept on seeing.

3. Present and future tenses (present, future, perfect completed, future-perfect) are called primary tenses; past tenses (imperfect, perfect simple, pluperfect) are called secondary tenses.

d. Mood   English and Latin have three moods (or attitudes of expression): indicative, subjunctive, and imperative. A verb-form in the indicative mood expresses a fact: *it rained yesterday*. A verb-form in the subjunctive mood expresses contingency or hypothetical action: *if only he were here; God bless you; we asked that he leave*. A verb-form in the imperative mood gives a direct command (or request): *pray for us! have mercy on us!*

e. Voice   Verb-forms in English and Latin may have one of two voices, the active or the passive. In the active voice, the action of the verb passes from the subject: *I yawned; he ran; he ran his father's business*. In the passive voice, the action of the verb passes to the subject: *the child was rocked to sleep; the safe was broken open by the thieves*. Only transitive verbs, those taking a direct object in the accusative case, may have passive forms as well as active.

f. Principal Parts   Verbs in English and Latin have basic forms which must be known first if all the possible forms are to be generated correctly. These are called principal parts. In English, each verb has five principal parts: *see, saw, seen, seeing, sees.*

see = present infinitive active
saw = past-simple active
seen = past participle

seeing = present participle
sees = third-person singular, present indicative active

In Latin, each verb has four principal parts: **videō, vidēre, vīdī, vīsus.**

videō = first-person singular, present indicative active 'I see;
  I am seeing'
vidēre = present infinitive active 'to see'
vīdī = first-person singular, perfect indicative active 'I saw;
  I have seen'
vīsus = perfect passive participle 'having been seen'

> *Note:*   It is assumed that the student already knows the prin-
> cipal parts of English verbs; therefore, Latin verbs have
> all their principal parts listed in the vocabularies, but
> are defined by the first only of the five English principal
> parts: **videō, vidēre, vīdī, vīsus** 'see.'

1. Finite Forms   Most verb-forms are capable of being used as the
predicate of a sentence. They are called finite forms because they are
limited by having a specific person, number, tense, mood, and voice
(participles and infinitives, for example, are not finite forms). The
first and third principal parts of **videō, vidēre, vīdī, vīsus** 'see' are
finite forms (**videō**: first-person singular, present indicative active;
vīdī: first-person singular, perfect indicative active), whereas the second and fourth are not (**vidēre**: present infinitive active; **vīsus**: perfect passive participle).

2. Infinitives   Infinitives may be seen as nouns formed from verbs
to convey the action of their verbs: *to be, to run, to see.* These verbal
nouns have tense and voice, but are not limited by having person,
number, or mood. English has a present and a past infinitive (to see,
to be seen; to have seen, to have been seen), but no future infinitive.
Latin has a present, a perfect, and a future infinitive. The second
principal part of **videō, vidēre, vīdī, vīsus** 'see' is an infinitive (**vidēre**:
present infinitive active).

3. Participles   Participles are adjectives formed from verbs to convey the action of their verbs: *running* water, a newly *elected* presi-

dent. While English has only two participles, the present and the past,* Latin has four: present active, perfect passive, future active, future passive. English does not have the equivalent of the future participles. The fourth principal part of **videō, vidēre, vīdī, vīsus** 'see' is a participle (**vīsus**: perfect passive participle).

4. Gerunds and Gerundives   Both English and Latin have gerunds; these are nouns formed from verbs to convey the action of their verbs. English uses the present participle as a gerund: *skiing* is fun; I hate *washing* dishes. English does not have a gerundive; in Latin, it is identical with the future passive participle. By using auxiliaries, English may make an approximation: *having to be seen.*

g. The Four Conjugations   To conjugate a verb is to generate its various possible forms. Verbs in Latin are classified according to their differing sets of conjugated forms. There are four conjugations in Latin, each immediately identifiable from the vowel in the penult of the second principal part (the present infinitive active). These are as follows:

first conjugation: **-ā-** (**laudāre**)
second conjugation: **-ē-** (**monēre**)
third conjugation: **-e-** (**dūcere**)
fourth conjugation: **-ī-** (**audīre**)

> *Notes:* 1. Thus **videō, vidēre, vīdī, vīsus** 'see' is a second conjugation verb.
> 2. Since the methods used to generate verb-forms are determined by a verb's conjugational classification, the student is advised to note clearly to which conjugation a verb belongs.
> 3. English does not have a system of conjugations. Its closest approximation is the division of verbs into weak and strong (a weak verb adds -*ed* to the present to form the past and the participle: *talk, talked,*

---

*That is, one (always) in -*ing*, the other (often) in -*d*, -*n*, or -*t*. The terms present and past are unsatisfactory, since the 'present' participle is used for the past progressive tense ('I was seeing') and the 'past' participle for the present passive tense ('I am seen'). Some grammarians prefer the neutral terms first and second.

Notes continued:
> *talked;* a strong verb alters the spelling of the present to form the past and the participle: *see, saw, seen; swim, swam, swum*).

21. The Present-Stem System: Three Tenses

In all four conjugations, the stem of the present infinitive (the second principal part) is the source of three tenses: the present, the imperfect, and the future. The present tense is formed from the present stem + the personal endings; the imperfect and the future tenses are formed from the present stem + a tense-making suffix + the personal endings.

22. Present Indicative Active: First Conjugation

To form the present indicative active of a first conjugation verb, from the present infinitive (the second principal part) remove the ending **-re**; then to this—the present stem—add the active personal endings: **-ō, -s, -t; -mus, -tis, -nt**. These endings each signal three things at once: the person, the number, and the voice.

laudō, laudāre, laudāvī, laudātus 'praise'
present infinitive: **laudāre**
present stem: **laudā-**
active personal endings: **-ō, -s, -t; -mus, -tis, -nt**

first-person singular: **laudā- + -ō = laudō**
second-person singular: **laudā- + -s = laudās**
third-person singular: **laudā- + -t = laudat**

first-person plural: **laudā- + -mus = laudāmus**
second-person plural: **laudā- + -tis = laudātis**
third-person plural: **laudā- + -nt = laudant**

The paradigm for these forms is as follows:

	SINGULAR	PLURAL
1	**laudō** ('I praise')	**laudāmus** ('we praise')
2	**laudās** ('you praise')	**laudātis** ('you praise')
3	**laudat** ('he/she/it praises')	**laudant** ('they praise')

Notes: 1. The **-ā-** of the stem is always dropped before the **-ō** ending of the first-person singular.
2. The endings **-t** and **-nt** always cause the **-ā-** of the stem to shorten.
3. Present simple translations alone have been given; present progressive translations, of course, are just as proper: 'I am praising, you are praising,' etc.
4. Since English relies on pronouns rather than personal endings, right from the start the student is advised to look upon the translation of verb-forms as a matter of analysis—the breaking up of the forms into their significant parts.

23. Word Order

Word order in Latin is not so closely tied to the basic meaning of a sentence as it is in English. For the most part, the inflection, or changing form, of Latin verbs and nouns constitutes the grammatical structure, whereas in English the word order contributes greatly to the grammatical structure. The form 'dog' gives no hint as to its possible use as a subject or an object; only in the word order of a sentence will the function of 'dog' be revealed: 'man bites dog'—object; 'dog bites man'—subject. These short sentences make clear the mutual relationships of their components: a noun beginning a sentence is construed as its subject; this noun is followed by the verb of the sentence; if there is an object in the sentence, it follows the verb: subject, verb, object. To change this order is to risk being misunderstood.

But in Latin, because the inflected forms carry with them information as to their function in the sentence, word order is often more a matter of emphasis and style: subject, verb, and object may occur in any order. There are some clear limitations: e.g., prepositions precede their cases; attributive adjectives are kept near their substantives.

In general, the beginning student is cautioned not to expect English word order in a Latin sentence; instead, an exact analysis of the inflectional endings should be made to uncover the basic meaning of a Latin sentence. With more experience, the student will learn to detect the subtle ancillary meanings which word order is capable of lending to Latin.

24. *Coordination (Compound Sentences)*

As in English, Latin sentences may be linked together to form compound sentences by the use of coordinating conjunctions; in English these include *and, but, for, nor,* and *or.* The use of a coordinating conjunction does not cause a sentence to lose its independent status: the sentences are merely joined; one does not become subordinate to the other.

Populus Deum laudat, *nam* bonus est.
'The people praise God, *for* He is good.'

25. *Accusative as Direct Object*

The accusative case may be used to express the direct object of a verb.

Populus *Deum* laudat.
'The people praise *God*.'

26. *Dative as Indirect Object*

The dative case may be used to express the indirect object of a verb of giving, telling, or showing.

Magister *puerō* praemium dat.
'The teacher is giving a reward *to the boy*.'
'The teacher is giving *the boy* a reward.'
[**dō, dare, dedī, datus** 'give']

27. *Ablative of Separation*

After verbs of freeing, separating, or depriving, an ablative of separation may occur, with or without a preposition (**ab** or **ex**).

Dominus populum (*ā*) *malō* līberat.
'The Lord frees His people *from evil*.'
[**līberō, līberāre, līberāvī, līberātus** 'free']

28. *Compounding of Verbs: Prepositions as Prefixes*

In English, prepositions are often used with simple verbs to make compound verbs. For example, the verb 'to cut' may take on more specialized meanings in combination with prepositions: cut *in*, cut *out*, cut *up*, cut *down*. Sometimes verbs have the prepositions attached to them as prefixes: to hold: to *up*hold; to run: to *out*run; to turn: to *over*turn; to stand: to *with*stand. This far less common method of compounding in English is the normative one in Latin.

With regard to the compounding of verbs in Latin, two phenomena are to be noticed: 1) assimilated spellings of the prepositions-as-prefixes; 2) vowel shifts in the verbs.

1) The more commonly compounded prepositions and their assimilated forms are these:

ā (ab, abs): ā-, ab-, abs-, au-
ad: a-, ac-, ad-, af-, ag-, al-, an-, ap-, ar-, as-, at-
circum: circu-, circum-
contrā: contrā-
cum: co-, cō-, col-, com-, con-, cōn-, cor-
dē: de-, dē-
ē (ex): ē-, ef-, ex-
in: i-, il-, im-, in-, īn-, ir-
inter: intel-, inter-
ob: o-, ob-, oc-, of-, op-, [obs >] os-
per: pel-, per-
post: post-
prae: prae-, prē-
prō: pro-, prō-
sub: su-, sub-, suc-, suf-, sug-, sum-, sup-, sur-, [subs >] sus-
super: super-
trāns: trā-, trāns-

Note: Inseparable prefixes (those which are not also used as prepositions) include **re-**, **dis-**, and **sē-**.

---

2) When compounded, verbs may shift their internal vowels. For example, **sacrō, sacrāre, sacrāvī, sacrātus** 'make holy, consecrate' compounded with **cum** becomes **cōnsecrō, cōnsecrāre, cōnsecrāvī**,

cōnsecrātus. (Note: Since -cr- does not make for position in prose, cōnsecrō is pronounced cónsecrō.)

The frequency of compound verbs constitutes a distinctive feature of ecclesiastical Latin. Often the compound is merely a strengthened form of the simple verb, and the difference in meaning is negligible. As a case in point, sacrō and cōnsecrō differ very little in meaning.

29. Parsing

The parsing of a sentence entails a complete analysis of its components; this includes identifying the parts of speech, and explaining in full their forms, functions, and interrelationships.

Populus Deum laudat.
'The people praise God.'

populus: nominative singular masculine, from the noun **populus, populī**, m. 'people'; subject of **laudat**.
Deum: accusative singular masculine, from the noun **Deus, Deī**, m. 'God'; direct object of **laudat**.
laudat: third-person singular, present indicative active, from the verb **laudō, laudāre, laudāvī, laudātus** 'praise'; agrees in number with the subject, **populus**; third person because it makes a statement about the subject; present indicative because it states a fact in present time; active voice because the action passes from the subject (to the object).

Since the mastery of Latin is a matter of analysis, a student's translation of a sentence must be the product of analysis, not of guesswork.

Vocabulary

ambulō, ambulāre, ambulāvī, ambulātus walk, take a walk; 'live'
cantō, cantāre, cantāvī, cantātus sing, chant
dō, dare, dedī, datus give
dōnō, dōnāre, dōnāvī, dōnātus give, grant; forgive

laudō, laudāre, laudāvī, laudātus praise
collaudō, collaudāre, collaudāvī, collaudātus praise exceedingly; praise together
līberō, līberāre, līberāvī, līberātus free

operō, operāre, operāvī,
operātus work

ōrō, ōrāre, ōrāvī, ōrātus pray

adōrō, adōrāre, adōrāvī, adōrātus worship, adore

exōrō, exōrāre, exōrāvī,
exōrātus beseech

rēgnō, rēgnāre, rēgnāvī, rēgnātus rule, reign

sacrō, sacrāre, sacrāvī, sacrātus
make holy, consecrate

cōnsecrō, cōnsecrāre, cōnsecrāvī, cōnsecrātus make
holy, consecrate

servō, servāre, servāvī, servātus keep, preserve

cōnservō, cōnservāre, cōn-
servāvī, cōnservātus keep,
preserve

observō, observāre, observāvī, observātus watch,
observe

vocō, vocāre, vocāvī, vocātus
call, invite

ēvocō, ēvocāre, ēvocāvī,
ēvocātus call forth

invocō, invocāre, invocāvī,
invocātus call upon,
invoke

stēlla, stēllae, f. star

via, viae, f. way, road, street

famulus, famulī, m. servant

documentum, documentī, n.
example

prīncipium, prīncipiī, n.
beginning

benedictus, -a, -um blessed,
blest

dīvīnus, -a, -um divine

jūstus, -a, -um righteous, just

sānctus, -a, -um hallowed, holy
  subst.: saint

enim (postpos. coord. conj.)
for; indeed

meritō (adv.) rightly,
deservedly

numquam (adv.) never

nunc (adv.) now

quoque (intensifying adv.) too,
also

semper (adv.) always

Vocabulary Notes

Ambulō means 'to walk,' but metaphorically it may mean 'to live,' as in the expression, 'to walk in the way of the Lord.' Ambulō, like most first conjugation verbs, has the pattern -ō, -āre, -āvī, -ātus.

Dō and dōnō basically mean 'give'; occasionally, dōnō means 'forgive.' Both take a direct and an indirect object: give something to someone. Dō, although a first conjugation verb, does not have principal parts which conform to the predominant pattern; note especially the short -a- in dare.

Collaudō is compounded of com- and laudō; com-, which here assimilates to col-, may either intensify the basic meaning ('completely') or add the notion 'jointly, together.'

Rēgnō is a denominative verb formed from rēgnum (Unit 3). Denominative verbs are most often derived from nouns and adjectives, and given the form of a first conjugation verb. Other such verbs—in this unit alone—are **dōnō**, **laudō**, **līberō**, **operō**, **ōrō**, **sacrō**, **servō**, and **vocō**.

Documentum 'example' is formed from the root of the verb **doceō** 'teach' (Unit 19) and the suffix **-mentum** 'instrument.'

Enim 'for' is weaker than **nam** (Unit 2); it is postpositive, i.e., it occurs toward the beginning of its clause, but never first. In contrast, **meritō** 'rightly, deservedly'—though an adverb—tends to stand at the beginning of its clause or phrase.

Quoque 'too, also' immediately follows the word it emphasizes.

Derivatives:	LATIN	ENGLISH
	ambulō	amble, ambulance, perambulator
	cantō	cant, chant, cantata
	dō	data
	dōnō	donation
	laudō	laud, laudatory
	līberō	liberate, deliver
	operō	operate
	ōrō	orison, orator, oratorio
	exōrō	inexorable
	rēgnō	regnant
	cōnsecrō	consecration
	cōnservō	conservation
	observō	observation
	vocō	vocation, vouch
	ēvocō	evocation
	invocō	invocation
	stēlla	Stella, stellar, constellation
	via	via, viaduct, viaticum
	famulus	famulus
	documentum	document
	prīncipium	principle
	benedictus	Benedict
	sānctus	sanctuary, saint, sanction
	nunc	quidnunc, nunc dimittis
	semper	sempiternal, semper paratus

Drills

I. Present indicative active: first conjugation. Translate; change to the singular or plural.

a. ambulāmus   f. rēgnat
b. cantās   g. cōnservās
c. dōnant   h. invocāmus
d. laudat   i. operant
e. adōrātis   j. collaudātis

II. Direct and indirect objects.

a. Discipulī populō exemplum dant.
b. Vir puerō librum dat.
c. Petrus praemium servō dat.
d. Aurum rēgīnae damus.
e. Magistrō dōnum dōnātis.

Exercises

I. 1. Sānctus, Sānctus, Sānctus Dominus Deus Sabaōth.
2. Apostolōs Chrīstus vocat.
3. In Missā populus Deī Dominum laudat.
4. Malīs virīs dōna nōn damus.
5. In viā Dominī ambulāmus.
6. Meritō Dominum collaudāmus; sānctus enim et bonus est.
7. Episcopus quoque prō ecclēsiā Deum invocat.
8. Dominus populum ā malō semper līberat.
9. In nostrīs animīs Chrīstus semper rēgnat.
10. Discipulī cum apostolīs operant.
11. Psalmum cōram Dominō cantāmus.
12. Ōrāmus prō mundī vītā.
13. Minister ad cēnam Dominī populum vocat.
14. Stēllam in caelō famulus laudat.
15. Verba impiōrum numquam jūstī observāmus.
16. Meritō enim Chrīstum, fīlium Deī, collaudās.
17. Clārum Marīae documentum est populō.
18. Nunc benedictī sabbatum cōnsecrant.
19. Ex agrīs Petrus puerōs ēvocat.

20. Ecclēsiae dōnāmus et prō populō operāmus.
21. Tū ('you') es Chrīstus fīlius Benedictī? Mk. xiv, 61.

II.   1. We pray to God.
2. God gives life to the world.
3. Good men always praise the Lord.
4. Our bishop consecrates the water and the wine.
5. God rules in heaven, the pope on earth.
6. In the beginning was the Word. Jn. i, 1.
7. The people rightly praise the Lord of Life.

Unit 6

30. Present Indicative Active: Second Conjugation

To form the present indicative active of a second conjugation verb, from the present infinitive (the second principal part) remove the ending **-re**; then add the active personal endings.

moneō, monēre, monuī, monitus 'warn, advise'
present infinitive: **monēre**
present stem: **monē-**

	SINGULAR	PLURAL
1	**moneō** ('I warn')	**monēmus** ('we warn')
2	**monēs** ('you warn')	**monētis** ('you warn')
3	**monet** ('he/she/it warns')	**monent** ('they warn')

Notes: 1. The stem vowel **-ē-** shortens before another vowel (**-ō**) in the first-person singular (see Section 1.a, Note 5).
2. The stem vowel shortens before the endings **-t** and **-nt**.

---

31. Present Indicative Active: Third Conjugation

There are two kinds of third conjugation verbs: the '**-ō**' type (e.g., **dūcō, dūc**e**re** . . .) and the '**-iō**' type (e.g., **capiō, cap**e**re** . . .).

a. '**-ō**' *Type*   To form the present indicative active of an '**-ō**' type verb of the third conjugation, remove the ending **-re** from the present infinitive and alter the stem vowel to **-i-** (but **-u-** for the third-person plural); then add the active personal endings.

dūcō, dūcere, dūxī, ductus 'lead'
present infinitive: **dūcere**
present stem: **dūce- > dūci-, dūcu-**

	SINGULAR	PLURAL
1	**dūcō** ('I lead')	**dūcimus** ('we lead')
2	**dūcis** ('you lead')	**dūcitis** ('you lead')
3	**dūcit** ('he/she/it leads')	**dūcunt** ('they lead')

Notes: 1. The stem vowel is dropped in the first-person singular.
2. The stem vowel **-e-** is weakened to **-i-** in all other forms except the third-person plural, where it weakens to **-u-**.

b. '-iō' Type To form the present indicative active of an '**-iō**' type verb of the third conjugation, remove the ending **-re** from the present infinitive and alter the stem vowel to **-i-** (but **-iu-** for the third-person plural); then add the active personal endings.

capiō, capere, cēpī, captus 'take, receive'
present infinitive: **capere**
present stem: **cape- > capi-, capiu-**

	SINGULAR	PLURAL
1	**capiō** ('I take')	**capimus** ('we take')
2	**capis** ('you take')	**capitis** ('you take')
3	**capit** ('he/she/it takes')	**capiunt** ('they take')

32. Present Indicative Active: Fourth Conjugation

To form the present indicative active of a fourth conjugation verb, remove the ending **-re** from the present infinitive; then add the active personal endings. The third-person plural adds **-u-** to the stem before the ending (causing the stem vowel to shorten).

audiō, audīre, audīvī, audītus 'hear'
present infinitive: **audīre**
present stem: **audī- (audiu-)**

SINGULAR	PLURAL
1 **audiō** ('I hear')	**audīmus** ('we hear')
2 **audīs** ('you hear')	**audītis** ('you hear')
3 **audit** ('he/she/it hears')	**audiunt** ('they hear')

> *Notes:* 1. The stem vowel shortens before another vowel in the first singular and the third plural.
> 2. The stem vowel shortens before the ending **-t**.

33. *Direct Questions (1)*

A direct statement may be converted into a direct question by attaching the enclitic particle **-ne** to the first word. But more often, context alone determines when a statement is to be construed as a question.

Vocatne Petrus discipulum?
'Is Peter calling the disciple?'

Angelī in caelīs Deum collaudant?
'Do the angels in heaven together praise God?'

These are sentence questions; far more frequently, a question is introduced by an interrogative word, such as the adverbs **ubi** 'where?' and **quārē** 'for what reason? why?'

Quārē Dominum nōn laudant?
'Why do they not praise the Lord?'

34. *Ablative of Means*

The ablative case of an inanimate noun may be used to express the means by which the action of a sentence is accomplished. Occasionally, the Latin of the Vulgate uses the preposition **in** with this construction.

Dominum *psalmīs* laudāmus.
'We praise the Lord *with (by means of) psalms.*'

Jūstī *in gladiō* rēgnant?
'Do righteous men rule *by (by means of) the sword?*'

35. *Ablative of Manner*

The ablative case of an abstract noun may be used to express the manner or style in which the action of a sentence is carried out. The preposition **cum** is always used if the noun is not modified by an adjective; the preposition may be omitted if the noun is modified.

Dominum *cum gaudiō* laudāmus.
'We praise the Lord *with joy (joyfully)*.'
Dominum *magnō (cum) gaudiō* laudāmus.
'*With great joy* we praise the Lord.'

Notes: 1. The ablative of manner may often be translated with an English adverb in *-ly* (since *-ly* means 'in a specified manner').
2. When both the preposition and an adjective are used with the ablative of manner, the adjective often begins the phrase: **magnō cum gaudiō**.

Vocabulary

dō:
  reddō, reddere, reddidī, redditus give back, render
  trādō, trādere, trādidī, trāditus give over, hand down, betray
fugō, fugāre, fugāvī, fugātus put to flight, chase away
dēleō, dēlēre, dēlēvī, dēlētus destroy, wipe out
habeō, habēre, habuī, habitus have, hold; consider
misceō, miscēre, miscuī, mixtus mix, mingle
moneō, monēre, monuī, monitus warn, advise; teach
agō, agere, ēgī, āctus do, drive, conduct

grātiās agere give thanks (to), thank (+ *dat.*)
bibō, bibere, bibī, bibitus drink
crēdō, crēdere, crēdidī, crēditus believe (in), trust (in)
dūcō, dūcere, dūxī, ductus lead
  ēdūcō, ēdūcere, ēdūxī, ēductus lead out
  indūcō, indūcere, indūxī, inductus lead into, bring into
  perdūcō, perdūcere, perdūxī, perductus lead through, bring to
  sēdūcō, sēdūcere, sēdūxī, sēductus deceive
jungō, jungere, jūnxī, jūnctus join, unite

conjungō, conjungere, conjūnxī, conjūnctus join,
unite

capiō, capere, cēpī, captus
take, receive; understand

accipiō, accipere, accēpī, acceptus take, get, receive

recipiō, recipere, recēpī, re-
ceptus take back, regain

faciō, facere, fēcī, factus do,
make

afficiō, afficere, affēcī, affectus affect

dēficiō, dēficere, dēfēcī, dēfectus fail, waste, vanish

efficiō, efficere, effēcī, effectus make, effect

audiō, audīre, audīvī (audiī),
audītus hear

exaudiō, exaudīre, exaudīvī
(exaudiī), exaudītus hear
(favorably)

veniō, venīre, vēnī, ventus
come

adveniō, advenīre, advēnī,
adventus come, arrive

conveniō, convenīre, con-
vēnī, conventus come
together; be fitting

inveniō, invenīre, invēnī, inventus come upon, find

Hebraeus, Hebraeī, m. Hebrew

nātus, nātī, m. son, child

domus, domī, f. home, house

exemplum, exemplī, n.
example

templum, templī, n. temple,
church

Aegyptius, -a, -um Egyptian

Chrīstiānus, -a, -um Christian

ēlēctus, -a, -um chosen, elect

adhūc (adv.) so far, till now,
still

aut (coord. conj.) or

aut . . . aut either . . . or

-ne (enclitic interrog. particle)
used in sentence questions

quārē (interrog. adv.) for what
reason? why?

Vocabulary Notes

Reddō and trādō (< trāns + dō) are compounds of dō 'give.' Reddō
has the inseparable prefix re(d)- ('back, again'); see Section 28.1, Note.
Although dō is a first conjugation verb, many of its compounds are of
the third conjugation.

Habeō has both a physical meaning, 'have, hold,' and a mental one,
'hold [in mind]: consider.' Compare 'we hold these truths . . .'

Moneō may take a personal accusative and an infinitive: monet
puerum operāre 'he advises the boy to work.'

Note that agere means 'do, drive, conduct,' but that grātiās agere is
an idiom meaning 'give thanks (to), thank'; the person thanked is
put into the dative case.

Crēdō may take a dative (crēdō puerō 'I trust [in] the boy') or in +
accusative (crēdimus in Deum 'we believe in God').

Dūcō 'lead' is one of many verbs which easily form compounds. **Sēdūcō** uses the inseparable prefix **sē-** 'apart from, astray'; hence, it means 'lead astray, deceive.'

Capiō has a physical meaning, 'take, receive,' and a mental, 'understand,' as in the English, 'if you take my meaning.'

Besides an accusative as direct object, **faciō** may take an accusative + infinitive, meaning 'to make or cause someone to do something': **facit puerum operāre** 'he makes (causes) the boy (to) work.'

Nātus 'son, child' is a noun derived from the verb **nāscor** 'to be born' (Unit 20).

Note that **domus** is a second declension *feminine* noun.

Chrīstiānus 'Christian' is an adjective compounded of the base of the noun **Chrīstus** + the adjectival suffix **-iānus, -a, -um** 'pertaining to, belonging to.'

Derivatives:	LATIN	ENGLISH
	reddō	render, rent
	trādō	tradition, traitor, extradite
	fugō	fugue
	dēleō	dele, delete
	habeō	habit, habeas corpus, able
	misceō	promiscuous, miscegenation, miscellany
	moneō	admonition, monitor
	agō	agent, actor, action, act
	bibō	bib, bibber, imbibe, beer
	crēdō	credo, creed, credit
	dūcō	Il Duce, duke, duct, ductile, aqueduct, educe, induce, induction
	jungō	join, joint, junction, conjoin, conjoint, conjunction
	capiō	cop, capture, caption, accept, recipe, recipient, receipt, reception
	faciō	fact, factor, affectation, deficit, defect, effective
	audiō	audio, audition, auditorium
	veniō	venue, venture, venireman, advent, convenient, convent, invent
	Hebraeus	Hebraic

Derivatives: LATIN   ENGLISH

nātus   innate, neonate, native, nation
domus   dome, domestic
exemplum   exemplum, exemplary
Chrīstiānus   cretin
ēlēctus   elite

Drills

I.   Present indicative active: second, third, and fourth conjugations. Translate; change the number.

reddītis — a. reddis *softe strong* f. capiunt *capio   capit*
b. dēlētis g. facis
c. habēmus h. audīmus
ire — d. agit i. advenīs
e. crēdō j. ēdūcitis
Ʌy you (ad out

II. Direct questions. *Are you calling the boy?*
puerumne
a. Puerum vocās?
b. Ambulatne ad ecclēsiam?
c. Hymnum cantant? Hymnum cantant.
d. Ad Jūdaeam advenit?
e. Verbum Deī servātis?

Exercises

Fugo fugare
4 to put to flight

I.   1. Prō Hebraeīs Dominus Aegyptiōs fugat.
2. Deō grātiās semper agimus.
3. Aeternīs praeceptīs Dominus populum monet.
4. Marīa nātum in templō invenit. *finds*
the son
5. Episcopus populum in ecclēsiam indūcit. *leads into*
in w/motion is accusative
6. Petrus cum discipulīs ad domum advenit.
7. Cum gaudiō vīnum bibimus vītae? *house*
unnecessary ablative of manner
8. Quārē apostolus Chrīstum malīs trādit? *for life*
9. Famulus malus puerum aurō sēdūcit.
10. In glōriā Chrīstus populum conjungit.
11. Praeceptīs pāpa ecclēsiam dūcit.
12. Nunc minister cum aquā vīnum miscet.

13. Populus Deī in ecclēsiam convenit et Missam agit noster
episcopus.
14. Aut psalmō aut sacrificiō glōriam collaudāmus Dominī.
15. Semper crēdunt ēlēctī in Deum? *accusative*
16. Magnō gaudiō Chrīstiānī doctrīnās Chrīstī audīmus.
17. Sacrificiō Fīliī Deus peccāta dēlet populī. *wipe away*
18. Sine Chrīstō dēficimus; populum enim servat.
19. Adhūc aurum ab impiīs capiunt? Impiī piōs exemplō bonō
nōn afficiunt.
20. Beātī et audiunt et cōnservant verba Dominī.
21. Dūcitne servus meus trāns agrum ad domum puerum?
22. In Chrīstō habēmus pium exemplum.
23. Cum Chrīstō mala numquam facimus (agimus).
24. Deum habēmus bonum et sānctum.
25. Vīnum minister magistrō dat?
26. Chrīstus gaudiō populum afficit.
27. Prīncipium Evangeliī puer capit?
28. In domum indūcit ancilla tuum nātum.
29. Vīnum nōn habent. Jn. ii, 3.
30. Venit hōra, et nunc est. Jn. v, 25.

II.   1. Is the wicked apostle betraying Christ?
2. Do we Christians have hatred of sin?
3. Our minister is making a sacrifice in behalf of the people.
4. Is Christ coming with glory?
5. We give thanks to the Lord, for he puts to flight the
wicked.
6. Is the servant giving back the gold to the master?

Unit 7

36. Present Indicative Passive: All Four Conjugations

Any transitive verb may occur in the passive voice. It forms its present indicative passive by adding to the present stem the passive personal endings. These endings signal the person, the number, and the voice.

PASSIVE PERSONAL ENDINGS

	SINGULAR	PLURAL
1	**-or (-r)**	**-mur**
2	**-ris, -re**	**-minī**
3	**-tur**	**-ntur**

> *Notes:* 1. The alternate first-person singular ending (**-r**) is not used in the present indicative.
> 2. In the second-person singular, both **-ris** and **-re** are found.

FIRST CONJUGATION:

laudō, laudāre, laudāvī, laudātus 'praise'
present infinitive: **laudāre**
present stem: **laudā-**

	SINGULAR	PLURAL
1	**laudor** ('I am praised')	**laudāmur** ('we are praised')
2	**laudāris, laudāre** ('you are praised')	**laudāminī** ('you are praised')
3	**laudātur** ('he/she/it is praised')	**laudantur** ('they are praised')

Notes: 1. The stem vowel drops before the ending **-or**.
        2. One form of the second-person singular is identical
           in spelling with the present infinitive; context will
           reveal which is intended.
        3. The stem vowel shortens before the ending **-ntur**.
        4. Present progressive translations are equally appropri-
           ate: 'I am being praised, you are being praised,' etc.

SECOND CONJUGATION:

moneō, monēre, monuī, monitus 'warn, advise'
present infinitive: **monēre**
present stem: **monē-**

	SINGULAR	PLURAL
1	**moneor** ('I am warned')	**monēmur** ('we are warned')
2	**monēris**, **monēre** ('you are warned')	**monēminī** ('you are warned')
3	**monētur** ('he/she/it is warned')	**monentur** ('they are warned')

Notes: 1. The stem vowel in the first singular shortens before
           another vowel.
        2. The stem vowel shortens before the ending **-ntur**.

THIRD CONJUGATION, '-ō' TYPE:

dūcō, dūcere, dūxī, ductus 'lead'
present infinitive: **dūcere**
present stem: **dūce-** > **dūci-, dūcu-**

	SINGULAR	PLURAL
1	**dūcor** ('I am led')	**dūcimur** ('we are led')
2	**dūceris**, **dūcere** ('you are led')	**dūciminī** ('you are led')
3	**dūcitur** ('he/she/it is led')	**dūcuntur** ('they are led')

Note: The stem vowel is dropped before the ending **-or**.

THIRD CONJUGATION, '-iō' TYPE:

capiō, capere, cēpī, captus 'take, receive'
present infinitive: **capere**
present stem: **cape-** > **capi-, capiu-**

SINGULAR	PLURAL
1 **capior** ('I am taken')	**capimur** ('we are taken')
2 **caperis, capere** ('you are taken')	**capiminī** ('you are taken')
3 **capitur** ('he/she/it is taken')	**capiuntur** ('they are taken')

> *Note:* In *all* third conjugation verbs, both second singular forms retain the original stem vowel (**-e-**).

FOURTH CONJUGATION:

audiō, audīre, audīvī, audītus 'hear'
present infinitive: **audīre**
present stem: **audī-** (**audiu-**)

SINGULAR	PLURAL
1 **audior** ('I am heard')	**audīmur** ('we are heard')
2 **audīris, audīre** ('you are heard')	**audīminī** ('you are heard')
3 **audītur** ('he/she/it is heard')	**audiuntur** ('they are heard')

> *Note:* The stem vowel in the first singular shortens before another vowel.

37. *Ablative of Personal Agency*

The ablative case may be used with a personal noun to express the doer or agent of a verb in the passive voice. The preposition **ā** (**ab, abs**) is always used in this construction.

> **Nostra peccāta *ā Chrīstō* dēlentur.**
> 'Our sins are destroyed *by Christ*.'

38. Ablative with Certain Adjectives

The adjectives **dīgnus, -a, -um** 'worthy (of),' **indīgnus, -a, -um** 'unworthy (of),' and **plēnus, -a, -um** 'full (of)' govern the ablative case.

Puer est *praemiō* dīgnus (indīgnus).
'The boy is worthy (not worthy) *of a reward*.'

Terra est *glōriā* Deī plēna.
'The earth is full *of the glory* of God.'

> *Note:*   Distinguish between the use of the preposition *of* to link these special adjectives with their ablatives and its use in general to translate the genitive case.

Vocabulary

celebrō, celebrāre, celebrāvī, celebrātus celebrate

concelebrō, concelebrāre, concelebrāvī, concelebrātus celebrate together

firmō, firmāre, firmāvī, firmātus strengthen, make steady

affirmō, affirmāre, affirmāvī, affirmātus prove, assert

cōnfirmō, cōnfirmāre, cōnfirmāvī, cōnfirmātus strengthen, uphold

sānō, sānāre, sānāvī, sānātus heal

dīcō, dīcere, dīxī, dictus say, tell *pass. also:* be called

benedīcō, benedīcere, benedīxī, benedictus speak well (of), bless

maledīcō, maledīcere, maledīxī, maledictus speak evil (of), curse

anima, animae, f. (*dat./abl. pl.*, **animābus**) soul, life

laetitia, laetitiae, f. gladness, joy

lītūrgia, lītūrgiae, f. (divine) service, liturgy

misericordia, misericordiae, f. mercy, kindness, pity

turba, turbae, f. crowd, multitude   MOB

victōria, victōriae, f. victory

diāconus, diāconī, m. deacon

respōnsum, respōnsī, n. answer, response

vōtum, vōtī, n. vow; prayer

cārus, -a, -um (+ *dat.*) dear, beloved

dīgnus, -a, -um (+ *abl.*) worthy (of)

indīgnus, -a, -um (+ *abl.*) unworthy (of)

firmus, -a, -um steadfast, firm

īnfirmus, -a, -um weak, sick

maestus, -a, -um sad
Nazarēnus, -a, -um
  of Nazareth, Nazarene,
  Nazorean
plēnus, -a, -um (+ abl.)
  full (of)
prīmus, -a, -um first
  in prīmīs at first, in the first
  place
ūniversus, -a, -um all, the
  whole

ūnus, -a, -um one; a, an
  ūnā (adv.) together
ā (ab, abs) (prep. + abl.) by
  (the agency of)
bene (adv.) well
Jēsūs, Jēsū, Jēsū, Jēsūm, Jēsū,
  m. (voc., Jēsū) Jesus, Joshua
male (adv.) badly, poorly
  male habēre be sick
propter (prep. + acc.) on account of, because of

Vocabulary Notes

Firmō 'strengthen, make steady' is the denominative verb formed from the adjective **firmus** 'steadfast, firm.'

Dīcō 'say, tell' takes either a dative of indirect object or **ad** + accusative: **dīcō populō** 'I tell the people,' **dīcō ad populum** 'I say to the people.' When it means 'tell' in the sense of 'give an order (to),' **dīcō** takes a dative + infinitive: **dīcit puerō operāre** 'he tells the boy to work.' In the passive voice, **dīcō** may mean 'be called'; as such, it is the equivalent of a copulative verb and takes a predicate nominative: **Petrus dīcitur pāpa** 'Peter is called pope.' [Likewise, **efficiō** (Unit 6) in the passive may function as a copulative: **Petrus efficitur pāpa** 'Peter is made (becomes) pope.'] The compounds **benedīcō** and **maledīcō** may take either a dative or an accusative: **benedīcit puerō/puerum** 'he blesses the boy.'

Anima has a dative/ablative plural in **-ābus**, to prevent its being confused with the dative/ablative plural of **animus** (Unit 4)—**animīs**. Any first declension noun whose base is identical with that of a second declension noun may use this alternate ending.

Laetitia means 'gladness, joy' as an outward expression of emotion. Cf. **gaudium** (Unit 3).

Lītūrgia, derived from the Greek, literally means 'work of the people.'

Diāconus 'deacon' is taken from the Greek for servant.

Cārus 'dear, beloved' may have its meaning supplemented by a dative: **cārus erat Marīae** 'he was dear to Mary.'

Besides its use with an ablative, **dīgnus** (or **indīgnus**) may occasionally be used with a genitive (in imitation of the Greek idiom).

An infinitive may also be used with these adjectives: **dīgnus est invocāre Deum** 'he is worthy to call upon God.'

Plēnus 'full of' takes an ablative, but sometimes a genitive: **plēna est grātiā/gratiae** 'she is full of grace.'

Ūniversus 'all, the whole' is the adjective from which the noun **ūniversum** (Unit 3) is derived.

Ūnus 'one' is sometimes the virtual equivalent of the indefinite article 'a, an.'

Unit 7 adds a new meaning to **ā (ab, abs)**: 'by (the agency of).' Cf. **ā (ab, abs)** in Unit 1.

Bene 'well' is the adverb derived from the adjective **bonus** (Unit 4).

The declension of **Jēsūs** is unique; its forms must be specially memorized.

Male 'badly, poorly,' the adverb from **malus** (Unit 4), when used with forms of **habeō**, yields the idiom 'to be sick.'

Derivatives:	LATIN	ENGLISH
	cōnfirmō	confirmation
	sānō	sane, sanatorium
	dīcō	indict, indite, dictum, diction, dictionary
	benedīcō	benediction
	maledīcō	malediction
	anima	animate, animation
	laetitia	Letitia
	misericordia	misericord
	turba	turbid, disturb, turbo-jet, turbulent
	diāconus	diaconate, deacon
	vōtum	vote, votary, votive
	dīgnus	deign, dignity
	indīgnus	indignity
	plēnus	plenary, plenty
	prīmus	prime
	ūnus	union, unity

Drills

I. Present indicative passive. Translate; change the number and retranslate.

a. audīris   e. monētur   i. trādiminī
b. capitur   f. dēlēminī   j. inveniuntur
c. jungor   g. fugāmur   k. exaudīmur
d. dūcuntur   h. ēdūcere   l. laudor

II.   Translate; change the voice and retranslate.

a. laudat   e. vocās   i. perdūcuntur
b. dōnāmur   f. habentur   j. capiō
c. līberāminī   g. miscētur   k. recipitur
d. servant   h. dūcitis   l. invenīs

Exercises

I.   1. Plēnī sunt caelī et terra glōriā tuā.
     2. Jēsūs Nazarēnus dīcitur Chrīstus.
     3. Puerō praemium ā magistrō datur.
     4. Jēsūs turbam sānat; multī enim male habent.
     5. Hodiē Missa ā cārō episcopō celebrātur.
     6. Dīgnī sumus misericordiā Deī?
     7. Puer īnfirmus vōtīs Petrī sānātur.
     8. Ūniversa Jūdaea ad domum advenit, et ā Jēsū peccāta dōnantur.
     9. Minister bene ōrat, et prīmum respōnsum ā populō dīcitur.
    10. In prīmīs īnfirmōs et maestōs sānat Jēsūs.
    11. Litūrgiā Deus ā populō laudātur.
    12. Propter Chrīstī victōriam apostolī erant plēnī laetitiā; et adhūc cum gaudiō populus Dominō semper benedīcit.
    13. Animābus jūstōrum semper benedīcimus?
    14. Ūnā cum populō diāconus dīgnus ad Deum ōrat.
    15. Cārus Jēsū apostolus Marīam in cēnāculum indūcit.
    16. Et dīgnī et indīgnī ā Deō cōnservantur.
    17. Ūna ancilla ad Jēsūm in domō venit, et benedīcitur.
    18. Magnā laetitiā psalmī ā discipulīs cantantur.
    19. Propter Fīlium Deī nostra nātūra ā peccātō līberātur.
    20. In nostrīs animīs Dominus rēgnat; nam dēlet nostra vitia et culpās.
    21. Ā famīliā puer Jēsūs cum magistrīs in templō invenitur.
    22. Līber ā prīmō diāconō recipitur.

[handwritten margin notes: "lead to a place / motion / accusative" and "Dative — not Abl / or Abl needs"]

23. In prīmīs famulus in domum dūcitur; ibi dīcunt famulō aquam capere.
24. Et tū ('you') cum hōc ('this') Nazarēnō, Jēsū, erās. Mk. xiv, 67.
25. Crēdō in ūnum Deum.
26. Lītūrgia Verbī nunc agitur?

II.
1. The good people are being led into the church by the new deacon; there the canticles of the Lord are joyfully sung.
2. Today the eternal victory of Christ is being well celebrated by his people.
3. The many gifts of the assembly are being received by the beloved minister.
4. The Lord of power and justice is rightly praised by all nature.
5. The man is not sad, but full of joy, for the sick in Judea are being healed by the blessed apostles.

Unit 8

39. Imperfect Indicative Active: All Four Conjugations

The imperfect is the past progressive tense. To form the imperfect indicative active of any verb, first construct the imperfect base: remove the ending **-re** from the present infinitive to isolate the present stem, lengthen the stem vowel, if it is short, and add the tense-making suffix **-bā-**. Then add the active personal endings (the first-person singular always uses the alternate ending **-m**, not **-ō**). Third conjugation verbs of the '**-iō**' type and fourth conjugation verbs alter the present stem to end in **-iē-**.

FIRST CONJUGATION:

laudō, laudāre, laudāvī, laudātus 'praise'
present stem: **laudā-**
imperfect base: **laudā-** + **-bā-** = **laudābā-**

	SINGULAR	PLURAL
1	**laudābam** ('I was praising')	**laudābāmus** ('we were praising')
2	**laudābās** ('you were praising')	**laudābātis** ('you were praising')
3	**laudābat** ('he/she/it was praising')	**laudābant** ('they were praising')

> *Notes:* 1. Since the progressive aspect also includes habitual or repeated action, these forms may thus be translated: 'I used to praise, I kept on praising.'
> 2. The endings **-m**, **-t**, and **-nt** shorten the vowel of the tense-making suffix. This is the case in the imperfect active forms of all other conjugations.

SECOND CONJUGATION:

moneō, monēre, monuī, monitus 'warn, advise'
present stem: **monē-**
imperfect base: **monē-** + **-bā-** = **monēbā-**

	SINGULAR	PLURAL
I	**monēbam** ('I was warning')	**monēbāmus** ('we were warning')
2	**monēbās** ('you were warning')	**monēbātis** ('you were warning')
3	**monēbat** ('he/she/it was warning')	**monēbant** ('they were warning')

THIRD CONJUGATION, '-ō' TYPE:

dūcō, dūcere, dūxī, ductus 'lead'
present stem: **dūce-** > **dūcē-**
imperfect base: **dūcē-** + **-bā-** = **dūcēbā-**

	SINGULAR	PLURAL
I	**dūcēbam** ('I was leading')	**dūcēbāmus** ('we were leading')
2	**dūcēbās** ('you were leading')	**dūcēbātis** ('you were leading')
3	**dūcēbat** ('he/she/it was leading')	**dūcēbant** ('they were leading')

THIRD CONJUGATION, '-iō' TYPE:

capiō, capere, cēpī, captus 'take, receive'
present stem: **cape-** > **capiē-**
imperfect base: **capiē-** + **-bā-** = **capiēbā-**

	SINGULAR	PLURAL
I	**capiēbam** ('I was taking')	**capiēbāmus** ('we were taking')
2	**capiēbās** ('you were taking')	**capiēbātis** ('you were taking')
3	**capiēbat** ('he/she/it was taking')	**capiēbant** ('they were taking')

FOURTH CONJUGATION:

audiō, audīre, audīvī, audītus 'hear'
present stem: audī- > audiē-
imperfect base: audiē- + -bā- = audiēbā-

	SINGULAR	PLURAL
1	audiēbam ('I was hearing')	audiēbāmus ('we were hearing')
2	audiēbās ('you were hearing')	audiēbātis ('you were hearing')
3	audiēbat ('he/she/it was hearing')	audiēbant ('they were hearing')

40. Imperfect Indicative Passive: All Four Conjugations

To form the imperfect indicative passive of any verb, first construct the imperfect base as detailed in Section 39; then add the passive personal endings (the first-person singular uses the alternate ending **-r**, not **-or**).

FIRST CONJUGATION:

laudō, laudāre, laudāvī, laudātus
imperfect base: laudābā-

	SINGULAR	PLURAL
1	laudābar ('I was being praised')	laudābāmur ('we were being praised')
2	laudābāris, laudābāre ('you were being praised')	laudābāminī ('you were being praised')
3	laudābātur ('he/she/it was being praised')	laudābantur ('they were being praised')

> *Note:* The endings **-r** and **-ntur** shorten the vowel of the tense-making suffix. This is the case in the imperfect passive forms of all other conjugations.

SECOND CONJUGATION:

moneō, monēre, monuī, monitus 'warn, advise'
imperfect base: monēbā-

SINGULAR	PLURAL
1 monēbar ('I was being warned')	monēbāmur ('we were being warned')
2 monēbāris, monēbāre ('you were being warned')	monēbāminī ('you were being warned')
3 monēbātur ('he/she/it was being warned')	monēbantur ('they were being warned')

THIRD CONJUGATION, '-ō' TYPE:

dūcō, dūcere, dūxī, ductus 'lead'
imperfect base: dūcēbā-

SINGULAR	PLURAL
1 dūcēbar ('I was being led')	dūcēbāmur ('we were being led')
2 dūcēbāris, dūcēbāre ('you were being led')	dūcēbāminī ('you were being led')
3 dūcēbātur ('he/she/it was being led')	dūcēbantur ('they were being led')

THIRD CONJUGATION, '-iō' TYPE:

capiō, capere, cēpī, captus 'take, receive'
imperfect base: capiēbā-

SINGULAR	PLURAL
1 capiēbar ('I was being taken')	capiēbāmur ('we were being taken')
2 capiēbāris, capiēbāre ('you were being taken')	capiēbāminī ('you were being taken')
3 capiēbātur ('he/she/it was being taken')	capiēbantur ('they were being taken')

FOURTH CONJUGATION:

audiō, audīre, audīvī, audītus 'hear'
imperfect base: audiēbā-

SINGULAR	PLURAL
1 audiēbar ('I was being heard')	audiēbāmur ('we were being heard')
2 audiēbāris, audiēbāre ('you were being heard')	audiēbāminī ('you were being heard')
3 audiēbātur ('he/she/it was being heard')	audiēbantur ('they were being heard')

41. Subordination (Complex Sentences)

A typical complex sentence contains two clauses: one independent and one dependent. Dependent, or subordinate, clauses are of three kinds: adverbial, adjectival, and substantive. An adverbial dependent clause is a sentence which has lost its independence by the addition of a certain kind of subordinating conjunction. In English, these include *after, although, because, if, since, when,* and *while.* The purpose of such subordinate clauses is to indicate a circumstance which sets the idea of the independent clause in a clearer light.

   1. It rained. The picnic was postponed.
   2. It rained and the picnic was postponed.
   3. Because it rained, the picnic was postponed.

The first example gives two independent clauses; the second links them to make a compound sentence (see Section 24). In both, the listener is left to sort out the relationship. But the third example, by subordinating the first clause to the second, clearly establishes their cause-and-effect relationship; in it, one clause is reduced to a dependent clause exerting the force of an adverb.

    In Latin, such adverbial clauses include temporal, concessive, conditional, and causal clauses.

42. Causal Clauses

A causal clause is an adverbial dependent clause which gives a reason for the action of the independent clause. It may be introduced by any of these subordinating conjunctions: **quia, quod, quoniam** 'because.'

> **Dominum laudāmus, *quia (quod, quoniam)* sānctus est.**
> 'We praise the Lord, *because* He is holy.'

43. Indirect Statements (1): Object Clauses

An indirect statement functions grammatically as a noun; in English it is commonly introduced by the subordinating conjunction *that.* Such a substantive clause may occasionally be used as a subject, but far more often is used as an object.

    An indirect statement in the form of an object clause in Latin occurs after a verb of saying, knowing, or thinking; it is introduced by a subordinating conjunction, **quod, quia, quoniam** 'that,' and may employ the indicative mood. It is the norm in both languages to make any logical adjustment in tense and personal reference.

DIRECT STATEMENT: **Chrīstiānus sum.**
'I am a Christian.'

INDIRECT STATEMENT: **Dīcēbat Petrō** *quia* (*quod, quoniam*) **Chrīstiānus erat.**
'He used to tell Peter *that* he was a Christian.'

Notes: 1. Although **quia, quod,** and **quoniam** mean both 'because' and 'that,' context will reveal whether their clause is adverbial (a causal clause) or substantive (an object clause).

2. **Dīcō,** as a verb of saying (or telling) takes an indirect object (**Petrō**) and a direct object (**quia Chrīstiānus erat**). See Section 26.

3. In imitation of Greek, an 'anticipatory' accusative may be found: **dīxit** *Jēsūm* **quoniam erat fīlius Deī** 'he said Jesus that he was the son of God' = **dīxit quoniam** *Jēsūs* **erat fīlius Deī** 'he said that Jesus was the son of God.'

4. A primary tense in the direct statement may be retained after a secondary main verb: **dīxit quod** *est* **Chrīstiānus** 'he said that he *was* a Christian.'

---

44. Ellipsis

In both English and Latin a word or words needed to complete a grammatical construction may be omitted when they can be understood from the preceding clauses. This common feature of language is called *ellipsis*: she sings as well as Amy [sings]; Dan is taller than I [am tall]; I went for a walk, but Meg didn't [go for a walk].

Bonī Deum laudant, sed malī nōn.
'Good men praise God, but evil men do not.'
[**sed** (coord. conj.) 'but, yet']

Vocabulary

-pleō, -plēre, -plēvī, -plētus fill, complete
  adimpleō, adimplēre, adimplēvī, adimplētus fulfill
  compleō, complēre, com-plēvī, complētus fulfill, accomplish
  impleō, implēre, implēvī, implētus fill, accomplish
  repleō, replēre, replēvī, re-plētus fill, complete
regō, regere, rēxī, rēctus rule, guide, govern
  corrigō, corrigere, corrēxī, corrēctus correct
  dīrigō, dīrigere, dīrēxī, dīrēctus direct
  ērigō, ērigere, ērēxī, ērēctus raise up, erect
incēnsum, incēnsī, n. incense
meritum, meritī, n. merit
silentium, silentiī, n. silence
angelicus, -a, -um angelic
contrītus, -a, -um contrite
cūnctus, -a, -um all
glōriōsus, -a, -um glorious
grātus, -a, -um (+ *dat.*) pleasing, agreeable

mīrus, -a, -um wonderful
mundus, -a, -um pure, clean
  immundus, -a, -um impure, unclean
sacrōsānctus, -a, -um most holy, venerable
salūtifer, -a, -um salutary, saving
supernus, -a, -um heavenly, celestial
terrēnus, -a, -um earthly
etiam (*intensifying adv.*) also; even
iterum (*adv.*) again
jam (*adv.*) already; now; soon
per (*prep.* + *acc.*) through
post (*prep.* + *acc.*) after, behind
quandō (*interrog. adv.*) when?
quia (*subord. conj.*) that; because
quod (*subord. conj.*) that; because
quoniam (*subord. conj.*) that; because
sed (*coord. conj.*) but, yet
tunc (*adv.*) then, at that time

Vocabulary Notes

The verb **-pleō** 'fill, complete' occurs only in compound form.

Dīrigō has the inseparable prefix **dis-** (**dī-**) 'apart, away.'

Meritum is a noun from which the adverb **meritō** (Unit 5) has been taken.

Angelicus 'angelic' is formed from the base of the noun **angelus** + the adjectival suffix **-icus, -a, -um** 'pertaining to.'

The adjective **glōriōsus** is compounded of the base of the noun **glōria** (Unit 1) + the adjectival suffix **-ōsus, -a, -um** 'full of.'

Distinguish between the homonyms **mundus, -a, -um** 'pure, clean' and **mundus, mundī,** m. 'world' (Unit 4).

Sacrōsānctus 'most holy, venerable' in its elements means 'consecrated with a religious ceremony.'

The adjective **supernus** 'heavenly, celestial' is derived from the preposition **super** 'above' (Unit 1).

The adjective **terrēnus** 'earthly' is made from **terra** (Unit 1) and the adjectival suffix **-ēnus, -a, -um** 'pertaining to.'

Jam tends to mean 'already' with any past tense, 'now' with the present, and 'soon' with a future.

Per (prep. + acc.), just as in English, may mean 'through' in four different senses: time, space, agency, and instrumentality: **per hōram** 'through an hour,' **per agrum** 'through the field,' **per Chrīstum** 'through Christ,' **per potentiam** 'through his power.'

Quod, quia, and **quoniam** mean 'that' or 'because'; occasionally, **eō quod** 'because' occurs.

Derivatives:	LATIN	ENGLISH
	-pleō	complete, complementary, replete, implement
	regō	regent, rector, incorrigible, corrigenda, dirigible
	grātus	grateful, ingrate
	mīrus	mirage, miracle, mirror
	sacrōsānctus	sacrosanct
	supernus	supernal
	terrēnus	terrain
	iterum	iterate
	per	perfect, percolator, perforation

Drills

I. Imperfect indicative. Translate; change the voice and retranslate.

a. cantābātur
b. dabāminī
c. laudābāre
d. līberābantur

e. dēlēbar
f. monēbāmur
g. agēbāre
h. dūcēbātur

i. perdūcēbāris
j. inveniēbāminī
k. sānābātur
l. cōnfirmābar

II. Imperfect indicative. Translate; change the number and re-translate.

a. dōnābat
b. laudābāminī
c. adōrābātur
d. efficiēbantur

e. vocābās
f. observābāmur
g. miscēbāris
h. recipiēbantur

i. inveniēbat
j. firmābās
k. sānābāminī
l. celebrābam

Exercises

I.
1. Potentiā Deī puer ērigēbātur (ērigitur).
2. Ā turbā angelicā caelōrum Deus laudābātur.
3. Per Christī potentiam populus ab apóstolīs sānābantur.
4. Domus maestō silentiō implēbātur, quoniam puer erat mortuus.
5. Apostolī gaudiō replēbantur, quia verbum Dominī adimplēbātur.
6. Quandō puer ā magistrō corrigēbātur? —Nōn hodiē.
7. Hebraeī glōriōsum Dominum psalmīs et incēnsō laudābant, quod mīra etiam prō populō complēbantur.
8. Diāconus dīcit quod Dominus vōta contrītōrum exaudit.
9. Contrītō animō Deō grātiās agēbāmus, sed malī nōn.
10. Cūnctī discipulī post Jēsūm in domum jam veniēbant.
11. Laetitia est et in supernīs et in terrēnīs, quia Dominus est bonus et magnus.
12. Puerī jam inveniēbant quod in librō mīrō sunt et hymnī et cantica.
13. Malus minister mundum sacrificium nōn faciēbat.
14. Nostrī ministrī dīcunt quoniam Christus erat et est et erit Dominus ūniversae nātūrae.
15. Iterum salūtiferīs praeceptīs Christī monēbāmur (monēmur).
16. Apostolus audiēbat quod Jēsūs erat (est) vīvus, sed nōn crēdēbat.
17. Semper dīcēbātis quia multī in Jūdaeā erant discipulī Christī.
18. Tunc discipulī cum Jēsū per agrōs ambulābant.
19. Per merita Jēsū sānābāmur et efficiēbāmur firmī.
20. Beātī sumus, quia Deō est fīlius pius in aeternum.
21. Hodiē verba antīquōrum cōram Jūdaeīs adimplentur.
22. Per sacrōsānctum sacrāmentum efficiēbāmur Dominō grātī.

23. Magna turba ad domum conveniēbat, quod audiēbant quia ibi erat Jēsūs Nazarēnus.
24. Tunc Petrus turbae benedīcēbat, et dīcēbat dē misericordiā Dominī nostrī Jēsū Chrīstī.
25. Sed venit hōra, et nunc est. Jn. iv, 23.

II.   1. They say that Peter was the first pope.
    2. You also used to praise God with psalms and canticles.
    3. We were always being strengthened by God's grace.
    4. There is hatred of sin but mercy for the contrite.
    5. Your true and living words are being heard through the world by all the people.

Unit 9

45. Future Indicative Active: First and Second Conjugations

The future indicative active for verbs of the first and second conjugations is compounded of the present stem + the tense-making suffix **-bi-** + the active personal endings.

FIRST CONJUGATION:

laudō, laudāre, laudāvī, laudātus 'praise'
present stem: **laudā-**
future base: **laudā-** + **-bi-** = **laudābi-**

	SINGULAR	PLURAL
1	**laudābō** ('I will praise')	**laudābimus** ('we will praise')
2	**laudābis** ('you will praise')	**laudābitis** ('you will praise')
3	**laudābit** ('he/she/it will praise')	**laudābunt** ('they will praise')

Note: The **-i-** of the suffix is absorbed in the first singular and changed to **-u-** in the third plural.

SECOND CONJUGATION:

moneō, monēre, monuī, monitus 'warn, advise'
present stem: **monē-**
future base: **monē-** + **-bi-** = **monēbi-**

	SINGULAR	PLURAL
1	**monēbō** ('I will warn')	**monēbimus** ('we will warn')
2	**monēbis** ('you will warn')	**monēbitis** ('you will warn')
3	**monēbit** ('he/she/it will warn')	**monēbunt** ('they will warn')

> *Note:* The **-i-** of the suffix is absorbed in the first singular and
> changed to **-u-** in the third plural.

46. Future Indicative Passive:
First and Second Conjugations

The future indicative passive for verbs of the first and second conjugations is compounded of the present stem + the tense-making suffix **-bi-** + the passive personal endings.

FIRST CONJUGATION:

laudō, laudāre, laudāvī, laudātus 'praise'
future base: **laudābi-**

	SINGULAR	PLURAL
1	**laudābor** ('I will be praised')	**laudābimur** ('we will be praised')
2	**laudāberis, laudābere** ('you will be praised')	**laudābiminī** ('you will be praised')
3	**laudābitur** ('he/she/it will be praised')	**laudābuntur** ('they will be praised')

> *Note:* The **-i-** of the suffix is absorbed in the first singular,
> changed to **-e-** in the second singular, and changed to
> **-u-** in the third plural. Cf. **erō** and **erunt.**

SECOND CONJUGATION:

moneō, monēre, monuī, monitus 'warn, advise'
future base: **monēbi-**

	SINGULAR	PLURAL
1	**monēbor** ('I will be warned')	**monēbimur** ('we will be warned')
2	**monēberis, monēbere** ('you will be warned')	**monēbiminī** ('you will be warned')
3	**monēbitur** ('he/she/it will be warned')	**monēbuntur** ('they will be warned')

> *Note:*   The **-i-** of the suffix is absorbed in the first singular, changed to **-e-** in the second singular, and changed to **-u-** in the third plural.

47. Future Indicative Active: Third and Fourth Conjugations

The future indicative base in the third and fourth conjugations ends in **-ē-**, lengthened from **-e-** of the present stem of the '**-ō**' type in the third conjugation, or added to the present stem in the fourth conjugation. The '**-iō**' type of the third conjugation has **-iē-**. The future indicative active of these conjugations is formed by adding the active personal endings to the future base.

THIRD CONJUGATION, '-ō' TYPE:

dūcō, dūcere, dūxī, ductus 'lead'
present stem: **dūce-**
future base: **dūcē-**

	SINGULAR	PLURAL
1	**dūcam** ('I will lead')	**dūcēmus** ('we will lead')
2	**dūcēs** ('you will lead')	**dūcētis** ('you will lead')
3	**dūcet** ('he/she/it will lead')	**dūcent** ('they will lead')

> *Notes:* 1. Short **-a-** appears as the tense sign in the first singular before the alternate ending **-m**.
> 2. Long **-e-** shortens before **-t** and **-nt**, as usual.

THIRD CONJUGATION, '-iō' TYPE:

capiō, capere, cēpī, captus 'take, receive'
present stem: **cape-**
future base: **capiē-**

	SINGULAR	PLURAL
1	**capiam** ('I will take')	**capiēmus** ('we will take')
2	**capiēs** ('you will take')	**capiētis** ('you will take')
3	**capiet** ('he/she/it will take')	**capient** ('they will take')

> *Notes:* 1. Short **-a-** appears as the tense sign in the first singular before the alternate ending **-m**.
> 2. Long **-e-** shortens before **-t** and **-nt**, as usual.

FOURTH CONJUGATION:

audiō, audīre, audīvī, audītus 'hear'
present stem: **audī-**
future base: **audiē-**

SINGULAR	PLURAL
1 **audiam** ('I will hear')	**audiēmus** ('we will hear')
2 **audiēs** ('you will hear')	**audiētis** ('you will hear')
3 **audiet** ('he/she/it will hear')	**audient** ('they will hear')

> *Notes:* 1. Short **-a-** appears as the tense sign in the first singular before the alternate ending **-m**.
> 2. Long **-e-** shortens before **-t** and **-nt**, as usual.

48. Future Indicative Passive: Third and Fourth Conjugations

The future indicative passive for verbs of the third and fourth conjugations is formed by adding the passive personal endings to the future base.

SINGULAR	PLURAL
1 **dūcar** ('I will be led')	**dūcēmur** ('we will be led')
2 **dūcēris, dūcēre** ('you will be led')	**dūcēminī** ('you will be led')
3 **dūcētur** ('he/she/it will be led')	**dūcentur** ('they will be led')
1 **capiar** ('I will be taken')	**capiēmur** ('we will be taken')
2 **capiēris, capiēre** ('you will be taken')	**capiēminī** ('you will be taken')
3 **capiētur** ('he/she/it will be taken')	**capientur** ('they will be taken')

	SINGULAR	PLURAL
1	**audiar** ('I will be heard')	**audiēmur** ('we will be heard')
2	**audiēris, audiēre** ('you will be heard')	**audiēminī** ('you will be heard')
3	**audiētur** ('he/she/it will be heard')	**audientur** ('they will be heard')

> *Note:* Again, **-a-** appears as the tense sign in the first-person singular.

49. Infinitive as Subject

Since an infinitive is a verbal noun (see Section 20f.2), it may be used as the subject of a sentence. A predicate adjective modifying a subject infinitive has a nominative singular neuter ending.

Bonum est *invocāre* Deum.
'*To call upon* God is good.'
'It is good *to call upon* God.'

> *Note:* In the second translation, the use of the expletive *it* allows the subject to be delayed.

50. Ablative of Respect (Specification)

The ablative of respect, or specification, indicates a specific category in terms of which a judgment is made.

Servus Dominī est *animō* beātus.
'The servant of the Lord is happy *in (respect to) spirit.*'

Vocabulary

adjuvō, adjuvāre, adjūvī, adjūtus help

fōrmō, fōrmāre, fōrmāvī, fōrmātus train, guide; fashion, form

intrō, intrāre, intrāvī, intrātus enter

satiō, satiāre, satiāvī, satiātus nourish, satisfy

sēparō, sēparāre, sēparāvī,
sēparātus separate
habeō:
perhibeō, perhibēre, per-
hibuī, perhibitus hold out,
produce, afford
videō, vidēre, vīdī, vīsus see;
realize
sciō, scīre, scīvī, scītus know
causa, causae, f. purpose,
reason
causā (improper prep. +
gen.) for the sake of
cēreus, cēreī, m. candle
socius, sociī, m. companion,
ally
mandātum, mandātī, n. order,
commandment
testimōnium, testimōniī, n.
witness, testimony
vestīgium, vestīgiī, n. footstep

tēctum, tēctī, n. roof, house
apostolicus, -a, -um apostolic
altus, -a, -um high, deep
catholicus, -a, -um universal,
catholic
vester, vestra, vestrum your,
yours (pl.)
autem (postpos. coord. conj.)
but, and
certē (adv.) surely, certainly;
at least
dīligenter (adv.) diligently
inter (prep. + acc.) between,
among
saepe (adv.) often
statim (adv.) immediately,
at once
sub (prep.: 1. + acc.; 2. + abl.)
1. (to a place) under 2. (in or
at a place) under
vērē (adv.) truly

Vocabulary Notes

The primitive verb from which **adjuvō** is formed—**juvō**, which
also means 'help'—is not formally presented in this text.

Intrō 'enter' may take an accusative, with or without a preposition
(**in** or **ad**): **intrat (in/ad) domum** 'he enters the house.'

It is hardly surprising that **videō** has both a physical and a mental
meaning: 'see; realize.' Cf. 'do you see that?'

The ablative of **causa** 'purpose, reason' may be used as an improper
preposition—**causā** 'for the sake of'—taking either a preceding genitive or an accompanying ablative of a possessive adjective: **Petrī
causā** 'for the sake of Peter,' **meā causā** 'for my sake.'

Altus indicates distance up or down; hence, 'high, deep.'

Catholicus is taken from the Greek for 'universal.'

Autem may be used to continue a narrative ('and') or to indicate a
weak adversative idea ('but').

Vērē 'truly' is the adverb formed from the adjective **vērus** (Unit 4).

Derivatives: LATIN   ENGLISH

adjuvō	adjutant general
fōrmō	formation
satiō	satiate, insatiable
videō	video, vision, visor
sciō	science, sciolism
cēreus	cerements
socius	sociology, associate, society
mandātum	mandate, mandatory
vestīgium	vestige
tēctum	detect
altus	alto, Terra Haute, altitude, exalted
inter	intermittent, international
sub	submit, submarine

Drills

I. Future indicative: first and second conjugations. Translate; change to the present and retranslate.

amulābitis

cantabitur

a. ambulābis   e. līberābimur   i. invocābimus
b. cantābuntur   f. operābō   j. fugābunt
c. dabit *he will give* g. servābiminī   k. monēbor
d. collaudābitis h. vocābere   l. habēberis

II. Future indicative: third and fourth conjugations. Translate; change to the present and retranslate.

bibimus

a. agētur   e. capiēmur *capimur*   i. regar
b. bibēmus   f. faciēs *facis*   j. maledīcentur
c. crēdent   g. veniētis   k. corrigēre
d. dūcet   h. adveniam *venie* *I will come* *adveniemus*   l. ēdūceminī

Exercises

I.   1. Animō autem bonī ā malīs sēparābuntur (sēparābantur).
     2. Mandāta Deī ā vestrō populō scientur (sciuntur).
     3. Dominum nostrum semper laudābimus, quoniam
        ūniversum certē regit.
     4. Puerī animō maestī in agrīs dīligenter operābunt?

5. Crēdimus in ūnam sānctam, catholicam et apostolicam Ecclēsiam.
6. Jēsūs sub tēctum servī intrābat, et statim puer sānābātur.
7. Petrus Marīam saepe vidēbat inter apostolī cārī sociōs.
8. Populī causā Petrus testimōnium dē Jēsū perhibēbit (perhibet, perhibēbat).
9. Vestrī sociī in mandātīs Dominī ā diācōnō fōrmābuntur.
10. Petrus videt quod bonum est hīc esse.
11. Scīmus quod ecclēsia dē Chrīstō Jēsū testimōnium semper dabit.
12. In viā vītae vestīgiīs Dominī semper perdūcēmur (perdūcimur, perdūcēbāmur).
13. Cēreī populō ā diācōnō dabuntur (dabantur, dantur).
14. Cēna Dominī populum satiābat (satiābit, satiat).
15. Apostolus dē agnō Deī testimōnium saepe perhibēbat.
16. Virōs in agrīs adjuvābunt puerī.
17. Gaudium discipulī plēnum, quia in potentiā Deī populum fōrmat.
18. Stēllam clāram vidēbant, et statim Altum Deum laudābant.
19. Petrus autem ē domō veniet, et vidēbit vestrōs sociōs.
20. Misericordia Deī est multae laetitiae causa.
21. Nātus inter magistrōs invenīētur (invenītur, inveniēbātur).
22. Vērē beātī sunt sociī, quoniam ab altō Deō et satiantur et adjuvantur.
23. Nātum vestrum in templō vidēbāmus; ibi autem mīra dīcēbat.
24. Quandō Dominus cum glōriā iterum veniet?
25. Scītis enim grātiam Dominī nostrī Jēsū Chrīstī. II Cor. viii, 9.

II.

1. The High God will be praised by the minister and the people.
2. It is good to work in behalf of the kingdom.
3. For the sake of the good servant Jesus will enter the house and heal the child.
4. In silence we will give thanks to the Lord.
5. Through the power of Jesus we will be freed from the evil one.

Unit 10

51. The Perfect-Active System: Three Tenses

In all four conjugations, the stem of the first-person singular, perfect indicative active (i.e., the third principal part) is the source of three indicative tenses: the perfect active, the pluperfect active, and the future-perfect active. The perfect active is formed from the perfect active stem + a set of endings unique to the perfect active; the pluperfect active and the future-perfect active are formed from the perfect active stem + a tense-making suffix + the active personal endings.

52. Perfect Indicative Active: All Four Conjugations

The perfect represents two tenses: the past simple ('I did') and the present completed ('I have done'). Context will determine which translation is more appropriate. (See Section 20c.)

The perfect indicative active is formed by removing the ending **-ī** from the third principal part to determine the stem, and then adding the following set of endings:

	SINGULAR	PLURAL
1	**-ī**	**-imus**
2	**-istī**	**-istis**
3	**-it**	**-ērunt**

For example:

laudō, laudāre, laudāvī, laudātus 'praise'
perfect stem: **laudāv-**

	SINGULAR	PLURAL
1	**laudāvī** ('I [have] praised')	**laudāvimus** ('we [have] praised')

	SINGULAR	PLURAL
2	**laudāvistī** ('you [have] praised')	**laudāvistis** ('you [have] praised')
3	**laudāvit** ('he/she/it [has] praised')	**laudāvērunt** ('they [have] praised')

> *Note:* Forms such as **laudāvistī** and **laudāvistis** may be contracted (**laudāstī**, **laudāstis**), with no difference in meaning.

sum, esse, fuī, futūrus 'be, exist'
perfect stem: **fu-**

	SINGULAR	PLURAL
1	**fuī** ('I was, I have been')	**fuimus** ('we were, have been')
2	**fuistī** ('you were, you have been')	**fuistis** ('you were, have been')
3	**fuit** ('he/she/it was, he/she/it has been')	**fuērunt** ('they were, have been')

53. Relative Pronoun/Interrogative Adjective: quī, quae, quod

As a relative pronoun, **quī, quae, quod** introduces an adjectival clause (see Section 41) which modifies the antecedent of the pronoun; it is translated by *who, whose, whom,* or *which,* depending on the case and the referent. As an interrogative adjective, it modifies a noun and asks a question; it is translated by *what* or *which.*

quī, quae, quod 'who, which; what? which?'

	SINGULAR			PLURAL		
	M.	F.	N.	M.	F.	N.
Nom.	quī	quae	quod	quī	quae	quae
Gen.	cujus	cujus	cujus	quōrum	quārum	quōrum
Dat.	cui	cui	cui	quibus	quibus	quibus
Acc.	quem	quam	quod	quōs	quās	quae
Abl.	quō	quā	quō	quibus	quibus	quibus

54. Uses of the Relative Pronoun

As a relative pronoun, **quī**, **quae**, **quod** is used in adjectival clauses and as a connective between sentences.

a. Adjectival Clauses   The relative pronoun, like an adjective, has gender, number, and case. It derives its gender and number from its antecedent (which may be either expressed or implied), but takes its case from its function in its own clause.

>**Deus, *quem* in psalmīs laudāmus, est bonus.**
>'God, *Whom* we praise in psalms, is good.'

Here **quem** introduces an adjectival clause modifying **Deus. Quem** is masculine and singular because its antecedent, **Deus**, is masculine and singular. But it is in the accusative case because in its own clause it is the direct object of **laudāmus.**

The antecedent of a relative pronoun may be left unexpressed.

>**Beātī, quī in viā Dominī ambulant.**
>'[Those] who walk in the way of the Lord are blessed.'

b. Connective Relative   A relative pronoun may be used as the equivalent of a conjunction (*and* or *or*) and a demonstrative pronoun (this one, that one, or simply, he, she, or it).

>**Discipulī in domum veniēbant. Quī cum laetitiā Jēsūm audiēbant.**
>'The disciples were coming into the house. And they were gladly listening to Jesus.'

55. Use of the Interrogative Adjective

The interrogative adjective, like any other adjective, agrees with the word it modifies in gender, number, and case.

>***Quī* minister hodiē missam celebrābat?**
>'*Which* minister was celebrating Mass today?'

Quī is masculine, singular, and nominative because **minister** is masculine, singular, and nominative.

Vocabulary

solvō, solvere, solvī, solūtus
set free; break up; pay back

    absolvō, absolvere, absolvī,
    absolūtus set free (from),
    absolve; finish

tollō, tollere, sustulī, sublātus
take away, lift up, take up

    extollō, extollere, extulī, —
    lift up, extol

fīniō, fīnīre, fīnīvī (fīniī),
fīnītus end, finish

Galilaea, Galilaeae, f. Galilee

annus, annī, m. year

clērus, clērī, m. clergy

dēbitum, dēbitī, n. debt

dēsīderium, dēsīderiī, n. want,
need, desire

dētrīmentum, dētrīmentī, n.
loss

imperium, imperiī, n. dominion, empire; precept,
command

ministerium, ministeriī, n.
ministry, service

spatium, spatiī, n. space

vinculum, vinculī, n. bond,
chain

excelsus, -a, -um high, lofty,
exalted

perpetuus, -a, -um everlasting,
perpetual

secundus, -a, -um next, second

ūnigenitus, -a, -um only begotten, only

allēlūjā (*Hebrew: interjection*)
alleluia (*cry of joy and
praise*)

ante (*prep. + acc.*) before

ecce (*interjection*) look! here!

eléīson (*Greek: imperative*)
have mercy!

hōsānnā (*Hebrew: interjection*) hosanna (*cry of praise*)

Kȳrie (*Greek: vocative*)
O Lord!

perenniter (*adv.*) constantly,
perennially

posteā (*adv.*) afterward,
later on

quī, quae, quod (1. *interrog.
adj.*; 2. *rel. pron.*) 1. which?
what? 2. who, which, that

secundum (*prep. + acc.*)
according to

subitō (*adv.*) suddenly

Vocabulary Notes

Clērus 'clergy' is taken from the Greek meaning 'inheritance'; the only inheritance of the Levites was the Lord.

Ministerium 'ministry, service' is an abstract noun formed from **minister** (Unit 2) and the abstract-noun-making suffix **-ium, -iī**.

Secundus literally means 'following'; hence, 'next, second.' From this adjective the preposition **secundum** 'according to' has been derived.

Ante 'before' has both a temporal and a spatial meaning: **ante an-num** 'a year before'; **ante domum** 'before (in front of) the home.'

When used in nominal sentences, **ecce** means 'here is': **ecce ancilla Dominī** 'here is the servant of the Lord.'

Eleīson, despite its long penult, retains its Greek accentuation: el*é*īson.

Quī, quae, quod has a more general meaning when suffixed by **-cumque**: **quīcumque, quaecumque, quodcumque** 'whichever, whoever, whatever.' When used with the preposition **cum** 'with' the ablative precedes and coalesces with it: **quōcum** 'with whom,' **quibuscum** 'with whom.' The relative may precede other prepositions, e.g., **quem propter** 'on account of which/whom.' A connective relative even precedes a subordinating conjunction: **Quī quoniam . . .** 'And because they . . .'

Derivatives:

LATIN	ENGLISH
solvō	solve, solution
absolvō	absolution
fīniō	finite, infinitive, definition
annus	annals, annual
clērus	cleric, clerical, clerk
dēbitum	debit, debt
dētrīmentum	detriment
imperium	empire, imperial
vinculum	vinculum (*math term*)
excelsus	excelsior
ante	antebellum, anticipate
quī	qui vive, quorum, qua, sine qua non
subitō	subito (*musical term*)

Drills

I. Give the principal parts of sum; adōrō; compleō; regō; accipiō; veniō. Fully conjugate the perfect active indicative of each.

II. Translate; change imperfect to perfect or perfect to imperfect and retranslate.

a. cantāvistis   c. vocābātis   e. faciēbam
b. laudābāmus   d. habuērunt   f. dūxistī

g. invēnit   i. sānāvī   k. replēvimus
h. crēdēbās   j. dīcēbat   l. vidēbant

Exercises

I. 1. Glōria in excelsīs Deō.
2. Miníster et servī ōrāvērunt: Kȳrie, eléīson!
3. Dominus, quī est bonus, dēsīderia populī semper scīvit. *perfgo*
4. Servus, quem scīs, ministrō et aquam et vīnum dedit. *perfgo*
5. Verba Chrīstī, quae audīmus, apostolī trādidērunt.
6. Quī discipulī in Galilaeā scīvērunt quod Jēsūs Nazarēnus erat fīlius ūnigenitus Deī?
7. Secundum tua verba perenniter operāvimus et ōrāvimus.
8. Cui servō nōn cārus fuit dominus?
9. Per ūnigenitum Fīlium Deus dēbita nostrōrum peccātōrum solvit.
10. Agnus Deī, quī tollit peccāta mundī, ā populō semper laudātur.
11. Hodiē Dominus Deus Fīlium ūnigenitum super cūnctōs in caelō et in terrā extulit. Allēlūjā!
12. Per Deī perpetuam misericordiam vincula peccātī tolluntur et solvuntur.
13. Quī discipulī vītam in Galilaeā fīnīvērunt?
14. Posteā Chrīstiānī dētrīmentō Petrī afficiēbantur.
15. Benedictus, quī venit ad cēnam Dominī. Hōsānnā in excelsīs!
16. Subitō puer imperium Dominī vīdit. Quī Deō grātiās egit. ⁷
17. Clērus ministeriō populī saepe adjuvātur.
18. Prīmus discipulus Petrum scīvit, sed secundus nōn.
19. Īnfirmī in domum intrāvērunt. Quī ā Jēsū sānābantur.
20. Per spatium multōrum annōrum apostolī Jēsū Chrīstī in Galilaeā vidēbantur. Quī enim in Jēsūm vērē crēdidērunt.
21. Per potentiam Dominī Petrus populum peccātīs absolvit.
22. Marīa nātum ante magistrōs vīdit (videt).
23. Virī, quibuscum Jēsūs trāns agrōs ambulābat, fuērunt discipulī.
24. Et iterum intrāvit Capharnaum. Mk. ii, 1.
25. Sciō quia Messiās venit—quī dīcitur Chrīstus. Jn. iv, 25.

II. 1. Which life is good and blessed?
2. The boy whom we saw is the child of the servant.

3. What servants of the Lord are without blame?
4. Here is the Lamb of God, who takes away the sin of the world. Jn. i, 29.
5. The disciple who helped the people ended his ministry in Judea.

Unit 11

56. *Pluperfect Indicative Active: All Four Conjugations*

The pluperfect is the past completed tense, translated in English with the auxiliary 'had.' To form the pluperfect indicative active of any verb, first construct the pluperfect base: remove the ending -ī from the third principal part to isolate the perfect-active stem, add the tense-making suffix **-erā-**, and add the active personal endings.

For example:

laudō, laudāre, laudāvī, laudātus 'praise'
perfect stem: **laudāv-**
pluperfect base: **laudāv-** + **-erā-** = **laudāverā-**

	SINGULAR	PLURAL
1	**laudāveram** ('I had praised')	**laudāverāmus** ('we had praised')
2	**laudāverās** ('you had praised')	**laudāverātis** ('you had praised')
3	**laudāverat** ('he/she/it had praised')	**laudāverant** ('they had praised')

57. *Future-Perfect Indicative Active: All Four Conjugations*

The future-perfect is the future completed tense, translated in English with the auxiliaries 'will have.' It is compounded of the perfect-active stem + the tense-making suffix **-eri-** + the active personal endings.

For example:

capiō, capere, cēpī, captus 'take, receive'
perfect stem: **cēp-**
future-perfect base: **cēp-** + **-eri-** = **cēperi-**

	SINGULAR	PLURAL
1	**cēperō** ('I will have taken')	**cēperimus** ('we will have taken')
2	**cēperis** ('you will have taken')	**cēperitis** ('you will have taken')
3	**cēperit** ('he/she/it will have taken')	**cēperint** ('they will have taken')

Note: The **-i-** of the suffix is dropped before the ending **-ō**.

58. Ablative of Cause

The ablative case (with or without a preposition) may be used to express the cause of an action or state.

Beātī sumus (ē) victōriā Dominī.
'We are happy *because of the victory* of the Lord.'

59. Direct Quotations

The exact words of a speaker may be quoted directly. In the traditional Vulgate Bible, quotation marks are not used; capitalization alone is used to indicate the beginning of a quotation.

a. No Change   The speaker's words are quoted with no change.

Puer dīxit, Mea famīlia est hīc.
'The boy said, "My family is here."'

b. No change, but introduced by **quia** *or* **quoniam**   The speaker's words are quoted with no change, but may be introduced by an untranslated sign-word, **quia** or **quoniam**.

Puer dīxit, Quia (Quoniam) mea famīlia est hīc.
'The boy said, "My family is here."'

Note: Following contemporary practices, the Nova Vulgata uses quotation marks and has eliminated the use of **quia** or **quoniam** to introduce direct quotations.

Vocabulary

-clīnō, -clīnāre, -clīnāvī,
-clīnātus bend
  inclīnō, inclīnāre, inclīnāvī,
  inclīnātus bow, lean
  forward
  reclīnō, reclīnāre, reclīnāvī,
  reclīnātus lean back,
  recline
exsultō, exsultāre, exsultāvī,
exsultātus rejoice, exult
glōrificō, glōrificāre, glōrificāvī, glōrificātus glorify
  conglōrificō, conglōrificāre,
  conglōrificāvī, con-
  glōrificātus glorify
  (exceedingly)
gregō, gregāre, gregāvī, gregātus gather, assemble
  aggregō, aggregāre, aggregāvī,
  aggregātus add to; join
  with
  congregō, congregāre, congregāvī, congregātus
  gather together, assemble
  sēgregō, sēgregāre, sēgregāvī,
  sēgregātus separate
parō, parāre, parāvī, parātus
provide, prepare
  praeparō, praeparāre,
  praeparāvī, praeparātus
  prepare
resultō, resultāre, resultāvī, resultātus resound, rebound
sānctificō, sānctificāre, sāncti-

ficāvī, sānctificātus make
holy, sanctify
aperiō, aperīre, aperuī, apertus
open; explain
Adam, Adae, m. Adam
aula, aulae, f. hall, church
columna, columnae, f. pillar,
column
creātūra, creātūrae, f. creation,
creature
flamma, flammae, f. flame
hostia, hostiae, f. sacrificial
offering, host
innocentia, innocentiae, f.
innocence
Pascha, Paschae, f. Passover,
Pesach, Pasch; Easter
prophēta, prophētae, m.
prophet
scrīptūra, scrīptūrae, f.
writing, scripture
cibus, cibī, m. food
Paulus, Paulī, m. Paul
dolōrōsus, -a, -um sorrowful
laetus, -a, -um joyful
parvus, -a, -um little, small
  parvulus, -a, -um little,
  small
tertius, -a, -um third
apud (prep. + acc.) in the
presence of, among, at the
house of
hinc (adv.) from here
ob (prep. + acc.) because of

Vocabulary Notes

The verb **-clīnō** 'bend' is used only in compounds. When used
without a direct object, **reclīnō** occurs in the passive (equivalent to
the Greek middle): **reclīnābantur** 'they were reclining.'

Exsultō and **resultō** are frequentative verbs derived from the primitive verb **saliō** 'leap.' For **exsultō** 'rejoice,' compare the expression, 'jump for joy.'

When **faciō** 'do, make' (Unit 6) is compounded with a noun or an adjective, it changes from the third conjugation to the first: **glōria** + **faciō** = **glōrificō** (**glōrificāre**, etc.) 'make glorious, glorify.' The same observation may be made about **sānctificō**.

Gregō is a denominative verb derived from the noun **grex** (Unit 18) meaning 'flock.'

The Hebrew nouns **Adam** and **Pascha** are declined as first declension nouns. **Adam**, in form, may be either nominative or accusative.

Creātūra literally means the 'act of or the result of the act of creating'; hence, 'creation, creature.' **Scrīptūra** uses the same noun-making suffix (**-ūra**).

Prophēta is taken from the Greek meaning 'one who speaks forth.'

Laetus is the adjective from which the noun **laetitia** (Unit 7) is formed.

There is little or no difference in meaning between **parvus** and **parvulus**; they are often used substantively to mean 'little one,' hence 'child.'

Derivatives:

LATIN	ENGLISH
inclīnō	incline, inclination
exsultō	exultation
aggregō	aggregate
congregō	congregate, congregation
sēgregō	segregation
aperiō	aperture
aula	aulic
cibus	ciborium
dolōrōsus	dolorous, doloroso (*musical term*)
tertius	tertiary

Drills

I. Pluperfect and future-perfect active. Translate; change the number and retranslate.

a. ambulāverat   c. dōnāverimus   e. dēlēverit
b. dederāmus   d. laudāverint   f. miscuerātis

g. ēgerant
h. dūxerō
i. dīxeris

j. affirmāveritis
k. adimplēverās
l. rēxerit

m. dīrēxerat
n. scīverāmus
o. solveram

II. Pluperfect and future-perfect active. Translate.

a. he had finished
b. we will have absolved
c. they had had
d. you will have seen
e. I had warned

f. I will have said
g. you (pl.) had taken
h. they will have healed
i. she had celebrated
j. he will have known

Exercises

I.

1. Quoniam Hebraeī columnam flammae vīdērunt, etiam *even*
   hodiē Pascham observant. *men*
2. Tunc caelī ante Jēsūm aperiēbantur.
3. Meritō ūniversa creātūra innocentiam Agnī laudāverit *will have praised*
   (laudābit).
4. Aula laetitiā populī resultāverat. *it had resounded — The hall had resounded b/c of the joy of the ppl* *e/ex understood prep.*
5. Jam Jēsūs populō intrāre in templum dīxerat.
6. Cūnctī apostolī in cēnāculō congregāverant, et ibi Deum
   perenniter conglōrificābant.
7. In prīncipiō erat Verbum, et Verbum erat apud Deum, et
   Deus erat Verbum. Jn. i, 1.
8. Ob Adae culpam prīmam habēmus Chrīstum Dominum.
9. Nam Chrīstus mortuōs ā vīvīs sēparāverit. *Ablative Separation — Future Perfect — separavi + ero erit...*
10. Paschā dolōrōsī efficiuntur laetī.
11. In Jūdaeā apostolus viam Dominī praeparāverat.
12. Quī semper et dīligenter operāverint prō Dominō,
    aeternum praemium habēbunt in rēgnō caelōrum.
13. Parvulī, quī ad Jēsūm in Petrī domō vēnerant,
    benedīcēbántur.
14. Sed ante annum Paulus Petrum in Galilaeā vīderat.
15. Parvus servus, quī cibum parāverat, scīvit cūnctōs quī
    vocābantur.
16. Paulus, magister in Jūdaeā clārus, scrīptūrās bene scīverat.
17. Populus, quī in aulā congregāverit, victōriā Chrīstī
    exsultābit.
18. Discipulī congregāvērunt in cēnāculō, et Petrus dīxit,
    Quia hodiē est magnum fēstum Dominī.

19. Paulus autem ad populum dīxit, Indīgnus sum esse etiam servus Dominī nostrī Jēsū Chrīstī.

20. Minister enim et servī sē (*refl.*) inclīnāverint et ad Deum Dominum creātūrae ōrāverint.

21. Quī prophēta sānctīs scrīptūrīs populum monuerat?

22. Hinc minister hostiam cōnsecrāvit (cōnsecrābit).

23. Dīxerat diāconus, Quoniam Paulus, cui erat potentia Deī, nōn fuerat ūnus prīmōrum apostolōrum.

24. Secundum Scrīptūrās beātī erunt in aeternum, quī mandāta Dominī observāverint.

25. Hostia sānctificābitur et efficiētur cibus aeternae vītae, quod nostrō ministrō Deus potentiam dedit.

26. Erat autem hōra tertia. Mk. xv, 25.

27. Dīcit eī ('to her') Jēsūs: "Bene dīxistī: 'Nōn habeō virum'; quīnque ('five') enim virōs habuistī, et nunc, quem habēs, nōn est tuus vir. Hoc ('this') vērē dīxistī." Jn. iv, 17–18.

II. 1. Had you known the innocence of the Lamb?

2. At the victory of the Son the multitude of angels will have rejoiced in the heavens.

3. The third minister said to Paul, "We have heard that you are the chosen of God."

4. Soon Paul, a contrite and sorrowful man, will have seen the power of the Lord.

5. In heaven the servants of the Word will be joyful, because they will have known the glory of the Lord.

Unit 12

60. The Auxiliary Verb possum 'be able': All Six Indicative Tenses

An important auxiliary verb is **possum, posse, potuī,** — 'be able, can.' Its present, imperfect, and future tenses are formed by adding **pot-** to those tenses of **sum**. (Before a consonant, **pot-** becomes **pos-**.)

		SINGULAR	PLURAL
PRESENT TENSE:	1	**possum** ('I can')	**possumus** ('we can')
	2	**potes** ('you can')	**potestis** ('you can')
	3	**potest** ('he/she/it can')	**possunt** ('they can')
IMPERFECT TENSE:	1	**poteram** ('I could')	**poterāmus** ('we could')
	2	**poterās** ('you could')	**poterātis** ('you could')
	3	**poterat** ('he/she/it could')	**poterant** ('they could')
FUTURE TENSE:	1	**poterō** ('I will be able')	**poterimus** ('we will be able')
	2	**poteris** ('you will be able')	**poteritis** ('you will be able')
	3	**poterit** ('he/she/it will be able')	**poterunt** ('they will be able')

The perfect, pluperfect, and future-perfect tenses are formed in the regular manner from the third principal part: **potuī, potuistī,** etc.; **potueram, potuerās,** etc.; **potuerō, potueris,** etc.

61. Complementary Infinitive

Certain verbs ordinarily need a present infinitive—i.e., the second principal part of a verb—to complete the meaning.

Dominum *laudāre* possumus.
'We are able *to praise* the Lord.'

62. Object Infinitive

Akin to the complementary infinitive is the object infinitive, i.e., an infinitive used as the object of a transitive verb.

Puerī sciunt *ōrāre*.
'The boys know (*how*) *to pray*.'

63. The Perfect-Passive System: Three Compound Tenses

In all four conjugations, the fourth principal part—the perfect passive participle—is the source of three indicative tenses: the perfect passive, the pluperfect passive, and the future-perfect passive. These tenses are formed by using the participle with the appropriate tense of **sum**. Thus each form of these tenses is made up of two words. The participle always agrees with the subject (whether expressed or implied) in gender, number, and case. Thus only the nominative endings **-us, -a, -um; -ī, -ae, -a** are used in the formation of these three tenses.

64. Perfect Indicative Passive: All Four Conjugations

The perfect indicative passive represents two tenses: the simple past passive ('it was done') and the present completed passive ('it has been done'). Context will determine the appropriate translation.

The perfect indicative passive is formed by using the fourth principal part in combination with the present tense of **sum**.
For example:

moneō, monēre, monuī, monitus 'warn, advise'

SINGULAR	PLURAL
I **monitus, -a, -um sum** ('I was/have been warned')	**monitī, -ae, -a sumus** ('we were/have been warned')

	SINGULAR	PLURAL
2	**monitus, -a, -um es** ('you were/have been warned')	**monitī, -ae, -a estis** ('you were/have been warned')
3	**monitus, -a, -um est** ('he/she/it was/has been warned')	**monitī, -ae, -a sunt** ('they were/have been warned')

Notes: 1. The student is cautioned not to confuse the present passive and the perfect passive. Compare **moneor** 'I am warned' and **monitus sum** 'I was warned.'
2. The perfect tense—**fuī, fuistī**, etc.—may be substituted for **sum, es, est**, etc., with no difference in meaning: **monitus sum (monitus fuī)** 'I was/have been warned.'
3. Occasionally, the form of **sum** precedes the participle, with no difference in meaning: **sum monitus = monitus sum.**

65. Uses of the Perfect Passive Participle

The perfect passive participle is essentially an adjective; several adjectives already learned originated as perfect passive participles: e.g., **sānctus, beātus, benedictus, ēlēctus**, and **contrītus**.

Besides its use in the formation of the compound tenses, this participle may be used exactly like an adjective, or with an adverbial force, the equivalent of a circumstantial clause (see Section 41). Like any adjective, it may be used as a substantive.

AS AN ADJECTIVE: **Laudāmus *glōrificātum* Deum.**
'We praise the *glorified* God.'

AS A SUBSTANTIVE: **Scīmus *adjūtōs* ā Petrō.**
'We know [*the ones*] (*having been*) *helped* by Peter.'

AS THE EQUIVALENT OF AN ADVERBIAL CLAUSE: **Puer, ā diāconō *monitus*, ecclēsiam intrāvit.**
'The boy, (*having been*) *warned* by the deacon, entered the church.'
'The boy, because/ although/ if/when he had been warned by the deacon, entered the church.'

Note that after the basic translation, 'having been _____,' the student may try various translations (depending on the context) which render the participle in a finite form. A perfect participle, when translated as a clause, is given a tense prior to that of the main verb. (Occasionally, where sense demands, it may be translated with a tense contemporaneous with the main verb.)

Vocabulary

clāmō, clāmāre, clāmāvī, clāmātus cry out, shout; call upon

acclāmō, acclāmāre, acclāmāvī, acclāmātus cry out, exclaim

exclāmō, exclāmāre, exclāmāvī, exclāmātus cry aloud, exclaim

gubernō, gubernāre, gubernāvī, gubernātus govern

dēbeō, dēbēre, dēbuī, dēbitus owe; ought (+ inf.)

valeō, valēre, valuī, — be well, be strong; be able (+ inf.)

videor, vidērī, —, vīsus sum be seen; seem (+ inf.)

dēsinō, dēsinere, dēsiī, dēsitus (+ inf.) cease

mittō, mittere, mīsī, missus send; cast; put

dīmittō, dīmittere, dīmīsī, dīmissus send away, release; forgive; permit

permittō, permittere, permīsī, permissus allow, permit (+ dat. and inf.)

submittō, submittere, submīsī, submissus lower; suborn, bribe

relinquō, relinquere, relīquī,

relictus leave (behind), abandon

regō:

surgō, surgere, surrēxī, surrēctus rise up, arise

īnsurgō, īnsurgere, īnsurrēxī, īnsurrēctus rise up

resurgō, resurgere, resurrēxī, resurrēctus rise up again

vīvō, vīvere, vīxī, vīctus live

capiō:

concipiō, concipere, concēpī, conceptus conceive

excipiō, excipere, excēpī, exceptus welcome

incipiō, incipere, incēpī, inceptus begin (+ inf.)

possum, posse, potuī, — be able, can (+ inf.)

collēcta, collēctae, f. collect; collection

Ēva, Ēvae, f. Eve

mēnsa, mēnsae, f. table; banquet

certus, -a, -um fixed, sure, certain

maximus, -a, -um greatest, very great

optimus, -a, -um best, very good

āmēn (*Hebrew*: 1. *indecl. adj.*;
2. *adv.*) 1. amen, true! (*word
of affirmation*) 2. truly
antequam (*subord. conj.*)
before
atque (**ac**) (*coord. conj.*) and
(also), and (even)
igitur (*conj.*) therefore, then

nimis (*adv.*) too (much)
postquam (*subord. conj.*) after
quīdam, quaedam, quiddam
(*indef. pron.*) a certain one,
a certain thing
quīdam, quaedam, quoddam
(*indef. adj.*) a certain
tamen (*adv.*) nevertheless

Vocabulary Notes

Dēbeō originated as a compound of **dē-** 'away from' and **habeō**
'have, hold' (Unit 6): a debtor holds what he owes away from his
creditor.

Note that **videor**, the passive of **videō** (Unit 9), means 'seem' when
used with an infinitive.

Surgō is compounded of **sub** + **regō** (**subrigō** > **surrigō** > **surgō**).

Incipiō means 'take upon' oneself, and so 'begin'; it takes an object
infinitive.

Certus is the adjective from which the adverb **certē** (Unit 9) is
formed.

The spelling **atque** is used before vowels or consonants; **ac** before
consonants only. **Atque** (**ac**) is used sparingly, to indicate that which
the listener could not anticipate from the context.

Postquam 'after' takes a perfect where formal English prefers the
pluperfect tense: **postquam puerum vīdit** 'after he had seen the boy.'

The indefinite adjective (**quīdam, quaedam, quoddam**) and the indefinite pronoun (**quīdam, quaedam, quiddam**) are identical in declension save for the spelling of the neuter singular nominative/
accusative. Both are formed from the relative pronoun/adjective,
quī, quae, quod (Unit 10) by the addition of the suffix **-dam**.

Tamen 'nevertheless' seldom comes first in its clause.

Derivatives:	LATIN	ENGLISH
	clāmō	claim; acclaim; exclaim
	gubernō	gubernatorial
	dēbeō	debenture (< dēbentur)
	valeō	valor, valid, avail, prevail
	dēsinō	desinence
	mittō	Mass, missile; permissive
	relinquō	relinquish, relic, relict

Derivatives: LATIN   ENGLISH

surgō   surge; insurrection; resurgence,
             Risorgimento

capiō   concept, conception; except;
             incipient, inception

possum   posse, possible, potent

mēnsa   Mensa, mensal

certus   certitude

maximus   maximum

optimus   optimum, Optimo cigars

Drills

I. Complementary infinitive with possum. Translate; change the number and retranslate.

a. vidēre potest
b. audīre poterāmus
c. scīre poterunt
d. parāre potuērunt
e. fīnīre possumus
f. reclīnāre potuerant

II. Give the principal parts of tollō; fīniō; aperiō; videō; ērigō; sānō. Fully conjugate the perfect indicative passive of each.

III. Complementary and object infinitive. Translate.

a. mittere dēbēmus
b. esse dēsiit
c. laudāre potuerat
d. miscēre valēbās
e. intrāre valēbunt
f. crēdere vidēminī
g. regere potuistis
h. invocāre dēbēbās
i. audīre dēsinam
j. cantāre puerō permittēbat
k. gregāre populō permittit
l. scīre vidēbantur

Exercises

I. 1. Per Jēsū potentiam Petrus valēbat populō dēbita dīmittere.
2. Nunc dīmittis servum tuum. Lk. ii, 29.
3. Certē Deum laudāre nōn dēsinēmus. Nam Dominus est in aeternum. Āmēn.
4. Postquam Paulus aulam relīquit, sub tēctum discipulī vēnit.

5. Ēva Adae ā Deō data.

6. Postquam Chrīstus Jēsūs ā mortuīs resurrēxit, vīvus in Galilaeā ā quibusdam discipulīs vīsus est.

7. Petrus puerō permīsit cibum et vīnum mittere ad famīliam.

8. Antequam minister collēctam ōrāvit, in silentiō sē (*refl.*) inclīnāvit.

9. Dīmissus ā Petrō, vir tamen ad Jēsūm acclāmābat.

10. Antequam apostolī ā Jēsū relictī sunt, accēpērunt potentiam peccātī.

11. Quoniam Jēsūs discipulīs verba salūtifera dedit, ad Deum ōrāre cum gaudiō dēbēmus.

12. Dē populī vītā scīre poterunt, sed sciētis dē Deī glōriā.

13. Quīdam discipulī, nōn nimis exceptī, Galilaeam relīquērunt.

14. Populus contrītus, ā Paulō bene monitus, incēpit secundum Jēsū praecepta vīvere.

15. In lītūrgiā misericordia Dominī ā populō saepe est laudāta.

16. Dē Jēsū vītā cārus apostolus scīvit mīra scrībere.

17. Jam Ēva prīmum fīlium concēperat.

18. Hodiē ante mēnsam Dominī convēnimus Chrīstiānī.

19. Optimum magister vīnum adhūc servāvit.

20. Ūniversum salūtiferā Deī potentiā semper rēctum fuit.

21. Discipulī igitur vīsī sunt certum capere praemium.

22. Malus servus, ā bonō monitus, nimis maledīcere dominō dēsiit.

23. Tunc optimus et maximus vir Jūdaeam gubernābat?

24. Puer aurum, quod Petrō dederat, subitō recēpit atque famīliae dedit.

25. In Jēsū adimplēta sunt verba antīquōrum prophētārum.

26. Beātī sunt quī parvulōs ante domum congregātōs adjuvāre possunt.

27. Et ūniversōrum vincula solūta sunt. Acts xvi, 26.

28. Ipsī ('to him') glōria et imperium in saecula saeculōrum. Āmēn. Rev. i, 6.

29. Āmēn, āmēn dīcō vōbīs ('to you'): Venit hōra, et nunc est. Jn. v, 25.

30. Vōbīs ('to you') datum est mystērium rēgnī Deī. Mk. iv, 11.

31. Ecce videō caelōs apertōs. Acts vii, 56.

II.   1. Will he be able to hear and do the words of Jesus?

2. The servant was sent by Paul to the assembly of God.

3. Today the joyful disciples will not cease to praise the very great power of the living God.

4. The little servant does not seem to know (how) to prepare a very good supper for Paul.

5. According to the Scriptures God permitted (to) His only son to wipe out the fault of Adam.

Unit 13

66. Pluperfect Indicative Passive: All Four Conjugations

The pluperfect indicative passive, the past completed tense, is always translated with the auxiliaries 'had been.' It is compounded of the perfect passive participle and the imperfect tense of **sum**.

For example:

dūcō, dūcere, dūxī, ductus 'lead'

	SINGULAR	PLURAL
1	**ductus, -a, -um eram** ('I had been led')	**ductī, -ae, -a erāmus** ('we had been led')
2	**ductus, -a, -um erās** ('you had been led')	**ductī, -ae, -a erātis** ('you had been led')
3	**ductus, -a, -um erat** ('he/she/it had been led')	**ductī, -ae, -a erant** ('they had been led')

> *Note:* The pluperfect tense—**fueram, fuerās**, etc.—may be substituted for **eram, erās**, etc., with no difference in meaning.

67. Future-Perfect Indicative Passive: All Four Conjugations

The future-perfect indicative passive, the future completed tense, is always translated with the auxiliaries 'will have been.' It is compounded of the perfect passive participle and the future tense of **sum**.

For example:

audiō, audīre, audīvī, audītus 'hear'

	SINGULAR	PLURAL
1	**audītus, -a, -um erō** ('I will have been heard')	**audītī, -ae, -a erimus** ('we will have been heard')

	SINGULAR	PLURAL
2	**audītus, -a, -um eris** ('you will have been heard')	**audītī, -ae, -a eritis** ('you will have been heard')
3	**audītus, -a, -um erit** ('he/she/it will have been heard')	**audītī, -ae, -a erunt** ('they will have been heard')

> *Note:* The future-perfect tense—**fuerō, fueris**, etc.—may be substituted for **erō, eris, erit**, etc., with no difference in meaning.

68. *Ablative Absolute*

The ablative absolute most often consists of a noun + a perfect passive participle in the ablative case (other less common forms will be seen later). As a subordinate construction, it occurs only as an addition to an independent clause (i.e., a complete sentence). But as its name "absolute" implies, it is not directly connected to either the subject or the object of the independent clause. [In the Vulgate, however, this rule is not always strictly observed.] Instead, it gives a circumstance which modifies the meaning of the sentence. The circumstance will vary: it may be temporal, concessive, causal, or conditional. Thus the ablative absolute serves as a substitute for an adverbial clause (see Section 41).

Since the precise circumstance intended by an ablative absolute depends on the context, the student should translate literally at first (using the formula 'with [*noun*] having been [*participle*]'), before trying other possibilities ('when, although, since, if'), which require a finite form of the verb in the English.

> **Cēnā praeparātā, puerī in domum intrāvērunt.**
> '*With dinner having been prepared*, the boys entered the house.'
> '*When, since, etc., dinner had been prepared, . . .*'

> *Note:* Since this form of the ablative absolute uses a passive participle, all translations, however free, should retain the passive voice. As usual, the perfect participle denotes an action prior to the main verb.

69. Temporal Clauses

Adverbial clauses of a purely temporal nature have verbs in the indicative mood; as in English, introductory time-words are used, e.g., **cum** 'when, after,' **ubi** 'when, as soon as,' **ut** 'when, as.'

> *Cum (ubi, ut) Jēsūs surrēxit*, **apostolī erant laetī.**
> 'When Jesus arose, the apostles were joyful.'

70. Synopsis of a Verb

A synopsis of a verb is a chart showing at a glance the different inflectional forms which the verb may have; it is usually drawn up to show forms of a chosen person and number.

Filling out a synopsis is an invaluable aid to remembering the various forms of any given verb. At this stage you know the six tenses of the indicative mood in both the active and the passive. But to prevent them from slipping away, you should fix them in your mind by the following procedure: take any transitive verb (i.e., one with passive as well as active forms) and write its four principal parts; choose a person and number; then fill out the twelve possible forms of the verb in the chosen person and number. As other forms are learned, this exercise should be expanded to include them. [A complete synopsis form may be found at the end of the morphological appendix.]

FOR EXAMPLE: The second-person singular of **vocō, vocāre, vocāvī, vocātus** 'call.' (Be sure to write out the English translation along with each form.)

The second-person singular of **vocō, vocāre, vocāvī, vocātus** 'call.'

INDICATIVE	ACTIVE	PASSIVE
Present:	**vocās** 'you call'	**vocāris, vocāre** 'you are called'
Imperfect:	**vocābās** 'you were calling'	**vocābāris, vocābāre** 'you were being called'
Future:	**vocābis** 'you will call'	**vocāberis, vocābere** 'you will be called'
Perfect:	**vocāvistī** 'you (have) called'	**vocātus, -a, -um es** 'you were/have been called'
Pluperfect:	**vocāverās** 'you had called'	**vocātus, -a, -um erās** 'you had been called'

INDICATIVE	ACTIVE	PASSIVE
Future-Perfect:	**vocāveris** 'you will have called'	**vocātus, -a, -um eris** 'you will have been called'

Vocabulary

cēnō, cēnāre, cēnāvī, cēnātus dine, eat supper

creō, creāre, creāvī, creātus create

dō:

  addō, addere, addidī, additus give to, add

  perdō, perdere, perdidī, perditus lose; destroy

incarnō, incarnāre, incarnāvī, incarnātus make into flesh, make incarnate

mūtō, mūtāre, mūtāvī, mūtātus change, exchange

  immūtō, immūtāre, immūtāvī, immūtātus transform

stō, stāre, stetī, status stand (still)

  astō, astāre, astitī, — stand by, stand near

  circumstō, circumstāre, circumstetī, — stand around, encircle

  īnstō, īnstāre, īnstitī, — urge; threaten (+ *dat.*)

  praestō, praestāre, praestitī (praestāvī), praestātus (praestitus) bestow; accomplish

  restō, restāre, restitī, — remain (behind)

-dō, -dere, -didī, -ditus put

  condō, condere, condidī, conditus found; hide

subdō, subdere, subdidī, subditus put under, put after, subject

pariō, parere, peperī, partus beget, produce, bear

speciō, specere, spexī, spectus look (at)

  aspiciō, aspicere, aspexī, aspectus look (at)

  circumspiciō, circumspicere, circumspexī, circumspectus look around

  dēspiciō, dēspicere, dēspexī, dēspectus look down on, despise

  respiciō, respicere, respexī, respectus look at, regard, watch

baptista, baptistae, m. baptizer, baptist

dextera, dexterae, f. right hand

tuba, tubae, f. trumpet

digitus, digitī, m. finger, toe

oculus, oculī, m. eye

brāchium, brāchiī, n. arm

dēsertus, -a, -um forsaken, deserted

  dēsertum, dēsertī, n. desert

Galilaeus, -a, -um Galilaean

Jūdaeus, -a, -um Jewish

Rōmānus, -a, -um Roman

cum (*subord. conj.*) when, after

dōnec (*subord. conj.*) while, as long as; till
dum (*subord. conj.*) while, as long as; till
etsī (*subord. conj.*) although, even if
nisi (*subord. conj.*) unless, if . . . not; except, but

prīmum (*adv.*) (at) first
sī (*subord. conj.*) if; whether
ubi (1. *subord. conj.*; 2. *relative adv.*) 1. when, as soon as 2. where, in which place
ubīque (*adv.*) everywhere, anywhere
ut (*subord. conj.*) when, as

Vocabulary Notes

Cēnō, a denominative verb from **cēna** (Unit 1), is intransitive, i.e., it does not take an object.

Addō and **perdō** are compounds of **dō** 'give.'

Incarnō is formed from the noun **carō, carnis**, f. 'flesh' (Unit 19).

The prefix of **immūtō** (**im-** = **in-**) is intensive (not negative or locative): **mūto** 'I change'; **immūtō** 'I transform.'

Stō 'stand' is sometimes the virtual equivalent of **sum** 'be': **mēnsae stant in aulā** 'the tables stand (= are) in the hall.'

The verb **-dō, -dere, -didī, -ditus** 'put' occurs only in compounds: e.g., **condō** 'found; hide' and **subdō** 'put under.'

While the simple verb **speciō** seldom occurs, it yields four important compounds: **aspiciō, circumspiciō, dēspiciō,** and **respiciō**.

Baptista is an agent noun borrowed from Greek.

Brāchium 'arm' is also spelled with two c's; when so spelled, the **-a-** is short by nature (but now long by position: **bracchium**).

Galilaeus and **Jūdaeus** are the adjectives from which the nouns **Galilaea** (Unit 10) and **Jūdaea** (Unit 2) are derived.

Cum 'with' (Unit 1) and **cum** 'when, after' are homonyms. Since their uses are so different, which is meant is always clear: **cum puerō** 'with the boy'; **cum puer videt** 'when the boy sees.' **Cum** 'when, after' is quite often used with the future or future-perfect indicative.

Dum, when it means 'while,' will often use the present, even if the main clause has a past tense: **dum** *ambulat*, **cantāvit** 'while he *walked*, he sang.'

Derivatives:	LATIN	ENGLISH
	mūtō	mutate, commutor
	stō	stay, status, state, station, substance, restive, the rest
	addō	add, addition

Derivatives: LATIN   ENGLISH
                condō   condiment, condition
                perdō   perdition
                pariō   parturition, postpartum blues
                speciō   spectator, aspect, despicable,
                                 respect
                dextera   ambidexter
                tuba   tuba
                digitus   digit, digital computer
                oculus   ocular, oculist, inveigle
                brāchium   brachial, bracer, brassiere, pretzel
                Jūdaeus   Judaic
                ubīque   ubiquity

Drills

I. Pluperfect and future-perfect passive. Translate; change the number and retranslate.

a. cantātus erit g. sānāta eris
b. data erant h. corrēctī fuerāmus
c. laudātī fuerint i. erit fōrmātum
d. sacrāta erat j. satiātae erunt
e. eritis vocātae k. vīsus eram
f. ductī erāmus l. missus erō

II. Pluperfect and future-perfect passive. Translate.

a. he had been abandoned f. I will have been helped
b. we will have been sent g. you (pl.) had been guided
c. they had been opened h. they will have been known
d. you will have been seen i. she had been strengthened
e. I had been separated j. he will have been healed

III. Ablative absolute. Translate literally.

a. stēllā vīsā f. pāpā laudātō
b. missō puerō g. populō congregātō
c. mēnsā praeparātā h. solūtīs dēbitīs
d. librīs captīs i. laetīs satiātīs
e. relictā domō j. īnfirmīs autem sānātīs

Exercises

I. 1. Hymnō dictō, apostolī domum relīquērunt.
  2. Antequam puer ad cēnam missus est, prīmum in dominī agrō cūnctīs cum servīs operāvit.
  3. Tunc Galilaeī ā Rōmānīs saepe dēspectī sunt, quoniam deōs Rōmānōrum nōn adōrābant.
  4. Cum verba Jēsū audīta erunt, quī vir nōn crēdet?
  5. Dum operat, ōrābat.
  6. Sī mandāta mea ā populō observāta fuerint, habēbunt vītam aeternam.
  7. Petrus populō mīra Dominī dīcet, dōnec Paulus advēnerit.
  8. Stēllā in caelō vīsā, virī ex agrīs vēnērunt atque adōrāvērunt nātum Jēsūm.
  9. Ut Jēsūs circumspexit, virī erant maestī et nōn ūnum verbum dīxērunt. Scīvērunt enim quod Jēsūs vēra dīxerat.
  10. Cum vīderint oculī meī Dominum, meam vītam fīnīre poterō.
  11. Ubi angelus Dominī vīsus erit, tuba victōriae super ūniversam terram audiētur.
  12. Etiam in dēsertō Jūdaeae baptista Jēsūm scīvit. Jēsū enim prīmum respectō, dīxit: Ecce agnus Deī.
  13. Etsī est parvulus, puer in domō restat.
  14. Baptistā autem trāditō, vēnit Jēsūs in Galilaeam, ubi populō Evangelium dīcere incēpit.
  15. Marīa prīmum nātum peperit, et vocātus est Jēsūs.
  16. Sānctus vir dexterā puerum cēpit et dūxit in domum.
  17. Ubi Jūdaeī digitum Deī in caelīs spexērunt, laetī potentiam misericordiamque laudāvērunt.
  18. In prīncipiō Deus mundum creāvit ac vītae praestitit dōnum.
  19. Nātūra immūtāta est nostra, ut Fīlius incarnātus est?
  20. Nātus in brāchiīs Marīae habitus fuerat.
  21. Postquam vir malus aurum condidit, ad dexteram Petrī in silentiō astitit.
  22. Vir, quī vītam perdidit, ā Jūdaeīs laudātus fuerat.
  23. Rōmānī quī circumsteterant puerō īnstābant.
  24. Nisi mea verba effecta fuerint, beātī nōn eritis.
  25. Chrīstiānīs ubīque inventīs, Paulus, bene satiātus, in domō Petrī cum gaudiō restābat.
  26. Meā culpā, meā culpā, meā maximā culpā.
  27. Et trāditus est Jēsū liber prophētae.
  28. Nōn est hīc, sed surrēxit. Lk. xxiv, 6.

II. 1. After the supper had been prepared (*translate in two ways*), Peter permitted the new disciple to stand at the right hand of Paul.

2. The people, who had been instructed by means of the saving precepts of Christ, were able to pray to God, who rules the universe.

3. When Paul will have arrived at the house, he will be seen by Peter the Galilaean.

4. After the apostle healed the second boy, the servant did not cease to praise the mercy of God.

Unit 14

71. *Third Declension Nouns: Masculine or Feminine*

While nouns of the first declension have **-ae** and those of the second declension have **-ī** in the genitive singular, nouns of the third declension have **-is**. The nominative singular form is so varied that it cannot be reduced to rule but must be learned as a vocabulary item.

To decline a masculine or feminine third declension noun, first derive the base by removing the ending **-is** from the genitive singular; then add the following endings:

	SINGULAR	PLURAL
Nom.	—	-ēs
Gen.	-is	-um
Dat.	-ī	-ibus
Acc.	-em	-ēs
Abl.	-e	-ibus

> *Notes:* 1. Since the dative singular (**-ī**) and the genitive plural (**-um**) endings are identical with the spellings used in other cases in the second declension, the student is cautioned to identify the declension of a noun before attempting to determine its case.
> 2. Although some endings in the plural are identically spelled, context will help to determine the intended case.

rēx, rēgis, m. 'king'; base: **rēg-**

	SINGULAR	PLURAL
Nom.	**rēx** ('the king')	**rēgēs** ('the kings')
Gen.	**rēgis** ('of the king')	**rēgum** ('of the kings')

	SINGULAR	PLURAL
Dat.	**rēgī** ('for/to the king')	**rēgibus** ('for/to the kings')
Acc.	**rēgem** ('the king')	**rēgēs** ('the kings')
Abl.	**rēge** ('from/with/in/by the king')	**rēgibus** ('from/with/in/by the kings')

māter, mātris, f. 'mother'; base: **mātr-**

Nom.	**māter** ('the mother')	**mātrēs** ('the mothers')
Gen.	**mātris** ('of the mother')	**mātrum** ('of the mothers')
Dat.	**mātrī** ('for/to the mother')	**mātribus** ('for/to the mothers')
Acc.	**mātrem** ('the mother')	**mātrēs** ('the mothers')
Abl.	**mātre** ('from/with/in/ by the mother')	**mātribus** ('from/with/in/by the mothers')

72. *Third Declension Nouns: Neuter*

Neuter nouns of the third declension use the same endings employed by masculine and feminine third declension nouns, except that the accusative singular duplicates the nominative singular (learned as a vocabulary item) and the nominative and accusative plural both end in **-a**.

	SINGULAR	PLURAL
Nom.	—	**-a**
Gen.	**-is**	**-um**
Dat.	**-ī**	**-ibus**
Acc.	—	**-a**
Abl.	**-e**	**-ibus**

corpus, corporis, n. 'body, corpse'; base: **corpor-**

	SINGULAR	PLURAL
Nom.	**corpus** ('the body')	**corpora** ('the bodies')
Gen.	**corporis** ('of the body')	**corporum** ('of the bodies')
Dat.	**corporī** ('for/to the body')	**corporibus** ('for/to the bodies')
Acc.	**corpus** ('the body')	**corpora** ('the bodies')
Abl.	**corpore** ('from/with/in/ by the body')	**corporibus** ('from/with/ in/by the bodies')

73. *Genitive of Description*

The genitive case of a noun, often accompanied by an adjective, is used to describe or explain another noun in the same phrase.

Sumus populus *misericordiae*?
'Are we a people *of mercy*?'

Prīmī Chrīstiānī erant hominēs *laetī animī*.
'The first Christians were persons of *joyful mind*.'
[**homō, hominis**, m. 'human being, person']

74. *Ablative of Description*

The ablative case of a noun, always accompanied by an adjective, is used to describe a person or thing.

Petrus erat vir *magnā animā*.
'Peter was a man *of great soul*.'

75. *Subjective and Objective Genitive*

The genitive case may be used subjectively when it names the subject of the action denoted by the noun to which it is connected. Likewise, the genitive may be used objectively when it names the object of the action denoted by the noun to which it is attached.

Propter *Deī* misericordiam *hominum* grātiās agimus.
'We give thanks on account of *God's* pity toward *human beings*.'

Here **Deī** is a subjective genitive because it denotes the one pitying, and **hominum** is an objective genitive because it denotes the ones receiving the pity.

76. *Dative of Reference: Advantage or Disadvantage*

The dative case may be used to refer to the interested or affected party of an action. Depending on whether the party benefits or suffers from the action, this use of the dative is called one of advantage or disadvantage.

Quae mala *meō populō* fēcistis?
'What evils have you done *to my people*?'

Chrīstus *omnibus hominibus* surrēxit.
'Christ has risen *for all human beings.*'

77. Apposition

A noun may be used to explain another noun; both nouns have the same case and the same syntactical relationship to the rest of the sentence.

Deum, nostrum Patrem, laudāmus.
'We praise *God,* our *Father.*'
[**pater, patris,** m. 'father']

Here **Deum** is an accusative, the direct object, and **Patrem** is an accusative, in apposition to **Deum.**

78. Concessive Clauses

Adverbial clauses of concession (see Section 41) have verbs in the indicative mood when introduced by such sign-words as **etsī** 'although, even if' (Unit 13) and **quamquam** 'although.'

Quamquam (etsī) sumus indīgnī, Deus tamen cūnctōs dīligit.
'*Although we are unworthy,* nevertheless God loves (us) all.'
[**dīligō, dīligere, dīlēxī, dīlēctus** 'love']

Vocabulary

dētergeō, dētergēre, dētersī, dētersus wipe away, cancel

inhaereō, inhaerēre, inhaesī, inhaesus cling to, adhere to (+ *dat.*)

legō, legere, lēgī, lēctus choose, select; read

  colligō, colligere, collēgī, collēctus gather up, take in, collect

  dīligō, dīligere, dīlēxī, dīlēctus love

  ēligō, ēligere, ēlēgī, ēlēctus choose, elect

scrībō, scrībere, scrīpsī, scrīptus write

  dēscrībō, dēscrībere, dēscrīpsī, dēscrīptus describe; enroll

capiō:

  suscipiō, suscipere, suscēpī, susceptus take up, pick up; accept

homō, hominis, m. human being, person

Jōannēs, Jōannis, m. John

pater, patris, m. father

prīnceps, prīncipis, m. chief, prince

redēmptor, redēmptōris, m. one who buys back: redeemer

rēx, rēgis, m. king

sacerdōs, sacerdōtis, m. priest

dēprecātiō, dēprecātiōnis, f. earnest prayer, supplication

māter, mātris, f. mother

ōrātiō, ōrātiōnis, f. prayer; speech

pāx, pācis, f. harmony, peace

virgō, virginis, f. virgin

voluntās, voluntātis, f. will

baptisma, baptismatis, n. baptism

corpus, corporis, n. body, corpse

genus, generis, n. kind; race; nation

lūmen, lūminis, n. light; pl., also: eyes

mūnus, mūneris, n. gift, offering; task, duty; pl., also: bribes

nōmen, nōminis, n. name

siccus, -a, -um dry

ruber, rubra, rubrum red

ergō (coord. conj.) therefore

ideō (adv.) therefore, on that account

quamquam (subord. conj.) although

Vocabulary Notes

Legō means both 'choose, select' and 'read,' since to read means to pick out words on a page—no easy task for the ancients, since the ideas of punctuation and spaces between words were late in coming. Note that the compounds **dīligō** and **intellegō** (Unit 31) have **-x-** (not **-g-**) in the third principal part: **dīlēxī; intellēxī.**

Suscipiō means 'take up (from below).' A Roman father acknowledged a newborn child as his own by picking it up; ecclesiastical Latin often uses this verb of God the Father taking up (and therefore acknowledging) our earnest prayers.

Jōannēs 'John' may also be spelled with an **-h-**: **Jōhannēs.**

Rēx 'king' is related to **regō** 'rule' (Unit 8).

Dēprecātiō 'supplication' and **ōrātiō** 'prayer' are nouns formed from perfect participles—from **dēprecor** 'beseech' (Unit 20) and **ōrō** 'pray' (Unit 5)—and the abstract-noun-making suffix **-iō, -iōnis.**

Baptisma, like **baptista** (Unit 13), is taken from the Greek.

Derivatives:	LATIN	ENGLISH
	dētergeō	deterge, detergent
	inhaereō	inherent
	legō	lesson, lecture, lectern, lection, lectionary
	dīligō	predilection

Derivatives:

LATIN	ENGLISH
ēligō	eligible
scrībō	scribe, script
suscipiō	intussusception, susceptible
homō	hominoid, hominid
pater	paternal
rēx	regal, royal
sacerdōs	sacerdotal
dēprecātiō	deprecation
māter	alma mater, matrix, maternal
ōrātiō	oration
pāx	peace, pacify
voluntās	voluntary
corpus	corps, corporal, corporation
genus	genus, gender, genre, generate
lūmen	lumen, luminous, luminary
mūnus	remuneration
nōmen	nominate, noun, nominal
siccus	desiccate, sec
ruber	rubric
quamquam	cancan

Drills

I. Third declension nouns: masculine and feminine. Identify the case; give all possibilities; translate; change the number and retranslate.

a. hominī
b. patre
c. redēmptōrum
d. rēgis
e. sacerdōtibus

f. dēprecātiōnēs
g. mātrem
h. ōrātiōne
i. pācem
j. virginibus

k. voluntātum
l. patris
m. rēx
n. ōrātiō
o. sacerdōtī

II. Third declension nouns: neuter. Identify the case; give all possibilities; translate; change the number and retranslate.

a. baptisma
b. corpora

c. generibus
d. lūminis

e. mūnera   h. lūminī
f. nōmine   i. baptismatum
g. genera   j. mūneribus

Exercises

I. 1. Quamquam prīnceps sacerdōtum verba Jēsū audīvit, inhaesit tamen antīquīs modīs, et nōn crēdidit.
    2. In templō Jēsūs ā librō prophētae ōrātiōnem lēgit.
    3. Ergō apostolī cibum collēgērunt et dedērunt populō.
    4. Scrīptō librō, apostolus iterum vēnit ad terram ubi ā Jēsū ante multōs annōs ēlectus erat.
    5. Scīs quia Jōannēs dīcēbātur dīlectus discipulus?
    6. Sī nostra dēprecātiō ā Patre suscepta erit, laetī erimus.
    7. Māter dolōrōsa corpus Jēsū in brāchiīs suscēpit; posteā corpus in terrā conditum est.
    8. Sānctus Petrus, homō pācis et bonae voluntātis, ēlectus est prīnceps cūnctōrum apostolōrum.
    9. Nostra peccāta ā Redēmptōre, Jēsū Chrīstō, dētersa sunt.
    10. Novus discipulus, quamquam ūnus apostolōrum nōn erat, hominibus cūnctīs Evangelium scrīpsit.
    11. Discipulī Evangelium Jēsū Chrīstī per ūniversās terrās semper lēctum est. Nam in librō vītam Jēsū dēscrīpsit.
    12. Tunc familia Jēsū ad Bēthlehem vēnit et dēscrīpta est.
    13. Postquam Jōannēs trāditus est, Jēsūs ministerium incēpit.
    14. Propter rēgem, hominem malō animō, familia terram patrum relīquit.
    15. Postquam sacerdōs noster ōrātiōnem lēgit, subdidimus: Āmēn.
    16. Marīa, et virgō et māter, ab hominibus cūnctīs laudāta.
    17. Sāncta familia per multōs annōs vīxit in terrā Aegyptiā, dum rēx impius in Galilaeā rēgnat.
    18. Nōmine Jēsū ā sacerdōte dictō, populus sē (refl.) inclīnāvit.
    19. Ubi lūmen est, vīta est.
    20. Deum dē Deō, lūmen dē lūmine, Deum vērum dē Deō vērō . . .
    21. Ideō Patrem invocāvimus et magnās Fīliō ēgimus grātiās.
    22. Baptismate Jōannis Jūdaeī peccātīs līberātī sunt.
    23. Prīmō Deī Testāmentō genus Jūdaeum effectum est ūniversō lūmen mundō.
    24. Hebraeī ā Dominō per aquam siccō vestīgiō rēctī sunt.

25. Aurum gladiīque, mūnera populī, rēgī jam data erant.
26. Postquam Paulus Rōmānīs scrīpsit, discipulus Paulō
    cēnam parāre poterat.
27. Hic ('this') est Jēsūs Rēx Jūdaeōrum. Mt. xxvii, 37.
28. Et ecce apertī sunt Jēsū caelī. Mt. iii, 16, adapted.

II.   1. Our priest, a man of peace, prayed for the Christian
          kings and princes.
       2. According to John, Jesus is the king of glory and the
          redeemer of human beings.
       3. John stood by when the Romans gave the body of Jesus to
          his mother Mary.
       4. If we call upon the name of the Father, he always receives
          our earnest prayer.
       5. Although the boy, the son of the king, was being trained
          by the priest, he did not adhere too much to the
          commandments of God.

Unit 15

79. Third Declension Nouns: Masculine or Feminine i-Stems

Some masculine and feminine nouns of the third declension belong to a subgroup called i-stem nouns. These nouns have **-ium** for the genitive plural ending.

MASCULINE AND FEMININE I-STEM NOUNS:

either have stems which end in two consonants, e.g., **pars, partis**, f. 'part'; stem: **part-** (but this is not the case if the second is l or r, e.g., **māter, mātris**, f. 'mother'; stem: **mātr-**),

or are parisyllabic (i.e., have an equal number of syllables) in the nominative and genitive singulars.

These nouns will be indicated in the vocabulary lists by the addition of the genitive plural, the one differing form: **pānis, pānis, pānium**, m. 'bread'; **pars, partis, partium**, f. 'part.'

80. Third Declension Nouns: Neuter i-Stems

A small number of neuter nouns of the third declension are members of the i-stem subgroup. Like masculine and feminine i-stems, they have **-ium** in the genitive plural, but they also have **-ī** (instead of **-e**) in the ablative singular and **-ia** in the nominative and accusative plural (instead of **-a**). Most neuter i-stems have nominatives in **-e**, **-ar**, or **-al**.

These neuter nouns will likewise be indicated in the vocabulary lists as i-stem nouns by the addition of the genitive plural: **mare, maris, marium**, n. 'sea.'

81. Partitive Genitive

The genitive case may be used to indicate the whole after a word denoting a part.

Petrus multōs *discipulōrum* in templum dūxit.
'Peter led many *of the disciples* into the temple.'

82. Dative with Certain Adjectives

The dative case may depend on an adjective meaning 'near to,' 'fit for,' 'pleasing to,' 'dear to,' or the like.

Nostrum sacrificium erit *Deō* grātum?
'Will our sacrifice be pleasing *to God*?'

83. Predicate Accusative

English has a construction called the objective complement in which a noun or adjective is used to complete the meaning of a noun or pronoun: 'we named *him president* of the club.' Latin has a similar usage called the predicate accusative, after such verbs as **faciō** and **habeō**. (See Section 7.5.)

Chrīstus Jēsūs Petrum *apostolum* fēcit.
'Christ Jesus made Peter his *apostle*.'

Ecclēsiam habēmus *sānctam*.
'We consider the church *holy*.'

84. Cognate Accusative

An accusative related in meaning to the verb which governs it is called a cognate accusative. 'To dream a dream' or 'to run a race' illustrates this construction in English.

Vītam bonam vīxit.
'He lived a good *life*.'

With the addition of the adjective, this brief sentence amounts to a transformation of **bene vīxit** 'he lived well.'

Vocabulary

**manдūcō, mandūcāre, man-
dūcāvī, mandūcātus** eat

sonō, sonāre, sonuī, sonitus
(make a) sound

  īnsonō, īnsonāre, īnsonuī, —
resound

  **personō, personāre, per-
sonuī, personitus** pro-
claim, resound

ambō, ambōnis, m. lectern,
ambo

cantor, cantōris, m. singer,
cantor

cruor, cruōris, m. blood
[from a wound]

lēctor, lēctōris, m. reader,
lector

pānis, pānis, pānium, m.
bread, loaf of bread

postis, postis, postium, m.
doorpost

sanguis, sanguinis, m. blood
[in general]

fīnis, fīnis, fīnium, m. & f.
end, boundary; *pl.*: territory,
district

particeps, participis, m. & f.
partaker, sharer

cālīgō, cālīginis, f. mist, gloom

inīquitās, inīquitātis, f.
wickedness

largitās, largitātis, f. bounty,
abundance

lēctiō, lēctiōnis, f. reading

mēns, mentis, mentium, f.
mind, intention

mors, mortis, mortium, f.
death

pars, partis, partium, f. part,
some

resurrēctiō, resurrēctiōnis, f.
rising again, resurrection

salūs, salūtis, f. safety, health,
salvation

cor, cordis, cordium, n. (*abl.
sing.,* **corde**) heart

mare, maris, marium, n. sea

aptus, -a, -um (+ *dat.* or **ad** +
acc.) fitting, suitable, apt

hūmānus, -a, -um human

proximus, -a, -um nearest
(+ *dat.*); *subst.*: neighbor

salvus, -a, -um safe, saved;
sound

prae (*prep.* + *abl.*) before, in
preference to; in comparison
with; in consequence of,
because of

praeter (*prep.* + *acc.*) except;
beyond, past

satis (1. *indecl. noun;* 2. *indecl. adj.;* 3. *adv.*) 1. enough
(of) (+ *partitive gen.*)
2. enough 3. enough,
sufficiently

Vocabulary Notes

  Ambō 'lectern' is derived from the Greek.

  Cruor specifically means 'blood' as it flows from a wound. Cf. English 'gore.' The more general **sanguis** 'blood' is the one more often used of Jesus and the shedding of his blood.

Particeps is a compound of **pars** 'part' and **capiō** 'take' (Unit 6).

Lēctor 'reader' and **lēctiō** 'reading' are formed from **legō** 'read' (Unit 14).

Resurrēctiō 'rising again' is taken from **resurgō** (Unit 12).

Note that **salūs** has three important interrelated meanings: safety, health, salvation.

Salvus + **facere** means 'make safe, i.e., save': **Jēsūs populum salvum fēcit** 'Jesus has saved the people.'

Depending on the usage, **satis** may function as a noun, an adjective, or an adverb: **habēmus satis cibī** 'we have enough food'; **pānēs sunt satis** 'the loaves are enough'; **Deum satis laudāmus?** 'do we praise God enough?'

Derivatives:

LATIN	ENGLISH
sonō	sonic boom
postis	at the post, post no bills
sanguis	sanguine, sangfroid, sangria
fīnis	finial, final, fine
particeps	participant
cālīgō	caliginous
inīquitās	iniquity
largitās	largesse
lēctiō	lection, lesson
mēns	mental
mors	mortal
pars	partial
salūs	salutary, salute
cor	cordial
mare	submarine, maritime
proximus	proximate, approximation
salvus	salvage, salvo, salver
prae	prelection, predict
praeter	preternatural
satis	satisfy, satisfaction

Drills

I. Additional third declension nouns, including i-stems. Identify the case; give all possibilities; translate; change the number and retranslate.

a. ambōnis f. mentium k. salūtibus
b. pānis g. lēctiōnī l. inīquitās
c. postium h. cordis m. cruōrem
d. sanguine i. maria n. mortēs
e. fīnēs j. marī o. cālīgō

II. Predicate accusative.

a. Virum prīncipem faciunt.
b. Jēsūm rēgem vocāmus.
c. Petrum bonum habēmus.
d. Bonum Deus creāvit mundum.
e. Jōannem ēlēgērunt pāpam.
f. Jōannēs Paulus ēlēctus est pāpa.

Exercises

I. 1. Multī hominum ā Jēsū sānātōrum grātiās Deō nōn ēgērunt.
2. Jōannēs viam Dominī parāvit; multī Jūdaeōrum, corde contrītī, ā Jōanne baptisma aquae accēpērunt; Jēsūs quoque ad Jōannem vēnit in baptisma; secundum Jōannem dēbēmus Jēsūm vocāre Agnum Deī.
3. Ad saeculī fīnem tuba jūstitiae īnsonuerit.
4. In prīmīs ad ambōnem lēctor prīmam lēctiōnem leget; hinc cantor canticum cantābit.
5. Sanguis agnī in postibus fēcit antīquōs Hebraeōs salvōs.
6. Ad Pascham laetī sumus, quoniam per resurrēctiōnem Redēmptōris effectī sumus novae vītae participēs.
7. Hebraeī, quōrum corda erant apta ad Dominī ministerium, per Mare Rubrum ductī sunt.
8. Fugātur cālīgō inīquitātis; lūmen Chrīstī ā cūnctīs hominibus vidētur. Allēlūjā.
9. Praeter cūnctōs hominēs Marīam, Stēllam Maris, laudāmus, quia Māter Deī est.
10. Nisi meum corpus mandūcāveritis et biberitis meum sanguinem, in rēgnum caelōrum nōn intrābitis.
11. Sanguine agnī in postibus Hebraeōrum vīsō, sub tēcta angelus Deī nōn intrāvit.
12. Propter Chrīstī victōriam mortis aula laetīs hymnīs personuit.
13. Turba satis pānis habuērunt? Nisi satis mandūcāverint, pars populī in viā dēficient.

14. Petrus prīmus Jēsūm vocāvit Chrīstum? Quamquam Petrus multa nōn scīvit, vīdit quod Jēsūs erat Dominus.
15. Virī, ā diācōnō fōrmātī, nunc sunt baptismatī aptī?
16. Jōannēs, Jēsū cordī proximus, ad dexteram Marīae astitit.
17. Morte Jēsū apostolī, quoniam erant hūmānī, effectī sunt maestī; sed resurrēctiōne, laetī.
18. Jēsūs, redēmptor hūmānī generis, prae cūnctīs ubīque laudātur.
19. Etsī mentem Deī scīre nōn semper possumus, bonī Dominō crēdunt.
20. Per bonī Dominī largitātem plēna est mēnsa nostra cibō.
21. Etiam pars hominum optimōrum ā malō sēductī sunt.
22. Audīvistī quia cūnctae creātūrae ā marī prīmum vēnērunt?
23. Post Evangeliī lēctiōnem populus respōnsum acclāmāvit.
24. Hūmānī, quī in mundō vīvimus, laudāmus Patrem, quī mundum condidit.
25. Episcopus Rōmānus, etsī homō bonus et jūstus, satis beātam vītam nōn vīxit.
26. Marīam Rēgīnam Caelī vocāmus, quoniam est Māter Deī.
27. Semper et ubīque misericordiam Dominī in mente habēbimus.
28. Aeternō cibō mandūcātō, ōrātiōnem subdimus ante Missae fīnem.
29. Relictā Galilaeā, iterum Jēsūs cum apostolīs ad fīnēs Jūdaeae vēnit.
30. Dominus mentēs nostrās ad superna dēsīderia ērigit.
31. Beātī mundō corde, quoniam ipsī ('they') Deum vidēbunt. Mt. v, 8.
32. Adōrāmus quod scīmus, quia salūs ex Jūdaeīs est. Jn. iv, 22.

II. 1. We are joyful because Jesus, the only Son of the Father, is a sharer of our human nature.
2. Many of the Galilaeans had not known that God chose Mary as the mother of Jesus.
3. The cantor sang a canticle sufficiently pleasing to the people.
4. Did many of the Jews call God the King of Kings?

Unit 16

85. Third Declension Adjectives

While some adjectives use the endings of the first and second declensions, others use the endings of the third declension only. This second type has three classes, depending on whether the nominative singular has one, two, or three separate forms.

Third declension adjectives are declined like i-stem nouns: in the ablative singular all three genders have **-ī**; in the genitive plural all three genders have **-ium**; in the nominative and accusative plural the neuter has **-ia**.

a. Three Endings in the Nominative Singular Since third declension nouns have *two* related sets of endings—a neuter and a non-neuter (i.e., masculine/feminine)—it is surprising to find that a small number of third declension adjectives have added a *third* ending *in one case*, the masculine nominative singular. The stem for these adjectives is found by dropping the **-is** ending from the feminine nominative singular. All three nominative forms will be listed in the vocabulary.

ācer, ācris, ācre 'sharp, bitter, ardent'; base: **ācr-**

	SINGULAR			PLURAL		
	Masc.	*Fem.*	*Neuter*	*Masc.*	*Fem.*	*Neuter*
Nom.	ācer	ācris	ācre	ācrēs	ācrēs	ācria
Gen.	ācris	ācris	ācris	ācrium	ācrium	ācrium
Dat.	ācrī	ācrī	ācrī	ācribus	ācribus	ācribus
Acc.	ācrem	ācrem	ācre	ācrēs	ācrēs	ācria
Abl.	ācrī	ācrī	ācrī	ācribus	ācribus	ācribus

b. Two Endings in the Nominative Singular Adjectives with two nominative singular forms—i.e., a masculine/feminine and a neuter—are the most common class of third declension adjectives. Both nominative forms are listed in the vocabulary. The stem is derived by dropping the **-is** ending from the masculine/feminine nominative singular.

omnis, omne 'every, all'; base: **omn-**

	SINGULAR		PLURAL	
	Masc./Fem.	*Neuter*	*Masc./Fem.*	*Neuter*
Nom.	**omnis**	**omne**	**omnēs**	**omnia**
Gen.	**omnis**	**omnis**	**omnium**	**omnium**
Dat.	**omnī**	**omnī**	**omnibus**	**omnibus**
Acc.	**omnem**	**omne**	**omnēs**	**omnia**
Abl.	**omnī**	**omnī**	**omnibus**	**omnibus**

c. One Ending in the Nominative Singular　Adjectives with one form in the nominative singular for all three genders are listed in the vocabulary with the genitive singular form. The base of these adjectives is derived by dropping the ending **-is** from the genitive singular.

fēlīx (*gen.*, **fēlīcis**) 'happy, blessed'; base: **fēlīc-**

	SINGULAR	PLURAL
	M./F./N.	*M./F./N.*
Nom.	**fēlīx**	**fēlīcēs** (M./F.); **fēlīcia** (N.)
Gen.	**fēlīcis**	**fēlīcium**
Dat.	**fēlīcī**	**fēlīcibus**
Acc.	**fēlīcem** (M./F.); **fēlīx** (N.)	**fēlīcēs** (M./F.); **fēlīcia** (N.)
Abl.	**fēlīcī**	**fēlīcibus**

86. Present Active Participles

Participles may be viewed as verbal adjectives (see Section 20f.3; cf. 65). Though built from verbs, they may modify a noun. For example, in the expressions 'glowing coals' and 'home-grown tomatoes' *glowing* and *grown*, derived from verbs, are used as adjectives. Present active participles in Latin are declined like third declension adjectives of one ending. These participles are formed by adding to the present stem of a verb the suffix **-ns** to form the nominative singular, and **-nt-** to form the base of the participle; to this base are added the endings of the third declension.

FIRST CONJUGATION:　**laudā- + -ns = laudāns** 'praising'
　　　　　　　　　　laudā- + -nt- + -is = laudantis

SECOND CONJUGATION:	monē- + -ns = monēns 'warning'
	monē- + -nt- + -is = monentis
THIRD CONJUGATION, '-ō' TYPE:	dūce- + -ns = dūcēns 'leading'
	dūce- + -nt- + -is = dūcentis
THIRD CONJUGATION, '-iō' TYPE:	capie- + -ns = capiēns 'taking'
	capie- + -nt- + -is = capientis
FOURTH CONJUGATION:	audie- + -ns = audiēns 'hearing'
	audie- + -nt- + -is = audientis

Notes: 1. The **'-iō'** verbs (third and fourth conjugation) have **-ie-** before the participial suffixes.
2. The ablative singular ending of the present active participle is usually **-e** (occasionally **-ī**).

---

87. *Uses of the Present Active Participle*

Present active participles are used in three ways:

a. Adjectival   These participles may modify nouns. Just as in English, they may either come with the noun or follow it, set off by commas. For example, in English, 'the struggling artist' and 'the artist, struggling to succeed, etc.,' are both regular uses of the participle as adjective.

Clāmāns vir ā Jēsū audītus est.
'The *shouting* man was heard by Jesus.'
Vir, *clāmāns*, ā Jēsū audītus est.
'The man, *shouting*, was heard by Jesus.'

Note: This second illustration may be translated with an English relative clause, since such a construction has adjectival force. Thus, 'The man[,] *who was shouting*[,] was heard by Jesus.' Any present participle, when translated as a clause, is given a tense contemporaneous with the main verb.

b. Adverbial   These participles may be used to take the place of various adverbial (therefore, subordinate) clauses of time, cause, concession, and purpose (see Section 41).

Vir, *clāmāns*, tamen ā Jēsū nōn audītus est.
'The man, *although he was shouting*, nevertheless was not heard by Jesus.'

Notes: 1. The example is a present participle illustrating its use as an adverbial clause of concession; here **tamen** is the clue to the concessive idea.

2. As usual, when the present participle is translated as a clause, it is given a tense which is contemporaneous with the main verb.

---

c. Ablative Absolute   Present participles, as well as perfect passive participles, may be used in the ablative absolute construction (see Section 68).

Petrō in domum *intrante*, Paulus restitit.
'With *Peter entering* . . .'
'When *Peter entered* the house, Paul remained behind.'

Petrō in domum *intrante*, Paulus restat.
'With *Peter entering* . . .'
'When *Peter enters* the house, Paul remains behind.'

Note again that the present participle denotes an action contemporaneous with the main verb.

---

88. Fourth Declension Nouns: Masculine (or Feminine)

Nouns of the fourth declension have **-ūs** in the genitive singular. Masculine (or feminine) nouns have **-us** in the nominative singular. Their endings, singular and plural, are the following:

	SINGULAR	PLURAL
Nom.	-us	-ūs
Gen.	-ūs	-uum
Dat.	-uī	-ibus
Acc.	-um	-ūs
Abl.	-ū	-ibus

> *Notes:* 1. The nominative and accusative singular are the same as those of the second declension masculine.
> 2. The dative and ablative plural are the same as those of the third declension.

rītus, rītūs, m. 'ceremony, rite'; base: **rīt-**

	SINGULAR	PLURAL
Nom.	**rītus** ('the rite')	**rītūs** ('the rites')
Gen.	**rītūs** ('of the rite')	**rītuum** ('of the rites')
Dat.	**rītuī** ('for/to the rite')	**rītibus** ('for/to the rites')
Acc.	**rītum** ('the rite')	**rītūs** ('the rites')
Abl.	**rītū** ('from/with/in/by the rite')	**rītibus** ('from/with/in/by the rites')

89. *Fourth Declension Nouns: Neuter*

Neuter nouns of the fourth declension have **-ū** in the nominative and accusative singular, **-ū** in the dative singular, and **-ua** in the nominative and accusative plural.

genū, genūs, n. 'knee'; base: **gen-**

	SINGULAR	PLURAL
Nom.	**genū** ('the knee')	**genua** ('the knees')
Gen.	**genūs** ('of the knee')	**genuum** ('of the knees')
Dat.	**genū** ('for/to the knee')	**genibus** ('for/to the knees')
Acc.	**genū** ('the knee')	**genua** ('the knees')
Abl.	**genū** ('from/with/in/by the knee')	**genibus** ('from/with/in/by the knees')

Vocabulary

fīgō, fīgere, fīxī, fīxus pierce, fix, fasten

    crucifīgō, crucifīgere, crucifīxī, crucifīxus fix to a cross, crucify

flectō, flectere, flexī, flexus bend, bow

    genūflectō, genūflectere, genūflexī, genūflexus bend the knee, genuflect, kneel (down)

frangō, frangere, frēgī, frāctus break

    cōnfringō, cōnfringere, cōnfrēgī, cōnfrāctus break in two, break in pieces

fundō, fundere, fūdī, fūsus pour

    cōnfundō, cōnfundere, cōnfūdī, cōnfūsus confound, confuse; put to shame

    effundō, effundere, effūdī, effūsus pour out, shed, spill

    īnfundō, īnfundere, īnfūdī, īnfūsus pour, infuse

    refundō, refundere, refūdī, refūsus pour back, restore, pay back

scandō, scandere, scandī, scānsus climb, mount

    ascendō, ascendere, ascendī, ascēnsus go up, come up, ascend

    dēscendō, dēscendere, dēscendī, dēscēnsus go down, come down, descend

calix, calicis, m. cup, chalice

cāritās, cāritātis, f. love, charity

crux, crucis, f. cross

passiō, passiōnis, f. suffering, passion

suāvitās, suāvitātis, f. sweetness

Pascha, Paschatis, n. Passover, Pesach, Pasch; Easter

pōtus, pōtūs, m. drink

rītus, rītūs, m. ceremony, rite

spīritus, spīritūs, m. breath; spirit

vultus, vultūs, m. face [i.e., countenance]

manus, manūs, f. hand

cornū, cornūs, n. horn; mountaintop

genū, genūs, n. knee

fēlīx (*gen.*, **fēlīcis**) happy, blessed

memor (*gen.*, **memoris**) mindful of (+ *gen.*)

omnipotēns (*gen.*, **omnipotentis**) all-powerful

omnis, omne every, all

paschālis, paschāle of Easter, Paschal

salūtāris, salūtāre saving, of salvation

similis, simile (+ *dat.*) like, similar (to)

dissimilis, dissimile (+ *dat.*) dissimilar, unlike

ācer, ācris, ācre sharp, bitter, ardent

intrā (*prep.* + *acc.*) within, among

quāpropter (*coord. conj.*) wherefore, and therefore

Vocabulary Notes

In some ancient texts the verb **genūflectō** is written as two words. In that event **genū** is to be construed as the direct object of **flectō**.

In the passive voice **cōnfundō** means 'be ashamed of' and takes the accusative case. This use imitates the Greek middle voice, which may take an accusative, just as the active voice does: **Petrus Paulum cōnfundēbātur** 'Peter was ashamed of Paul.'

Besides as terms for 'coming down from or going up' to heaven, **ascendō** and **dēscendō** are also used of 'going to or coming from' the big city (on high ground) or 'getting in or out' of a boat.

Note that **cāritās** is an abstract noun formed from the base of the adjective **cārus** (Unit 7) + the noun-making suffix **-itās, -itātis**. The early Christians chose this word for 'love,' to avoid the unwanted connotations attaching to others, such as **amor**.

Pascha, Paschatis, n. and **Pascha, Paschae**, f. (Unit 11) are identical in origin and meaning. These words are heteroclites (i.e., words identical in base which use the endings of two different declensions).

Note that **manus** is a feminine noun. To remember this, recall that **dextera** 'right hand' (Unit 13) is feminine: **dextera (manus)**. Most other non-neuter words of the fourth declension are masculine.

Memor takes the genitive case. In general, words meaning 'forgetting or remembering' take this case.

Omnipotēns is a compound of two third-declension adjectives, **omnis** and **potēns** (Unit 20).

Note that **salūtāris** is an adjective built on the noun **salūs, salūtis**, f. (Unit 15). The suffix **-āris, -e** means 'pertaining to.'

Similis and **dissimilis** are two more adjectives which take the dative case (see Section 82) (occasionally the genitive occurs).

Derivatives:	LATIN	ENGLISH
	fīgō	fixture, fixation
	crucifīgō	crucifix, crucifixion
	flectō	reflect, flex
	frangō	frangible, fracture, fraction
	fundō	fusion, fusible
	effundō	effusive
	īnfundō	funnel
	refundō	refund, refuse
	scandō	scansion
	ascendō	ascension, ascendant, ascendent

Derivatives: LATIN   ENGLISH

dēscendō	descendant, descendent, condescension
crux	crux, crucial, crisscross (i.e., Christ's cross)
suāvitās	suavity
pōtus	potable water
vultus	volte-face
manus	manual, maintain
cornū	cornucopia, corner, cornet, cornea
genū	genuine
fēlīx	felicitous
memor	memorable
omnipotēns	omnipotent
omnis	bus (from dat. pl., omnibus), Dodge Omni
salūtāris	salutary
similis	simile
ācer	acrid, acrimonious
intrā	intramurals

Drills

I. Third declension adjectives. Identify the case of each phrase; translate; change the number.

A. omnis, omne 'every, all'
1. omnis homō
2. nōminis omnis
3. omnem lēctiōnem
4. omnibus baptismatibus
5. omnī ecclēsiae
6. omnēs pāpae
7. angelō omnī
8. omnium apostolōrum
9. omnī Missā
10. omnia mandāta

B. ācer, ācris, ācre 'bitter'
1. servus ācer
2. rēgīna ācris
3. ācris rēgīnae
4. ācrī diāconō
5. dōnum ācre

C. fēlīx (gen., fēlīcis) 'happy'
1. fēlīcī famīliae
2. famīliae fēlīcis
3. fēlīcēs discipulōs
4. fēlīx rēgnum
5. saecula fēlīcia

II.   Present active participles. Translate; identify each participle.

1. Paulus vīdit Petrum ambulantem in viā.
2. Vidēns Jēsūm, vir clāmāvit.
3. Beātī quī, audientēs, verbum Dominī faciunt.
4. Servus cēnam parābat Paulō venientī in domum.
5. Ōrāmus prō in Dominō vīventibus.
6. Paulus vocāvit ūnum hominum ex ecclēsiā venientium.

Exercises

I.
1. In nōmine Patris et Fīliī et Spīritūs Sānctī. Āmēn.
2. Et sanguis meus vērus est pōtus. Jn. vi, 55.
3. Apostolī dedērunt pānēs mīrōs hominibus in terrā reclīnātīs.
4. Corpus vestrum templum est Spīritūs Sānctī, quī in vōbīs ('you') est, quem habetis ā Deō, et nōn estis vestrī. I Cor. vi, 19.
5. Tunc Jēsūs et apostolī intrā domum erant, mandūcantēs Pascha. Ūnus autem Dominum jam trādiderat.
6. Parvula ancilla, adveniēns ad Jēsūm, cum innocentiā dīxit: Sciō quia sānāre potes male habentēs. Nōn sānābis mātrem meam? Et Jēsūs domum intrāvit et mātrem ancillae sānāvit.
7. a. Dum Jēsūs autem ambulat ad mare, vīdit Petrum.
   b. Dōnec Jēsūs autem ambulābat ad mare, vīdit Petrum.
   c. Jēsūs autem, ambulāns ad mare, vīdit Petrum monentem fēlīcem populum.
8. Et vīdit omnis populus eum ('him') ambulantem et laudantem Deum. Acts iii, 9.
9. Discipulī autem collēgērunt cōnfrāctōs pānēs ā populō relictōs.
10. Glōria Patrī et Fīliō et Spīrituī Sānctō.
11. Accēpit pānem et grātiās agēns frēgit et dīxit: "*Hoc* ('this') *est corpus meum.*" I Cor. xi, 23–24.
12. "*Hic* ('this') *calix novum testāmentum est in meō sanguine.*" I Cor. xi, 25.
13. Chrīstus Jēsūs enim effūdit sanguinem prō mundī vītā.
14. Nōs ('we') autem nōn spīritum mundī accēpimus, sed Spīritum, quī ex Deō est. I Cor. ii, 12.
15. In ōrātiōne genūflectentēs, semper laudābimus Dominum, quī passiōne et morte in cruce et resurrēctiōne mundum salvum fēcit.

16. Vīnō autem in calicem fūsō, Jēsūs benedīxit et dedit apostolīs, dīcēns: Hīc est meus sanguis. Sī biberitis, vīvētis in aeternum.

17. Quis ('who') nōs ('us') sēparābit ā cāritāte Chrīstī? Rom. viii, 35.

18. Jēsūs memor autem Patris omnipotentis ascendit in templum atque aspexit vultūs ōrantium. Et intrā templum invēnit multōs, et fēlīcēs et ācrēs.

19. Paschālis rītūs memorēs vidēmus suāvitātem et misericordiam et cāritātem Deī Patris.

20. Et Petrus invēnit Jēsūm in cornū ōrantem prō omnibus hominibus.

21. Vēnit Fīlius hominis mandūcāns et bibēns. Mt. xi, 19.

22. Jūstōrum autem animae in manū Deī sunt. Wisdom iii, 1.

23. Quāpropter salūtāre praeceptum Dominī fēlīcēs audīvimus, et dīligimus omnēs, et nōbīs ('to us') similēs et dissimilēs.

24. Jēsūs, reclīnātus in cēnāculō, cum apostolīs pānem frangēbat.

25. Per omnia saecula saeculōrum.

II.   1. Although all had eaten, nevertheless they were not happy.

2. When he will have ascended to the Father, Jesus will be ashamed of the men not hearing the Father's words.

3. By his cross and resurrection Jesus has saved the world.

4. Taking the sick man by the hand, Peter led (him) into the house, where he gave the man a drink of wine.

5. Mindful of our faults, we praise the mercy of the living Lord.

Unit 17

90. The Irregular Verb volō 'wish': All Six Indicative Tenses

Since a verb is assigned to a conjugation according to the form of its second principal part, a glance at the present infinitive of **volō**, **velle**, **voluī**, — 'wish, want, be willing' shows that it is irregular: **velle**.

The forms of the present indicative cannot be synthesized from the stem of its present infinitive; the forms must be observed and memorized.

PRESENT INDICATIVE

	SINGULAR	PLURAL
1	**volō** ('I wish')	**volumus** ('we wish')
2	**vīs** ('you wish')	**vultis** ('you wish')
3	**vult** ('he/she/it wishes')	**volunt** ('they wish')

The imperfect and future indicative tenses are formed *as if* from a regular third conjugation verb with the infinitive *volere. Once this is known, the forms are easily generated. Thus, the imperfect indicative: **volēbam**, **volēbās**, etc.; the future indicative: **volam**, **volēs**, **volet**, etc. (See Sections 39 and 47.)

In the perfect-active system **volō** is entirely regular: the perfect, pluperfect, and future-perfect are formed in the regular way from the stem of the third principal part. Thus, the perfect: **voluī**, **voluistī**, etc.; the pluperfect: **volueram**, **voluerās**, etc.; the future-perfect: **voluerō**, **volueris**, etc.

91. The Irregular Verb eō 'go': All Six Indicative Tenses

Although at first glance the present infinitive of **eō**, **īre**, **īvī** (**iī**), **itus** 'go' appears to place it among fourth conjugation verbs, it is irregular; the present indicative must be observed and memorized.

PRESENT INDICATIVE

	SINGULAR	PLURAL
1	eō ('I go')	īmus ('we go')
2	īs ('you go')	ītis ('you go')
3	it ('he/she/it goes')	eunt ('they go')

> *Note:* The monosyllabic forms **īs** and **it**, when uncompounded, are rare; other verbs, such as **ambulō** (Unit 5) and **vādō** (Unit 24), supply substitutes for these two forms.

The imperfect indicative is formed from the stem **ī-** (very rarely **iē-**). Thus **ībam, ībās, ībat**, etc. (Compare the formation in a regular fourth conjugation verb—**audiēbam, audiēbās**, etc.—where **-ē-** is always added to the present stem.) The future indicative also uses this stem (**ī-**), but employs the future suffix **-bi-**, like a first or second conjugation verb.

IMPERFECT INDICATIVE

	SINGULAR	PLURAL
1	ībam ('I was going')	ībāmus ('we were going')
2	ībās ('you were going')	ībātis ('you were going')
3	ībat ('he/she/it was going')	ībant ('they were going')

FUTURE INDICATIVE

	SINGULAR	PLURAL
1	ībō ('I will go')	ībimus ('we will go')
2	ībis ('you will go')	ībitis ('you will go')
3	ībit ('he/she/it will go')	ībunt ('they will go')

Like any verb, **eō** has a regular perfect-active system. Either form of the third principal part—**īvī** or **iī**—yields the perfect, pluperfect, and future-perfect tenses in accordance with the rules. When the shorter stem is used, the second-person forms of the perfect are contracted: **iistī > īstī; iistis > īstis**.

92. *Accusative of Place to/into Which*

The accusative case is used with the prepositions **ad** or **in** to express motion toward or into a place. The preposition may be omitted with **domus** 'house' or with the names of big cities.

Et veniunt *ad domum*. Mk. iii, 20.
'And they come *to the house*.'

Petrus introiit (*in*) *domum*.
'Peter entered (*into*) *the house*.'
[**introeō, introīre, introīvī (introiī), introitus** 'go within, enter']

Petrus īvit (*in*) *Rōmam* (*Hierosolymam*).
'Peter went *to Rome* (*to Jerusalem*).'
[**Rōma, Rōmae,** f. 'Rome'; **Hierosolyma, Hierosolymae,** f.
'Jerusalem']

93. *Ablative of Place Where*

The ablative case is used with the preposition **in** to express the place
in which something happens.

Apostolī *in cēnāculō* convēnerant.
'The apostles had come together *in the upper room*.'

94. *Ablative of Place from Which/out of Which*

The ablative case is used with the prepositions **ā (ab, abs)** and **ē (ex)**
to express motion away from or out of a place.

Paulus vēnit *ā Rōmā* (*ab Hierosolymīs*).
'Paul came *from Rome* (*from Jerusalem*).'

Petrus vēnit *ē templō*.
'Peter came *out of the temple*.'

95. *Locative Case*

The concept of place where, when applied to big cities, may be expressed by the locative case. Nouns of the first and second declensions use an ending which is identical with the genitive singular.
Nouns occurring only in the plural use an ending which is identical
with the ablative plural.

Rōmae.
'At Rome.'

Ephesī.
'At Ephesus.'
[**Ephesus, Ephesī,** m. 'Ephesus']

Athēnīs.
'At Athens.'
[**Athēnae, Athēnārum**, f. 'Athens']
Hierosolymīs.
'At Jerusalem.'

Note: When the indeclinable noun **Jerūsalem** occurs, the preposition is always expressed: **in Jerūsalem** 'in Jerusalem.'

Vocabulary

**nūntiō, nūntiāre, nūntiāvī,
nūntiātus** declare, announce
**annūntiō, annūntiāre, an-
nūntiāvī, annūntiātus**
announce
**plācō, plācāre, plācāvī,
plācātus** appease; reconcile
**pūrgō, pūrgāre, pūrgāvī, pūr-
gātus** purify, purge
**vīvificō, vīvificāre, vīvificāvī,
vīvificātus** bring to life,
make live
mittō:
  **admittō, admittere, admīsī,
  admissus** join, admit;
  allow, permit
  **āmittō, āmittere, āmīsī,
  āmissus** send off; lose
  **ēmittō, ēmittere, ēmīsī,
  ēmissus** send out
  **remittō, remittere, remīsī,
  remissus** send back;
  forgive
eō, īre, īvī (iī), itus go
  **abeō, abīre, abīvī (abiī),
  abitus** go away, leave
  adeō, adīre, adīvī (adiī),

  aditus go to, approach
**circumeō, circumīre,
  circumīvī (circumiī),
  circumitus** go about
**exeō, exīre, exīvī (exiī),
  exitus** go out, leave
ineō, inīre, inīvī (iniī), initus
  go in, enter (upon)
**intereō, interīre, interīvī (in-
  teriī), interitus** perish, die
**introeō, introīre, introīvī (in-
  troiī), introitus** go within,
  enter
**obeō, obīre, obīvī (obiī),
  obitus** go to meet; die
**pereō, perīre, perīvī (periī),
  peritus** perish, die, be lost
**pertrānseō, pertrānsīre, per-
  trānsīvī (pertrānsiī), per-
  trānsitus** go all about, go
  away; pierce
**praeeō, praeīre, praeīvī
  (praeiī), praeitus** go before
**prōdeō, prōdīre, prōdīvī
  (prōdiī), prōditus** go forth
**redeō, redīre, redīvī (rediī),
  reditus** go back, return

subeō, subīre, subīvī (subiī),
  subitus go under, submit
  to; climb
trānseō, trānsīre, trānsīvī
  (trānsiī), trānsitus
  go across, pass through;
  pass away
sum:
  adsum (assum), adesse,
    affuī, — be present
  prōsum, prōdesse, prōfuī, —
    avail, profit, be advan-
    tageous (to) (+ dat.)
volō, velle, voluī, — want,
  wish, be willing
Rōma, Rōmae, f. Rome
locus, locī, m. (pl., loca) place
salvātor, salvātōris, m. savior
dīlēctiō, dīlēctiōnis, f. love
laus, laudis, f. praise
pietās, pietātis, f. goodness;
  tenderness, pity
remissiō, remissiōnis, f.
  forgiveness, remission
tellūs, tellūris, f. earth
adventus, adventūs, m.
  coming, advent

frūctus, frūctūs, m. fruit
clēmēns (gen., clēmentis)
  merciful
supplex (gen., supplicis)
  suppliant
vetus (gen., veteris) old,
  ancient; former
acceptābilis, acceptābile
  acceptable
episcopālis, episcopāle
  of a bishop, episcopal
invīsibilis, invīsibile spiritual,
  invisible
vīsibilis, vīsibile tangible,
  visible
Jerūsalem (Hebrew: indecl.
  noun; also, Hierosolyma,
  Hierosolymae, f. and Hierosolyma, Hierosolymōrum,
  n.) Jerusalem
ūsque (adv.) as far as, all
  the way
  ūsque ad (+ acc.) even to,
  up to, all the way to

Vocabulary Notes

When **admittō** means 'allow, permit' it takes an object infinitive.
Āmittō may indicate either intentional or accidental action, 'send off' or 'lose.'

The present participle of **eō** is **iēns** (gen., **euntis**). The **m** in **circumeō** may be dropped: **circueō, circuīre, circuīvī (circuiī), circuitus**. Note that some compounds of **eō**—**intereō; obeō; pereō**—are employed euphemistically to mean 'die.' The **d** in **prōdeō** and **redeō** is epenthetical, i.e., inserted to make the words easier to say. Besides 'to go under' **subeō** may also mean 'climb' in the sense of 'to go up from under.' (Cf. **suscipiō**, Unit 14.)

As the infinitive shows, **prōsum** uses an epenthetical **d** when the form of **sum** begins with a vowel: **prōdes; prōderō**, etc.

The present participle of **volō** is **volēns** (*gen.*, **volentis**). **Volō** may take a direct object or an object infinitive: **Vīsne pānem?** 'Do you want the bread?' **Volō meum fīlium vidēre.** 'I wish to see my son.'

Vetus 'old' is the antonym of 'new,' not the antonym of 'young': **vetus testāmentum** 'old testament'; **novum testāmentum** 'new testament.'

Note that the Latin for 'Jerusalem' falls into three classes: indeclinable noun, first declension noun, and second declension plural noun. The concept of place to which often uses the accusative of the first declension form: **Hierosolymam**; place where uses either the locative of the second declension plural form, **Hierosolymīs**, or the preposition with the indeclinable form, **in Jerūsalem**.

Derivatives:	LATIN	ENGLISH
	nūntiō	papal nuncio (from the noun nūntius)
	annūntiō	annunciation
	plācō	placate
	pūrgō	purgatory
	vīvificō	vivify
	mittō	Mass, missal, missile
	admittō	admission, admissible
	ēmittō	emission, emissary
	remittō	remit
	eō	adit, exit, circuit, initial, introit, obituary, perish, subito, transit
	volō	volition, velleity
	locus	locus, location, locale, locomotive
	salvātor	Salvatore, El Salvador
	dīlēctiō	predilection
	laus	laud, Lauds, laudatory
	pietās	piety, pity, the Pieta
	tellūs	tellurium
	frūctus	fructify, usufruct
	clēmēns	clement, inclement
	vetus	veteran
	episcopālis	Episcopalian

Drills

I.   The irregular verb volō 'wish.'

1. Volō cum discipulīs meīs Pascha facere.
2. Vīs Pascha facere?
3. Paulus vult domum Petrī venīre.
4. Volumus pānem, nōn vīnum.
5. Vultis lēctiōnem audīre?
6. Apostolī volunt Paulum relinquere.
7. Diāconus episcopum vidēre volēbat.
8. Voletne diāconus episcopum vidēre?
9. Populus sacerdōtem rītum complēre volēbat (volēbant).
10. Quārē ad mare venīre voluistī?

II.   The irregular verb eō 'go.'

1. Eō ad meum Patrem.
2. Abīs ā templō?
3. Petrus ad apostolōs init.
4. Īmus ē domō.
5. Ībātis in Galilaeam?
6. Virī ex ecclēsiā exeunt.
7. Ībunt Hierosolymam.
8. Īstis Chrīstiānī Rōmam?
9. Iērunt in aulam.
10. Volō domum īre.

Exercises

I.   1. Postquam turbae satis mandūcāvērunt, apostolī iērunt et omnēs pānēs relictōs collēgērunt.

2. Quī enim voluerit animam suam ('his') salvam facere, perdet eam ('it'); quī autem perdiderit animam suam propter mē ('me') et evangelium, salvam faciet eam. Mk. viii, 35.

3. Vērē dīgnum et jūstum est, invīsibilem Deum Patrem omnipotentem Fīliumque ūnigenitum, Dominum nostrum Jēsūm Chrīstum, personāre. →to proclaim

4. a. Jēsūs in mundum inīvit in remissiōnem peccātōrum nostrōrum, et prō omnibus crucifīxus est.

   b. Jēsūs, quī in mundum inīvit in remissiōnem

peccātōrum nostrōrum, prō omnibus hominibus crucifīxus est.

c. Jēsūs Salvātor, iniēns in mundum in remissiōnem peccātōrum, voluntātem Patris clēmentis fēcit.

5. Ō dīlēctiō cāritātis! Pater noster enim Fīlium ūnigenitum mīsit.

6. Crēdō in ūnum Deum, Patrem omnipotentem, factōrem ('maker') caelī et terrae, vīsibilium omnium et invīsibilium.

7. Supplicēs igitur volumus ad Dominum pietātis acceptābile sacrificium facere.

8. Angelus Dominī ad Marīam annūntiāvit: Quod māter Deī eris.

9. Paulō autem volente intrāre in populum, nōn permīsērunt discipulī. Acts xix, 30.

10. Librī veteris testāmentī ac novī, in numerō multī, prōsunt omnibus crēdentibus in Deum.

11. Jēsūs circuībat Galilaeam, et populum monēbat. Posteā rediit Hierosolymam, ubi dīxit apostolīs dē morte et resurrēctiōne.

12. Sciēbat autem et Jūdās, quī trādēbat eum ('him'), locum. Jn. xviii, 2.

13. Scrīptum est in librō veteris testāmentī prīmō quoniam Deus spīritum ēmīsit et vīvificāvit Adam.

14. Diāconus, dēprecātiōnēs prō populō effundēns, laudem cēreī dīligenter implēvit.

15. Paulus, adventum glōriōsum Fīliī nūntiāns, cōnfundēbat Jūdaeōs quī in templō aderant.

16. Sānctus Petrus, servus et apostolus Jēsū Chrīstī, Rōmae prīmus episcopālem potentiam habēbat.

17. Volō ergō virōs ōrāre in omnī locō. I Tim. ii, 8.

18. Noster pānis, frūctus tellūris, ā sacerdōte benedictus, erit omnibus pānis vītae aeternae.

19. Deō volente, omnis nātūra pūrgābitur (pūrgāta erit).

20. Ob fēlīcem culpam Adae, Jēsūs vēnit in mundum atque Patrī omnēs fīliōs Adae plācāvit.

21. Apostolī, ā Jēsū āmissī, male habentēs sānāre et peccāta remittere valēbant.

22. Petrus autem et Jōannēs ascendēbant in templum ad hōram ōrātiōnis nōnam ('ninth'). Acts iii, 1.

II.   1. After Peter went away from Rome, he came to Jerusalem, because he wanted to see Paul about clean and unclean food.

2. Paul wishes to go to the temple and announce the Lord Jesus, that he is the Son of God.

3. At Athens, it was not permitted for Paul to go in to the people.   passive

4. Paul, although he was confounding the chief of the priests in Jerusalem, wished to go away and announce the coming of the Savior to the people in Rome.

(1) Postea Petrus abiit / abibat a Roma venit Hierolosymam quia volebat / voluit videre Paulam de mundo et immundo cibo.

(2) Paulus vult ire ad templum et annuntiare Dominum Jesum, quia est Filius Dei.

(3) ~~Athenae~~ AthenTS non permittebatur / permissum est Paulo, inire ad populum,

(4) Paulus, quamquam confundebat principem sacerdotum ~~erat~~ Hierolosymae voluit abire ~~et~~ annuntiareque adventum ~~adventum~~ salvatoris populo ~~in~~ Romae.

Unit 18

96. *Future Active Participle*

Besides the present active and the perfect passive, Latin has future participles of both voices. To form the future active participle, simply insert the suffix **-ūr-** between the base of the perfect passive participle and the ending:

> **laudāt-** + **-ūr-**: **laudātūrus, -a, -um**
> **monit-** + **-ūr-**: **monitūrus, -a, -um**
> **duct-** + **-ūr-**: **ductūrus, -a, -um**
> **capt-** + **-ūr-**: **captūrus, -a, -um**
> **audīt-** + **-ūr-**: **audītūrus, -a, -um**

Since these participles refer to a time subsequent to that of the main verb, they may be translated with the expressions 'intending to' or 'about to'; thus, 'intending to praise,' 'about to lead,' etc. Since they are active in form and meaning, these participles may take a direct object: **laudātūrus Deum** 'about to praise God'; **audītūrus ōrātiōnem** 'intending to hear the prayer.' Thus future participles often convey the idea of likelihood or purpose.

97. *Future Passive Participle*

To form the future passive participle, add **-ndus, -nda, -ndum** to the stem of the present infinitive; i-stem verbs will have **-ie-**:

> **laudā-** + **-nd-**: **laudandus, -a, -um**
> **monē-** + **-nd-**: **monendus, -a, -um**
> **dūce-** + **-nd-**: **dūcendus, -a, -um**
> **capie-** + **-nd-**: **capiendus, -a, -um**
> **audie-** + **-nd-**: **audiendus, -a, -um**

Note that all stem vowels are short before **-nd-**. These participles may be translated with the phrases 'about to be,' 'having to be.' Future passive participles often convey the added notion of duty, propriety, or necessity—an action which 'has to be done' or 'should be done.'

98. Periphrastic Conjugations

While the future active and passive participles are verbal adjectives and may be used as such, they are most often joined with the verb **sum** to form compound tenses which are the grammatical equivalents of the regular tenses. These compound tenses are called periphrastics. As in all compound tenses, the endings are restricted to the nominative (**-us, -a, -um; -ī, -ae, -a**) since they always refer back to the subject, whether it is expressed or implied.

a. Active Periphrastic   The active periphrastic conjugation is compounded of the future active participle in the nominative case and **sum** in the required tense.

Present: **laudātūrus sum.**   'I am going to praise.'
Imperfect: **laudātūrus eram.**   'I was intending to praise.'
Pluperfect: **laudātūrus fueram.**   'I had been about to praise.'
                   etc.

Note that the participle determines only the voice of the compound verb form; the form of **sum** determines the person, number, tense, and mood.

b. Passive Periphrastic   The passive periphrastic conjugation is composed of the future passive participle in the nominative case and **sum** in the required tense.

Present: **audiendus est.**   'he is having to be heard.'
                                    'he must be heard.'
Future: **audienda erit.**   'she will have to be heard.'
               etc.

Note, again, that the form of the participle determines only the voice.
    Care should be taken to distinguish these periphrastics from the three regular compound tenses: e.g., **audītī sunt** 'they were heard/have been heard,' but **audītūrī sunt** 'they are about to hear,' **audiendī sunt** 'they should/must/ought to be heard,' etc.

99. Dative of Personal Agency with Passive Periphrastics

Since the dative is the case of the interested party, passive periphrastics quite logically use this case to indicate the one on whom the obligation or necessity of the action rests; this is called the dative of personal agency.

Psalmus *populō* cantandus est.
'A psalm is having to be chanted *by the people*.'
'A psalm must be chanted *by the people*.'

Paulus *rēgī* audiendus erat.
'Paul was having to be heard *by the king*.'
'Paul had to be heard *by the king*.'

Note: The dative of personal agency is occasionally found even with the regular compound tenses, in imitation of the Greek practice with perfect or pluperfect passives: **nihil dīgnum morte āctum est eī** (Lk. xxiii, 15) 'nothing worthy of death has been done *by him*.'

100. Review of Participles

Theoretically, since there are two voices and three tenses, Latin should have six participles. But in practice it lacks two, a present passive and a perfect active.

Participles, when used as adjectives, express relative time; i.e., they indicate a time relative to that of the action of the main verb. The present participle expresses a time simultaneous with that of the main verb; the perfect, either a time prior to or simultaneous with that of the main verb (since the perfect is both the past simple and the present perfect); and the future, a time subsequent to that of the main verb.

	ACTIVE	PASSIVE
Present:	**laudāns** (*gen.*, **laudantis**) ('praising')	None
Perfect:	None	**laudātus, -a, -um** ('having been praised')
Future:	**laudātūrus, -a, -um** ('about to praise,' 'intending to praise')	**laudandus, -a, -um** ('having to be praised')

Latin makes up for these missing participles by inverting the voice or by using a finite verb. For example, the active idea, 'having seen the apostle,' may easily be inverted and thus expressed: **apostolō vīsō** 'the apostle having been seen'; or it may be expressed in an adverbial clause by a finite verb introduced by a subordinating conjunction: **postquam apostolum vīdit** 'after he had seen the apostle.'

Vocabulary

baptizō, baptizāre, baptizāvī, baptizātus immerse, baptize

evangelizō, evangelizāre, evangelizāvī, evangelizātus preach the Gospel

cēdō, cēdere, cessī, cessus go; yield

> **accēdō, accēdere, accessī, accessus** go to, approach

> **concēdō, concēdere, concessī, concessus** yield; grant

> **discēdō, discēdere, discessī, discessus** depart

> **incēdō, incēdere, incessī, incessus** go, walk

> **praecēdō, praecēdere, praecessī, praecessus** go before; lead the way

> **prōcēdō, prōcēdere, prōcessī, prōcessus** go forth, proceed

> **recēdō, recēdere, recessī, recessus** go back, depart

claudō, claudere, clausī, clausus shut, close

> **conclūdō, conclūdere, conclūsī, conclūsus** shut up; conclude

tendō, tendere, tetendī, tentus (tēnsus) stretch, extend

extendō, extendere, extendī, extentus (extēnsus) stretch out

intendō, intendere, intendī, intentus (intēnsus) aim (at), look at intently

ostendō, ostendere, ostendī, ostentus (ostēnsus) show; explain

faciō:

> **interficiō, interficere, interfēcī, interfectus** do away with, kill

> **perficiō, perficere, perfēcī, perfectus** do completely, finish, accomplish

> **sufficiō, sufficere, suffēcī, suffectus** be enough, be sufficient

custōdiō, custōdīre, custōdīvī (custōdiī), custōdītus guard, watch over

veniō:

> **perveniō, pervenīre, pervēnī, perventus** arrive; attain

> **subveniō, subvenīre, subvēnī, subventus** (+ *dat.*) come upon; assist, come to help

> **superveniō, supervenīre, supervēnī, superventus**

come upon, overtake
(+ *dat.*); come up, arrive
clēmentia, clēmentiae, f.
mercy, clemency
Lēvīta (Lēvītēs), Lēvītae, m.
deacon, Levite
Lūcās, Lūcae, m. Luke
sapientia, sapientiae, f.
wisdom
tenebrae, tenebrārum, f. *pl.*
darkness, gloom
grex, gregis, m. flock
pāstor, pāstōris, m. shepherd;
pastor
ars, artis, artium, f. (practical)
knowledge, art
ascēnsiō, ascēnsiōnis, f.
going up, ascension

hūmānitās, hūmānitātis, f.
humanity
lēx, lēgis, f. law, Torah
altāre, altāris, altārium, n.
altar
benīgnus, -a, -um kindly
cōtīdiānus, -a, -um daily
cōtīdiē (*adv.*) daily
dēvōtus, -a, -um devout,
devoted
fēstus, -a, -um festal
indēficiēns (*gen.,* **indēficientis**)
unfailing
circum (*prep.* + *acc.*) around,
about
inde (*adv.*) from there;
from then

Vocabulary Notes

The **z** in **baptizō** and **evangelizō** is a rare letter in Latin, occurring only in words borrowed from Greek. Since it has the value of two consonants (see Section 1c, Note 4), the **z** in these words causes the preceding **i** to get the accent: **baptízō, evangelízō.** When **evangelizō** takes a direct object, translate 'announce the good news of.'

The basic meaning of **cēdō** is 'to go'; when it means 'yield to' or 'give in to' it takes the dative. All its many compounds expand on the idea of 'to go,' with the exception of **concēdō** 'yield; grant.'

When the preposition **ob** (Unit 11) is used as a prefix, it means 'out in front of'; **ostendō** is a compound of **tendō** and **obs** (a by-form of **ob**) with the **b** dropped: 'stretch' (something) 'out in front of' (someone); hence, 'show; explain.' Consequently, **ostendō** may take a direct and an indirect object.

Note that the noun **clēmentia** is built from the base of **clēmēns** (*gen.,* **clēmentis**) (Unit 17) + the abstract-noun-making suffix, **-ia.**

Tenebrae occurs only in the plural; translate in the singular: 'darkness, gloom.'

Grex, gregis, m. 'flock' is the source of the denominative verb **gregō** (Unit 11).

Ascēnsiō is formed from the perfect passive participle of **ascendō** (Unit 16): **ascēns-** + **-iō** (**-iōnis**).

Hūmānitās is the abstract noun made from the adjective **hūmānus** (Unit 15): **hūmān-** + **-itās** (**-itātis**).

Altāre is the neuter of an adjective used substantively; it is ultimately derived from the simpler adjective **altus** (Unit 9).

The noun **fēstum** (Unit 3) is the adjective **fēstus** used as a substantive.

The adjective **indēficiēns** is a post-classical coinage from the present participle of **dēficiō** (Unit 6). The prefix **in-** is here the inseparable particle meaning 'without, not.'

Derivatives:	LATIN	ENGLISH
	evangelizō	evangelize, evangelization
	cēdō	cede, accede, concede, precede, proceed, processional, recede, recessional
	claudō	clause, clausula, conclusive, conclusion
	tendō	tend, tension, extend, intend, ostensible, ostentatious
	perficiō	perfect
	sufficiō	suffice, sufficient
	custōdiō	custodian, custody
	subveniō	subvention
	superveniō	supervene
	sapientia	sapience
	tenebrae	Tenebrae, tenebrific, tenebrous
	grex	gregarious
	lēx	legal, loyal, legitimate, legislator
	benīgnus	benign tumor
	cōtīdiānus	quotidian
	circum	circumcision, circumstance, circumlocution

Drills

I. Form the future active and passive participles of each verb; translate:

1. dō, dare, dedī, datus
2. dēleō, dēlēre, dēlēvī, dēlētus
3. agō, agere, ēgī, āctus

4. suscipiō, suscipere, suscēpī, susceptus
5. fīniō, fīnīre, fīnīvī (fīniī), fīnītus
6. extollō, extollere, extulī, —

II.   Periphrastic conjugations.
Ablative of accompaniment
1. Chrīstus cum glōriā ventūrus est.
2. Marīa ōrātūra erat.
3. Diāconus prīmam lēctiōnem lēctūrus fuerat.
4. Prīma lēctiō diāconō legenda erit.
5. Vīnum servō miscendum est.
6. Pānēs apostolīs colligendī erant.

Exercises

I.   1. Quīcumque facit lēgem secundum Patris voluntātem ad
        aeternam glōriam perventūrus est in rēgnō caelōrum.
     2. Rītū inceptō, dēvōtī conveniunt circum fēstum altāre
        Dominī, arte hūmānitātis factum.
     3. Nōn vēnī solvere Lēgem aut Prophētās; nōn vēnī solvere,
        sed adimplēre. Mt. v, 17.
     4. Pater benīgnus hūmānitātī pānem cōtīdiānum semper dat.
     5. Post Jēsū ascēnsiōnem apostolī Galilaeae astitērunt,
        aspicientēs in caelōs.
     6. Prīmā lēctiōne lēctā, prīncipium Evangeliī secundum
        Lūcam Lēvītae legendum erat. Lēctiōne fīnītā, populus
        acclāmāvit.
     7. Vir autem, Jēsūm intendēns, exclāmāvit: Quia mē ('me')
        salvum facere potes. Concēdēs igitur indīgnō hominī
        clēmentiam tuam?
     8. Sapientia clēmentiaque Deī omnibus Chrīstiānīs semper
        et ubīque laudandae sunt.
     9. Etsī in tenebrīs incēdentēs, tamen Chrīstum, lūmen
        indēficiēns, habēmus. Quī enim populō viam semper
        ostendit.
    10. Dominus Jēsūs apostolīs saepe ostendēbat quod mors ejus
        ('his') in salūtem mundī suffectūra erat.
    11. Ubi dē monte dēscendit et supervēnit Jēsūs, statim incēpit
        apostolīs ventūram mortem ostendere.
    12. Jēsūs autem nōn volēbat in Jūdaeā circuīre, quia Jūdaeī
        dīcēbant quod interficiendus erat.
    13. Ut apostolī in cēnāculō conclūsī sunt, Jēsūs, vinculīs
        mortis solūtīs, accessit et dīxit: Ecce adsum.

14. Baptizātus autem Jēsūs, cōnfestim (= statim) ascendit dē aquā. Mt. iii, 16.
15. Missā inceptā, sacerdōs dīcēbat: Introībō ad altāre Deī.
16. Jōannēs baptista dīxit quoniam Jēsū baptizandus fuit.
17. Postquam autem resurrēxerō, praecēdam vōs ('you') in Galilaeam. Mt. xxvi, 32.
18. Tunc sacerdōs, manibus extēnsīs, dīcit ōrātiōnem.
19. Et respiciēns Jēsūm ambulantem dīcit: "Ecce agnus Deī." Jn. i, 36.
20. Crēdimus in Spīritum Sānctum, Dominum et vīvificantem, quī ex Patre Fīliōque prōcēdit.
21. Corpus Chrīstī custōdiet mē ('me') in vītam aeternam.
22. Perficere autem bonum, nōn inveniō.
23. Inde angelus Dominī accessūrus est ad pāstōrēs in agrīs gregēs custōdientēs.
24. Ecce enim evangelizō vōbīs ('to you') gaudium magnum, quod erit omnī populō. Evangelium secundum Lūcam ii, 10.
25. Ego ('I') sum Alpha et Ōmega, dīcit Dominus Deus, quī est et quī erat et quī ventūrus est, Omnipotēns. Rev. i, 8.
26. Beātī quī ambulant in lēge Dominī.

II. 1. Paul will have to be seen by Peter, who is about to arrive at Rome.
2. The flock must be guarded by the good shepherd.
3. The kindly priest, having stretched out his hands, was about to pray for all humanity.
4. Jesus said that the contrite had to be baptized by the apostles.
5. Luke knew that he was going to write a book about the Savior.
6. The devout will see the darkness of the world put to flight by the unfailing light of wisdom and clemency.

Unit 19

101. *Fifth Declension Nouns*

Nouns of the fifth declension have **-eī** in the genitive singular. With few exceptions, this is a feminine declension. The endings, singular and plural, are the following:

	SINGULAR	PLURAL
Nom.	**-ēs**	**-ēs**
Gen.	**-eī (-ēī)**	**-ērum**
Dat.	**-eī (-ēī)**	**-ēbus**
Acc.	**-em**	**-ēs**
Abl.	**-ē**	**-ēbus**

> *Notes:* 1. Each ending begins with the letter **e**.
> 2. The alternate genitive and dative singular endings are used when the base of the noun ends in a vowel: **diēs, diēī**, m. & f. 'day.'

rēs, reī, f. 'thing'; base: **r-**

	SINGULAR	PLURAL
Nom.	**rēs** ('the thing')	**rēs** ('the things')
Gen.	**reī** ('of the thing')	**rērum** ('of the things')
Dat.	**reī** ('for/to the thing')	**rēbus** ('for/to the things')
Acc.	**rem** ('the thing')	**rēs** ('the things')
Abl.	**rē** ('from/with/in/by the thing')	**rēbus** ('from/with/in/by the things')

102. Direct Commands (or Requests) (1): Imperative Mood

The third kind of sentence, the direct command (or request) (see Section 7), is expressed by the imperative mood. The tense of an imperative is present; its forms are restricted to the second person.

a. Present Imperative Active: All Four Conjugations   The second-person singular present imperative active is identical with the present stem. The plural is formed by adding **-te**; the stem vowel of third conjugation verbs shifts from **-e-** to **-i-** before **-te**.

	SINGULAR	PLURAL
2	**laudā!** 'praise!'	**laudāte!** 'praise!'
2	**monē!** 'warn!'	**monēte!** 'warn!'
2	****dūce!** 'lead!'	**dūcite!** 'lead!'
2	**cape!** 'take!'	**capite!** 'take!'
2	**audī!** 'hear!'	**audīte!** 'hear!'

> *Notes:*   1. **Dūce** always occurs without the stem vowel—**dūc**.
> 2. There is a little-used future tense in the imperative mood. The monosyllabic **scī**—from **sciō** (Unit 9)—is often replaced by a future form—**scītō**—with little or no difference in meaning.
> 3. The imperative forms of **sum** are **es** and **este**. The singular is often replaced by a future form—**estō**; the plural may be replaced by a future form—**estōte**. In either event there is little difference in meaning.
> 4. The imperatives of **eō** 'go' are **ī** and **īte**; **ī** is not used unless compounded: **exī**, **adī**, etc.
> 5. There are no imperatives of **volō** 'wish' or **possum** 'be able.'

b. Present Imperative Passive: All Four Conjugations   The second-person present imperative passive is identical with the second-person present indicative passive in both numbers; in the singular, the shorter ending only is used: **-re**.

	SINGULAR	PLURAL
2	**laudāre!** 'be praised!'	**laudāminī!** 'be praised!'
2	**monēre!** 'be warned!'	**monēminī!** 'be warned!'
2	**dūcere!** 'be led!'	**dūciminī!** 'be led!'
2	**capere!** 'be taken!'	**capiminī!** 'be taken!'
2	**audīre!** 'be heard!'	**audīminī!** 'be heard!'

Notes: 1. The singular form is spelled like the present infinitive active.

2. Context will help to distinguish these passive imperatives from infinitives and indicative forms.

103. Vocative Case

Direct address (of a person, place, or thing) is conveyed by the vocative case. Both nouns and adjectives have vocatives. All forms, both singular and plural, are identical with the nominative, except for second declension masculine nouns in the singular, where the ending is **-e**.

Ō bona māter! 'O good mother!'
Ō fēlīcēs rēgēs! 'O happy kings!'
Domine ūniversī! 'Lord of the universe!'
Cāre apostole! 'O beloved apostle!'

The major exceptions are these:

1. Second declension nouns in **-ius** drop the **-us** ending and lengthen the **-i-** of the stem.
2. Second declension nouns in **-ir** or **-er** use the nominative case.
3. The vocative of **meus** (**-a, -um**) is either **meus** or **mī**.
4. **Deus** and **agnus** use the nominative case.
5. The vocative of **Jēsūs** is **Jēsū**.

Jēsū, fīlī Patris! 'O Jesus, son of the Father!'
Magister mī! 'O my master!'
Deus meus! 'O my God!'
Agnus Deī! 'Lamb of God!'

104. Personal Pronouns

Latin has pronouns of the first and second persons to express the speaker and the person addressed. Because these forms are irregular, they must be carefully observed and memorized. The nominatives are always emphatic (since the verb ending already indicates the person intended).

a. First-Person Pronoun

	SINGULAR	PLURAL
Nom.	ego ('I')	nōs ('we')
Gen.	meī ('of me')	nostrī / nostrum } ('of us')
Dat.	mihi ('for/to me')	nōbīs ('for/to us')
Acc.	mē ('me')	nōs ('us')
Abl.	mē ('from/with/in/by me')	nōbīs ('from/with/in/by us')

> *Notes:* 1. The preposition **cum** is appended to the ablatives: **mēcum** 'with me'; **nōbīscum** 'with us.'
> 2. **Nostrī** is used for the objective genitive (see Section 75): **Deī dīlēctiō nostrī** 'God's love of us'; **nostrum** is used for the partitive (see Section 81): **multī nostrum** 'many of us.'

b. Second-Person Pronoun

	SINGULAR	PLURAL
Nom.	tū ('you')	vōs ('you')
Gen.	tuī ('of you')	vestrī / vestrum } ('of you')
Dat.	tibi ('for/to you')	vōbīs ('for/to you')
Acc.	tē ('you')	vōs ('you')
Abl.	tē ('from/with/in/by you')	vōbīs ('from/with/in/by you')

> *Notes:* 1. Here, too, the preposition **cum**, when used, is appended to the ablative forms: **tēcum** 'with you'; **vōbīscum** 'with you.'
> 2. **Vestrī** is used like **nostrī**, **vestrum** like **nostrum**: Deī **dīlēctiō vestrī** 'God's love of you'; **multī vestrum** 'many of you.' Note that both forms have **-e-**; all other plurals, **-ō-**.

105. Double Accusative

A small number of verbs meaning 'ask (for)' or 'teach' take a double object, an accusative of the thing and an accusative of the person.

Diāconus *puerōs Evangelium* docēbat.
'The deacon used to teach *the boys the Gospel.*'
[**doceō, docēre, docuī, doctus** 'teach']

Vocabulary

cūrō, cūrāre, cūrāvī, cūrātus
heal, cure; care for
dēsīderō, dēsīderāre, dē-sīderāvī, dēsīderātus desire
vulnerō, vulnerāre, vulnerāvī, vulnerātus wound
appāreō, appārēre, appāruī, appāritus show forth, appear
doceō, docēre, docuī, doctus
teach
alō, alere, aluī, altus nourish
cadō, cadere, cecidī, cāsus
fall (down)
incidō, incidere, incidī, —
fall into; happen
frāter, frātris, m. brother
pēs, pedis, m. foot
auris, auris, aurium, f. (*abl. sing.*, **aure** *or* **aurī**) ear

carō, carnis, f. flesh
mulier, mulieris, f. woman, wife
prex, precis, f. entreaty, prayer
caput, capitis, n. head
latus, lateris, n. side
ōs, ōris, n. mouth
diēs, diēī, m. & f. day
fidēs, fideī, f. faith, faithfulness
rēs, reī, f. thing
spēs, speī, f. hope
dīlēctus, -a, -um beloved
dulcis, dulce sweet; kind
fidēlis, fidēle faithful; believing
supersubstantiālis, supersubstantiāle life-sustaining

deinde (*adv.*) then, next, thereupon
ego, **meī** (*pron.*) I

sūrsum (*adv.*) on high, upward
tū, **tuī** (*pron.*) you

Vocabulary Notes

Like many first conjugation verbs, **cūrō**, **dēsīderō**, and **vulnerō** are denominatives—from **cūra** (Unit 22), **dēsīderium** (Unit 10), and **vulnus**, **vulneris**, n. 'wound' (not formally presented).

Dēsīderō may take a direct object or an object infinitive: **dēsīderō pānem** 'I desire bread'; **dēsīderō vidēre Petrum** 'I desire to see Peter.'

Doceō, besides taking a double accusative of person and thing, may also take a double object of person and infinitive: **docēbat puerum legere** 'he was teaching the boy (how) to read.'

Frāter 'brother' is a code-word for 'fellow-Christian.'

The verb **incarnō** (Unit 13) is derived from **carō**, **carnis**, f. 'flesh.'

Mulier means 'woman' or 'wife,' much as **vir** (Unit 3) means 'man' or 'husband.'

Though usually masculine and thus exceptional in the fifth declension, **diēs** is feminine when a specific day is meant. Note that since the base ends in a vowel the lengthened genitive and dative endings are used—**diēī** and **diēī**.

Fidēs and **fidēlis** both combine the meanings of 'belief' and 'loyalty to one's beliefs.'

Rēs is nearly as variable in meaning as English 'thing'; it acquires its specific meaning from the context. Some of its more frequent significations are these: matters, affairs, circumstances, property, reality, the state.

The nominatives **ego** and **tū** are emphatic forms, best translated verbally by tone of voice or in writing by italics: *I, you.*

Derivatives:	LATIN	ENGLISH
	cūrō	curative, curator
	dēsīderō	desideratum, desire
	vulnerō	vulnerable
	appāreō	appear, apparent, apparition
	doceō	docile, doctor
	alō	alimentary, alimony
	cadō	cadence, cadenza, case
	incidō	incident
	frāter	fraternal, friar

Derivatives:

LATIN	ENGLISH
pēs	pedal, pedometer
auris	aural, auricle
carō	carnal, carnation, carnival
mulier	muliebrity
prex	precarious, imprecation
caput	chief, capital, chapter, chef, achieve, cattle
latus	lateral, unilateral
ōs	oral, oracle
diēs	per diem, diurnal
fidēs	faith
rēs	real, realty, reality, rebus (a puzzle made *with things*)
spēs	Esperanto, desperate
dīlēctus	predilection
dulcis	dulcimer, dulcet
fidēlis	fidelity
ego	ego, egoist, egotist
sūrsum	sursum corda
tū	Te Deum

Drills

I. Imperative mood; vocative case. Translate; change the number.

1. ambulā, fīlī! walk, son
2. cantāte, chorī angelōrum!
3. observāte! watch
4. incipite!
5. habēminī! passive
6. jungere!
7. venī! Come
8. adeste (adestōte), fidēlēs!
9. dīc! fac!*
10. rege!
11. exaudī, Domine!
12. virī, sānāminī!

II. Personal pronouns. Translate; where possible, change the number.

1. Ego tē videō.
2. Tū mē vidēs.

[*Note that the stem vowel is also omitted with dīcō and faciō.]

3. Vōs estis memorēs meī? *objective genitive*
4. Nōs ōrāvimus prō vōbīs. → te
vos 5. Tū veniēs mēcum?
6. Nōs ūnum vestrum ēlēgimus. *partitive genitive*
nobis 7. Vōs mihi librum dedistis? 🡒 *indirect* ←
8. Laus tibi, Chrīste.
9. Propter tuī dīlēctiōnem vēnī ego. → *objective*
10. Pāx vōbīscum.

4 subjunctive

Exercises

I.   1. Agnus Deī, quī tollis peccāta mundī, dōnā nōbīs pācem.
2. Fīlī, dīmittuntur tibi peccāta tua. Mk. ii, 5.
3. Deinde dīlēctus apostolus discipulīs dīxit rēs quae in secundā diē inciderant Hierosolymīs.
4. Pānis autem, quem ego dabō, carō mea est prō mundī vītā. Jn. vi, 51.
5. ℣. Dominus vōbīscum. ℟. Et cum spīritū tuō.
℣. Sūrsum corda. ℟. Habēmus ad Dominum.
6. Cūrāns nōs, Jēsūs in latere vulnerātus est et effūdit sanguinem salūtis.
7. Benedicta tū inter mulierēs. Lk. i, 42.
8. Ā quibus custōdientēs vōs bene agētis. Acts xv, 29.
9. Tū crēdis in Fīlium hominis? Jn. ix, 35.
10. Effundentēs precēs nostrās, dēsīderāmus fidēlēs tuam salūtem nostrī, Ō dulcis Jēsū! Venī, Domine Jēsū!
11. Jūstus ex fide vīvet. Gal. iii, 11.
12. Volō autem vōs scīre quod omnis virī caput Chrīstus est, caput autem mulieris vir, caput vērō ('but') Chrīstī Deus. I Cor. xi, 3.
13. Relinque ibi mūnus tuum ante altāre. Mt. v, 24.
14. Laudō autem vōs[, frātrēs,]* quod omnia ('in all respects') meī memorēs estis. I Cor. xi, 2.
15. Cōtīdiē alimur tuā dīlēctiōne, Ō Domine: vērē tū docuistī nōs tuam salūtem.
16. Dīcit eī ('to him') mulier: Domine, videō quia prophēta es tū. Jn. iv, 19.

*Not in the Greek original; traditional in Latin texts, but removed by the Nova Vulgata editors.

17. Pānem nostrum supersubstantiālem dā nōbīs hodiē. Mt. vi, 11.

18. Grātiās agō Deō meō semper prō vōbīs in grātiā Deī, quae data est vōbīs in Chrīstō Jēsū. I Cor. i, 4.

19. Domine, docē nōs ōrāre, sīcut ('as') et Jōannēs docuit discipulōs suōs ('his'). Lk. xi, 1.

20. Dīmitte eam ('her'), quia clāmat post nōs. Mt. xv, 23.

21. Crēditis quia possum hoc ('this') facere? Mt. ix, 28.

22. Et ēlēgērunt Stephanum, virum plēnum fidē et Spīritū Sānctō. Acts vi, 5.

23. Dominus Jēsūs interficiet spīritū ōris. II Thess. ii, 8.

24. Tū ergō, sī adōrāveris cōram mē, erit tua omnis. Lk. iv, 7.

25. Carō enim mea vērus est cibus, et sanguis meus vērus est pōtus. Jn. vi, 55.

26. Spēs autem, quae vidētur, nōn est spēs. Rom. viii, 24.

27. Dīxit Jēsūs: "Facite hominēs discumbere ('sit down')." Jn. vi, 10.

28. Hodiē implēta est haec ('this') Scrīptūra in auribus vestrīs. Lk. iv, 21.

29. Oculōs habentēs nōn vidētis, et aurēs habentēs nōn audītis? Mk. viii, 18.

30. Quae est māter mea et frātrēs meī? Mk. iii, 33.

31. Āmēn dīcō vōbīs: Ūnus vestrum mē trāditūrus est. Mt. xxvi, 21.

32. Omnia mihi trādita sunt ā Patre meō. Mt. xi, 27.

33. Dīxit ergō Jēsūs Petrō: "Mitte gladium in vagīnam ('scabbard'); calicem, quem dedit mihi Pater, nōn bibam illum ('it')?" Jn. xviii, 11.

34. Īte, Missa est.

35. Magister dīcit: . . apud tē faciō Pascha cum discipulīs meīs. Mt. xxvi, 18.

36. Pānem nostrum cōtīdiānum dā nōbīs cōtīdiē, et dīmitte nōbīs peccāta nostra. Lk. xi, 3–4.

37. Sāncta Marīa, ōrā prō nōbīs.

   Sāncte Petre, ōrā prō nōbīs.

   Omnēs sānctī Discipulī Dominī, ōrāte prō nōbīs.

   Chrīste, audī nōs.

   Chrīste, exaudī nōs.

   Kȳrie, eléison.

   Chrīste, eléison.

   Kȳrie, eléison.

II.　　1. Lord, teach us your ways.
　　　　2. Brothers, fall on your knees and worship the Lord!
　　　　3. O Lord, grant us the grace of a happy death.
　　　　4. Love your neighbor, my son.
　　　　5. When *you* will have arrived at the temple, send your servant to me.
　　　　6. Will *I* put my finger into the Master's side?

Unit 20

106. Deponent Verbs

Deponent verbs have passive forms, but active meanings. Conversely stated, these verbs have no active forms and no passive meanings. They occur in all four conjugations:

1: **mīror, mīrārī, —, mīrātus sum** 'wonder (at)'
2: **misereor, miserērī, —, misertus sum** 'have pity (on)'
3: **nāscor, nāscī, —, nātus sum** 'be born'
   patior, patī, —, passus sum 'suffer'
4: **orior, orīrī, —, ortus sum** 'spring up, arise'

Notes: 1. Deponent verbs have only three principal parts, since there is no perfect active form.
2. Like other verbs, deponents are classified according to the form of the second principal part, the present infinitive. These end in **-ārī** in the first conjugation, **-ērī** in the second, **-ī** in the third (whether '**-ō**' type or '**-iō**' type), and **-īrī** in the fourth.
3. The last principal part is conventionally given with **sum**, showing the perfect indicative form. Without **sum**, this is of course the perfect participle, which has an active meaning.
4. *Exceptions in Voice:*
   a. Deponents have present participles; these of course are active in form as well as in meaning: **mīrāns** (*gen.*, **mīrantis**) 'wondering (at),' etc.
   b. Deponents have both future participles: **mīrātūrus** 'about to wonder (at),' **mīrandus** 'having to be wondered at.'

Dominus miserētur nōbīs.
'The Lord has pity on us.'

Jēsūs propter peccāta nostra passus est.
'Jesus suffered on account of our sins.'

107. Semi-Deponent Verbs

A very small number of verbs are deponent in their perfect system only. They have active and passive forms and meanings in the present-stem system, but only passive forms with active meanings in the tenses formed from the perfect participle.

2: **audeō, audēre; —, ausus sum** 'dare'
2: **gaudeō, gaudēre; —, gāvīsus sum** 'rejoice'
3: **cōnfīdō, cōnfīdere; —, cōnfīsus sum** 'trust'

Audēmus ad Patrem ōrāre.
'We dare to pray to the Father.'

Ausī sumus ad Patrem ōrāre.
'We dared to pray to the Father.'

108. Subjunctive Mood: An Overview

The subjunctive is the mood of contingency or hypothetical action. It expresses what may happen or might have happened. Although it is mostly used in a variety of subordinate clauses, the subjunctive may also be employed independently to express certain forms of statements, commands, and questions. English makes very little use of its own subjunctive mood ('till death do us part,' 'thy kingdom come,' 'if I were king,' etc.), preferring instead to employ a number of auxiliary verbs: 'should, would, may, might, could.' Depending on the precise construction, the Latin subjunctive may be translated with the aid of one or another of these English auxiliaries. Until the various uses of the subjunctive are quite clear, the student is advised to translate with the precise translation formula given for each construction.

There are only four tenses of the subjunctive mood: present, perfect; imperfect, pluperfect. The subjunctive has no need of a future or a future-perfect tense; the mood itself (especially in its present and imperfect tenses) conveys the notion of what may or might be possible. The negative, for the most part, is **nē** (although in certain clear cases **nōn** is used, just as in the indicative). A subjunctive clause may be introduced by a sign-word, such as **utinam** or **ut**.

109. Present Subjunctive: First Conjugation

The sign of the present subjunctive in the first conjugation is the letter **-ē-**; it replaces the stem vowel **-ā-**.

No translation is presented in subjunctive paradigms, since the exact meaning, often supplemented by English auxiliaries, is determined by the use.

a. Active   All active forms of the subjunctive mood for the first conjugation are compounded of the present stem in **-ē-** and the active personal endings; the alternate **-m** is used in the first-person singular.

	SINGULAR	PLURAL
1	**laudem**	**laudēmus**
2	**laudēs**	**laudētis**
3	**laudet**	**laudent**

> *Notes:* 1. Long **-e-** is shortened before **-m, -t**, and **-nt**.
> 2. Since first-conjugation present subjunctives look like second-conjugation present indicative forms (cf. **monēmus**), the student is advised to determine the conjugation before analyzing any verb-form.

b. Passive   The passive forms use the passive personal endings. The **-ē-** appears throughout.

	SINGULAR	PLURAL
1	**lauder**	**laudēmur**
2	**laudēris, laudēre**	**laudēminī**
3	**laudētur**	**laudentur**

> *Notes:* 1. Long **-e-** is shortened before **-r** and **-ntur**.
> 2. As in the indicative, the second-person singular uses both alternate forms.

110. *Direct Commands (or Requests) (2)*

Besides the imperative mood (see Section 102), certain subjunctive and indicative constructions may also express direct commands (or requests).

a. Hortatory Subjunctive   When rousing or exhorting oneself and others to possible action, the speaker may use the first-person plural of the present subjunctive.
    Translation formula: 'Let us . .'

Cantēmus Dominō canticum novum!
'Let us sing to the Lord a new song!'

Baptizēmur ā Jōanne!
'Let us be baptized by John!'

> *Note:*   Occasionally the first-person singular is found: **cantem**
> 'let me sing.'

b. Optative Subjunctive   Attainable wishes (in the present or for the future) may be expressed by the present subjunctive. Occasionally this optative use of the subjunctive is introduced by the sign-word **utinam.**
    Translation formula: 'Would that . . may . .' *or* 'May . .'

Dominum semper glōrificem!
'Would that I may always glorify the Lord!'
'May I always glorify the Lord!'

Mūtēs tuōs modōs!
'Would that you may change your ways!'
'May you change your ways!'

Utinam Aegyptiī fugentur!
'Would that the Egyptians may be put to flight!'
'May the Egyptians be put to flight!'

c. Jussive Future Indicative   The future indicative may be used for commands which are binding for an indefinite period of time; they are to be heeded both now and in the future. Like the imperative mood, this jussive use of the future indicative occurs only in the second person.

Translation formula: 'You shall . .'

Dīligēs proximum tuum.
'You shall love your neighbor.'

111. How to Answer Syntax Questions (2)

Thus far, syntax questions have inquired about nouns and adjectives only; these have focused on the case and the reason for the case (see Section 19). Now that the subjunctive mood—with its four tenses and its many uses—is being introduced, from now on syntax questions will also include verbs. Such questions will concentrate on two of the five facts about each finite verb-form, the tense and the mood, and ask the reasons for the tense and the mood. They help to focus the student's attention on the inalterable fact that precise syntactical analysis must always precede any attempt at translation.

Vocabulary

mīror, mīrārī, —, mīrātus sum wonder (at), be amazed (at)
admīror, admīrārī, —, admīrātus sum wonder at, be amazed at
peccō, peccāre, peccāvī, peccātus sin
precor, precārī, —, precātus sum ask, pray
dēprecor, dēprecārī, —, dēprecātus sum beseech
audeō, audēre; —, ausus sum dare, have the courage
gaudeō, gaudēre; —, gāvīsus sum rejoice, be glad
misereor, miserērī, —, misertus sum (+ gen. or dat.) have pity (on)
cōnfīdō, cōnfīdere; —, cōnfīsus

sum (+ dat.) trust (in), confide (in), hope (in)
nāscor, nāscī, —, nātus sum be born
morior, mori, —, mortuus sum die
patior, patī, —, passus sum suffer; allow
orior, orīrī, —, ortus sum spring up, arise, appear
lacrima, lacrimae, f. tear
memoria, memoriae, f. remembrance, memory
ignis, ignis, ignium, m. (abl. sing., **igne** or **ignī**) fire
peccātor, peccātōris, m. sinner
arbor, arboris, f. tree
benedictiō, benedictiōnis, f. blessing, benediction

nox, noctis, noctium, f. night
potestās, potestātis, f. power, authority
opus, operis, n. work, deed
  opus est = it is necessary, there is a need (+ *inf.* or *abl.*)
scelus, sceleris, n. crime, sin
miser, misera, miserum wretched, pitiable
paternus, -a, -um of a father, paternal
innocēns (*gen.,* **innocentis**) clean, pure, innocent

potēns (*gen.,* **potentis**) powerful (in), having power (over)
cōnsubstantiālis, cōnsubstantiāle (+ *dat.*) of the same nature (as), consubstantial (with)
nihil (**nīl**) (1. *indecl. noun;* 2. *adv.*) 1. nothing 2. not at all
valdē (*adv.*) greatly, very (much)
vērō (*adv.*) indeed; but indeed

Vocabulary Notes

Mīror is a denominative verb from the adjective **mīrus** (Unit 8); it is used both transitively and intransitively.

Peccātum (Unit 3) is a noun made from the perfect passive participle of **peccō**. **Peccātor** is the agent noun formed from **peccō**.

Precor is a denominative verb formed from **prex** (Unit 19). It takes an accusative of the person asked and an infinitive of the action requested: **precor Marīam ōrāre prō mē** 'I ask Mary to pray for me.'

Dēprecor is an intensive form of **precor,** much as 'beseech' is an intensive form of 'seek.'

Audeō may take an object, but more commonly it takes an object infinitive: **audēmus dīcere** 'we dare to say.' Be careful to distinguish this verb from **audiō, audīre, audīvī, audītus** 'hear.'

Gaudeō is often followed by an ablative of cause (see Section 58). The noun **gaudium** (Unit 3) is formed from the same root from which this verb is made.

Misereor is a second conjugation denominative verb built on **miser.** It takes a dative or a genitive: **miserēre nōbīs** (**nostrī**) 'have mercy on us.'

As with many verbs taking the dative, **cōnfīdō** may instead be followed by a prepositional phrase (such as **in Dominō** 'in the Lord').

The future participle active of **morior** is **moritūrus, -a, -um;** its perfect participle is the source of the adjective **mortuus** (Unit 4).

Patior may take an object or an accusative and object infinitive:

Petrus patitur parvulōs ad Jēsūm venīre 'Peter allows the children to come to Jesus.' The noun **passiō** (Unit 16) is derived from the perfect participle.

The future participle active of **orior** is **oritūrus, -a, -um**; the third-person singular present indicative is **orĭtur**; the present active participle, **oriēns** (*gen.*, **orientis**), is often used substantively, 'east, orient.'

Memoria is an abstract noun formed from the adjective **memor** (Unit 16) and the noun-making suffix **-ia, -iae**, f.

Benedictiō is composed of the base of the perfect passive participle of **benedīcō** (Unit 7) and the noun-making suffix **-iō, -iōnis**, f.

Potestās and **potēns** often take an objective genitive: **potēns**—in reality, the present participle of **possum**—may govern a complementary infinitive.

Opus means 'work, deed,' but when used with **est** it means 'there is a need.' It may take a referential dative + either an infinitive or an ablative (of means): **opus est mihi librum legere** 'there is a need to me to read a book, I must read a book'; **opus est mihi pāne** 'there is a need to me by means of bread, I need bread.' Rarely, the nominative is found: **pānis est opus nōbīs** 'bread is a need to us, we need bread.'

Paternus is an adjective built on **pater** (Unit 14).

Cōnsubstantiālis is a word coined by the Church (probably by the Carthaginian theologian, Tertullian, 160?–230?) to describe a crucial aspect of Trinitarian doctrine.

Nihil, or **nīl**, is used as an indeclinable noun or as an adverb: **nihil ēgī** 'I have done nothing'; **verba Petrī nihil audīta sunt** 'the words of Peter were not at all heard.'

Notice that **vērō** 'indeed,' an adverb derived from the adjective **vērus** (Unit 4), may also have an adversative force—'but indeed.' A postpositive, it occurs as the second or third word of its clause.

Derivatives:	LATIN	ENGLISH
	admīror	admire, admiration
	peccō	impeccable, peccant
	audeō	audacity
	cōnfīdō	confidence
	nāscor	natal, nation, nature
	morior	moribund, morgue
	patior	patient, passive
	orior	orient, orientation

Derivatives:

LATIN	ENGLISH
lacrima	lacrimation, lachrymose
memoria	memorial, in memoriam
ignis	ignite, ignition, igneous
arbor	arboretum, arboreal
nox	nocturnal, equinox
opus	magnum opus, operate
miser	miser, misery, miserable
paternus	paternity
potēns	potent, impotent
nihil	nihilism, nihil obstat

Drills

I. Deponent and semi-deponent verbs.

    1. Form the four participles; translate.
        a. admīror, admīrārī, —, admīrātus sum 'wonder at'
        b. audeō, audēre; —, ausus sum 'dare'

    2. Identify the form; translate.
        a. admīrātur   d. audet
        b. admīrābātur   e. audēbit
        c. admīrātus est   f. ausus eram

II. Present subjunctive: first conjugation. Translate; where possible, change to the indicative and retranslate.

    a. Laudēmus Dominum!
    b. Līberēmus servōs!
    c. Utinam Deus servet nōs!
    d. Tua fidēs firmētur!
    e. Vocēmur ad Dominī cēnam!

Exercises

I.   1. Fīlius hominis trāditur in manūs peccātōrum. Mt. xxvi, 45.
    2. Praeceptīs salūtāribus monitī, audēmus dīcere:
    3. Pater noster, quī es in caelīs, sānctificētur nōmen tuum. Mt. vi, 9.
    4. Miserī dēprecēmur Dominum scelera nostra fugāre!

5. Utinam Corpus et Sanguis Dominī Jēsū Chrīstī nōs ab omnibus inīquitātibus nostrīs līberent!

6. Turba mīra opera Jēsū admīrāta est.

7. Dominō dēmus pānem nostrum, frūctum terrae et operis manuum hominum.

8. Petrus mīrābātur quod populus Dominō nihil cōnfīdēbat.

9. Utinam paterna dīlēctiō nōs semper servet!

10. Paulus, verba atque opera Jēsū in memoriā habēns, evangelizāre erat potēns.

11. Opus est sacerdōtī prō populō benedictiōnem Dominī invocāre.

12. Lūmen mundī ortum est et fugāvit peccātōrum tenebrās.

13. Homō miser, lacrimās effundēns, dīxit quod fīlius moriēbātur.

14. Ipse ('he') vōs baptizābit in Spīritū Sānctō et ignī. Mt. iii, 11.

15. Haec ('this') nox est, quae hodiē per ūniversum mundum in Chrīstō crēdentēs reddit grātiae.

16. . . Deum dē Deō, lūmen dē lūmine, Deum vērum dē Deō vērō, genitum ('begotten'), nōn factum, cōnsubstantiālem Patrī: per quem omnia facta sunt.

17. Ideo precor beātam Marīam semper Virginem, omnēs Angelōs, et Sānctōs, et vōs, frātrēs, ōrāre prō mē ad Dominum Deum nostrum.

18. Dominus enim Jēsūs crucifīxus, passus et mortuus est prō mundī vītā.

19. Ō Domine, et fac mē tuīs semper inhaerēre mandātīs.

20. Nātus est vōbīs hodiē Salvātor, quī est Chrīstus Dominus. Lk. ii, 11.

21. Ego baptizāvī vōs aquā; ille ('he') vērō baptizābit vōs Spīritū Sānctō. Mk. 1, 8.

22. Quārē cum peccātōribus mandūcat et bibit Magister vester?

23. Peccāvī trādēns sanguinem innocentem. Mt. xxvii, 4.

24. Eōdem tempore ('at the same time') nātus est Mōysēs et erat fōrmōsus ('handsome') cōram Deō. Acts vii, 20.

25. Tunc Jēsūs apostolīs dedit potestātem spīrituum malōrum.

26. Nam et ego homō sub potestāte. Mt. viii, 9.

27. Et aspiciēns dīcēbat: "Videō hominēs, quia velut ('just like') arborēs videō ambulantēs." Mk. viii, 24.

28. Et ecce nihil dīgnum morte āctum est ā Nazarēnō.

29. Exī ā mē, quia homō peccātor sum, Domine. Lk. v, 8.
30. Videntēs autem stēllam gāvīsī sunt gaudiō magnō valdē. Mt. ii, 10.
31. Agnus Deī, quī tollis peccāta mundī, miserēre nōbīs.

II.   1. May our faith be strengthened daily!
     2. Let us pray to the Lord to grant us peace.
     3. The wretched apostle dared to betray Jesus.
     4. Let us rejoice because the Lord has taken pity on us.
     5. Why was it necessary for John to baptize Jesus? (*Express the idea of necessity in two ways: 1. opus est; 2. the passive periphrastic.*)

Unit 21

112. Present Subjunctive: Second, Third, and Fourth Conjugations

The letter **-ā-** is the sign of the present subjunctive in the second, third, and fourth conjugations. In the second and fourth it is added to the present stem—**moneā-**, **audiā-**; in the third, it replaces the stem vowel (the '**-iō**' type has **-iā-**)—**dūcā-**, **capiā-**.

a. Active To form the present active subjunctive of these conjugations, add the active personal endings to the modified stem. The **-ā-** is shortened before **-m**, **-t**, and **-nt**, as usual.

SECOND CONJUGATION:		SINGULAR	PLURAL
	1	moneam	moneāmus
	2	moneās	moneātis
	3	moneat	moneant

> *Note:* The stem **monē-** becomes **mone-** in all forms, under the rule that a long vowel is shortened when followed by another vowel (see Section 1a.5).

		SINGULAR	PLURAL
THIRD CONJUGATION, '**-ō**' TYPE:	1	dūcam	dūcāmus
	2	dūcās	dūcātis
	3	dūcat	dūcant
THIRD CONJUGATION, '**-iō**' TYPE:	1	capiam	capiāmus
	2	capiās	capiātis
	3	capiat	capiant

FOURTH CONJUGATION:	1	audiam	audiāmus
	2	audiās	audiātis
	3	audiat	audiant

> *Note:* The stem **audī-** is shortened to **audi-** in all forms.

b. Passive   To form the present passive subjunctive of these conjugations, add the passive personal endings to the modified stem. The **-ā-** is shortened before **-r** and **-ntur**.

SECOND CONJUGATION:		SINGULAR	PLURAL
	1	monear	moneāmur
	2	moneāris, moneāre	moneāminī
	3	moneātur	moneantur

> *Note:* As in the active, the stem **monē-** is shortened to **mone-** in all forms.

THIRD CONJUGATION, '-ō' TYPE:	1	dūcar	dūcāmur
	2	dūcāris, ducāre	dūcāminī
	3	dūcātur	dūcantur
THIRD CONJUGATION, '-iō' TYPE:	1	capiar	capiāmur
	2	capiāris, capiāre	capiāminī
	3	capiātur	capiantur
FOURTH CONJUGATION:	1	audiar	audiāmur
	2	audiāris, audiāre	audiāminī
	3	audiātur	audiantur

> *Note:* The stem **audī-** is shortened to **audi-** in all forms.

113. Direct Commands (or Requests) (3): Jussive Subjunctive

The present subjunctive may be used in the third person to give a command (cf. Sections 102 and 110). This use is called the jussive subjunctive.

Translation formula: 'Let . .'

Populus gaudeat!
'Let the people rejoice!'

Crucifīgātur!
'Let him be crucified!'

> *Note:* English usage requires that the understood subject of **crucifīgātur** be translated into the English objective case—'him.'

114. Direct Questions (2): Deliberative Subjunctive

Occasionally the present subjunctive is used to ask what course of action one is to adopt (cf. Section 33).

Translation formula: 'Am I to . .' 'Are we to . .' 'Should . .'

Quod dōnum ad Dominum dēmus?
'What gift are we to give to the Lord?'
'What gift should we give to the Lord?'

Nōn mittam diāconōs Rōmam?
'Am I not to send the deacons to Rome?'
'Should I not send the deacons to Rome?'

115. Conditional Clauses (1)

Thus far, independent uses of the subjunctive mood have been presented. But the most frequent use of the subjunctive is in a dependent clause.

A frequent form of subordination is the conditional clause, one which states a condition or contingency ('if, unless, in the event that, on condition that') on which the action of the main clause hinges. Depending on the type of conditional idea in mind, the indicative or the subjunctive is required.

A conditional clause and the independent clause on which it grammatically depends together comprise what is called a conditional sentence; the conditional clause is called the protasis, the main clause the apodosis. The words which introduce the protasis have already been met (in Unit 13)—**sī** or **nisi** (the negative form, although **sī . . nōn** may also occur). Conditional sentences may be so constructed as to refer to past, present, or future action, and to imply possibility or impossibility of fulfillment.

a. Simple   A simple conditional clause indicates a contingency, without implying anything about its fulfillment: 'if a book is popular, he reads it'; 'if the car broke down, they were late.' The verb of a simple conditional clause uses either the present or any past tense; the verb of the apodosis may take any logical form.

Sī Dominum invocāmus, nōs audit.
'If we call upon the Lord, He hears us.'
Nisi lēgem faciēbant, nōn jūstī erant.
'If they were not keeping the law, they were not righteous.'
Sī beātus es, Deō grātiās age!
'If you are happy, (then) thank God!'

b. Future   A future conditional clause imagines an action in the future. There are two subclasses, the more vivid and the less vivid, depending on the degree of clarity or confidence with which the speaker sees the action.

1. More Vivid   A future more vivid conditional clause has an indicative in either the future or the future-perfect tense (the second is the more emphatic). The verb of the apodosis is ordinarily a future indicative, although other equivalent forms, such as a jussive subjunctive, may occur.
Translation formula: 'if . . does, (then) will do.'

> *Note:*   English usage requires that the Latin future or future-perfect in the protasis be translated by the English present. (In general, English substitutes the present for the future in any subordinate clause.)

Sī voluntātem Deī faciet, salvus efficiētur.
'If he does the will of God, he will be saved.'

Nisi voluntātem Deī fēcerimus, in rēgnum caelōrum nōn
introībimus.
'Unless we (first) do the will of God, we will not enter into the
kingdom of heaven.'

Sī Petrus vēnerit, cum Paulō cēnet!
'If Peter comes, let him dine with Paul!'

2. *Less Vivid*   A future less vivid conditional clause has a verb in
the present *subjunctive*. The verb of the apodosis is ordinarily a
present indicative or a present subjunctive.

TRANSLATION FORMULA:

Protasis: 'if . . should do,'
Apodosis (Ind.): '(then) . . does.'
          (Subj.): '(then) . . would do.'

Sī agnus ūnus āmittātur, pāstor bonus est maestus.
'If one lamb should be lost, the good shepherd is sad.'

Sī Petrus domum intret, frātrēs ōrantēs videat.
'If Peter should enter the house, he would see his brothers
praying.'

Note: The use of the subjunctive in the apodosis constitutes
what is termed the potential subjunctive. This use is
rare by itself, but common enough in a conditional
sentence.

Vocabulary

cōnor, cōnārī, —, cōnātus sum
  (+ *inf.*) try, strive
exspectō, exspectāre,
  exspectāvī, exspectātus
  look for, wait for
lacrimor, lacrimārī, —,
  lacrimātus sum weep
laetor, laetārī, —, laetātus sum
  rejoice, be glad

collaetor, collaetārī, —,
  collaetātus sum rejoice
  together
miseror, miserārī, —,
  miserātus sum bewail, pity
sōlor, sōlārī, —, sōlātus sum
  console, comfort
cōnsōlor, cōnsōlārī, —,
  cōnsōlātus sum

or

cōnsōlō, cōnsōlāre, cōn-
    sōlāvī, cōnsōlātus console,
    comfort
amplector, amplectī, —,
    amplexus sum embrace
fungor, fungī, —, fūnctus sum
    (+ *abl.*) perform
nōscō, nōscere, nōvī, nōtus
    present-stem system: get ac-
    quainted with, get to know
    perfect system: know
    agnōscō, agnōscere, agnōvī,
        agnitus know, recognize,
        acknowledge
    cognōscō, cognōscere, cog-
        nōvī, cognitus *present-
        stem system*: get ac-
        quainted with, get to
        know *perfect system*:
        know
    praenōscō, praenōscere,
        praenōvī, praenōtus know
        beforehand, foreknow
gradior, gradī, —, gressus sum
    walk, step
    aggredior, aggredī, —,
        aggressus sum approach
    ēgredior, ēgredī, —, ēgressus
        sum come out, go out
    ingredior, ingredī, —, in-
        gressus sum walk along,
        come in
    regredior, regredī, —,
    regressus sum go back,
        return
tangō, tangere, tetigī, tāctus
    touch
sepeliō, sepelīre, sepelīvī
    (sepeliī), sepultus bury
vestiō, vestīre, vestīvī (vestiī),
    vestītus clothe
caelicola, caelicolae, m.
    heaven-dweller
corōna, corōnae, f. wreath,
    crown
sēmita, sēmitae, f. path
substantia, substantiae, f.
    nature, substance
ovis, ovis, ovium, f. sheep
affectus, affectūs, m. devotion,
    affection; sense
cōnspectus, cōnspectūs, m.
    sight, presence
flētus, flētūs, m. weeping
assiduus, -a, -um constant,
    unceasing
līber, lībera, līberum free
senex (*gen.*, senis) old *subst.*:
    old man
neque (nec) (*coord. conj.*)
    and not, nor
    neque (nec) . . neque (nec)
        neither . . nor
quattuor (*indecl. adj.*) four
septem (*indecl. adj.*) seven

Vocabulary Notes

Apart from its prefix, **exspectō** is a frequentative form of **speciō,
specere, spexī, spectus** 'look (at)' (Unit 13). Frequentative verbs denote repeated action, and are formed by adding first conjugation endings to the base of a perfect passive participle.

Lacrimor is the denominative verb formed from **lacrima** (Unit 20).

Laetor and **collaetor** (denominatives of **laetus**, Unit 11), often take an ablative of cause: **adventū Dominī laetāmur** 'we rejoice because of the coming of the Lord.'

Distinguish **miseror** (another denominative from **miser**, Unit 20) from **misereor** (Unit 20); **miseror** takes the accusative: **Jēsūs mulierem miserātus est** 'Jesus pitied the woman.'

Note that the compound of **sōlor** may be either **cōnsōlor** or **cōnsōlō**, with no difference in meaning.

Amplector 'embrace' has both a literal and a figurative meaning: 'embrace a person' or 'embrace an idea, a cause, a project, etc.'

Note that **fungor** has its object in the ablative case (a form of the ablative of means): **sacerdōs rītū fūnctus est** 'the priest performed the ceremony.'

The **-sc-** in **nōscō** shows that it is an inceptive verb in its present-stem system: 'begin to know.' Consequently, the perfect has the force of a present: '(now) know.' Compare: **novum testāmentum nōscimus** 'we are getting to know the New Testament'; **novum testāmentum nōvimus** 'we know the New Testament.' Notice that the compounds of **nōscō** may preserve the **g** of the archaic spelling, *gnōscō. **Nōscō** and **cognōscō** may take an object infinitive: **diāconus legere nōvit** 'the deacon knows how to read.'

Ingredior has two basic meanings, depending on the sense attached to the prefix **in-**: intensive ('walk along') or motion toward ('walk into, come in').

Substantia is a word of post-classical origin: the noun-making suffix **-ia** has been added to the present participial base of the verb **substō** [sub + stō (Unit 13)].

As is often the case with fourth declension nouns, **affectus**, **cōnspectus**, and **flētus** have been formed from the perfect passive participles of verbs: **afficiō** (Unit 6), **speciō** (Unit 13), **fleō** (Unit 25).

Assiduus literally means 'inclined to sit at (a place).' The adjective-forming suffix **-uus** has been added to the present stem of **sedeō** (Unit 23) prefixed by **ad-**. Hence the meaning: 'constant, unceasing.'

Although **senex** is an adjective of a single ending, its major use is as a substantive: 'old man.'

The adjective **līber** 'free' is the source of the denominative verb **līberō** (Unit 5).

Neque, or **nec**, regularly stands in place of **et nōn**. **Nec** rarely stands before a vowel.

Derivatives:

LATIN	ENGLISH
cōnor	conation, conative
exspectō	expect, expectation
lacrimor	lachrymator
laetor	Laetare Sunday
miseror	commiserate
cōnsōlor	consolation
amplector	amplexicaul
fungor	function
nōscō	notion, notice
cognōscō	cognitive, cognition, cognizance, recognize
gradior	gradient, aggression, egress, ingredient, ingress, regression, regress
tangō	tangent, tangible, tact, tactile, tangential
sepeliō	sepulcher, sepulture
vestiō	vestment, invest
corōna	corona, coroner, coronary
ovis	ovine
affectus	affect, affected
cōnspectus	conspectus
assiduus	assiduous, assiduity
līber	liberal
senex	senile, senator
septem	September

Drills Person, tense, mood, voice, number

I. Present subjunctive: second, third, and fourth conjugations.
    1. Identify the form; change the number.
    2. Change to the indicative.

    a. misereātur   f. habeāmus   k. veniēs
    b. trādant   g. agāmus   l. dīcātur
    c. trādent   h. jungāminī   m. nāscāmur → we should arise
    d. trādunt   i. sciātis   n. audiant
    e. dēleātur   j. veniās   o. tollās

II. Conditional clauses. Identify the kind of conditional clause;
translate.

    If Paul Rome we send (handwritten)

1. Sī Paulum Rōmam mittimus, Petrum videt. *sees* (handwritten)
2. Sī Paulum Rōmam mittēmus, Petrum vidēbit. *will see* (handwritten)
3. Sī Paulum Rōmam mīserimus, Petrum vidēbit.
4. Sī Paulum Rōmam mittāmus, Petrum videat.
5. Nisi Paulum mīsimus, Rōmam nōn iit.
6. Sī puerī nōn operāverint, nōn cēnābunt.

Exercises

I.

1. Sī ergō filius vōs līberāverit, vērē līberī eritis. Jn. viii, 36.
2. Sī ego testimōnium perhibeō dē mēipsō (= mē),
   testimōnium meum nōn est vērum. Jn. v, 31.
3. Benedīcat vōs omnipotēns Deus, Pater et Fīlius et Spīritus
   Sānctus.
4. Nam Deus dīxit: "*Honōrā* ('honor') *patrem et mātrem*"
   et: "*Quī maledīxerit patrī vel* (= aut) *mātrī, morte
   moriātur.*" Mt. xv, 4.
5. Sed turba haec ('this'), quae nōn nōvit lēgem, maledictī
   sunt! Jn. vii, 49.
6. Neque mē scītis neque Patrem meum. Jn. viii, 19.
7. Et extendēns manum, tetigit eum ('him'). Mt. viii, 3.
8. Jēsūs autem plēnus Spīritū Sānctō regressus est ā Jordāne
   et agēbātur in Spīritū in dēsertō. Lk. iv, 1.
9. Vēnit enim Jōannēs neque mandūcāns neque bibēns.
   Mt. xi, 18.
10. Quod ergō Deus conjūnxit, homō nōn sēparet. Mt. xix, 6.
11. Corpus Dominī nostrī Jēsū Chrīstī custōdiat animam
    tuam in vītam aeternam.
12. Nōs enim spīritū ex fidē spem jūstitiae exspectāmus.
    Gal. v, 5.
13. Sī vēritātem ('truth') dīcō, quārē vōs nōn crēditis mihi?
    Jn. viii, 46.
14. Exsultet jam angelica turba caelōrum: exsultent dīvina
    mystēria: et prō tantī ('so great') Rēgis victōria tuba
    īnsonet salūtāris.
15. Frātrēs, agnōscāmus peccāta nostra.
16. Misereātur nostrī omnipotēns Deus, et, dīmissīs peccātīs
    nostrīs, perdūcat nōs ad vītam aeternam.
17. Et exspectō resurrēctiōnem mortuōrum, et vītam ventūrī
    saeculī.

18. Posteā, sī habenda sit ('should be'), legitur secunda lēctiō.
19. Suscipiat Dominus sacrificium dē manibus tuīs ad laudem et glōriam nōminis suī ('his own').
20. *N.* Grātiās agāmus Dominō Deō nostrō.
    R. Dīgnum et jūstum est.
21. Tū es quī ventūrus es? Mt. xi, 3.
22. Āmēn, āmēn dīcō vōbīs: Nisi mandūcāveritis carnem Fīliī hominis et biberitis ejus ('of him') sanguinem, nōn habētis vītam in vōbīsmetipsīs (= vōbīs). Jn. vi, 53.
23. Dīxī ergō vōbīs quia moriēminī in peccātīs vestrīs; sī enim nōn crēdideritis quia ego sum, moriēminī in peccātīs vestrīs. Jn. viii, 24.
24. Marīa lacrimāta ac Fīlium amplexa est.
25. Cōnēmur contrītō cum corde ad Dominum precārī.
26. Jēsūs passus et sepultus est, et resurrēxit tertiā diē, secundum Scrīptūrās.
27. Mulier cōnsōlāta est senem, quī dētrīmentum fīliī miserābātur.
28. Collaetēmur sānctīs caelicolīs, quī corōnam glōriae habent.
29. Beātī quī cōnspectum Dominī cognōvērunt et gradiuntur in sēmitīs ejus ('of him').
30. Jēsūs, flētū quattuor mulierum tāctus, regressus et eās ('them') sōlātus est.
31. Pāstor senex, septem ovēs dūcēns, ad montem ingrediēbātur.
32. Dēsīderiīs nostrīs ā Dominō praenōtīs, efficiāmur populus assiduī affectūs.
33. Sacerdōs rītibus fungātur quibus substantia nostra alitur. Neque alere dēsinant!

II.   1. If Peter returns to Rome, will he find his brothers faithful to the teachings of Jesus?
2. Jesus knew beforehand that he was about to die.
3. Let the dead bury the dead!
4. Would that all men may get to know the peace of Christ!
5. Should we try to console the weeping woman?

Readings

1. The Gloria.

Glōria in excelsīs Deō et in terrā pāx hominibus bonae voluntātis. Laudāmus tē, benedīcimus tē, adōrāmus tē, glōrificāmus

tē, grātiās agimus tibi propter magnam glōriam tuam, Domine
Deus, Rēx caelestis,[1] Deus Pater omnipotēns. Domine Fīlī ūni-
genite, Jēsū Chrīste, Domine Deus, Agnus Deī, Fīlius Patris, quī
tollis peccāta mundī, miserēre nōbīs; quī tollis peccāta mundī,
suscipe dēprecātiōnem nostram. Quī sedēs[2] ad dexteram Patris,
miserēre nōbīs. Quoniam tū sōlus[3] Sānctus, tū sōlus Dominus,
tū sōlus Altissimus,[4] Jēsū Chrīste, cum Sānctō Spīritū: in glōriā
Deī Patris. Āmēn.

[1]**caelestis, caeleste** heavenly [2]**sedeō, sedēre, sēdī, sessus** sit [3]**sōlus, -a, -um** only,
alone [4]**altissimus, -a, -um**: superlative of **altus, -a, -um**

2. Lēctiō sānctī Evangeliī secundum Marcum i, 40–42. Jesus cures
a leper. Et venit ad eum[1] leprōsus[2] dēprecāns eum[1] et genū
flectēns et dīcēns eī:[3] "Sī vīs, potes mē mundāre."[4] Et misertus
extendēns manum suam[5] tetigit eum[1] et ait[6] illī:[7] "Volō, mundāre!";[4] et statim discessit ab eō[8] lepra,[9] et mundātus est.[4]

[1]**eum** 'him' [2]**leprōsus, -a, -um** leprous [3]**eī** 'to him' [4]**mundō, mundāre, mundāvī,
mundātus** cleanse [5]**suam** 'his' [6]**ait** 'he says' [7]**illī** 'to him' [8]**eō** 'him' [9]**lepra, leprae,
f.** leprosy

Unit 22

116. Imperfect Subjunctive

All verbs, whether regular or not, form the imperfect tense of the subjunctive mood in the same manner: the entire second principal part, with the final **e** lengthened, is used as the base; to this are added the personal endings.

a. Active Active forms of the imperfect subjunctive are compounded of the modified second principal part and the active personal endings. The **-ē-** is shortened, as usual, before **-m**, **-t**, and **-nt**.

laudārem	monērem	dūcerem
laudārēs	monērēs	dūcerēs
laudāret	monēret	dūceret
laudārēmus	monērēmus	dūcerēmus
laudārētis	monērētis	dūcerētis
laudārent	monērent	dūcerent
caperem	audīrem	essem
caperēs	audīrēs	essēs
caperet	audīret	esset
caperēmus	audīrēmus	essēmus
caperētis	audīrētis	essētis
caperent	audīrent	essent
possem	īrem	vellem
possēs	īrēs	vellēs
posset	īret	vellet
possēmus	īrēmus	vellēmus
possētis	īrētis	vellētis
possent	īrent	vellent

b. Passive   Passive forms of the imperfect subjunctive are compounded of the modified second principal part and the passive personal endings. The -ē- is shortened, as usual, before -r and -ntur.

laudārer	monērer	dūcerer
laudārēris/-re	monērēris/-re	dūcerēris/-re
laudārētur	monērētur	dūcerētur
laudārēmur	monērēmur	dūcerēmur
laudārēminī	monērēminī	dūcerēminī
laudārentur	monērentur	dūcerentur
caperer	audīrer	mīrārer
caperēris/-re	audīrēris/-re	mīrārēris/-re
caperētur	audīrētur	mīrārētur
caperēmur	audīrēmur	mīrārēmur
caperēminī	audīrēminī	mīrārēminī
caperentur	audīrentur	mīrārentur

Note that the deponent verb **mīror, mīrārī, —, mīrātus sum** forms its imperfect subjunctive *as if* it had an active infinitive (****mīrāre**). This is true of all deponent verbs: e.g., **patior, patī, —, passus sum**, a verb of the third conjugation, first reconstructs the *hypothetical* present active infinitive (****patere**) before adding the passive personal endings—**paterer, paterēris/-re, paterētur**, etc.

117. Sequences of Tenses: Subordinate Use of Subjunctives

Although the subjunctive mood may be used as the verb of an independent clause (see Sections 110, 113, 114, 134, and 153b), its chief use is as the verb of a subordinate clause (cf. Section 115). As its etymology declares, it is the mood which 'tends to be subjoined.'

Subjunctives occur in subordinate clauses of condition, purpose, result, and the like, and in indirect forms of statements, commands, and questions.

Which subjunctive tense to employ in a subordinate clause—the present, imperfect, perfect, or pluperfect—is determined partly by the tense of the verb in the main clause, and partly by the time relationship of the subordinate verb to the main verb.

Subordinate clauses requiring the subjunctive must use a present or a perfect if the main verb is *primary*, and an imperfect or a pluperfect if the main verb is *secondary*. The primary tenses are those which refer to present or future time: the present, future, future-perfect, and perfect (with completed aspect, 'has/have'); the secondary tenses are those which refer to past time: the imperfect, perfect (with simple aspect), and pluperfect.

A present subjunctive indicates time contemporaneous with or subsequent to a primary main verb; a perfect subjunctive, time prior to a primary main verb. These relationships constitute primary sequence.

An imperfect subjunctive indicates time contemporaneous with or subsequent to a secondary main verb; a pluperfect subjunctive, time prior to a secondary main verb. These relationships constitute secondary sequence.

> *Note:*   The terms 'contemporaneous' time and 'simultaneous' time may be used interchangeably; cf. Section 100.

INDEPENDENT CLAUSE	SUBORDINATE CLAUSE	
	Contemp./Subseq.	*Prior*

1. Any *primary* tense:
  Present
  Future
  Perfect (completed)
  Future-Perfect
	Present
	Subjunctive
		Perfect
		Subjunctive

2. Any *secondary* tense:
  Imperfect
  Perfect (simple)
  Pluperfect
	Imperfect
	Subjunctive
		Pluperfect
		Subjunctive

The operation of these sequences of tenses has already been illustrated in part by the future less vivid conditional sentence (Section 115b.2): a present tense in the apodosis, or main clause, is accompanied in the protasis, or subordinate clause, by a present subjunctive (signaling time contemporaneous with a primary tense).

118. Purpose Clauses

The statement of an action may be accompanied by a subordinate clause which expresses the purpose or intention of the action; such a clause answers the question *why*: Paul went to Rome in order that he might see Peter. Why did Paul go to Rome? 'in order that he might see Peter.'

Purpose clauses always use the subjunctive mood. Since the goal or aim expressed in the purpose clause is necessarily *subsequent* in time to that of the main verb, by the rules of the sequences of tenses, only the present or the imperfect tense can logically occur, depending on whether the main verb is a primary or a secondary tense. (See the chart above.)

a. Adverbial Most purpose clauses are strictly adverbial, answering only the question *why*. The sign-words for the adverbial purpose clause are **ut** for the affirmative and **nē** for the negative; they occur only at the beginning of a clause.

Primary sequence:
Translation formula: 'in order that . . may'

Paulus in domum { intrat / intrābit / intrāvit / intrāverit } **ut Petrum videat.**

'Paul (enters/will enter/has entered/will have entered) the house in order that he may see Peter.'

Jēsūs in domum intrāvit nē ā turbā videātur.
'Jesus has entered the house in order that he may not be seen by the crowd.'

Secondary sequence:
Translation formula: 'in order that . . might'

Paulus in domum { intrābat / intrāvit / intrāverat } **ut Petrum vidēret.**

'Paul (was entering/entered/had entered) the house in order that he might see Peter.'

Jēsūs in domum intrābat nē ā turbā vidērētur.
'Jesus was entering the house in order that he might not be seen by the crowd.'

b. Relative   The relative purpose clause answers the question *who* (or *whom*) as well as *why*; here the relative pronoun (**quī, quae, quod**) replaces the sign-word **ut**; the antecedent is expressed in the main clause. Occasionally a relative adverb (e.g., **ubi**) introduces a relative purpose clause.

To avoid ambiguity, it is often better to translate a relative purpose clause either with the formula prescribed for an adverbial purpose clause, i.e., 'in order that . . may/might' (rather than 'who may/might') or with the English infinitive of purpose.

> **Paulus quattuor diāconōs mīsit, quī Petrum vidērent.**
> ['Paul sent the four deacons who might see Peter.']
> 'Paul sent the four deacons in order that they might see Peter.'
> 'Paul sent the four deacons to see Peter.'
>
> **Paulus diāconem Rōmam mīsit, ubi Petrum vidēret.**
> ['Paul sent the deacon to Rome, where he might see Peter.']
> 'Paul sent the deacon to Rome in order that there he might see Peter.'
> 'Paul sent the deacon to Rome to see Peter there.'

119. Infinitive of Purpose

As in English, the infinitive (often following a main verb of motion) may be employed for the expression of an aim, intention, or purpose.

> **Paulus Rōmam vēnit Petrum vidēre.**
> 'Paul came to Rome to see Peter.'

120. Indirect Commands (or Requests)

After a verb of ordering or asking, an indirect command (or request) may be conveyed either by **ut** + subjunctive or by an accusative + infinitive.

Translation formula: 'that . .' *or* 'to . .'

a. Subjunctive   An indirect command (or request) may take the form of a substantive clause with **ut** + the subjunctive mood. Since the action of an indirect command must be subsequent to that of the main verb, only the present or the imperfect subjunctive may appear (depending on the sequence in operation). The negative is **nē**.

Dēprecēmur Deum ut peccāta nostra nōbīs dīmittat.
'Let us beseech God that he forgive us our sins.'
'Let us beseech God to forgive us our sins.'

Deum ōrāmus nē dēficiāmus.
'We pray God that we not fail.'

Jēsūs dīxit apostolīs ut pānēs colligerent.
'Jesus told the apostles to collect the loaves.'

It is important to note that an indirect command (or request) is a *noun* clause, functioning as the direct object of the main verb, whereas a purpose clause is *adverbial*. In this last example, **dīxit** has both an indirect object (**apostolīs**) and a direct object (**ut pānēs colligerent**).

b. Infinitive   An indirect command (or request) may take the form of an accusative + infinitive construction. This is in reality a double accusative—the person asked and the action requested.

Diāconus jussit populum ōrāre.
'The deacon bade the people (to) pray.'
[**jubeō, jubēre, jussī, jussus** 'command, ask, bid']

Vocabulary

dīgnor, dīgnārī, —, dīgnātus sum consider worthwhile, deign

dēdīgnor, dēdīgnārī, —, dēdīgnātus sum scorn, disdain

jūdicō, jūdicāre, jūdicāvī, jūdicātus judge

dījūdicō, dījūdicāre, dījūdicāvī, dījūdicātus discern, distinguish

memoror, memorārī, —, memorātus sum (+ *gen.* or *acc.*) be mindful of, remember

postulō, postulāre, postulāvī, postulātus ask (for), pray for; require

praedicō, praedicāre, praedicāvī, praedicātus preach, proclaim

rogō, rogāre, rogāvī, rogātus ask (for), pray, beseech

interrogō, interrogāre, interrogāvī, interrogātus ask, inquire

fateor, fatērī, —, fassus sum acknowledge, confess (+ *acc.*); praise (+ *dat.*)

cōnfiteor, cōnfitērī, —, cōnfessus sum confess (+ *acc.*); praise (+ *dat.*)

**profiteor, profitērī, —,
profēssus sum** profess
jubeō, jubēre, jussī, jussus
command, ask, bid
**respondeō, respondēre, re-
spondī, respōnsus** answer,
respond (to) (+ *dat.*)
loquor, loquī, —, locūtus sum
speak
   **alloquor, alloquī, —, al-
locūtus sum** speak to,
address (+ *acc.*)
**petō, petere, petīvī (petiī),
petītus** ask (for), entreat
sequor, sequī, —, secūtus sum
follow
   **assequor, assequī, —,
assecūtus sum** follow
   **cōnsequor, cōnsequī, —,
cōnsecūtus sum** follow;
obtain
   **persequor, persequī, —,
persecūtus sum** pursue,
track down; persecute
   **prōsequor, prōsequī, —,
prōsecūtus sum** proceed
(with), go through (with)
ūtor, ūtī, —, ūsus sum (+ *abl.*)
use, enjoy, be friends with

cūra, cūrae, f. care, concern
spīna, spīnae, f. thorn
antistes, antistitis, m. bishop
cīvitās, cīvitātis, f. city
clāritās, clāritātis, f. light,
brightness; glory, fame
intercessiō, intercessiōnis, f.
intercession
cantus, cantūs, m. chant
introitus, introitūs, m. a going
in, introit
plānctus, plānctūs, m.
mourning
serēnus, -a, -um bright, serene
commūnis, commūne common; unclean
major, majus (*gen.*, **majōris**)
greater, older
nē (*subord. conj.*) in order that
. . not (*introducing negative
purpose + subj.*); that . . not
(*introducing indirect command + subj.*)
ut (*subord. conj.*) in order that
(*introducing purpose clause
+ subj.*); that (*introducing
indirect command + subj.*)

Vocabulary Notes

Dīgnor (the denominative from **dīgnus**, Unit 4) may take an object
infinitive: **dīgnor Rōmam vidēre** 'I consider (it) worthwhile to see
Rome'; or an accusative and ablative: **dīgnor Petrum laude** 'I consider
Peter worthy of praise.'

Several verbs, some already seen, introduce indirect commands.
Postulō, rogō, petō, ōrō (Unit 5), **precor** (Unit 20), and **moneō** (Unit 6)
may take either construction: **ut** + subjunctive or accusative + infinitive. **Jubeō** takes only accusative + infinitive; **dīcō**, only **ut** +
subjunctive. Most verbs of asking also take a double accusative (see
Section 105).

Cūra is the noun from which **cūrō** (Unit 19) has been formed. Distinguish between the English derivative 'cure' and the meaning of **cūra** 'care, concern.'

Antistes is a compound of **ante** + **stō** 'stand in front.'

Clāritās is compounded of the base of **clārus** (Unit 4) and the noun-forming suffix **-itās, -itātis,** f.; cf. English 'bright' + noun-forming suffix '-ness' = 'brightness.'

Note that **intercessiō** (from **cēdō**, Unit 18) literally means 'a going between.'

Major ('greater') is the comparative of **magnus** ('great'). It illustrates a curious orthographical rule: intervocalic *j* is written singly though pronounced doubly (majjor). Thus the preceding vowel is always long by position.

Derivatives:	LATIN	ENGLISH
	dīgnor	indignation
	jūdicō	adjudicate
	memoror	commemoration
	postulō	postulate
	praedicō	preach, predicament, predicate
	rogō	rogation days, interrogation
	cōnfiteor	Confiteor, confess
	jubeō	jussive subjunctive
	respondeō	responsorial psalm
	loquor	locution
	petō	compete, competition
	sequor	sequence, consequence, prosecutor
	spīna	spine
	cantus	cant
	major	major, majority

Drills

I. Purpose clauses.

1. Vir clāmat ut audiātur.
2. Vir clāmāvit ut audīrētur.
3. Vir clāmāvit ut audiātur.

4. Servus in domum intrat ut cēnam praeparet.
5. Servus ā domō exīverat nē ā magistrō vocārētur.
6. Jēsūs apostolōs mīsit quī evangelizārent.
7. Habēmus satis cibī mandūcāre?
8. Jōannēs vēnit testimōnium dē Jēsū perhibēre.

II. Indirect commands.

1. Dēprecēmur Marīam prō nōbīs ōrāre.
2. Ōrēmus Deum nōbīs dēbita nostra dīmittere.
3. Ōrāmus Deum ut nōbīs dēbita nostra dīmittat.
4. Paulus monuit frātrēs ut mandāta servārent.
5. Jēsūs apostolīs dīxit ut evangelizārent.
6. Jēsūs jussit apostolōs evangelizāre.
7. Petāmus ā Deō ut nōs respiciat.
   [petō, petere, petīvī (petiī), petītus 'ask (for), entreat']
8. Petimus Deum nōs respicere.
9. Petīvimus ā Patre pānem nostrum cotīdiānum.
10. Puer magistrum librum rogāvit.
    [rogō, rogāre, rogāvī, rogātus 'ask (for)']
11. Sacerdōtēs Rōmānōs mōnuerant nē templum dēlērent.

Exercises

I.
1. Nōn enim mīsit mē Chrīstus baptizāre sed evangelizāre. I Cor. i, 17.
2. Plānctus mulierum ad lacrimās et cūram Jēsūm mōvit.
3. Omnis ergō quī cōnfitēbitur mē cōram hominibus, cōnfitēbor et ego eum ('him') cōram Patre meō, quī est in caelīs. Mt. x, 32.
4. Tollat crucem et sequātur mē.
5. Nōn vēnī vocāre jūstōs sed peccātōrēs. Mk. ii, 17.
6. Commūne aut immundum numquam introīvit in ōs meum. Acts xi, 8.
7. Statimque tunc Paulum dīmīsērunt frātrēs, ut īret ūsque ad mare. Acts xvii, 14.
8. Cōnfiteor tibi, Pater, Domine caelī et terrae. Mt. xi, 25.
9. Nōs autem nōn spīritum mundī accēpimus, sed Spīritum, quī ex Deō est, ut sciāmus quae ā Deō dōnāta sunt nōbīs. I Cor. ii, 12.

10. Glōrificāte ergō Deum in corpore vestrō. I Cor. vi, 20.

11. Ego enim sum minimus ('least') apostolōrum, quī nōn sum dīgnus vocārī ('to be called') apostolus, quoniam persecūtus sum ecclēsiam Deī. I Cor. xv, 9.

12. Nōn enim coūtuntur (co- + ūtuntur) Jūdaeī Samarītānīs. Jn. iv, 9.

13. Respondit mulier et dīxit eī ('him'): "Nōn habeō virum." Jn. iv, 17.

14. Ego sum, quī loquor tēcum. Jn. iv, 26.

15. Ego cibum habeō mandūcāre, quem vōs nescītis (= nōn scītis). Jn. iv, 32.

16. Ex cīvitāte autem illā ('that') multī crēdidērunt in eum ('him') Samarītānōrum propter verbum mulieris testimōnium perhibentis: "Dīxit mihi omnia, quae-cumque fēcī!" Jn. iv, 39.

17. Per Marīae et omnium sānctōrum intercessiōnem, rogēmus Patrem ut nōs respicere dīgnētur.

18. Pater, nostrī memorāns, Fīlium mīsit, quī ā sceleribus nostrīs nōs līberāret.

19. Sī jūdicēmus, jūdicēmur.

20. Profiteāmur fidem nostram in Chrīstō Jēsū.

21. Fatentēs culpās, Deum remissiōnem postulāvērunt.

22. Apostolī Jēsūm interrogābant dē Patris misericordiā.

23. Jēsūs mulierem nōn dēdīgnātus sed allocūtus est.

24. Jōannēs prīmum vēnit ut major sequerētur.

25. Et cōtīdiē Jēsūs in templō praedicābat, ut voluntātem Patris faceret.

26. Corōna spīnōrum glōriae corōna.

27. Deinde antistes noster introitum Missae diēī lēgit.

28. Cantibus laetīs frātrēs cōnfitentur Dominō.

29. Ad Majōrem Deī Glōriam (motto of the Society of Jesus).

30. Jubeāmus Dominum nōs servāre nē āmittāmur.

31. Petāmus ā Jēsū ut clāritās vultūs serēnī nōbīs appāreat.

II.   1. Peter, tracking down Jesus, found (him) praying.

2. Jesus had gone out in order that he might pray.

3. Peter bade the Lord (to) return to the city.

4. But the Lord asked Peter to go to the nearest city.

Readings

1. The Confiteor (old style).

Cōnfiteor Deō omnipotentī, beātae Marīae semper Virginī, beātō Michāēlī[1] Archangelō, beātō Jōannī Baptistae, sānctīs Apostolīs Petrō et Paulō, omnibus Sānctīs, et vōbīs, frātrēs: quia peccāvī nimis cōgitātiōne,[2] verbō, et opere; meā culpā, meā culpā, meā maximā culpā. Ideō precor beātam Marīam semper Virginem, beātum Michāēlem Archangelum, beātum Jōannem Baptistam, sānctōs Apostolōs Petrum et Paulum, omnēs Sānctōs, et vōs, frātrēs, ōrāre prō mē ad Dominum Deum nostrum.

[1] **Michāēl, Michāēlis**, m. Michael [2] **cōgitātiō, cōgitātiōnis**, f. thought

2. Lēctiō prīncipiī sānctī Evangeliī secundum Jōannem i, 1–9.

In prīncipiō erat Verbum, et Verbum erat apud Deum, et Deus erat Verbum. Hoc[1] erat in prīncipiō apud Deum. Omnia per ipsum[2] facta sunt, et sine ipsō[3] factum est nihil; quod factum est in ipsō[3] vīta erat, et vīta erat lūx[4] hominum, et lūx[4] in tenebrīs lūcet,[5] et tenebrae eam[6] nōn comprehendērunt.[7] Fuit homō missus ā Deō, cui nōmen erat Jōannēs; hic[8] vēnit in testimōnium, ut testimōnium perhibēret dē lūmine, ut omnēs crēderent per illum.[9] Nōn erat ille[10] lūx,[4] sed ut testimōnium perhibēret dē lūmine. Erat[11] lūx[4] vēra, quae illūminat[12] omnem hominem, veniēns[11] in mundum.

[1] **hoc** 'this' [2] **ipsum** 'him' [3] **ipsō** 'him' [4] **lūx, lūcis**, f. light [5] **lūceō, lūcēre, lūxī, —** shine [6] **eam** 'it' [7] **comprehendō, comprehendere, comprehendī, comprehēnsus** overtake, overcome [8] **hic** 'he' [9] **illum** 'him' [10] **ille** *'the'* [11] **erat veniēns** = **veniēbat** [12] **illūminō, illūmināre, illūmināvī, illūminātus** make shine, illuminate; enlighten

Unit 23

121. Present Subjunctives of sum and possum

The present subjunctive of **sum** is compounded of the stem **sī-** and the personal endings; for **possum** the stem is **possī-**. Long **i** is shortened before **-m**, **-t**, and **-nt**, as usual.

sim	sīmus	possim	possīmus
sīs	sītis	possīs	possītis
sit	sint	possit	possint

122. Emphatic Demonstrative Pronouns/Adjectives: hic and ille

In English the demonstratives 'this' and 'that' may be used as pronouns or as adjectives: 'this is good,' 'this pie is good'; 'that is good,' 'that pie is good.' So too in Latin: **hic, haec, hoc** 'this' and **ille, illa, illud** 'that' may be used either as pronouns or as adjectives. Such words specify or single out a particular person or thing; hence, the term 'demonstrative.' Their declensions are somewhat irregular, and so must be carefully learned.

hic, haec, hoc 'this'

	SINGULAR			PLURAL		
	M.	F.	N.	M.	F.	N.
Nom.	hic	haec	hoc	hī	hae	haec
Gen.	hujus	hujus	hujus	hōrum	hārum	hōrum
Dat.	huic	huic	huic	hīs	hīs	hīs
Acc.	hunc	hanc	hoc	hōs	hās	haec
Abl.	hōc	hāc	hōc	hīs	hīs	hīs

ille, illa, illud 'that'

	SINGULAR			PLURAL		
	M.	F.	N.	M.	F.	N.
Nom.	ille	illa	illud	illī	illae	illa
Gen.	illīus	illīus	illīus	illōrum	illārum	illōrum
Dat.	illī	illī	illī	illīs	illīs	illīs
Acc.	illum	illam	illud	illōs	illās	illa
Abl.	illō	illā	illō	illīs	illīs	illīs

123. Unemphatic Demonstrative Pronouns/Adjectives: is and iste

The demonstrative pronouns/adjectives **is**, **ea**, **id** and **iste**, **ista**, **istud** mean 'this' or 'that,' depending on the context. Less emphatic than **hic** or **ille**, they are used to refer again to a person or thing previously mentioned.

is, ea, id 'this, that'

	SINGULAR			PLURAL		
	M.	F.	N.	M.	F.	N.
Nom.	is	ea	id	eī	eae	ea
Gen.	ejus	ejus	ejus	eōrum	eārum	eōrum
Dat.	eī	eī	eī	eīs	eīs	eīs
Acc.	eum	eam	id	eōs	eās	ea
Abl.	eō	eā	eō	eīs	eīs	eīs

> *Note:* Latin often makes up for its lack of a third-person pro-
> noun by using **is, ea, id**; in such cases it is translated as
> 'he, his, him, she, it, they,' etc. Likewise, its need of a
> third-person pronominal adjective (his, her, its; their) is
> met by the use of the genitives: **ejus** 'of him, of her, of
> it' = 'his, her, its'; **eōrum** (m./n.) 'of them' = 'their';
> **eārum** (f.) 'of them' = 'their.'

The demonstrative **iste, ista, istud** 'this, that,' almost identical in meaning to **is, ea, id**, sometimes has the added meaning of 'that *of yours.*'

iste, ista, istud 'this, that (of yours)'

	SINGULAR			PLURAL		
	M.	F.	N.	M.	F.	N.
Nom.	iste	ista	istud	istī	istae	ista
Gen.	istīus	istīus	istīus	istōrum	istārum	istōrum
Dat.	istī	istī	istī	istīs	istīs	istīs
Acc.	istum	istam	istud	istōs	istās	ista
Abl.	istō	istā	istō	istīs	istīs	istīs

> Note that **ille, illa, illud** (Section 122) and **iste, ista, istud** are declined exactly alike.

124. Result Clauses

The statement of an action or quality may be accompanied by a subordinate clause which expresses the consequence, effect, or result of the action or quality. Thus two clauses are linked, giving cause and effect. Result clauses use the subjunctive mood: the present tense in primary sequence or the imperfect in secondary sequence.

Often a word of degree or manner ('so, so great, of such a kind') occurs in the main clause, anticipating the result clause: **tālis, tāle** 'such, of such a sort,' **tantus, -a, -um** 'so, so great,' **ita** 'so, thus, in this way,' **sīc** 'so, thus,' **tam** 'so, to such a degree.' If such a word is omitted from the main clause, it may be supplied from the context.

Translation formula: 'that . .'

a. Adverbial Most result clauses are strictly adverbial, answering only the question, With what consequence? The sign-words for the adverbial result clause are **ut** for the affirmative and **ut . . nōn** for the negative.

Deus mundum sīc dīlēxit, ut Fīlium nōbīs daret.
'God so loved the world that he gave us his Son.'

Fidēlis et jūstus est ut remittat nōbīs peccāta nostra. I. Jn. i, 9.
'He is (so) faithful and just that he forgives us our sins.'

Pāstor bonus ovēs custōdit ita ut nōn āmittantur.
'The good shepherd guards his sheep so that they are not lost.'

b. Relative   The relative result clause answers the question *who* as well as *with what consequence*. The relative pronoun (**quī, quae, quod**) replaces the sign-word **ut**; the antecedent is expressed in the main clause. Here **quī** is equivalent to **ut is** 'that he.'

Deus mundum sīc dīlēxit, quī Fīlium mitteret.
'God so loved the world, that he sent his Son.'

Notes: 1. A *substantive* clause of result may be introduced by **facere, efficere**, or the like. Translate 'see to it' or 'bring it about.'

   Deus effēcit ut Hebraeī mare trānsīrent.
   'God saw to it (brought it about) that the Hebrews crossed the sea.'

   2. Besides the infinitive, **volō** takes a subjunctive construction (without **ut**); this may also be considered a substantive clause of result.

   Vultis respondeam?
   'Do you wish that I answer?'

---

125. *Characterizing Relative Clauses*

To express an action which is typical or characteristic of a person or thing, a relative clause with the subjunctive may be used. The main clause may simply indicate existence (**est quī** 'there is one who') or may include an adjective such as **dīgnus** or **indīgnus**.

Translation formula: '(the sort) who . .' *or* '(the sort) to . .'

Paulus est quī in viīs Dominī ambulet.
'Paul is (the sort) who walks in the ways of the Lord.'

Petrus erat dīgnus quī apostolōs dūceret.
'Peter was (the sort) worthy to lead the apostles.'

Note that the present or imperfect subjunctive is used in accordance with the sequences of tenses.

Vocabulary

amō, amāre, amāvī, amātus
love

illūminō, illūmināre, illūmināvī, illūminātus make
shine, illuminate; enlighten

operor, operārī, —, operātus
sum work, perform

    cooperor, cooperārī, —,
    cooperātus sum work to-
    gether, cooperate (with)

sedeō, sedēre, sēdī, sessus
sit (down), be seated

tueor, tuērī, —, tuitus sum
watch, protect, uphold

lābor, lābī, —, lāpsus sum
slide, (slip and) fall

largior, largīrī, —, largītus sum
grant, bestow

dēlicia, dēliciae, f. pleasure,
delight

factor, factōris, m. maker,
doer

ōrdō, ōrdinis, m. rank, order

cōgitātiō, cōgitātiōnis, f.
thought

commemorātiō, commemo-
rātiōnis, f. remembrance,
commemoration

vītis, vītis, vītium, f. vine,
grapevine

sēnsus, sēnsūs, m. feeling,
sense; understanding, mind

quālis, quāle (of) what kind (of)

quantus, -a, -um how much,
how great

sextus, -a, -um sixth

tālis, tāle such, of such a sort

tantus, -a, -um so much,
so great

hic, haec, hoc (*demon. pron. &*
adj.) this

ille, illa, illud (*demon. pron. &*
adj.) that

is, ea, id (*unemphatic demon.*
pron. & adj.) this, that,
[= he, she, it]

iste, ista, istud (*unemphatic*
demon. pron. & adj.)
this, that (of yours)

ita (*adv.*) so, thus, in this way

sīc (*adv.*) so, thus

sīcut (1. *adv.*; 2. *subord. conj.*)
1. like 2. (just) as

    sīcut . . et (just) as . . (so) too

tam (*adv.*) so, to such a degree

Vocabulary Notes

Amō may take an object infinitive: **amat cantāre** 'he loves (likes)
to sing.' Because of its connotations, **amō** is used rather sparingly in
the Vulgate (51 times, whereas **dīligō** [Unit 14] appears 422 times).

Lābor 'slide, (slip and) fall' may further mean 'fall away from the
true faith, become apostate.'

Dēlicia may appear in the plural with a singular meaning (this is
the only classical usage).

The adverbs **ita**, **tam**, and **sīc** are not used interchangeably: **ita** may
modify adverbs, adjectives, and verbs; **tam**, adverbs and adjectives;
sīc, verbs only.

Derivatives:

LATIN	ENGLISH
amō	amour, amatory
illūminō	illumination
operor	operate
sedeō	sediment, papal see, sedentary
tueor	tuition, tutor
lābor	lapsed Catholic
dēlicia	delicious
factor	factor, factory
ōrdō	ordinal, ordinary
cōgitātiō	cogitation
vītis	viticulture, vise
quālis	quality
quantus	quantity, quantum
sextus	sextant
tālis	tales (*law term*)
tantus	tantamount
hic	ad hoc committee
is	id

Drills

I. hic, haec, hoc 'this'; ille, illa, illud 'that.' Identify the case; change the number.

1. hujus spīnae
2. illārum cūrārum
3. huic puerō
4. hīs mulieribus
5. illī rēgī
6. illī rēgēs
7. hunc virum
8. hoc vitium
9. illam cīvitātem
10. hōc modō
11. hāc corōnā
12. illīus patris
13. illud opus
14. haec scelera
15. huic memoriae
16. haec māter
17. hī caelicolae
18. illīs arboribus
19. ille peccātor
20. haec nox

II. Result clauses.

1. Marīa est tam maesta, ut Jēsūm agnōscere nōn possit.
2. Vir fidē erat ita plēnus, ut sānārētur.
3. Jēsūs sīc locūtus est, ut mulier Dominum eum vocāret.

4. Is ita ōrat, ut Deus eum audiat.
5. Eī sīc passī sunt, ut eīs Dominus miserērētur.

III. Characterizing relative clauses.

1. Is est quī bene cantet.
2. Eae mulierēs erant quae semper lacrimārentur.
3. Eī sunt indīgnī quī ad altāre Deī adveniant.
4. Nōvistī ōrātiōnem quae Dominum glōrificet?
5. Eī sunt quī vōbīscum cōnfringant pānem?
6. Sunt quī in Jēsūm nōn crēdant.

Exercises

I.

1. Glōria Patrī, et Fīliō, et Spīrituī Sānctō. Sīcut erat in prīncipiō, et nunc, et semper, et in saecula saeculōrum. Āmēn.
2. Hoc facite in meam commemorātiōnem. Lk. xxii, 19.
3. Ille vōs docēbit omnia. Jn. xiv, 26.
4. Scīmus autem quoniam dīligentibus Deum omnia cooperantur in bonum, hīs, quī secundum prōpositum ('decree') vocātī sunt. Rom. viii, 28.
5. Is erat quī Jēsūm trādere vellet.
6. Vidēs quoniam fidēs cooperābātur operibus illīus? James ii, 22.
7. Estō fidēlis ūsque ad mortem, et dabō tibi corōnam vītae. Rev. ii, 10.
8. Et cum ōrātis nōn eritis sīcut hypocritae ('hypocrites'), quī amant in synagōgīs ('synagogues') et in angulīs plateārum ('street corners') stantēs ōrāre, ut videantur ab hominibus. Mt. vi, 5.
9. Ego sum vītis vēra. Jn. xv, 1.
10. Sīc trānsit glōria mundī (spoken during the coronation of a new pope).
11. Haec nox est, dē quā scrīptum est: Et nox sīcut diēs illūminābitur: Et nox illūminātiō ('light') mea in dēliciīs meīs.
12. Haec nox reddit innocentiam lāpsīs et maestīs laetitiam.
13. Et sānātus est puer in hōrā illā. Mt. viii, 13.
14. Ecce faciam illōs, ut veniant et adōrent ante pedēs tuōs et scient quia ego dīlēxī tē. Rev. iii, 9.
15. Sīc enim dīlēxit Deus mundum, ut Fīlium suum ('his')

ūnigenitum daret, ut omnis, quī crēdit in eum, nōn pereat, sed habeat vītam aeternam. Jn. iii, 16.

16. Sī cōnfiteāmur peccāta nostra, fidēlis est et jūstus, ut remittat nōbīs peccāta. I Jn. i, 9.

17. Fīlius autem hominis nōn habet, ubi caput reclīnet. Mt. viii, 20.

18. Et vīso eō rogābant, ut trānsīret ā fīnibus eōrum. Mt. viii, 34.

19. Nisi factōrēs verbī sīmus, nōn sīmus salvī.

20. Tū es sacerdōs in aeternum secundum ōrdinem Melchisedech. Heb. v, 6.

21. Illae mulierēs parvulōs sīc tuitae sunt, ut omnēs eās bonās mātrēs vocārent.

22. Misertus autem dominus servī illīus dīmīsit eum et dēbitum dīmīsit eī. Mt. xviii, 27.

23. Nisi bona opera operātus eris, rēgnum caelōrum nōn cōnsequēris.

24. Rēgnum meum nōn est dē mundō hōc. Jn. xviii, 36.

25. Quis ('who') enim cognōvit sēnsum Dominī? I Cor. ii, 16.

26. Ita et istī nunc nōn crēdidērunt propter vestram misericordiam, ut et ipsī ('they') nunc misericordiam cōnsequantur. Rom. xi, 31.

27. Quī videt mē, videt eum, quī mīsit mē. Jn. xii, 45.

28. Haec tibi omnia dabō, sī cadēns adōrāveris mē. Mt. iv, 9.

29. Nam et Pater tālēs quaerit ('seeks'), quī adōrent eum. Jn. iv, 23.

30. Dē corde enim exeunt cōgitātiōnēs malae. Mt. xv, 19.

31. Pāx Dominī sit semper vōbīscum.

32. Discēdite ā mē, quī operāminī inīquitātem. Mt. vii, 23.

33. Quālia et quanta sunt opera Dominī!

34. Prō tantī Rēgis victōriā tuba īnsonet salūtāris!

35. In sextā hōrā eī ad cīvitātem regressī sunt, ubi rēx, sedēns in jūdiciō ('judgment'), eīs grātiam largīrētur.

II. 1. So great is God's concern for us that we are able to rejoice always.

2. There are those who pray in order that they may be praised by men.

3. Are there those who are so wretched that they are not able to believe in Christ?

4. The boys so worked together among the grapevines with unceasing care, that they were not able to sit down to eat dinner.

Readings

1. The Nicene Creed.

Crēdō in ūnum Deum, Patrem omnipotentem, factōrem caelī et terrae, vīsibilium omnium et invīsibilium. Et in ūnum Dominum Jēsūm Chrīstum, Fīlium Deī ūnigenitum, et ex Patre nātum ante omnia saecula. Deum dē Deō, lūmen dē lūmine, Deum vērum dē Deō vērō, genitum,[1] nōn factum, cōnsubstantiālem Patrī: per quem omnia facta sunt. Quī propter nōs hominēs et propter nostram salūtem dēscendit dē caelīs. Et incarnātus est dē Spīritū Sānctō ex Marīā Virgine, et homō factus est. Crucifīxus etiam prō nōbīs sub Pontiō Pīlātō[2]; passus et sepultus est, et resurrēxit tertiā diē, secundum Scrīptūrās, et ascendit in caelum, sedet ad dexteram Patris. Et iterum ventūrus est cum glōriā jūdicāre vīvōs et mortuōs, cujus rēgnī nōn erit fīnis. Et in Spīritum Sānctum, Dominum et vīvificantem; quī ex Patre Fīliōque prōcēdit. Quī cum Patre et Fīliō simul[3] adōrātur et conglōrificātur; quī locūtus est per prophētās. Et ūnam sānctam, catholicam et apostolicam Ecclēsiam. Cōnfiteor ūnum baptisma in remissiōnem peccātōrum. Et exspectō resurrēctiōnem mortuōrum, et vītam ventūrī saeculī.

[1] **genō, genere, genuī, genitus** cause to live, beget [2] **Pontius, -ī, Pīlātus, -ī,** m. Pontius Pilatus, 'Pilate,' Roman procurator of Judea, A.D. c.26–c.36 [3] **simul** (*adv.*) together, at the same time

2. Lēctiō sānctī Evangeliī secundum Jōannem i, 10–13.

In mundō erat,
et mundus per ipsum[1] factus est,
et mundus eum nōn cognōvit.
In propria[2] vēnit,
et suī[3] eum nōn recēpērunt.
Quotquot[4] autem recēpērunt eum,
dedit eīs potestātem fīliōs Deī fierī,[5]
hīs, quī crēdunt in nōmine ejus, quī nōn ex sanguinibus neque ex voluntāte carnis neque ex voluntāte virī, sed ex Deō nātī sunt.

[1] **ipsum** 'him' [2] **proprius, -a, -um** one's own [3] **suī** 'his own' [4] **quotquot** (*indecl. adj.*) however many [5] **fierī** 'to become'

Unit 24

126. Present Subjunctives of eō and volō

The present subjunctive of the irregular verb **eō** has three elements: the stem **e-**, the sign of the present subjunctive, **-ā-**, and the personal endings.

eam	**eāmus**
eās	**eātis**
eat	**eant**

When uncompounded, several of these forms often give way to the equivalent forms of **vādō**, **vādere**, —, — 'go, walk, hurry': **vādam**, **vādās**, **vādat**; **eāmus**, **eātis**, **vādant**.

The present subjunctive of the irregular verb **volō** is compounded of the stem **velī-** and the personal endings.

velim	**velīmus**
velīs	**velītis**
velit	**velint**

127. Intensive Pronoun/Adjective: ipse

In English the element '-self' is used to intensify the meaning of a pronoun or a noun: 'I did it myself (I myself did it),' 'the boy did it himself (the boy himself did it).' The intensive pronoun/adjective **ipse**, **ipsa**, **ipsum** '-self' is used in a similar fashion; it may also appear alone, with the personal pronoun understood.

	SINGULAR			PLURAL		
	M.	F.	N.	M.	F.	N.
Nom.	**ipse**	**ipsa**	**ipsum**	**ipsī**	**ipsae**	**ipsa**
Gen.	**ipsīus**	**ipsīus**	**ipsīus**	**ipsōrum**	**ipsārum**	**ipsōrum**
Dat.	**ipsī**	**ipsī**	**ipsī**	**ipsīs**	**ipsīs**	**ipsīs**

	SINGULAR			PLURAL		
	M.	F.	N.	M.	F.	N.
Acc.	ipsum	ipsam	ipsum	ipsōs	ipsās	ipsa
Abl.	ipsō	ipsā	ipsō	ipsīs	ipsīs	ipsīs

Ego ipse hoc fēcī.
'*I* myself did this (*I* did this myself).'

Puer ipse hoc fēcit.
'The boy himself did this (the boy did this himself).'

Ipsa hoc fēcit.
'She herself did this (she did this herself).'

Jēsūs sānāvit mulierēs ipsās.
'Jesus healed the women themselves.'

In ipsum crēdimus.
'We believe in *him*.'

Note the translation of **ipsum**: 'him himself' is avoided in English in favor of the simple pronoun said with greater stress (or italicized in print).

The pronominal suffix **-met** has an equivalent intensive force when attached to a pronoun.

Egomet Rōmam ībō.
'I myself will go to Rome.'
'I will go to Rome myself.'
'*I* will go to Rome.'

Here, **egomet** is triply emphatic: **ego** is always emphatic (see Section 104); **-met** intensifies; the first position in a sentence is the most emphatic.

In the Nova Vulgata **ipse**, **ipsa**, **ipsum** is treated as a suffix after personal pronouns: e.g., **tēipsum**, **vōsmetipsōs**, **vōbīsmetipsīs**, etc.

128. Conditional Clauses (2): Present Contrafactual

In English a conditional clause which implies that something is not at present true employs the past tense: 'if I *were* home [but just now I am not], I would be eating dinner now.' So too in Latin: a conditional clause spoken in the present concerning something which is not at the moment true uses the imperfect subjunctive. This is called the present contrafactual conditional clause. The apodosis (i.e., the main clause) may also use the imperfect subjunctive.

Translation formula: 'were . . , would . .'

Sī Paulus esset hīc, fēlīcēs essēmus.
'If Paul were here, we would be happy.'

The implication is clear: 'Paul is *not now* present, and so we are *not now* happy.' The statement is contrary to fact, in present time: hence, the imperfect subjunctive.

129. Gerundives

The future passive participle (see Section 97) is sometimes called the gerundive. This verbal adjective (e.g., **laudandus, -a, -um** '[having] to be praised') modifies a noun in any case *except* the nominative (which is reserved for the formation of the passive periphrastic conjugation [see Section 98b]). The gerundive is a *passive* construction where English prefers the active.

Petrō erat dēsīderium Paulī videndī.
['To Peter there was the desire of Paul to-be-seen.']
'Peter had the desire of seeing Paul.'

Jōannēs vēnit ad populum baptizandum.
['John came for the people to-be-baptized.']
'John came to baptize the people.'

Jōannēs vēnit populī baptizandī causā.
['John came for the sake of the people to-be-baptized.']
'John came to baptize the people.'

Note that in the last two examples **ad** + gerundive and gerundive + **causā** are equivalent to purpose clauses, a construction to which the *future* passive participle quite naturally lends itself.

130. Gerunds

A gerund is the neuter singular of a gerundive used *substantively* and with an *active* meaning. Like the gerundive, it may occur in any case except the nominative. As a noun formed from a verb, it may take an object.

The English gerund, in -ing, translates the Latin gerund exactly.
Unlike in English, there are no passive gerunds.

Nom. —
Gen. ōrandī 'of praying'
Dat. ōrandō 'for/to praying'
Acc. ōrandum 'praying'
Abl. ōrandō 'from/with/in/by praying'

> *Notes:* 1. The above is merely illustrative: nearly every verb
>   has a gerund.
>   2. The gerund makes up for the lack of a nominative by
>   using the infinitive (also a verbal noun): **ōrāre est
>   bonum** 'to pray is good,' 'praying is good.'
>   3. The gerund of **eō** is **eundī, -ō, -um, -ō.**

Jēsūs in montem subīvit ad ōrandum.
'Jesus went up into the mountain for praying (to pray).'

Mandūcandō vīvimus.
'We live by eating.'

Paulus vēnit ad videndum frātrēs in Chrīstō.
'Paul came for seeing (to see) his brothers in Christ.'

Diāconus ad ambōnem accessit Evangelium legendī causā.
'The deacon approached the ambo for the sake of reading (to read)
  the Gospel.'

Vocabulary

illūstrō, illūstrāre, illūstrāvī,
  illūstrātus illuminate;
  enlighten, explain
portō, portāre, portāvī,
  portātus carry
accendō, accendere, accendī,
  accēnsus kindle, set on fire
canō, canere, cecinī, cantus
  sing; prophesy

concinō, concinere, con-
  cinuī, concentus sing
plangō, plangere, plānxī,
  plānctus bewail, mourn
pōnō, pōnere, posuī, positus
  put, place, set
dēpōnō, dēpōnere, dēposuī,
  dēpositus set down,
  lay down; remove

impōnō, impōnere, imposuī,
impositus put upon
prōpōnō, prōpōnere, prō-
posuī, prōpositus set be-
fore; propose
repōnō, repōnere, reposuī,
repositus put back, re-
place; lay aside; bury
vādō, vādere, —, — go, walk,
hurry
capiō:
praecipiō, praecipere,
praecēpī, praeceptus
command; instruct, teach
Olīvētum, Olīvētī, n. Olivet
[a hill east of Jerusalem]
creātor, creātōris, m. maker,
creator
mīles, mīlitis, m. soldier
mōns, montis, montium, m.
mountain, hill
cōnsors, cōnsortis, cōnsortium, m. or f. sharer
commixtiō, commixtiōnis, f.
mingling

lūx, lūcis, f. light
vēritās, vēritātis, f. truth
crīmen, crīminis, n. guilt, sin
dexter, dextera, dexterum right
paucī, -ae, -a few, a few
caelestis, caeleste heavenly,
divine
mītis, mīte mild, meek
cōnfestim (adv.) at once,
immediately
ipse, ipsa, ipsum (intensive
pron. & adj.) -self, [= he,
she, it]
octō (indecl. adj.) eight
octōgintā (indecl. adj.) eighty
quidem (intensifying adv.)
indeed, at any rate
quīnque (indecl. adj.) five
simul (adv.) together, at the
same time
simul ac or atque (subord.
conj.) as soon as

Vocabulary Notes

The frequentative form of **canō** is **cantō** (Unit 5).

Plānctus (Unit 22) is a fourth declension noun formed on the fourth principal part of **plangō**.

Pōnere genū means 'to kneel.'

Vādō replaces monosyllabic forms of **eō**: **vādis** for **īs**, **vādit** for **it**, **vāde!** for **ī!**

Praecipiō takes the dative with both indirect command construc-tions—dative with **ut** + subjunctive, dative with infinitive: **praecipiō tibi (ut exeās) (exīre)** 'I command you to leave.'

Creātor is the agent noun formed from **creō** (Unit 13).

Vēritās is the noun built from the adjective **vērus** (Unit 4).

Outside of the masculine nominative singular, **dexter, dextera, dexterum** may have syncopated forms: **dextra** for **dextera**, **dextrum** for **dexterum**, etc.

When **paucī** (rarely) occurs in the singular, it means 'little': e.g., **pauca spēs est** 'there is little hope.'

Quidem, together with **vērō** (Unit 20) or **autem** (Unit 9) in succeeding clauses, is translated 'on the one hand . . on the other hand,' in imitation of a Greek idiom. It follows the emphatic word.

Simul ac *or* **atque** may be spelled as one word: **simulac/simulatque**. It takes the indicative mood.

Derivatives:

LATIN	ENGLISH
illūstrō	illustration, illustrative
canō	bel canto singing
plangō	plangent
pōnō	posit, position, deponent, deposit, imposition, proponent
portō	porter, transportation
vādō	invade, evade, vade mecum
praecipiō	precept, preceptive
mīles	militia, military
mōns	mount, Montana
cōnsors	prince consort
lūx	lux, lucid
vēritās	verity
crīmen	crime, criminal
dexter	dexterity, ambidextrous
paucī	paucity
caelestis	celestial, celesta
mītis	mitigate
ipse	ipso facto, solipsism
octō	octet, octave
quīnque	quinquefoliate, quinquennium
simul	simultaneous, simulcast

Drills

I. Present contrafactual conditional clauses (sentences).

1. Sī pāstor malus ovēs tuērētur, āmitterentur.
2. Sī rēx morerētur, famīlia regrederētur.
3. Nisi ille esset apostolus, Jēsūm nōn trāderet.
4. Sī in Chrīstum crēderēs, nunc laetārēris.
5. Sacerdōs rītū jam fungerētur, sī esset hīc.

II. Gerundives and gerunds.

   1. Ad ōrātiōnem fīniendam populus dīcunt: Āmēn.
   2. Legendō nōscimus multa.
   3. Librīs legendīs nōscimus multa.
   4. Ipse apostolīs dedit potestātem sānandī.
   5. Jēsūs exiit apostolōs vocandī causā.
   6. Prō virō maledīcendō Jēsūs eum benedīxit.
   7. Prō virum maledīcendō Jēsūs eum benedīxit.
   8. Malī locūtī sunt dē Jēsū interficiendō.
   9. Ipsī in cēnāculum intrāvērunt ad Pascha mandūcandum.
   10. Stēllam videndō rēgēs exsultāvērunt.
   11. Eundō in dēsertum Jōannēs satiāre poterat populī dēsīderium baptizandī.

Exercises

I.
   1. Beātī mītēs, quoniam ipsī possidēbunt ('will possess') terram. Mt. v, 4.
   2. Et praecēpit turbae sedēre super terram.
   3. Ut autem sciātis quia potestātem habet Fīlius hominis in terrā dīmittendī peccāta . . : Tibi dīcō: Surge, tolle grabātum ('cot') tuum et vāde in domum tuam. Mk. ii, 10–11.
   4. Et hymnō dictō, exiērunt in montem Olīvētī. Mt. xxvi, 30.
   5. Illō diē in nōmine meō petētis, et nōn dīcō vōbīs quia ego rogābō Patrem dē vōbīs; ipse enim Pater amat vōs, quia vōs mē amāstis et crēdidistis quia ego ā Deō exīvī. Exīvī ā Patre et vēnī in mundum; iterum relinquō mundum et vādō ad Patrem. Jn. xvi, 26–28.
   6. Vidēte autem vōsmetipsōs. Mk. xiii, 9.
   7. Salvum fac tēmetipsum dēscendēns dē cruce. Mk. xv, 30.
   8. Ō Domine, Creātor Spīritus, accende in cordibus nostrīs ignem dīlēctiōnis tuae.
   9. Prophētae ad sēnsum Deī illūstrandum cecinērunt.
   10. Jēsū repositō, quīnque mulierēs plangēbant valdē.
   11. Vērē homō hic Fīlius Deī erat. Mk. xv, 39.
   12. In hoc enim vocātī estis, quia et Chrīstus passus est prō vōbīs vōbīs relinquēns exemplum, ut sequāminī vestīgia ejus. I Pet. ii, 21.
   13. Paucī, id est octō animae, salvae factae sunt per aquam. I Pet. iii, 20.
   14. Sed, quemadmodum ('to the extent that') commūnicātis

('you share') Chrīstī passiōnibus, gaudēte, ut et in
revēlātiōne glōriae ejus gaudeātis exsultantēs. I Pet. iv, 13.

15. Ipsī imperium in saecula saeculōrum. Āmēn. I Pet. v, 11.

16. Sufficit, vēnit hōra: ecce trāditur Fīlius hominis in manūs
peccātōrum. Surgite, eāmus; ecce, quī mē trādit, prope
('near') est. Mk. xiv, 41–42.

17. Spīritus quidem prōmptus ('ready'), carō vērō īnfirma
('weak'). Mk. xiv, 38.

18. Et pōnentēs genua adōrābant eum. Mk. xv, 19.

19. Propter quod rogō vōs accipere cibum, hoc enim prō salūte
vestrā est. Acts xxvii, 34.

20. Trānseāmus ūsque Bēthlehem et videāmus hoc verbum,
quod factum est, quod Dominus ostendit nōbīs. Lk. ii, 15.

21. Meus cibus est, ut faciam voluntātem ejus, quī mīsit mē,
et ut perficiam opus ejus. Jn. iv, 34.

22. Nōn est hīc: surrēxit enim, sīcut dīxit. Venīte, vidēte
locum, ubi positus erat. Mt. xxviii, 6.

23. Multī enim sunt vocātī, paucī vērō ēlēctī. Mt. xxii, 14.

24. Omnia ergō, quaecumque vultis, ut faciant vōbīs
hominēs, ita et vōs facite eīs; haec est enim Lēx et
Prophētae. Mt. vii, 12.

25. Et ēgressus est rūrsus ('again') ad mare; omnisque turba
veniēbat ad eum, et docēbat eōs. Mk. ii, 13.

26. Prīmus homō dē terrā terrēnus, secundus homō dē caelō.
Quālis terrēnus, tālēs et terrēnī, et quālis caelestis, tālēs
et caelestēs; et sīcut portāvimus imāginem ('image')
terrēnī, portābimus et imāginem caelestis. I Cor. xv,
47–49.

27. Deus autem speī repleat vōs omnī gaudiō et pāce in
crēdendō. Rom. xv, 13.

28. Ex ipsō et per ipsum et in ipsum omnia. Ipsī glōria in
saecula. Āmēn. Rom. xi, 36.

29. Et ūnus ex illīs nōn cadet super terram sine Patre vestrō.
Mt. x, 29.

30. Vōs mīsistis ad Jōannem, et testimōnium perhibuit
vēritātī; ego autem nōn ab homine testimōnium accipiō,
sed haec dīcō, ut vōs salvī sītis. Jn. v, 33–34.

31. Beātī mundō corde, quoniam ipsī Deum vidēbunt. Mt. v, 8.

32. Ecce videō caelōs apertōs et Fīlium hominis ā dextrīs
stantem Deī. Acts vii, 56.

33. Neque mē scītis neque Patrem meum; sī mē scīrētis,
forsitan ('perhaps') et Patrem meum scīrētis. Jn. viii, 19.

34. Rogō autem tē, permitte mihi loquī ad populum.
Acts xxi, 39.

35. Vōs estis lūx mundī. Mt. v, 14.
36. Sī enim crēderētis Mōysī, crēderētis forsitan ('perhaps')
    et mihi. Jn. v, 46.
37. Erant enim, quī veniēbant et redībant multī, et nec
    mandūcandī spatium habēbant. Mk. vi, 31.
38. Cōnfestim igitur mīsī ad tē, et tū bene fēcistī veniendō.
    Acts x, 33.
39. Ipsī enim audīvimus et scīmus quia hic est vērē Salvātor
    mundī! Jn. iv, 42.
40. Quī habet aurēs [audiendī,] audiat. Mt. xiii, 9.
41. Dīligēs proximum tuum sīcut tēipsum. Mt. xxii, 39.
42. Sī dīligerētis mē, gaudērētis quia vādō ad Patrem, quia
    Pater major mē ('than I') est. Jn. xiv, 28.
43. Per hujus aquae et vīnī mystērium ejus efficiāmur
    dīvīnitātis cōnsortēs.
44. Haec commixtiō Corporis et Sanguinis Dominī nostrī Jēsū
    Chrīstī sit accipientibus nōbīs in vītam aeternam.
45. Simulatque octōgintā mīlitēs in cīvitātem iniērunt,
    mulierēs dē crīminibus eōrum exclāmāvērunt.

II. 1. Jesus sat down to break bread with the apostles. [*Use an
         ad + gerundive construction.*]
      2. If we were putting our faith in the Lord, we would be
         joyfully awaiting his coming.
      3. As soon as Jesus arrived in the city, he went to the temple
         to teach. [*Use a gerund + causā construction.*]
      4. By climbing the mountain and at the same time tracking
         him down, Peter was able to find Jesus himself.

Readings

1. Preface for the Nativity.
   Vērē dīgnum et jūstum est, aequum[1] et salūtāre, nōs tibi semper,
   et ubīque grātiās agere: Domine sāncte, Pater omnipotēns,
   aeterne Deus: Quia per incarnātī Verbī mystērium, nova mentis
   nostrae oculīs lūx tuae clāritātis īnfulsit[2]: ut, dum vīsibiliter[3]
   Deum cognōscimus, per hunc in invīsibilium amōrem[4] rapiā-
   mur.[5] Et ideō cum Angelīs et Archangelīs, cum Thronīs[6] et

[1] **aequus, -a, -um** equal, fair [2] **īnfulgeō, īnfulgēre, īnfulsī, —** shine on (+ *dat.*)
[3] **vīsibiliter**: *adverb from* **vīsibilis, -e** [4] **amor, amōris,** m. love [5] **rapiō, rapere, rapuī,**
raptus seize, take up, carry up [6] **thronus, thronī,** m. throne

Dominātiōnibus,[7] cumque omnī mīlitiā[8] caelestis exercitūs,[9] hymnum glōriae tuae canimus, sine fīne dīcentēs: Sānctus, sānctus, sānctus . .

[7] **dominātiō, dominātiōnis**, f. dominion [8] **mīlitia, mīlitiae**, f. armed forces, soldiery [9] **exercitus, exercitūs**, m. army

2. Lēctiō sānctī Evangeliī secundum Jōannem i, 14–18.
Et Verbum carō factum est
et habitāvit[1] in nōbīs,
et vīdimus glōriam ejus,
glōriam quasi[2] Ūnigenitī ā Patre,
plēnum grātiae et vēritātis.
Jōannēs testimōnium perhibet dē ipsō et clāmat dīcēns: "Hic erat, quem dīxī: Quī post mē ventūrus est, ante mē factus est, quia prior mē[3] erat."
Et dē plēnitūdine[4] ejus nōs omnēs accēpimus,
et grātiam prō grātiā;
quia lēx per Mōysēn[5] data est, grātia et vēritās per Jēsūm Chrīstum facta est. Deum nēmō[6] vīdit umquam[7]; ūnigenitus Deus, quī est in sinū[8] Patris, ipse ēnārrāvit.[9]

[1] **habitō, habitāre, habitāvī, habitātus** live, dwell [2] **quasi** (*adv.*) as if, as it were [3] **prior mē** 'earlier than I, before me' [4] **plēnitūdō, plēnitūdinis**, f. fullness [5] **Mōysēs, Mōysae**, m. Moses [6] **nēmō** 'no one' [7] **umquam** (*adv.*) ever [8] **sinus, sinūs**, m. bosom: loving protection [9] **ēnārrō, ēnārrāre, ēnārrāvī, ēnārrātus** tell, narrate, explain

Unit 25

131. Pluperfect Subjunctive

The pluperfect subjunctive of any verb is formed from a perfect base or participle, in combination with the imperfect subjunctive of **sum** (**essem, essēs, esset**, etc.).

a. **Active**   The active forms of the pluperfect subjunctive are compounded of the base of the perfect active and the imperfect subjunctive of **sum**, slightly respelled; i.e., initial **e-** becomes **-i-**.

laudāvissem	monuissem	dūxissem
laudāvissēs	monuissēs	dūxissēs
laudāvisset	monuisset	dūxisset
laudāvissēmus	monuissēmus	dūxissēmus
laudāvissētis	monuissētis	dūxissētis
laudāvissent	monuissent	dūxissent
cēpissem	audīvissem	īssem
cēpissēs	audīvissēs	īssēs
cēpisset	audīvisset	īsset
cēpissēmus	audīvissēmus	īssēmus
cēpissētis	audīvissētis	īssētis
cēpissent	audīvissent	īssent

> *Note:*   When the shorter perfect base of **eō** is used, double **i** is contracted to **ī**: **iissem** > **īssem**; this is true of any third principal part in **-īvī(-iī)**: e.g., **audiissem** > **audīssem**.

b. **Passive**   The passive forms of the pluperfect subjunctive are made up of the perfect passive participle and the imperfect subjunctive of **sum**.

laudātus, -a, -um essem	monitus, -a, -um essem
laudātus, -a, -um essēs	monitus, -a, -um essēs
laudātus, -a, -um esset	monitus, -a, -um esset
laudātī, -ae, -a essēmus	monitī, -ae, -a essēmus
laudātī, -ae, -a essētis	monitī, -ae, -a essētis
laudātī, -ae, -a essent	monitī, -ae, -a essent
ductus, -a, -um essem	captus, -a, -um essem
ductus, -a, -um essēs	captus, -a, -um essēs
ductus, -a, -um esset	captus, -a, -um esset
ductī, -ae, -a essēmus	captī, -ae, -a essēmus
ductī, -ae, -a essētis	captī, -ae, -a essētis
ductī, -ae, -a essent	captī, -ae, -a essent

auditus, -a, -um essem
auditus, -a, -um essēs
auditus, -a, -um esset
audītī, -ae, -a essēmus
audītī, -ae, -a essētis
audītī, -ae, -a essent

132. *Conditional Clauses (3): Past Contrafactual*

In English a conditional clause which implies that something was not true at some time in the past employs the pluperfect: 'if I *had known* that you were sick [but at that time I did not], I would have visited you then.' So too in Latin: a conditional clause stating something not true at some time past uses the pluperfect subjunctive. This is called the past contrafactual conditional clause. The apodosis (i.e., the main clause) may also use the pluperfect subjunctive.

Translation formula: 'had . . , would have . .'

Sī Paulus fuisset hīc, fēlīcēs fuissēmus.
'If Paul had been here, we would have been happy.'

Nisi Fīlius Deī in mundum missus esset, salvī nōn factī essēmus.
'If the Son of God had not been sent into the world, we would not have been saved.'

133. Clauses of Fearing

A verb of fearing may have as its object a subjunctive clause introduced by **nē** or **ut**. Since in a verb of fearing there is the implied desire for the *opposite* of a state or action, **nē** quite logically introduces an affirmative clause and **ut** a negative.

> **Paulus timet nē Rōmānī Petrum interfectūrī sint.**
> 'Paul fears that the Romans are going to kill Peter.'
> [**timeō, timēre, timuī,** — 'fear, be afraid (of)']
>
> **Paulus timuit ut Corinthiī essent fidēlēs.**
> 'Paul feared that the Corinthians were not being faithful.'

134. Unattainable Wishes

A wish for an action still possible uses the present subjunctive (see the optative subjunctive, Section 110b). But a wish for an action unattainable or impossible uses either the imperfect or the pluperfect subjunctive. The sign-word **utinam** is frequently used to introduce an unattainable wish.

a. Present Time   Like the present contrafactual conditional clause (see Section 128), an unattainable wish in present time uses the imperfect subjunctive.
   Translation formula: 'Would that . . were' *or* 'I wish that . . were'

> **Utinam Petrus adhūc vīveret!**
> 'Would that/I wish that Peter were still living!'

b. Past Time   Like the past contrafactual conditional clause (see Section 132), an unattainable wish referring to past time uses the pluperfect subjunctive.
   Translation formula: 'Would that . . had' *or* 'I wish that . . had'

> **Utinam Petrum vīdissēs!**
> 'Would that/I wish that you had seen Peter!'

135. Indirect Statements (2):
Object Clauses with Subjunctives

Indirect statements in the form of object clauses introduced by **quod**, **quia**, **quoniam** 'that' may take the indicative (see Section 43); this is called the retained indicative. But the use of the subjunctive mood in such clauses emphasizes the grammatical subordination of the indirect statement.

> **Invēnimus quod Paulus Rōmam jam īsset.**
> 'We discovered that Paul had already gone to Rome.'

> **Crēdunt quia Chrīstus sit Dominus.**
> 'They believe that Christ is Lord.'

Vocabulary

fleō, flēre, flēvī, flētus weep, lament

timeō, timēre, timuī, — fear, be afraid (of)

currō, currere, cucurrī, cursus run, hasten

    occurrō, occurrere, occurrī, occursus run up to, meet up with (+ *dat.*)

    succurrō, succurrere, succurrī, succursus run to the aid of, aid, succor (+ *dat.*)

dēfendō, dēfendere, dēfendī, dēfēnsus defend

dīcō:

    addīcō, addīcere, addīxī, addictus adjudge, condemn

    contrādīcō, contrādīcere, contrādīxī, contrādictus dispute, contradict (+ *dat.*)

    praedīcō, praedīcere, praedīxī, praedictus say earlier, foretell, predict

poscō, poscere, poposcī, — ask, beseech

    dēposcō, dēposcere, dēpoposcī, — beseech, demand

fugiō, fugere, fūgī, fugitus flee (from)

fīlia, fīliae, f. daughter

patria, patriae, f. native land, country

venia, veniae, f. indulgence, kindness

diabolus, diabolī, m. devil

dolor, dolōris, m. sorrow, pain

honor, honōris, m. honor

imperātor, imperātōris, m. general, emperor

effūsiō, effūsiōnis, f. outpouring

oblātiō, oblātiōnis, f. offering

ūnitās, ūnitātis, f. unity

necessārius, -a, -um needful, fateful; needed (+ *dat.*)

dīves (*gen.*, **dīvitis**) rich,
wealthy

pauper (*gen.*, **pauperis**) poor,
not wealthy

sōlemnis, sōlemne annual,
solemn, customary

avē! (*imperative;* *pl.*, **avēte**)
hail! hello! goodbye!
greetings!

circā (*prep.* + *acc.*) around

extrā (*prep.* + *acc.*) beyond,
outside

nē (*subord. conj.*) that (*intro-*

*ducing an affirmative clause
of fearing + subj.*)

perpetuō (*adv.*) uninterruptedly, perpetually

salvē! (*imperative;* *pl.*, **salvēte**)
hail! farewell! hello! good-
bye! greetings!

_ **sīve** (**seu**) (*subord. conj.*) or if
sīve (**seu**) .. **sīve** (**seu**)
if .. or if; whether .. or

ut (*subord. conj.*) that .. not
(*introducing a negative
clause of fearing + subj.*)

Vocabulary Notes

Besides a clause of fearing, **timeō** may take a direct object or an object infinitive: **Petrum timeō** 'I fear Peter'; **vir nōn timuit Jēsūm alloquī** 'the man was not afraid to address Jesus.'

Note that both **currō** and **poscō** form the perfect active by reduplicating the first two letters of the base: *cucurrī*, *poposcī*.

Whether **fugiō** is used to mean 'flee' or 'flee from,' it takes the accusative (not the ablative): **Petrus mīlitem fūgit** 'Peter fled (from) the soldier.'

Fīlia 'daughter' and **fīlius** 'son' share the same base. The dative/ablative pl. of **fīlia** is **fīliābus**. Cf. **anima** (Unit 7).

Patria is an adjectival form used substantively (from **patrius, -a, -um** 'of father, paternal,' from **pater** 'father' [Unit 14]). It is feminine because the understood noun is **terra** 'land.'

Effūsiō is the noun formed from the verb **effundō** (Unit 16).

The first meaning of **sōlemnis** is 'annual'; that which is celebrated annually is a 'solemn' feast. Hence, when used generally, it means 'customary.'

Avē (pl., **avēte**) and **salvē** (pl., **salvēte**) are interchangeable words of greeting and leave-taking. These are imperative forms from verbs otherwise very little used (i.e., **aveō** and **salveō**).

Sīve (**seu**) .. **sīve** (**seu**) introduce alternative conditional clauses, which may take any logical form. Often the alternatives consist of just a single word each: **sīve dīves sīve pauper, Petrus est fēlīx** 'whether rich or poor, Peter is happy.'

Derivatives:

LATIN	ENGLISH
timeō	timid, timorous
currō	course, current
occurrō	occur, occurrence
addīcō	addict
fugiō	fugitive, fugacious
fīlia	filial
patria	expatriate, repatriate
venia	venial
diabolus	diabolic, diabolism
dolor	dolorous, dolorimetry
effūsiō	effusion
oblatiō	oblation
necessārius	necessary
dīves	Dives
pauper	pauper, poor
avē	Ave
circā	circa, circadian
extrā	extraneous, extrapolate

Drills

I. Past contrafactual conditional clauses (sentences).

1. Sī diāconus ad aulam vēnisset, eum vīdissēmus.
2. Sī librum lēgissēs, hoc scīvissēs.
3. Nisi vir sānātus esset, mortuus esset.
4. Ovēs āmissae essent, sī pāstor eās nōn tuitus esset.
5. Sī nōs adjūvissētis, nunc bene facerēmus.

II. Clauses of fearing.

1. Timuērunt nē Petrus Paulum vīdisset.
2. Timuī ut Petrus Paulum vidēret (vīsūrus esset).
3. Paulus timēbat ut dē Jēsū audīssent.
4. Populus timent ut satis cibī habitūrī sint.
5. Nōn timēs nē Rōmānī mīlitēs tē trāditūrī sint?

Exercises

I.
1. Ō certē necessārium Adae peccātum, quod Chrīstī morte dēlētum est!
2. Per ipsum, et cum ipsō, et in ipsō, est tibi Deō Patrī omnipotentī, in ūnitāte Spīritūs Sānctī, omnis honor et glōria per omnia saecula saeculōrum. Āmēn.
3. Et relinquentēs eum omnēs fūgērunt. Mk. xiv, 50.
4. Bonum erat eī, sī nātus nōn fuisset homō ille. Mt. xxvi, 24.
5. Domine, sī fuissēs hīc, nōn esset mortuus frāter meus! Jn. xi, 32.
6. Sī enim data esset lēx, quae posset vīvificāre, vērē ex lēge esset jūstitia. Gal. iii, 21.
7. Nōn est prophēta sine honōre nisi in patriā et in domō suā ('his own'). Mt. xiii, 57.
8. Avē, grātiā plēna, Dominus tēcum [benedicta tū in mulieribus]. Lk. i, 28.
9. Respice etiam ad dēvōtum Imperātōrem nostrum!
10. Jūdaeī timēbant nē discipulī Jēsū sublātūrī essent corpus ejus.
11. Turba dēpoposcērunt ut Jēsūs ad mortem addīcerētur.
12. Sī nōn esset hic malefactor ('evil-doer'), nōn tibi trādidissēmus eum. Jn. xviii, 30.
13. Respondit Jēsūs et dīxit eī: "Sī scīrēs dōnum Deī et quis ('someone') est, quī dīcit tibi: 'Dā mihi bibere,' tū forsitan ('perhaps') petīssēs ab eō et dedisset tibi aquam vīvam." Jn. iv, 10.
14. Tunc discipulī omnēs, relictō eō, fūgērunt. Mt. xxvi, 56.
15. Nam et sī sunt, quī dīcantur diī sīve in caelō sīve in terrā, sīquidem sunt diī multī et dominī multī, nōbīs tamen ūnus Deus Pater, ex quō omnia et nōs in illum, et ūnus Dominus Jēsūs Chrīstus, per quem omnia et nōs per ipsum. I Cor. viii, 5–6.
16. Vōs ex patre Diabolō estis et dēsīderia patris vestrī vultis facere. Jn. viii, 44.
17. Sīve enim vīvimus, Dominō vīvimus, sīve morimur, Dominō morimur. Sīve ergō vīvimus, sīve morimur, Dominī sumus. Rom. xiv, 8.
18. Sī enim cognōvissent, numquam Dominum glōriae crucifīxissent. I Cor. ii, 8.
19. Extrā cīvitātem fīliae Jerūsalem, dolōre plēnae, ad crucem Jēsū flēbant.
20. Beātī pauperēs spīritū, quoniam ipsōrum est rēgnum caelōrum. Mt. v, 3.

21. Jēsūs surrēxit, sīcut praedīxit, allēlūjā.
22. Dominus cum veniā accipiat oblātiōnem nostram!
23. Salvē, Michāēl Archangele! Nōs ā diabolō semper dēfendās!
24. Occurrit Petrus Jēsū contrādīcentī cum Jūdaeīs.
25. Stantēs circā Jēsū corpus, mulierēs lacrimārum cum effūsiōne flēbant, clāmantēs: Quārē Dominus est mortuus? Utinam adhūc vīveret!
26. Dīves perpetuō timēbat ut sōlemne vōtum esset satis.

II.   1. Would that the Roman soldiers had defended the city!
2. Did the deacon beseech the Father that he regard us with indulgence?
3. Did you fear that the priest was not going to aid the people?
4. If Peter had not fled from the city, he would have been handed over to the Romans.
5. The daughter of the poor man would have died if Jesus had not come to the house and healed her.
6. The boy would still be safe if he had not met up with the evil men.

Readings

1.   The Salve Regina (Hermann Contractus, c. 1054).

Salvē, Rēgīna, Māter misericordiae, vīta, dulcēdō,[1] et spēs nostra, salvē. Ad tē clāmāmus exsulēs[2] filiī Hēvae. Ad tē suspīrāmus,[3] gementēs[4] et flentēs in hāc lacrimārum valle.[5] Eia[6] ergō, advocāta[7] nostra, illōs tuōs misericordēs[8] oculōs ad nōs converte.[9] Et Jēsūm benedictum frūctum ventris[10] tuī nōbīs post hoc exsilium[11] ostende. Ō clēmēns, Ō pia, Ō dulcis Virgō Marīa.

℣. Ōrā prō nōbīs, sāncta Deī Genetrīx.[12]
R. Ut dīgnī efficiāmur prōmissiōnibus[13] Chrīstī.

[1]**dulcēdō, dulcēdinis**, f. sweetness [2]**exsul, exsulis**, m. or f. a banished person, an exile [3]**suspīrō, suspīrāre, suspīrāvī, suspīrātus** breathe deeply, sigh [4]**gemō, gemere, gemuī, gemitus** groan, sigh, mourn [5]**vallis (vallēs), vallis**, f. valley, vale [6]**eia** (*interjection*) come on! [7]**advocāta, advocātae**, f. advocate [8]**misericors** (*gen.*, **misericordis**) compassionate, merciful [9]**convertō, convertere, convertī, conversus** *here*, turn [10]**venter, ventris**, m. belly; womb [11]**exsilium, exsiliī**, n. banishment, exile [12]**genetrīx, genetrīcis**, f. mother [13]**prōmissiō, prōmissiōnis**, f. promise

2. Lēctiō sānctī Evangeliī secundum Lūcam i, 26–28.
The Annunciation.

In mēnse[1] autem sextō missus est angelus Gabriēl ā Deō in cīvitātem Galilaeae, cui nōmen Nazareth, ad virginem dēspōnsātam[2] virō, cui nōmen erat Jōsēph dē domō Dāvid, et nōmen virginis Marīa. Et ingressus angelus ad eam dīxit: "Avē, grātiā plēna, Dominus tēcum" [benedicta tū in mulieribus].

[1] **mēnsis, mēnsis,** m. month [2] **dēspōnsātus, -a, -um** engaged

Unit 26

136. Perfect Subjunctive

The perfect subjunctive is formed from a perfect base or participle.

a. Active The active forms of the perfect subjunctive are compounded of the base of the perfect active, the suffix **-eri-**, and the active personal endings.

laudāverim	monuerim	dūxerim
laudāveris	monueris	dūxeris
laudāverit	monuerit	dūxerit
laudāverimus	monuerimus	dūxerimus
laudāveritis	monueritis	dūxeritis
laudāverint	monuerint	dūxerint
cēperim	audīverim	fuerim
cēperis	audīveris	fueris
cēperit	audīverit	fuerit
cēperimus	audīverimus	fuerimus
cēperitis	audīveritis	fueritis
cēperint	audīverint	fuerint

> *Note:* Although these forms are largely identical with those of the future-perfect indicative, context will help to distinguish them.

b. Passive The passive forms of the perfect subjunctive are made up of the perfect participle and the present subjunctive of **sum**.

laudātus, -a, -um sim	monitus, -a, -um sim
laudātus, -a, -um sīs	monitus, -a, -um sīs
laudātus, -a, -um sit	monitus, -a, -um sit

laudātī, -ae, -a sīmus	monitī, -ae, -a sīmus
laudātī, -ae, -a sītis	monitī, -ae, -a sītis
laudātī, -ae, -a sint	monitī, -ae, -a sint
ductus, -a, -um sim	captus, -a, -um sim
ductus, -a, -um sīs	captus, -a, -um sīs
ductus, -a, -um sit	captus, -a, -um sit
ductī, -ae, -a sīmus	captī, -ae, -a sīmus
ductī, -ae, -a sītis	captī, -ae, -a sītis
ductī, -ae, -a sint	captī, -ae, -a sint

auditus, -a, -um sim
auditus, -a, -um sīs
auditus, -a, -um sit

audītī, -ae, -a sīmus
audītī, -ae, -a sītis
audītī, -ae, -a sint

137. Direct Questions (3)

As Section 33 points out, a direct statement may be converted into a direct question by the addition of a question mark or by the suffixing of the enclitic particle **-ne** to the one word whose meaning calls the question into being. The answer may be either affirmative or negative.

a. Affirmative Answer Implied   When the speaker desires that his listener agree to the truth of a proposition, he may cast it in the form of a direct question introduced by **nōnne**, the signal that an affirmative answer is expected.

> **Nōnne Chrīstus iterum ventūrus est?**
> 'Christ is going to come again, is he not?'
> 'Is it not the case that Christ is going to come again?'

> Note that **nōnne** = **nōn** + **-ne**.

b. Negative Answer Implied   When the speaker desires that his listener assent to the falsity of a proposition, he may express it as a direct question introduced by **numquid**, the sign that a negative answer is expected.

Numquid Paulus Hierosolymīs interfectus est?
'Paul was not killed in Jerusalem, was he?'
'Is it not the case that Paul was not killed in Jerusalem?'

138. Indirect Questions

As in English, direct questions may be converted into dependent clauses, with a change in personal reference where logical: 'Where are my slippers?' indirectly quoted may become 'Your father is asking where his slippers are.' Cf. Section 7.

a. Introductory Words   Indirect questions may be introduced by **sī** 'if, whether' or any interrogative pronoun, adjective, or adverb.

b. Subjunctive   Since an indirect question is a subordinate clause, the mood of subordination, the subjunctive, is often used in place of an original indicative.

DIRECT: **Quārē Paulus Rōmam iit?**
'Why did Paul go to Rome?'

INDIRECT: **Discipulus rogat quārē Paulus Rōmam ierit.**
'The disciple is asking why Paul went to Rome.'

Note that the perfect subjunctive is required because it represents prior time in primary sequence (see Section 117).

c. Retained Indicative   An original indicative of a direct question may be retained when a question is indirectly expressed. English has no means to convey this nuance.

Discipulus rogat quārē Paulus Rōmam iit.
'The disciple is asking why Paul went to Rome.'

139. Dōnec *and* dum *Clauses*

Contemporaneity ('while, as long as') or expectancy ('until') may be expressed by clauses introduced by **dōnec** or **dum**. The indicative or the subjunctive occurs in these clauses, with no difference in meaning. Context determines whether time simultaneous or subsequent is intended.

Dōnec (dum) Paulus rediit, frātrēs erant maestī.
'Until Paul returned, his brothers were sad.'

Dōnec (dum) vīta est, spēs est.
'While/as long as there is life, there is hope.'

Missam nōn incipiēmus, dum (dōnec) antistes adveniat.
'We will not begin the Mass until the bishop arrives.'

Petrō occurrērunt, dum in viā ambulārent.
'They met Peter while they were walking on the road.'

140. *Interrogative Pronoun:* quis, quid

The interrogative pronoun **quis, quid** 'who, what' has plural forms which are identical with those of the interrogative adjective (see Section 53). The singular is as follows:

	M./F.	N.
Nom.	**quis** ('who?')	**quid** ('what?')
Gen.	**cujus** ('whose?')	**cujus** ('of what?')
Dat.	**cui** ('for/to whom?')	**cui** ('for/to what?')
Acc.	**quem** ('whom?')	**quid** ('what?')
Abl.	**quō** ('from/with/in/by whom?')	**quō** ('from/with/in/by what?')

Quis mē vocat?
'Who is calling me?'

Cujus liber est?
'Whose book is this?'

Ā quō Jēsūs trāditus est?
'By whom was Jesus betrayed?'

Quī sunt hī Chrīstiānī?
'Who are these Christians?'

Quibuscum Jēsūs Pascham mandūcāvit?
'With whom did Jesus eat the Pasch?'

Note that the preposition **cum** follows **quō** or **quibus** and coalesces with it: **quōcum, quibuscum.** Cf. Section 104.

---

141. Adverbial Accusative

Certain neuter pronouns and adjectives occur in the accusative case with an adverbial force. Among these are the following:

[ut] **quid** 'as to what, why'
nihil 'as to nothing, not at all'
quod sī 'as to which if, but if'
quod nisi 'as to which unless, but unless'
omnia 'as to all things, in all respects'

Quid in cīvitātem iniērunt?
'Why did they go into the city?'

Illī lēgem nihil faciunt.
'Those people do not keep the law at all.'

Quod sī Patrem invocāveritis, vōs audiet.
'But if you call upon the Father, he will hear you.'

Semper gaudeō, quoniam omnia fidēlēs remanētis.
'Always I rejoice because in all respects you are remaining faithful.'

Vocabulary

labōrō, labōrāre, labōrāvī, labōrātus work, labor

praestōlor, praestōlārī, —, praestōlātus sum wait for (+ *dat.* or *acc.*)

spīrō, spīrāre, spīrāvī, spīrātus breathe
    exspīrō, exspīrāre, exspīrāvī, exspīrātus die, expire

nesciō, nescīre, nescīvī (nesciī), nescītus not to know, be ignorant

indulgentia, indulgentiae, f. forgiveness, pardon, concession

lūcifer, lūciferī, m. daystar, morning star

patrōnus, patrōnī, m. defender, advocate

triumphus, triumphī, m. triumph

dēbitor, dēbitōris, m. debtor

doctor, doctōris, m. teacher

martyr, martyris, m. witness, martyr

acquīsītiō, acquīsītiōnis, f. purchase, acquisition

cōnsuētūdō, cōnsuētūdinis, f. custom

dogma, dogmatis, n. decision, dogma

iter, itineris, n. journey

peregrīnāns (*gen.*, **peregrīnan-**

tis) traveling *subst.*: (foreign) traveler, pilgrim

fortis, forte strong

spīrituālis, spīrituāle spiritual, of the spirit

an (1. *coord.* [*or subord.*] *conj.*, *introducing the second of two [in]direct questions*; 2. *interrog. adv.*) 1. or 2. can it be that?

dōnec (*subord. conj.*) while, as long as; until

dum (*subord. conj.*) while, as long as; until

numquid (*interrog. adv.*) *introduces a question expecting a negative reply*

quandō (1. *interrog. adv.*; 2. *subord. conj.*) 1. when? 2. when

quid (*interrog. adv.*) why? how? wherefore?

  ut quid (*interrog. adv.*) as to what? to what purpose? why?

quis, quid (1. *interrog. pron.*; 2. *indef. pron., after* **sī, nisi, numquid, nē**) 1. who? what? 2. someone, something; anyone, anything

quōmodo (*interrog. adv.*) in what manner? how?

Vocabulary Notes

Labōrō 'work' is unrelated to **lābor** 'fall' (Unit 23).

Nesciō is the verb **sciō** (Unit 6) with the negative prefix **ne-**. It has a shorter perfect active form—**nesciī**—whereas **sciō** only has the longer form—**scīvī**.

Lūcifer 'daystar' literally means 'light-bearer.'

Dēbitor is the agent noun from **dēbeō** (Unit 12).

Doctor is the agent noun from **doceō** 'teach' (Unit 19).

Spīrituālis, spīrituāle may also be spelled without the **-u-**.

When **quis, quid** 'who? what?' is not used to ask a question and occurs in a clause introduced by **sī, nisi, numquid,** or **nē**, it means 'someone, something; anyone, anything.' A related word with these latter meanings (i.e., **aliquis, aliquid**) will be presented in Unit 31.

Derivatives:	LATIN	ENGLISH
	labōrō	elaboration, laboratory
	spīrō	spiracle, spirant
	nesciō	nice, nescience
	indulgentia	plenary indulgence
	lūcifer	Lucifer, luciferin
	patrōnus	patron, patronage
	doctor	Doctor of the Church, doctoral

Derivatives:

LATIN	ENGLISH
iter	itinerary, itinerant
peregrīnāns	peregrination, peregrine falcon
fortis	fort, fortitude, fortissimo
quis	quiddity, quidnunc, quid pro quo

Drills

I. Indirect questions.

1. Scīs sī Paulus advēnerit?
2. Rogāvit quārē mulierēs plangerent.
3. Petrus scīvit ubi Jēsūs docuisset.
4. Discipulus rogābat quandō Paulus interfectus est ā Rōmānīs.
5. Audīstis sī Paulus Petrum vidēbit?

II. Quis, quid.

1. Sī quis esse salvus vult, mē sequātur.
2. Nisi quis huic miserō succurrerit, certē moriētur.
3. Ā quō liber scrīptus est? An ā Jōanne?
4. Quōcum Petrus cēnābat?
5. Quibus verbīs apostolī ā Jēsū doctī sunt?
6. Quae fēsta celebrās?
7. Quid in agrō vīdistī?
8. Quid pānem nōn cēpit?
9. Cui corōnam dabunt?
10. Quem Rēgem Jūdaeōrum vocābant?
11. Quōrum est rēgnum caelōrum?
12. Quis est mea māter? Quī sunt meī frātrēs?

Exercises

I.

1. Et interrogābat quis esset et quid fēcisset. Acts xxi, 33.
2. Quem vultis dīmittam vōbīs: Barabbam an Jēsum, quī dīcitur Chrīstus? Mt. xxvii, 17.
3. Numquid Paulus crucifīxus est prō vōbīs, aut in nōmine Paulī baptizātī estis? I Cor. i, 13.
4. Sī terrēna dīxī vōbīs, et nōn crēditis, quōmodo, sī dīxerō vōbīs caelestia, crēdētis? Jn. iii, 12.

However there is a custom for you, such that I release one unto you during the passover, do you wish therefore that I release the king of the Jews.

Exercises 229

5. Est autem cōnsuētūdō vōbīs, ut ūnum dīmittam vōbīs in Pascha; vultis ergo dīmittam vōbīs rēgem Jūdaeōrum? Jn. xviii, 39.

6. Quis nōs sēparābit ā cāritāte Chrīstī? Rom. viii, 35.

7. Sī quis vidētur prophēta esse aut spīritālis, cognōscat, quae scrībō vōbīs, quia Dominī est mandātum. I Cor. xiv, 37.

8. Ō homō, sed tū quis es, quī respondeās Deō? Rom. ix, 20.

9. Laudō autem vōs quod omnia meī memorēs estis. I Cor. xi, 2.

10. Et ēgressus ībat secundum cōnsuētūdinem in montem Olīvārum (= Olīvētī). Lk. xxii, 39.

11. Dīcō enim vōbīs: Nōn mandūcābō illud, dōnec impleātur in rēgnō Deī. Lk. xxii, 16.

12. Ecclēsiam tuam, peregrīnantem in terrā, in fidē et cāritāte firmāre dignēris cum famulō tuō Pāpā nostrō Jōanne Paulō et Episcopō nostrō N., cum episcopālī ōrdine et ūniversō clērō et omnī populō acquīsītiōnis tuae.

13. Lūciferō ortō, in nōs in dogma resurrēctiōnis crēdentēs nova vīta spīrāta est.

14. Quōmodo igitur apertī sunt oculī tibi? Jn. ix, 10.

15. An nescītis quoniam corpus vestrum templum est Spīritūs Sānctī, quī in vōbīs est, quem habētis ā Deō, et nōn estis vestrī? I Cor. vi, 19.

16. Nōnne Mōysēs dedit vōbīs lēgem? Jn. vii, 19.

17. Hoc autem dīcō secundum indulgentiam, nōn secundum imperium. I Cor. vii, 6.

18. An nescītis quoniam sānctī dē mundō jūdicābunt? I Cor. vi, 2.

19. Quid mē interrogās? Interroga eōs, quī audiērunt quid locūtus sum ipsīs; ecce hī sciunt, quae dīxerim ego. Jn. xviii, 21.

20. Et sī quis vōbīs dīxerit: "Quid facitis hoc?," dīcite: "Dominō necessārius est." Mk. xi, 3.

21. Respondēns autem Jūdās, quī trādidit eum, dīxit: "Numquid ego sum, Rabbī?" Mt. xxvi, 25.

22. Et observābant eum, sī sabbatīs cūrāret illum. Mk. iii, 2.

23. Et dīmitte nōbīs dēbita nostra, sīcut et nōs dīmittimus dēbitōribus nostrīs. Mt. vi, 12.

24. Dum Jēsū doctōrī praestōlantur, discipulī, stantēs in fidē fortēs, in domō ōrābant.

25. Magister, quid bonī faciam, ut habeam vītam aeternam? Mt. xix, 16.

26. Sāncte Petre, patrōne noster, dūc martyrēs labōrantēs prō Dominō ad triumphum.

27. Manifestum ('clear') enim quod ex Jūdā ortus sit Dominus noster. Heb. vii, 14.

28. Peregrīnantēs in terrā facimus iter ad rēgnum caelōrum.

29. Ergō, frātrēs, dēbitōrēs sumus, nōn carnī, ut secundum carnem vīvāmus. Rom. viii, 12.

30. Quid mihi prōdest? sī mortuī nōn resurgunt, *mandūcēmus et bibāmus, crās* ('tomorrow') *enim moriēmur.* I Cor. xv, 32.

31. Quōmodo potest hic nōbīs carnem suam ('his own') dare ad mandūcandum? Jn. vi, 52.

32. Quid ergō dīcēmus ad haec? Sī Deus prō nōbīs, quis contrā ('against') nōs? Rom. viii, 31.

33. Sed et sī quid patiminī propter jūstitiam, beātī! I Pet. iii, 14.

34. Mystērium fideī: mortem tuam annūntiāmus, Domine, et tuam resurrēctiōnem cōnfitēmur, dōnec veniās.

35. Quōmodo autem nunc videat nescīmus, aut quis ejus aperuit oculōs nōs nescīmus. Jn. ix, 21.

36. Quis reddere potest, id quod perditum est?

37. Et ecce clāmāvērunt dīcentēs: "Quid nōbīs et tibi, Fīlī Deī?" Mt. viii, 29.

38. Nam semper pauperēs habētis vōbīscum, mē autem nōn semper habētis. Mt. xxvi, 11.

II. 1. Do you know when Jesus breathed life into the daughter of the Roman soldier?
2. While we are working, we are praying.
3. In behalf of whom did the first martyrs die?
4. The boy is asking his teacher why the martyr was not buried according to the custom of the Jews.
5. a) Did John write this book?
   b) John wrote this book, didn't he?
   c) John didn't write this book, did he?

Readings

1. The Last Supper, as understood by Paul, I Cor. xi, 23–26.
Ego enim accēpī ā Dominō, quod et trādidī vōbīs, quoniam Dominus Jēsūs, in quā nocte[1] trādēbātur, accēpit pānem et grātiās

[1] in quā nocte = in nocte in quā

agēns frēgit et dīxit: *"Hoc est corpus meum, quod prō vōbīs est;*
hoc facite in meam commemorātiōnem"; similiter[2] et calicem,
postquam cēnātum est, dīcēns: *"Hic calix novum testāmentum*
est in meō sanguine; hoc facite, quotiēnscumque[3] bibētis, in
meam commemorātiōnem." Quotiēnscumque[3] enim mandūcā-
bitis pānem hunc et calicem bibētis, mortem Dominī annūn-
tiātis dōnec veniat.

[2]**similiter**: *adv. from* **similis, -e** [3]**quotiēnscumque** (*adv.*) as often as

2. Avē, rēgīna caelōrum,
    avē, domina[1] angelōrum,
    salvē, rādīx,[2] salvē, porta,[3]
    ex quā mundō lūx est orta:
    gaudē, virgō glōriōsa,
    super omnēs speciōsa,[4]
    valē, Ō valdē decōra,[5]
    et prō nōbīs Chrīstum exōrā.

[1]**domina, dominae**, f. mistress, lady [2]**rādīx, rādīcis**, f. root, source [3]**porta, portae**,
f. gate [4]**speciōsus, -a, -um** beautiful [5]**decōrus, -a, -um** fitting, decorous

Unit 27

142. Comparison of Adjectives: Positive, Comparative, and Superlative

In English, the positive degree of an adjective is the uncompared form: 'Daniel is *tall*.' The comparative degree involves a comparison between two: 'Daniel is *taller* than Stephen.' The superlative degree is the extreme degree of an adjective, usually involving three or more (whether expressed or implied): 'Of all his brothers Daniel is the *tallest*.' The suffixes *-er* and *-est* are regularly added to the positive degree of an adjective to make the other two degrees: tall, taller, tallest; where this suffixing would be awkward, *more* and *most* are used instead: *more* delightful (not *delightfuler), *most* delightful (not *delightfulest). Some adjectives in English have irregular comparisons: e.g., good, better, best (not good, *gooder, *goodest).

Latin, too, has a) suffixes which indicate the comparative and superlative degrees, b) adjectives which are irregular in their comparison, and c) occasionally, separate adverbs to do the work of the comparative and superlative suffixes.

a. Forms   Any adjective of either type (i.e., first/second declension adjectives or third declension adjectives) is declined as a third declension adjective of two endings when used in the comparative degree. This is formed by adding the suffix **-iōr-** to the adjective base before adding the endings of the third declension; the masculine/feminine nominative singular has **-ior**, the neuter nominative singular **-ius**.

beātus, -a, -um 'blessed/happy'; **beātior, beātius** 'happier'

SINGULAR		PLURAL	
M./F.	N.	M./F.	N.
beātior	beātius	beātiōrēs	beātiōra
beātiōris	beātiōris	beātiōrum	beātiōrum

SINGULAR		PLURAL	
M./F.	N.	M./F.	N.
beātiōrī	beātiōrī	beātiōribus	beātiōribus
beātiōrem	beātius	beātiōrēs	beātiōra
beātiōre	beātiōre	beātiōribus	beātiōribus

fēlīx (*gen.*, **fēlīcis**) 'happy, blessed'; **fēlīcior, fēlīcius** 'happier'

SINGULAR		PLURAL	
M./F.	N.	M./F.	N.
fēlīcior	fēlīcius	fēlīciōrēs	fēlīciōra
fēlīciōris	fēlīciōris	fēlīciōrum	fēlīciōrum
fēlīciōrī	fēlīciōrī	fēlīciōribus	fēlīciōribus
fēlīciōrem	fēlīcius	fēlīciōrēs	fēlīciōra
fēlīciōre	fēlīciōre	fēlīciōribus	fēlīciōribus

> *Note:* Although comparatives use third declension endings, they are not declined like i-stem nouns (see Section 85).

Any adjective of either type is declined as a first/second declension adjective when used in the superlative degree. This is formed by adding the suffix **-issim-** to the adjective base before adding the endings of the first and second declensions.

beātus, -a, -um 'blessed, happy':
  beātissimus, -a, -um 'happiest'

fēlīx (*gen.*, **fēlīcis**) 'happy, blessed':
  fēlīcissimus, -a, -um 'happiest'

> *Notes:* 1. Adjectives in **-er** in the masculine nominative singular add *to this form* (not to the adjective base) the suffix **-rim-**: **ācer, ācris, ācre: ācerrimus, -a, -um.**
> 2. Adjectives ending in **-ilis** in the masculine/feminine nominative singular add to the base **-lim-**: **similis, -e: simillimus, -a, -um.**

Some common adjectives have irregular comparisons:

bonus, -a, -um	**melior, melius**	**optimus, -a, -um**
'good'	'better'	'best'

Fraser   *U S*

malus, -a, -um 'bad'	pejor, pejus 'worse'	pessimus, -a, -um 'worst'
magnus, -a, -um 'great'	major, majus 'greater'	maximus, -a, -um 'greatest'
multus, -a, -um 'much, many'	plūs (indecl.); plūrēs, plūra 'more'	plūrimus, -a, -um 'most, very many'
parvus, -a, -um 'small'	minor, minus 'smaller'	minimus, -a, -um 'smallest'
prope (adv.) 'near'	propior, propius 'nearer'	proximus, -a, -um 'nearest, next'
prae, prō (prep.) 'before'	prior, prius 'former, earlier'	prīmus, -a, -um 'first'
superus, -a, -um 'above'	superior, superius 'higher, upper'	suprēmus, -a, -um summus, -a, -um 'highest'

b. Uses   In general, these three degrees are used as they are in English, i.e., when comparison is expressed or implied: **beātior vir** 'a happier man' (than another), **beātissimus vir** 'the happiest man' (of all). But when the comparison is more remote, then 'rather' and 'very' may be used to translate the comparative and the superlative: **beātior vir** 'a rather happy man,' **beātissimus vir** 'a very happy man.'

When the comparative degree is used to express an *explicit* comparison, the adverb **quam** 'than' may be used; the comparands have the same case on either side of **quam**: *Petrus* **erat fēlīcior quam** *Jōannēs* '*Peter* was happier than *John*.' Note that in both languages there is ellipsis: **Petrus erat fēlīcior quam Jōannēs [erat fēlīx]** 'Peter was happier than John [was happy].'

Occasionally the comparative degree is employed where English would prefer the superlative degree: *major* **est cāritās** 'the *greatest* is charity.'

When the superlative degree is used, it may be strengthened by a partitive genitive: **Petrus erat fēlīcissimus omnium apostolōrum** 'Peter was the happiest of all the apostles.'

Notes: 1. The equivalent of the comparative or the superlative may be formed by using the adverbs **magis** 'more' or **maximē** 'most' with the *positive* degree: **magis beātus** 'happier'; **maximē beātus** 'happiest.'

Notes continued:
>   2. When **novus, -a, -um** 'new, recent' is used in the superlative it often means 'last, latest': **in novissimō diē** 'on the last day.'
>   3. Note that such a phrase as **ante/super omnēs bonus** 'good before/over all' is a periphrasis for 'best of all.'

---

143. *Ablative of Comparison*

The second of the two comparands in a comparison may employ the ablative case; this construction does not use **quam**.

> **Petrus erat fēlīcior *Jōanne.***
> 'Peter was happier than *John.*'

> *Note:* This ablative construction is used only if the first comparand is in either the nominative or the accusative case; otherwise, to avoid confusion, the **quam** construction is employed.

---

144. *Ablative of Degree of Difference*

The ablative of a noun or a neuter adjective indicating some measurement or intensity may accompany an adjective in the comparative or superlative degree.

> **Haec mēnsa est *pede* altior quam illa.**
> 'This table is higher *by a foot* than that one.'
> 'This table is a foot higher than that one.'

> **Petrus erat *multō* fēlīcior quam Jōannēs.**
> 'Peter was happier *by much* than John.'
> 'Peter was much happier than John.'

> **Illa diēs erat *multō* maestissima omnium.**
> 'That day was (*by*) *much* the saddest one of all.'

Vocabulary

lavō, lavāre, lāvī, lautus (lōtus)
wash; *pass.*, be washed,
bathe

fulgeō, fulgēre, fulsī, — shine,
glow

 **circumfulgeō, circumfulgēre,
circumfulsī, —** shine
around

 refulgeō, refulgēre, refulsī, —
shine brightly, gleam

mereō, merēre, meruī, meritus
be worthy, deserve

emō, emere, ēmī, ēmptus buy

 **redimō, redimere, redēmī,
redēmptus** buy back,
redeem

pāscō, pāscere, pāvī, pāstus
feed

**statuō, statuere, statuī, sta-
tūtus** establish, appoint,
determine

 **cōnstituō, cōnstituere, cōn-
stituī, cōnstitūtus** decree,
ordain

īra, īrae, f. anger, wrath

synagōga, synagōgae, f.
congregation, synagogue

Pontius Pīlātus, Pontiī Pīlātī,
m. Pontius Pilatus, Pilate

pretium, pretiī, n. price;
ransom

sīgnum, sīgnī, n. sign; miracle

labor, labōris, m. work, labor

odor, odōris, m. aroma, odor

gēns, gentis, gentium, f. nation; *pl.*, nations, Gentiles

virtūs, virtūtis, f. excellence,
virtue; power, strength;
pl., miracles

vōx, vōcis, f. sound, voice

salūtāre, salūtāris, salūtārium,
n. salvation

tempus, temporis, n. time

faciēs, faciēī, f. face [i.e.,
appearance]

genitus, -a, -um begotten,
engendered

suāvis, suāve sweet

ait; aiunt (*defective verb*)
he says; they say

magis (*adv.*) more

nōndum (*adv.*) not yet

quam (1. *adv.*; 2. *coord. conj.*)
1. how, how much; as . . as
possible (*with positive or
superlative*) 2. than (*in
comparisons*)

quō (*interrog. & rel. adv.*)
(to) where

tantum (*adv.*) only

unde (*interrog. & rel. adv.*)
from where

Vocabulary Notes

The third principal part of **lavō**, a first conjugation verb, is **lāvī** (not
*lavāvī). **Lautus** and **lōtus** are alternative spellings of the perfect passive participle. When used in the passive, **lavō** may have a reflexive
force (like that of the Greek middle voice): 'to wash oneself, to bathe.'

Mereō is often followed by an object infinitive: **mereō facere** 'I
deserve to do.' This is the equivalent of **meritō faciō** 'I rightly/
deservedly do.'

Statuō may take the indirect command construction, **ut** + subjunctive.

In works written from a Jewish perspective, **gēns** in the plural may mean 'Gentiles,' i.e., non-Jews; but from a Christian perspective, 'heathens,' i.e., non-Christians.

Salūtāre is the neuter of the adjective **salūtāris, -e** (Unit 16) used substantively.

Ait and **aiunt** are present tense forms, but often are used to represent a past tense: 'he says, he said; they say, they said.'

Besides being employed in comparisons, **quam** may modify an adjective, often in an exclamation: **quam bonus es!** 'how good you are!' It may also intensify a positive or a superlative with the meaning 'as . . as possible': **puer erat quam laetus/laetissimus** 'the boy was as joyful as possible.'

Quō refers to motion to which; **unde**, motion from which.

Tantum means 'only' in the sense 'just so much and no more.'

Derivatives:	LATIN	ENGLISH
	lavō	Lavabo, lavatory, lotion, laundry
	refulgeō	refulgent
	mereō	merit, emeritus
	emō	caveat emptor
	redimō	redeem, redemption
	pāscō	pasture, pasta
	statuō	statute
	cōnstituō	constituent, constitution
	īra	ire, irate, irascible
	pretium	praise, price, prize
	gēns	gentle, genteel, jaunty
	tempus	tempo, temporary, temporal, tense
	faciēs	prima facie, facet
	genitus	genital
	suāvis	suave

Drills

I. Comparative and superlative adjectives.

1. Hic Lēvīta est omnium fidēlissimus.
2. Quis dīgnior est quam tū?

3. Cārissimī frātrēs, quid est mīrius Jēsū resurrēctiōne?
4. Glōria in altissimīs Deō.
5. Illa ecclēsia erat marī proxima.
6. In novissimō diē omnēs resurgēmus.
7. Nōs creātī sumus paulō minōrēs quam angelī.
8. Quis habet dīlēctiōnem majōrem hāc?
9. Plūrēs hominēs in templum conveniēbant.
10. Seniōrēs Jēsūm observābant.
11. Hī sunt multō pejōrēs illīs.
12. Dā hoc miserrimō in vōbīs.
13. Ego Alpha et Ōmega, prīmus et novissimus, prīncipium et
    fīnis. Rev. xxii, 13.

Exercises

I.
1. Et veniēns in patriam suam ('his own'), docēbat eōs in
   synagōgā eōrum, ita ut mīrārentur et dīcerent: "Unde huic
   sapientia haec et virtūtēs?" Mt. xiii, 54.
2. [Crēdō in] Deum dē Deō, lūmen dē lūmine, Deum vērum
   dē Deō vērō, genitum, nōn factum.
3. Grātiās agimus Deō semper prō omnibus vōbīs,
   memoriam facientēs in ōrātiōnibus nostrīs, sine
   intermissiōne ('interruption') memorēs operis fideī vestrae
   et labōris cāritātis. I Thess. i, 2–3.
4. Ō inaestimābilis ('priceless') dīlēctiō cāritātis: ut servum
   redimerēs, Fīlium trādidistī!
5. Et clāritās Deī circumfulsit illōs. Lk. ii, 9.
6. Tempus meum nōndum adest, tempus autem vestrum
   semper est parātum. Jn. vii, 6.
7. Quī amat patrem aut mātrem plūs quam mē, nōn est mē
   dīgnus. Mt. x, 37.
8. Dīxit ergō eīs Pīlātus: "Accipite eum vōs et secundum
   lēgem vestram jūdicāte eum!" Jn. xviii, 31.
9. Ēmptī enim estis pretiō! Glōrificāte ergō Deum in corpore
   vestrō. I Cor. vi, 20.
10. Quī ergō solverit ūnum dē mandātīs istīs minimīs et
    docuerit sīc hominēs, minimus vocābitur in rēgnō
    caelōrum. Mt. v, 19.
11. Respondit Pīlātus: "Numquid ego Jūdaeus sum?"
    Jn. xviii, 35.
12. Posuī tē in lūcem gentium. Acts xiii, 47.

13. Sī dīligerētis mē, gaudērētis quia vādō ad Patrem, quia Pater major mē est. Jn. xiv, 28.

14. Jugum ('yoke') enim meum suāve est. Mt. xi, 30.

15. Beātius est magis dare quam accipere! Acts xx, 35.

16. "Simōn Jōannis, dīligis mē plūs hīs?" Dīcit eī: "Etiam, Domine, tū scīs quia amō tē." Dīcit eī: "Pāsce agnōs meōs." Jn. xxi, 15.

17. Venit ergō ad Simōnem Petrum. Dīcit eī: "Domine, tū mihi lavās pedēs?" Respondit Jēsus et dīcit eī: "Quod ego faciō, tū nescīs modo ('just now'), sciēs autem posteā." Dīcit eī Petrus: "Nōn lavābis mihi pedēs in aeternum!" Respondit Jēsūs eī: "Sī nōn lāverō tē, nōn habēs partem mēcum." Dīcit eī Simōn Petrus: "Domine, nōn tantum pedēs meōs, sed et manūs et caput!" Jn. xiii, 6–9.

18. Haec dīxit Īsaiās ('Isaiah'), quia vīdit glōriam ejus et locūtus est de eō. Jn. xii, 41.

19. Domine, nescīmus quō vādis; quōmodo possumus viam scīre? Jn. xiv, 5.

20. Spīritus, ubi vult, spīrat, et vōcem ejus audīs, sed nōn scīs unde veniat et quō vādat; sīc est omnis, quī nātus est ex Spīritū. Jn. iii, 8.

21. Et ait illī: "Ego veniam et cūrābō eum." Et respondēns centuriō ('centurion') ait: "Domine, nōn sum dīgnus, ut intrēs sub tēctum meum, sed tantum dīc verbō, et sānābitur puer meus. Nam et ego homō sub potestāte, habēns sub mē mīlitēs, et dīcō huic: 'Vāde,' et vādit, et aliī ('to another'): 'Venī,' et venit, et servō meō: 'Fac hoc,' et facit." Audiēns autem Jēsūs, mīrātus est et sequentibus sē ('him') dīxit: "Āmēn dīcō vōbīs: Apud nūllum (= 'never') invēnī tantam fidem in Israēl." Mt. viii, 7–10.

22. Dīrigātur, Domine, ōrātiō mea, sīcut incēnsum, in cōnspectū tuō.

23. Dīcit illīs Pīlātus: "Quid igitur faciam dē Jēsū, quī dīcitur Chrīstus?" Dīcunt omnēs: "Crucifīgātur!" Ait autem: "Quid enim malī fēcit?" At illī magis clāmābant dīcentēs: "Crucifīgātur!" Mt. xxvii, 22–23.

24. Sit autem omnis homō vēlōx ('quick') ad audiendum, tardus ('slow') autem ad loquendum et tardus ad īram; īra enim virī jūstitiam Deī nōn operātur. James i, 19–20.

25. Circumībō altāre tuum, Domine, ut audiam vōcem laudis tuī.

26. Ego semper docuī in synagōgā et in templō, quō omnēs Jūdaeī conveniunt. Jn. xviii, 20.

27. Quō hic itūrus est, quia nōs nōn inveniēmus eum? Jn. vii, 35.

28. [Et cōnstituistī eum super opera manuum tuārum.] Heb. ii, 7.

29. Dīcit eī Simōn Petrus: "Domine, quō vādis?" Respondit Jēsūs: "Quō vādō, nōn potes mē modo ('now') sequī, sequēris autem posteā." Jn. xiii, 36.

30. Eme ea, quae opus sunt nōbīs ad diem fēstum. Jn. xiii, 29.

31. Āmēn dīcō vōbīs: Nōn surrēxit inter nātōs mulierum major Jōanne Baptistā; quī autem minor est in rēgnō caelōrum, major est illō. Mt. xi, 11.

32. In illō tempore respondēns Jēsūs dīxit: "Cōnfiteor tibi, Pater, Domine caelī et terrae." Mt. xi, 25.

33. Baptismum (= baptisma) Jōannis unde erat? Ā caelō an ex hominibus? Mt. xxi, 25.

34. At (= sed) illī īnstābant vōcibus magnīs postulantēs, ut crucifīgerētur. Lk. xxiii, 23.

35. Major autem ex hīs est cāritās. I Cor. xiii, 13.

36. Multīs passeribus ('sparrows') meliōrēs estis vōs. Mt. x, 31.

37. Statuērunt, ut ascenderent Paulus et Barnabās. Acts xv, 2.

38. Euntēs ergō docēte omnēs gentēs. Mt. xxviii, 19.

39. Virī frātrēs, vōs scītis quoniam ab antīquīs diēbus in vōbīs ēlēgit Deus per ōs meum audīre gentēs verbum evangeliī et crēdere. Acts, xv, 7.

40. Quī post mē ventūrus est, ante mē factus est, quia prior mē erat. Jn. i, 15.

41. Ō fēlīx culpa, quae tālem ac tantum meruit habēre Redēmptōrem!

42. Faciem quidem caelī dījūdicāre nōstis (= nōvistis), sīgna autem temporum nōn potestis. Mt. xvi, 3.

43. Et exsultāvit spīritus meus in Deō salvātōre meō. Lk. i, 47.

44. Et in odōrem suāvitātis acceptus, supernīs lūmināribus ('lights') misceātur!

45. Laudāte Dominum, omnēs gentēs; laudāte eum, omnēs populī. Ps. cxvii, 1.

II.   1. Which is the greatest commandment of all?

2. The elders and the priests of the temple were watching Jesus, to see what he would do.

3. May the rather sweet odor of this incense, blessed by you, ascend to you, O Lord.

4. What is more important (i.e., greater) than the love of God and neighbor?

Readings

1. The Marriage Feast at Cana, Jn. ii, 1–11.

Et diē tertiō nuptiae[1] factae sunt in Cana[2] Galilaeae, et erat māter Jēsū ibi; vocātus est autem et Jēsūs et discipulī ejus ad nuptiās.[1] Et dēficiente vīnō, dīcit māter Jēsū ad eum: "Vīnum nōn habent." Et dīcit eī Jēsūs: "Quid mihi et tibi, mulier? Nōndum vēnit hōra mea." Dīcit māter ejus ministrīs: "Quodcumque dīxerit vōbīs, facite." Erant autem ibi lapideae[3] hydriae[4] sex[5] positae secundum pūrificātiōnem[6] Jūdaeōrum, capientēs[7] singulae[8] metrētās[9] bīnās[10] vel ternās.[11] Dīcit eīs Jēsūs: "Implēte hydriās[4] aquā." Et implēvērunt eās ūsque ad summum.[12] Et dīcit eīs: "Haurīte[13] nunc et ferte[14] architrīclīnō."[15] Illī autem tulērunt.[16] Ut autem gustāvit[17] architrīclīnus[15] aquam vīnum factam et nōn sciēbat unde esset, ministrī autem sciēbant, quī haurierant[13] aquam, vocat spōnsum[18] architrīclīnus[15] et dīcit eī: "Omnis homō prīmum bonum vīnum pōnit et, cum inēbriātī fuerint,[19] id quod dēterius[20] est; tū servāstī bonum vīnum ūsque adhūc." Hoc fēcit initium[21] sīgnōrum Jēsūs in Cana Galilaeae et manifestāvit[22] glōriam suam,[23] et crēdidērunt in eum discipulī ejus.

[1]**nuptiae, nuptiārum,** f. marriage, wedding [2]**Cana** (*indecl. noun*) Cana, village 4 miles NE of Nazareth [3]**lapideus, -a, -um** (made of) stone [4]**hydria, hydriae,** f. water jar [5]**sex** (*indecl. adj.*) six [6]**pūrificātiō, pūrificātiōnis,** f. ceremonial washing [7]**capientēs** *here,* holding (cf. capacity) [8]**singulī, -ae, -a,** each one [9]**metrēta, metrētae,** f. a liquid measure (about 9 gallons) [10]**bīnī, -ae, -a** two each [11]**ternī, -ae, -a** three each [12]**summum, summī,** n. the top [13]**hauriō, haurīre, hausī, haustus** draw out [14]**ferte** 'bring' [15]**architrīclīnus, architrīclīnī,** m. head waiter [16]**tulērunt** 'they brought' [17]**gustō, gustāre, gustāvī, gustātus** taste [18]**spōnsus, spōnsī,** m. bridegroom [19]**inēbriō, inēbriāre, inēbriāvī, inēbriātus** intoxicate, make drunk [inēbriātī fuerint = inēbriātī sint] [20]**dēterius** (*comp. adj.*) 'worse, less good' [21]**initium, initiī,** n. beginning [22]**manifestō, manifestāre, manifestāvī, manifestātus** make clear, reveal [23]**suam** 'his own'

2. Rēgīna caelī, laetāre, allēlūjā,
   quia quem meruistī portāre, allēlūjā,
   resurrēxit sīcut dīxit, allēlūjā,
   ōrā prō nōbīs Deum, allēlūjā.

3. The Family of Jesus, Mk. iii, 31–35.

Et venit māter ejus et frātrēs ejus et forīs[1] stantēs mīsērunt ad eum vocantēs eum. Et sedēbat circā eum turba, et dīcunt eī:

[1]**forīs** (*adv.*) outside

"Ecce māter tua et frātrēs tuī et sorōrēs[2] tuae forīs[1] quaerunt[3] tē." Et respondēns eīs ait: "Quae est māter mea, et frātrēs meī?" Et circumspiciēns eōs quī in circuitū[4] ejus sedēbant, ait: "Ecce māter mea et frātrēs meī. Quī enim fēcerit voluntātem Deī, hic frāter meus et soror[2] mea et māter est."

[2] **soror, sorōris,** f. sister [3] **quaerō, quaerere, quaesīvī, quaesītus** ask for, seek [4] **circuitus, circuitūs,** m. circle

Unit 28

145. *Reflexive Adjective and Pronoun:* suus; —, suī

An adjective or pronoun which refers to the subject of a sentence is termed a reflexive. In the first and second persons, the reflexive forms are identical with the first and second person pronouns and pronominal adjectives: **ego dīligō** *mē* 'I love *myself*'; **tū dīligis** *tē* 'you love *yourself*'; **ego habeō** *meum* **librum** 'I have *my* (*own*) book'; **tū habēs** *tuum* **librum** 'you have *your* (*own*) book,' etc.

But in the third person there are separate forms for the reflexive: the adjective **suus, -a, -um** 'one's own' and the pronoun —, **suī** 'oneself.' **Suus, -a, -um** is an adjective of the first and second declensions. The third person reflexive pronoun is declined as follows:

SINGULAR/PLURAL

Nom.	—
Gen.	**suī**
Dat.	**sibi**
Acc.	**sē**
Abl.	**sē**

Notes: 1. Logically, this pronoun has no nominative form, since its use is confined to the reflexive idea.
2. These forms—**suus, -a, -um** and —, **suī**—are used to refer either to a singular or to a plural subject.
3. The adjective has nominative forms, since its referend may also occur as the subject in the preceding clause.
4. As it is with other pronouns, the preposition **cum** is used enclitically: **sēcum.**

Hic dīligit sē.
'This man loves himself.'

Hae dīligunt sē.
'These women love themselves.'

Hī dīligunt suōs frātrēs.
'These men love their (own) brothers.'

Vēnit, sed suī eum nōn cognōvērunt.
'He came, but his own people did not know him.'

Note that in this last example **suī**, the reflexive adjective used substantively, is the nominative subject of its own sentence; a reflexive form has been used because it refers to the subject of the preceding clause. **Eum**, the object of **cognōvērunt**, is not a reflexive because it does not refer to the subject of its sentence.

In English 'he saw his brothers' is ambiguous: is 'his' reflexive or not? In Latin there is no ambiguity: **vīdit frātrēs ejus** 'he saw the brothers of that man'; **vīdit suōs frātrēs** 'he saw his (own) brothers.'

146. Six Partly Irregular Adjectives

Some otherwise regular adjectives of the first and second declensions are irregular only in their genitive and dative singular forms. The most common are **alius, alia, aliud** 'other, another'; **alter, altera, alterum** 'the other (of two)'; **nūllus, nūlla, nūllum** 'not any, no'; **sōlus, sōla, sōlum** 'only, alone'; **tōtus, tōta, tōtum** 'all, the whole'; **ūnus, ūna, ūnum** 'one; a, an' (already introduced in Unit 7).

ūnus, -a, -um 'one; a, an'

SINGULAR

	M.	F.	N.
Nom.	ūnus	ūna	ūnum
Gen.	ūn*īus*	ūn*īus*	ūn*īus*
Dat.	ūn*ī*	ūn*ī*	ūn*ī*
Acc.	ūnum	ūnam	ūnum
Abl.	ūnō	ūnā	ūnō

> *Notes:* 1. **ūnus, -a, -um** (quite logically) has no plural; the plurals of the other five adjectives are regular, if they occur.
>
> 2. These genitive and dative singular forms have already been encountered in the demonstrative and intensive pronouns (see Sections 122, 123, and 127).

147. Comparison of Adverbs

For the *positive* degree, adjectives of the first and second declensions form their adverbs by adding **-ē** to the base; third declensions add **-iter** to the base. For all comparative forms of adjectives the adverb of the *comparative* degree is identical with the neuter accusative singular. For all *superlative* degree of the adverb is formed by adding **-ē** to the base of the superlative form of the adjective.

aptus, -a, -um: ('suitable')	**aptē** ('suitably')	**aptius** ('more suitably')	**aptissimē** ('most suitably')
suāvis, suāve: ('sweet')	**suāviter** ('sweetly')	**suāvius** ('more sweetly')	**suāvissimē** ('most sweetly')

> *Notes:* 1. Exceptions occur, but only in the formation of the positive degree. These are the three main types: a) those in **-um** (the neuter accusative singular), e.g., **tantum** 'only' or **multum** 'much'; b) those in **-ō** (the neuter ablative singular), e.g., **meritō** 'rightly'; c) those in **-e**, e.g., **bene** 'well' and **male** 'poorly, badly.'
>
> 2. **Novissimē** 'most recently' may mean 'finally, at last.' Cf. Section 142b, Note 2.
>
> 3. **Quam** may be used with a positive or superlative degree of an adverb: **quam suāviter/suāvissimē** 'as sweetly as possible.'

148. Cum *Clauses*

The subordinating conjunction **cum** has several distinct uses: it may be used to introduce purely temporal clauses, 'when' (see Section 69), temporal-circumstantial clauses, '(under the circumstances) when,' causal clauses, 'since,' and concessive clauses, 'although.' These last three constructions employ the subjunctive mood. Here English with its different subordinators is far less ambiguous; the precise translation of **cum** must be determined from a careful study of the context.

TEMPORAL-CIRCUMSTANTIAL: **Cum Jēsūs turbam docēret, quīdam eum accessit.**

'(Under the circumstances) when Jesus was teaching the crowd, a certain man approached him.'

CAUSAL: **Cum vir esset fēlīx, prae gaudiō clāmāvit.**

'Since the man was happy, he shouted for joy.'

CONCESSIVE: **Cum virī male habērent, labōrāre (tamen) nōn dēsiērunt.**

'Although the men were sick, (nevertheless) they did not stop working.'

Note that the recognition of the concessive use may be made easier by the presence of **tamen** in the main clause. Such is the case with the similarly adaptable construction, the ablative absolute (see Section 68).

Vocabulary

curvo, curvāre, curvāvī, curvātus bend; humble

fundō, fundāre, fundāvī, fundātus establish, found

magnificō, magnificāre, magnificāvī, magnificātus extol, praise, glorify

venerō, venerāre, venerāvī, venerātus

or

veneror, venerārī, —, venerātus sum worship, venerate

ardeō, ardēre, arsī, arsus burn

doleō, dolēre, doluī, dolitus grieve, suffer, feel pain

condoleō, condolēre, —, — feel severe pain, suffer

greatly; feel another's pain,
empathize with

moveō, movēre, mōvī, mōtus
move; affect

faciō:

   **īnficiō, īnficere, īnfēcī, īn-
fectus** infect, pollute

   **prōficiō, prōficere, prōfēcī,
prōfectus** avail; prevail

   **reficiō, reficere, refēcī, re-
fectus** refresh; repair

lingua, linguae, f. tongue;
language

umbra, umbrae, f. shadow,
shade

testis, testis, testium, m.
witness

praefātiō, praefātiōnis, f.
preface

prōtēctiō, prōtēctiōnis, f.
protection

quiēs, quiētis, f. peace, rest,
quiet

tentātiō, tentātiōnis, f.
temptation, trial

amplus, -a, -um abundant,
ample

   amplius (*comp. adv.*)
(any) more

perfectus, -a, -um perfect

suus, -a, -um (*third-person refl.
pron. adj.*) one's [own] (i.e.,
his/her/its/their [own])

gravis, grave heavy; serious,
grievous

trīstis, trīste sad, sorrowful,
gloomy

alius, alia, aliud other, another

alter, altera, alterum the other
(of two), the second

nūllus, -a, -um not any, no

sōlus, -a, -um only, alone

tōtus, -a, -um all, the whole

contrā (*prep. + acc.*) against,
opposite (to)

cum (*subord. conj.*) when,
after (+ *ind.*); (under the
circumstances) when, since,
although (+ *subj.*)

invicem (1. *adv.*; 2. *indecl.
reciprocal refl. pron.*)
   1. in turn 2. one another

—, suī (*refl. pron.*) oneself
(i.e., himself, herself, itself,
themselves)

Vocabulary Notes

Distinguish between **fundō, fundere, fūdī, fūsus** 'pour' (Unit 16)
and **fundō, fundāre, fundāvī, fundātus** 'establish, found.'

Magnificō is a multiple-base compound: **magnus** 'great' + a form
of **faciō** 'make.' See Vocabulary Notes, Unit 11.

Veneror, a deponent verb, has a collateral form, **venerō**. Context
will reveal whether a passive form is active or passive in meaning:
Dominus venerātus est 'the Lord was worshiped'; **Dominum venerātus est** 'he worshiped the Lord.'

Perhaps the most frequent form of **amplus** is its comparative adverb **amplius** 'any more, more.'

Perfectus is in reality the perfect passive participle of **perficiō** (Unit 18).

Suus 'one's own' takes its specific translation from its context, 'his own, her own, its own, their own,' depending on the gender and number of its referend.

Invicem, essentially an adverb, is often used in ecclesiastical texts as an indeclinable reciprocal reflexive pronoun; as such it may be used with a preposition: **ad invicem** 'to one another,' **ab invicem** 'from one another,' etc.

Alius and **alter** may be used in succeeding, coordinated clauses: **alius . . alius** 'one . . another'; **alter . . alter** 'the one . . the other.'

Like **suus**, the reflexive pronoun —, **suī** 'oneself' takes its exact translation from the gender and number of its referend: 'himself, herself, itself, themselves.'

Derivatives:	LATIN	ENGLISH
	curvō	curve, curb
	fundō	fundamental, foundation
	magnificō	Magnificat, magnification
	ardeō	ardent, arson
	condoleō	condole, condolences
	moveō	motion, motive
	prōficiō	proficient, profit
	reficiō	refectory
	lingua	bilingual, linguist
	umbra	umbrella, adumbration
	testis	intestate, testes
	gravis	grave, gravity
	trīstis	tristful queen
	alius	inter alia, et al., alias
	alter	alter ego, alter, alternate
	amplus	amplitude, amplification
	nūllus	null, nullity
	sōlus	sole, solo, solitary
	tōtus	factotum, total
	contrā	contrary, counterfeit, contretemps, contradict
	—, suī	suicide, sui generis

Drills

I. Reflexives.

1. Pontius Pīlātus ā culpā sē līberāvit.
2. Apostolī pānēs sēcum nōn portābunt.
3. Mulier sibi bibere dabat.
4. Memorēs suī timuērunt Jēsūm.
5. Cōnfitēbantur sua peccāta.
6. Prō suā mātre Jēsūs aquam in vīnum mūtāvit.
7. Jēsūs ab ūnō ē suīs apostolīs trāditus est.
8. Fīlia ejus suum librum āmīsit.
9. Jēsūs cognōvit in sēmet ipsō virtūtem quae exierat dē sē.
10. Petrus in domum intrāvit, et suī erant ibi.

II. Cum clauses.

spoke to the woman

1. Cum Samarītāna esset, mulierem Jēsūs allocūtus est.
2. Cum Petrus Hierosolymīs esset, Paulum vīdit.
3. Cum cēnāvērunt, tunc ē domō exiērunt.
4. Cum vocātī essent, Dominum secūtī sunt.
5. Mulierēs condolēbant, cum Jēsūm crucifīxum vīdērent.

Exercises

I.   1. Cum ergō vēnisset in Galilaeam, *he had come into* excēpērunt eum *they waited for him* Galilaeī, cum omnia vīdissent, quae fēcerat Hierosolymīs in diē fēstō. Jn. iv, 45. *they had seen was met*
    2. Et cum haec dīxisset, positīs genibus suīs, cum omnibus illīs ōrāvit. Acts xx, 36.
    3. Ūnus autem ex illīs, ut vīdit quia sānātus est, regressus est cum magnā vōce magnificāns Deum. Lk. xvii, 15.
    4. Quōmodo potest homō nāscī, cum senex sit? Jn. iii, 4.
    5. Cum autem dēscendisset dē monte, secūtae sunt eum turbae multae. Mt. viii, 1.
    6. Quid hic sīc loquitur? Blasphēmat! Quis potest dīmittere peccāta nisi sōlus Deus? Mk. ii, 7.
    7. Alius autem dē discipulīs ejus ait illī: "Domine, permitte mē prīmum īre et sepelīre patrem meum." Mt. viii, 21.
    8. Et respondit ad illum Jēsūs: "Scrīptum est: 'Nōn in pāne sōlō vīvet homō[, sed in omnī verbō Deī].'" Lk. iv, 4.

9. Quī cum pervēnisset, et vīdisset grātiam Deī, gāvīsus est.

10. Magna est vēritās, et prōficit, cum multī ā diabolō īnfectī eī contrādīcant.

11. Et prōcēdens inde vīdit aliōs duōs ('two') frātrēs, Jacōbum Zebedaeī et Jōannem frātrem ejus, in nāvī ('boat') cum Zebedaeō patre eōrum reficientēs rētia ('nets') sua, et vocāvit eōs. Mt. iv, 21.

12. Quī enim voluerit animam suam salvam facere, perdet illam; quī autem perdiderit animam suam propter mē, hic salvam faciet illam. Lk. ix, 24.

13. Alter cēdit gravī tentātiōnī, alter nōn.

14. Et nūllam causam mortis invenientēs petiērunt ā Pīlātō, ut interficerētur. Acts xiii, 28.

15. Vidēns autem turbās, ascendit in montem; et cum sēdisset, accessērunt ad eum discipulī ejus. Mt. v, 1.

16. Mulier suī corporis potestātem nōn habet sed vir; similiter autem et vir suī corporis potestātem nōn habet sed mulier. I Cor. vii, 4.

17. Quī nōn est mēcum, contrā mē est. Mt. xii, 30.

18. Līberābit mē Dominus ab omnī opere malō et salvum faciet in rēgnum suum caeleste; cui glōria in saecula saeculōrum. Āmēn. II Tim. iv, 18.

19. Tibi sōlī peccāvī et malum cōram tē fēcī. Ps. li, 6.

20. Trīstēs mulierēs, condolentēs, quiētem rogābant.

21. Āmēn, āmēn dīcō vōbīs: Nōn est servus major dominō suō, neque apostolus major eō, quī mīsit illum. Jn. xiii, 16.

22. Et regressus est Jēsūs in virtūte Spīritūs in Galilaeam. Et fāma ('report') exiit per ūniversam regiōnem dē illō. Et ipse docēbat in synagōgīs eōrum et magnificābātur ab omnibus. Lk. iv, 14–15.

23. Et replētī sunt omnēs in synagōgā irā haec audientēs. Lk. iv, 28.

24. Propter nostrī prōtēctiōnem Dominum venerēmur.

25. Surgēns autem dē synagōgā introīvit in domum Simōnis. Lk. iv, 38.

26. Patria mihi vītā meā multō est cārior.

27. Sacerdōs ūnā cum populō ipsam praefātiōnem conclūdit.

28. Quī enim mandūcat et bibit, jūdicium sibi mandūcat et bibit nōn dījūdicāns corpus. I Cor. xi, 29.

29. Volō autem omnēs vōs loquī linguīs, magis autem prophētāre ('to prophesy'); major autem est quī prophētat ('prophesies') quam quī loquitur linguīs. I Cor. xiv, 5.

30. Quī enim loquitur linguā, nōn hominibus loquitur, sed

Deō; nēmō ('no one') enim audit, spīritū autem loquitur mystēria. I Cor. xiv, 2.

31. Haec nox fugat odia et imperia curvat.

32. Et sī trādiderō corpus meum ut glōrier ('boast'), cāritātem autem nōn habuerō, nihil mihi prōdest. I Cor. xiii, 3.

33. Iterum mīsit aliōs servōs plūrēs priōribus, et fēcērunt illīs similiter. Mt. xxi, 36.

34. Cum [Jēsūm] nōn vīderitis, dīligitis. I Pet. i, 8.

35. Jēsūs autem amplius nihil respondit, ita ut mīrārētur Pīlātus. Mk. xv, 5.

36. Et tū, puer, prophēta Altissimī vocāberis: praeībis enim *ante faciem Dominī parāre viās ejus, illūmināre hīs, quī in tenebrīs et in umbrā mortis sedent,* ad dīrigendōs pedēs nostrōs in viam pācis. Lk. i, 76, 79.

37. Et ait Marīa: "Magnificat anima mea Dominum." Lk. i, 46.

38. Tū in prīncipiō, Domine, terram fundāstī; et opera manuum tuārum sunt caelī. Heb. i, 10.

39. Ait autem illī: *"Dīligēs Dominum Deum tuum in tōtō corde tuō et in tōtā animā tuā* et in tōtā mente tuā: hoc est magnum et prīmum mandātum. Secundum autem simile est huic: *Dīligēs proximum tuum sīcut tēipsum."* Mt. xxii, 37—39.

40. Accendat in nōbīs Dominus ignem suī amōris ('love'), et flammam aeternae cāritātis.

41. Et dīxērunt ad invicem: "Nōnne cor nostrum ardēns erat in nōbīs, dum loquerētur in viā et aperīret nōbīs Scrīptūrās?" Lk. xxiv, 32.

42. Ego mīsī vōs metere ('to reap'), quod vōs nōn labōrāstis; aliī labōrāvērunt, et vōs in labōrem eōrum introīstis. Jn. iv, 38.

43. Melius est enim benefacientēs, sī velit voluntās Deī, patī quam malefacientēs. I Pet. iii, 17.

44. Ideōque et nōs tantam habentēs circumpositam nōbīs nūbem ('cloud') testium, dēpōnentēs omne pondus ('burden') et circumstāns nōs peccātum, per patientiam cūrrāmus prōpositum nōbīs certāmen ('contest'). Heb. xii, 1.

45. Quam cum vīdisset Dominus, misericordiā mōtus super eā dīxit illī: "Nōlī ('don't') flēre!" Lk. vii, 13.

46. Quid enim prōdest hominī, sī lucrētur ('should gain') mundum tōtum et dētrīmentum faciat animae suae? Mk. viii, 36.

47. Fīlius enim hominis ventūrus est in glōriā Patris suī cum angelīs suīs. Mt. xvi, 27.

48. Jōannēs autem, cum audīsset in vinculīs opera Chrīstī, mittēns per discipulōs suōs ait illī: "Tū es, quī ventūrus es, an alium exspectāmus?" Mt. xi, 2–3.

49. Et circumībat Jēsūs tōtam Galilaeam, docēns in synagōgīs eōrum et praedicāns evangelium rēgnī. Mt. iv, 23.

50. Ipse enim Jēsūs testimōnium perhibuit quia prophēta in suā patriā honōrem nōn habet. Jn. iv, 44.

51. Sī vīs perfectus esse, vāde, vende ('sell') quae habēs, et dā pauperibus. Mt. xix, 21.

52. Dīcit eī mulier: "Sciō quia Messiās venit—quī dīcitur Chrīstus—; cum vēnerit ille, nōbīs annūntiābit omnia." Jn. iv, 25.

53. Aliī dīcēbant: "Hic est Chrīstus!"; quīdam autem dīcēbant: "Numquid ā Galilaeā Chrīstus venit?" Jn. vii, 41.

54. Ad verba quae sequuntur, ūsque ad *factus est*, omnēs sē inclīnant.

II.   1. Some speak in tongues; others preach the Gospel. For the gifts of the Holy Spirit are many. [*Use aliī . . aliī.*]

2. Since we have heard the words of Jesus, let us love one another.

3. There is no hope for those who do not call upon their Father.

4. The deacon prayed most devoutly that God would refresh our minds and hearts.

Readings

1.   The Calling of the First Apostles, Mk. i, 16–20.
Et praeteriēns[1] secus[2] mare Galilaeae vīdit Simōnem[3] et An-drēam[4] frātrem Simōnis[3] mittentēs [rētia[5]] in mare; erant enim piscātōrēs.[6] Et dīxit eīs Jēsūs: "Venīte post mē, et faciam vōs fierī[7] piscātōrēs[6] hominum." Et prōtinus,[8] relictīs rētibus,[5] secūtī sunt eum. Et prōgressus[9] pusillum[10] vīdit Jacōbum[11] Zebedaeī[12] et Jōannem frātrem ejus, et ipsōs in nāvī[13] compōnentēs[14] rētia,[5] et statim vocāvit illōs. Et, relictō patre suō Zebedaeō in nāvī[13] cum mercennāriīs,[15] abiērunt eum.

[1] **praeteriēns** < **praeter** + **eō** [2] **secus** (*prep.* + *acc.*) along, beside [3] **Simōn, Simōnis,** m. Simon (i.e., Peter) [4] **Andrēas, Andreae,** m. Andrew [5] **rēte, rētis, rētium,** n. net [6] **piscātor, piscātōris,** m. fisherman [7] **fierī** 'become' [8] **prōtinus** (*adv.*) right away, on the spot [9] **prōgressus** < **prō** + **gradior** [10] **pusillum** (*adv.*) a little [11] **Jacōbus, Jacōbī,** m. James [12] **Zebedaeus, Zebedaeī,** m. Zebedee [13] **nāvis, nāvis, nāvium,** f. ship, boat [14] **compōnentēs** < **com-** + **pōnō** [15] **mercennārius, mercennāriī,** m. hired man, paid worker

2. Two Blind Men, Mt. ix, 27–31.

Et trānseunte inde Jēsū, secūtī sunt eum duo[1] caecī[2] clāmantēs et dīcentēs: "Miserēre nostrī, fīlī Dāvid!" Cum autem vēnisset domum, accessērunt ad eum caecī,[2] et dīcit eīs Jēsūs: "Crēditis quia possum hoc facere?" Dīcunt eī: "Utīque,[3] Domine." Tunc tetigit oculōs eōrum dīcēns: "Secundum fidem vestram fīat[4] vōbīs." Et apertī sunt oculī illōrum. Et comminātus est[5] illīs Jēsūs dīcēns: "Vidēte, nē quis sciat." Illī autem exeuntēs diffāmāvērunt[6] eum in ūniversā terrā illā.

[1] **duo** 'two' [2] **caecus, -a, -um** blind [3] **utīque** (*adv.*) certainly, by all means, at any rate [4] **fīat** 'let it be done' [5] **comminor, comminārī, —, comminātus sum** threaten, sternly warn [6] **diffāmō, diffāmāre, diffāmāvī, diffāmātus** spread the news (concerning)

Unit 29

149. Indefinite Pronouns and Adjectives:
quis; aliquis; aliquī, etc.

When **quis**, **quid** 'who, what' is used as an indefinite pronoun 'someone, something' (see Unit 26, vocabulary notes), it may be preceded by **sī**, **nisi**, **numquid**, or **nē**; if not, it has **ali-** prefixed to it: **aliquis**, **aliquid** 'someone, something.' The adjectival form is declined exactly like the relative pronoun (see Section 53), except that the feminine nominative singular is spelled **-qua** (not **-quae**): **aliquī**, **aliqua**, **aliquod** 'some, any.'

When the relative pronoun **quī**, **quae**, **quod** 'who, which' is itself used indefinitely, it is unchanged except for the replacement of **quae** by **qua**: **quī**, **qua**, **quod** 'some, any.' Other indefinites formed from the relative pronoun are **quīcumque**, **quaecumque**, **quodcumque** 'whoever, whatever' (see Section 53); **quīdam**, **quaedam**, **quiddam** 'a certain one or thing' (Unit 12); **quīdam**, **quaedam**, **quoddam** 'a certain' (Unit 12).

> **Quis, quid** 'who? what?' leads to:
>> **quis, quid** 'someone, something' [may be preceded by **sī**, **nisi**, **numquid**, or **nē**]
>> **aliquis, aliquid** 'someone, something'
>
> **Quī, quae, quod** 'who, which' leads to:
>> **quī, qua, quod** 'some, any' [may be preceded by **sī**, **nisi**, **numquid**, or **nē**]
>> **aliquī, aliqua, aliquod** 'some, any'
>> **quīcumque, quaecumque, quodcumque** 'whoever, whatever'
>> **quīdam, quaedam, quiddam** 'a certain one or thing' [pronoun]
>> **quīdam, quaedam, quoddam** 'a certain' [adjective]

150. Dative of Purpose; Double Dative Construction

The dative case may be used to express purpose or effect intended.

Hic odiō mē habet.
'This man holds me for the purpose of hatred.'
'This man hates me.'

The dative of purpose is often used with another dative, a dative of
reference. This is called the double dative construction.

Jēsūs est salūtī nōbīs.
'Jesus is for the purpose of salvation with reference to us.'
'Jesus serves as our salvation.'
'Jesus is our salvation.'

151. Review of Clauses: Time, Cause, and Concession

Clauses of time, cause, and concession use a variety of subordinating
conjunctions with either the indicative or the subjunctive mood.

a. Time   Temporal clauses introduced by **cum** 'when,' **ubi** 'when,
as soon as,' **ut** 'when, as,' **quandō**, 'when,' **simul atque (simul ac)** 'as
soon as,' and **postquam** 'after' take the indicative only.

Temporal clauses introduced by **antequam** 'before,' **priusquam** 'before,' **dum** 'while, as long as; until,' and **dōnec** 'while, as long as; until' may take either the indicative or the subjunctive, with no difference in meaning.

Temporal clauses introduced by **cum** '(under the circumstances)
when' take the subjunctive only.

> *Note:*   **-cumque** may be suffixed to **ubi**, **ut**, and **quandō** to add a
> generalizing force: **ubicumque, utcumque, quandōcum-**
> **que** 'whenever.' Cf. **quī** 'who': **quīcumque** 'whoever.'

b. Cause   Causal clauses introduced by **quia, quoniam,** or **quod**
'because' take either the indicative or the subjunctive. The indicative is used to express actual cause; the subjunctive, to express either
actual or alleged cause.

Causal clauses introduced by **cum** 'since' take the subjunctive only.

c. Concession Concessive clauses introduced by **etsī**, **licet**, or **quamquam** 'although' may take either the indicative or the subjunctive, with no distinction in meaning.

Concessive clauses introduced by **cum** 'although' take the subjunctive only.

d. Ablative Absolute A participle (see Sections 65 and 87b), or a participial construction (i.e., the ablative absolute [see Sections 68 and 87c]), may be used as the equivalent of a clause of time, cause, or concession.

Since no specific sign-word accompanies a participle to indicate its use, the context must be examined with care to determine the precise meaning.

Vocabulary

corōnō, corōnāre, corōnāvī, corōnātus crown

mōnstrō, mōnstrāre, mōnstrāvī, mōnstrātus show; command

dēmōnstrō, dēmōnstrāre, dēmōnstrāvī, dēmōnstrātus show, reveal

supplicō, supplicāre, supplicāvī, supplicātus (humbly) beseech

suscitō, suscitāre, suscitāvī, suscitātus awaken, raise up

resuscitō, resuscitāre, resuscitāvī, resuscitātus reawaken, raise up again

crēscō, crēscere, crēvī, crētus grow, increase

gerō, gerere, gessī, gestus bear, manage, conduct

struō, struere, strūxi, strūctus build

dēstruō, dēstruere, dēstrūxī, dēstrūctus destroy

īnstruō, īnstruere, īnstrūxī, īnstrūctus instruct

sūmō, sūmere, sūmpsī, sūmptus take, obtain

assūmō, assūmere, assūmpsī, assūmptus take up

cūria, cūriae, f. court, curia

figūra, figūrae, f. fashion, figure

Magdalēna, Magdalēnae, f. Magdalen

psalmista, psalmistae, m. psalmist

jūdicium, jūdiciī, n. judgment

timor, timōris, m. fear

timōrātus, -a, -um God-fearing, devout, reverent

hospes, hospitis, m. & f. host; guest

cautiō, cautiōnis, f. bill, bail

conclūsiō, conclūsiōnis, f. conclusion

lampas, lampadis, f. (*acc.,*
  lampada) lamp, torch; flame
omissiō, omissiōnis, f.
  omission
sānctificātiō, sānctificātiōnis,
  f. holiness; holy mystery
pretiōsus, -a, -um precious
vespertīnus, -a, -um (of)
  evening
humilis, humile lowly, humble

aliquī, aliqua, aliquod (*indef.*
  pron. adj.) some, any
aliquis, aliquid (*indef. pron.*)
  someone, something; any-
  one, anything
licet (*subord. conj.*) <u>although</u>
priusquam (*subord. conj.*)
  before
utīque (*adv.*) certainly, by all
  means, at any rate

Vocabulary Notes

Corōnō is the denominative verb formed from **corōna** (Unit 21).

Mōnstrō, as a verb of showing (see Section 26), takes an indirect and a direct object; the object may be an object infinitive: **mōnstrāvit nōbīs viam** 'he showed us the way'; **mōnstrāvit nōbīs ōrāre** 'he showed us (how) to pray.'

Supplicō is the denominative verb formed from the adjective **supplex** (Unit 17).

The Greek nominative singular ending of **Magdalēna** also occurs: **Magdalēnē.**

Timor and **timōrātus** are derived from **timeō** (Unit 25).

Conclūsiō is the abstract noun derived from **conclūdō** (Unit 18).

The accusative singular of **lampas** is **lampada,** a transliteration of its Greek original.

Sānctificātiō is the abstract noun derived from **sānctificō** (Unit 11).

Pretiōsus is compounded of the base of **pretium** 'price' (Unit 27) and the suffix **-ōsus** 'full of.'

Humilis forms its superlative with the suffix **-limus: humillimus.** See Section 142a, Note 2.

Though used as a subordinating conjunction, **licet** is properly a verb (to be formally presented in Unit 34).

Priusquam may be spelled as two words; a subordinating conjunction, it is formed in the same manner as **postquam** and **antequam** (Unit 12).

Derivatives: LATIN   ENGLISH
             corōnō   coronary, coronation
             mōnstrō   monster, monstrance
             dēmōnstrō   demonstrative, demonstration

Derivatives:

LATIN	ENGLISH
supplicō	supplication
resuscitō	resuscitation
crēscō	accrue, increase, crescent, increment, concrete
gerō	gesture, digest, suggest
struō	structure, construe
dēstruō	destroy, destruction
sūmō	sumptuous
assūmō	Assumption, assume
Magdalēna	maudlin
jūdicium	judicious
timor	timorous
hospes	hospital, hostel, hotel
cautiō	caution
sānctificātiō	sanctification
vespertīnus	vespertine

Drills

I. Indefinite pronouns and adjectives.

1. Quodcumque minimīs facitis, mihi facitis.
2. Petrus alicui in viā locūtus est?
3. Sī quid vidēs, dīc mihi.
4. Aliqua mulier tibi librum relīquit.
5. Quīcumque aurēs habent, audiant. *jussive*
6. Tū rogābās aliquid bonī?
7. Quīdam ad Jēsūm accessit.
8. Aurum aliquibus mīlitibus datum est.

II. Clauses of time, cause, and concession.

1. Ubi hōra vēnit, Jēsūs ōrābat.
2. Priusquam abeās, vāde ad Petrum.
3. Quia esset senex, Jōannēs cum frātribus īre nōn poterat.
4. Cum Jēsūm audīre vellet, vir synagōgam introīvit.
5. Licet nihil baptizāret, sed Paulus evangelizābat.
6. Etsī essent peccātōrēs, Jēsūs cum eīs mandūcāvit.
7. Cum Jēsūs ōrāre in montem subīret, apostolī illum secūtī sunt.

8. Quoniam Jēsūs est Salvātor noster, eum semper et ubīque laudāmus.

Exercises

I.   1. Ō bone Jēsū, miserēre nōbīs quia tū creāstī nōs, tū redēmistī nōs sanguine tuō pretiōsissimō.

2. Jēsū, Salvātor mundī, tuīs famulīs subvenī, quōs pretiōsō sanguine redēmistī.

3. Et eritis odiō omnibus gentibus propter nōmen meum. Mt. xxiv, 9.

4. Ōsculābantur ('were kissing') eum dolentēs maximē in verbō, quod dīxerat, quoniam amplius faciem ejus nōn essent vīsūrī. Acts xx, 38.

5. Jacōb dīlēxī, Ēsau autem odiō habuī. Rom. ix, 13.

6. Nam cum līber essem ex omnibus, omnium mē servum fēcī. I Cor. ix, 19.

7. Quamquam Jēsūs nōn baptizāret sed discipulī ejus. Jn. iv, 2.

8. Quis enim cognōvit sēnsum Dominī, quī īnstruat eum? Nōs autem sēnsum Chrīstī habēmus. I Cor. ii, 16.

9. Lēgem ergō dēstruimus per fidem? Absit, sed lēgem statuimus. Rom. iii, 31.

10. Audīvimus enim eum dīcentem quoniam Jēsūs Nazarēnus hic dēstruet locum istum et mūtābit cōnsuētūdinēs, quās trādidit nōbīs Mōysēs. Acts vi, 14.

11. Quod sī nōsmetipsōs dījūdicārēmus, nōn utīque jūdicārēmur. I Cor. xi, 31.

12. Glōriā et honōre corōnāstī eum[, et cōnstituistī eum super opera manuum tuārum]. Heb. ii, 7.

13. Et hoc est testimōnium Jōannis, quandō mīsērunt ad eum Jūdaeī ab Hierosolymīs sacerdōtēs et Lēvītās, ut interrogārent eum: "Tū quis es?" Jn. i, 19.

14. Et dīxit eī Nathanaēl: "Ā Nazareth potest aliquid bonī esse?" Dīcit eī Philippus: "Venī et vidē." Jn. i, 46.

15. Domine, dēscende priusquam moriātur puer meus. Jn. iv, 49.

16. Pater enim dīligit Fīlium et omnia dēmōnstrat eī, quae ipse facit, et majōra hīs dēmōnstrābit eī opera, ut vōs mīrēminī. Sīcut enim Pater suscitat mortuōs et vīvificat, sīc et Fīlius, quōs vult, vīvificat. Jn. v, 20–21.

17. Āmēn, āmēn dīcō vōbīs: Venit hōra, et nunc est, quandō mortuī audient vōcem Fīliī Deī et, quī audierint, vīvent. Sīcut enim Pater habet vītam in sēmetipsō, sīc dedit et

Fīliō vītam habēre in sēmetipsō; et potestātem dedit eī
et jūdicium facere, quia Fīlius hominis est. Jn. v, 25–27.

18. Ego vēnī in nōmine Patris meī, et nōn accipitis mē; sī
alius vēnerit in nōmine suō, illum accipiētis. Jn. v, 43.

19. Hic enim erat trāditūrus eum, cum esset ūnus ex
Duodecim ('twelve'). Jn. vi, 71.

20. Dē turbā autem multī crēdidērunt in eum et dīcēbant:
"Chrīstus cum vēnerit, numquid plūra sīgna faciet quam
quae hic fēcit?" Jn. vii, 31.

21. Ego autem quia vēritātem dīcō nōn crēditis mihi.
Jn. viii, 45.

22. Proptereā ('therefore') mē Pater dīligit, quia ego pōnō
animam meam, ut iterum sūmam eam. Jn. x, 17.

23. At (= sed) ubi vēnit plēnitūdō ('fullness') temporis, mīsit
Deus Fīlium suum, factum ex muliere, factum sub lēge,
ut eōs, quī sub lēge erant, redimeret. Gal. iv, 4–5.

24. Et mandūcantibus illīs, accēpit pānem et benedīcēns frēgit
et dedit eīs et ait: "Sūmite; hoc est corpus meum." Et
acceptō calice, grātiās agēns dedit eīs, et bibērunt ex illō
omnēs. Et ait illīs: "Hic est sanguis meus novī testāmentī,
quī prō multīs effunditur." Mk. xiv, 22–24.

25. Haec est autem voluntās ejus, quī mīsit mē, ut omne,
quod dedit mihi, nōn perdam ex eō, sed resuscitem illud
in novissimō diē. Jn. vi, 39.

26. Dīrigātur, Domine, ōrātiō mea, sīcut incēnsum, in
cōnspectū tuō: ēlevātiō ('lifting up') manuum meārum,
sacrificium vespertīnum. Ps. cxli, 2.

27. Sepeliērunt autem Stephanum virī timōrātī et fēcērunt
plānctum magnum super illum. Acts viii, 2.

28. Sed licet nōs aut angelus dē caelō evangelizet vōbīs
praeterquam ('before') quod evangelizāvimus vōbīs,
anathema sit! Gal. i, 8.

29. Cōnfiteor Deō omnipotentī, et vōbīs, frātrēs, quia peccāvī
nimis cōgitātiōne, verbō, opere, et omissiōne.

30. Psalmista seu cantor psalmum dīcit.

31. Ad Missae conclūsiōnem populus acclāmat: Deō grātiās.

32. Jēsūs veteris peccātī cautiōnem piō cruōre dētersit.

33. In hujus igitur noctis grātiā, suscipe, sāncte Pater, incēnsī
hujus sacrificium vespertīnum.

34. Hujus igitur sānctificātiō noctis fugat scelera, culpās lavat:
et reddit innocentiam lāpsīs et maestīs laetitiam.

35. Diāconus accendat hanc pretiōsam lampada!

36. Humilēs hospitēs timōre implētī sunt.

37. Et Jēsūs prōficiēbat sapientiā et aetāte ('age') et grātiā apud Deum et hominēs. Lk. ii, 52.

38. Tē aeternum Patrem omnis terra venerātur.

39. Post haec Marīa Magdalēna Jēsūm agnōvit.

40. Et cum stātis in ōrātiōne, dīmitte, sī quid habētis adversus ('against') aliquem, ut et Pater vester, quī in caelīs est, dīmittat vōbīs peccāta vestra. Mk. xi, 25.

41. Et ait discipulīs suīs: "Sedēte hīc, dōnec ōrem." Et assūmit Petrum et Jacōbum et Jōannem sēcum. Mk. xiv, 32–33.

42. Reddite omnibus dēbita: . . cui timōrem timōrem, cui honōrem honōrem. Rom. xiii, 7.

43. Ō quanta quālia sunt illa sabbata, Quae semper celebrat superna cūria. Peter Abelard.

44. Ecce figūram Jēsū, crēscentem dōnec tōtum mundum amplectātur.

45. Humilēs supplicēmus Deum et bene gerāmus!

46. Hoc est autem jūdicium: Lūx vēnit in mundum, et dīlēxērunt hominēs magis tenebrās quam lūcem; erant enim eōrum mala opera. Jn. iii, 19.

II. 1. Although the disciples could not buy much bread, the whole crowd had something to eat.

2. Since Jesus had been sent by the Father, he showed the apostles how to preach the Gospel.

3. When Jesus took the cup, he blessed it and gave it to the apostles.

4. After she was taken up into heaven, Mary was crowned with glory and honor.

5. Before we were redeemed with the precious blood, we had no hope of salvation.

Readings

1. The Second Sign at Cana, Jn. iv, 46–54.

Vēnit ergō iterum in Cana Galilaeae, ubi fēcit aquam vīnum. Et erat quīdam rēgius,[1] cujus fīlius īnfirmābātur[2] Capharnaum; hic cum audīsset quia Jēsūs advēnerit ā Jūdaeā in Galilaeam, abiit ad eum et rogābat, ut dēscenderet et sānāret fīlium ejus; incipiēbat

[1] rēgius, rēgiī, m. royal official [2] īnfirmō, īnfirmāre, īnfirmāvī, īnfirmātus make weak, enfeeble; pass., be sick

enim morī. Dīxit ergō Jēsūs ad eum: "Nisi sīgna et prōdigia[3] vīderitis, nōn crēdetis." Dīcit ad eum rēgius[1]: "Domine, dē-scende priusquam moriātur puer meus." Dīcit eī Jēsūs: "Vāde, fīlius tuus vīvit." Crēdidit homō sermōnī,[4] quem dīxit eī Jēsūs, et ībat. Jam autem eō dēscendente, servī ejus occurrērunt eī dīcentēs quia puer ejus vīvit. Interrogābat ergō hōram ab eīs, in quā melius habuerit.[5] Dīxērunt ergō eī: "Heri[6] hōrā septimā[7] relīquit eum febris."[8] Cognōvit ergō pater quia illā hōrā erat, in quā dīxit eī Jēsūs: "Fīlius tuus vīvit," et crēdidit ipse et domus ejus tōta. Hoc iterum secundum sīgnum fēcit Jēsūs, cum vēnisset ā Jūdaeā in Galilaeam.

[3] **prōdigium, prōdigiī**, n. omen, wonder [4] **sermō, sermōnis**, m. word, saying [5] **melius habēre** 'get better, be better' [6] **heri** (*adv.*) yesterday [7] **septimus, -a, -um** seventh [8] **febris, febris, febrium**, f. fever

2. The Conditions for Following Jesus, Mt. viii, 19–22.

Et accēdēns ūnus scrība[1] ait illī: "Magister, sequar tē quōcum-que[2] ieris." Et dīcit eī Jēsūs: "Vulpēs[3] foveās[4] habent et volucrēs[5] caelī tabernācula,[6] Fīlius autem hominis nōn habet, ubi caput reclīnet." Alius autem dē discipulīs ejus ait illī: "Domine, per-mitte mē prīmum īre et sepelīre patrem meum." Jēsūs autem ait illī: "Sequere mē et dīmitte mortuōs sepelīre mortuōs suōs."

[1] **scrība, scrībae**, m. scribe [2] **quōcumque** < **quō** 'to where' + **-cumque** [3] **vulpēs, vulpis, vulpium**, f. fox [4] **fovea, foveae**, f. pit, lair [5] **volucris, volucris**, f. bird [6] **ta-bernāculum, tabernāculī**, n. hut, nest

Unit 30

152. Present Infinitives: Active and Passive

The second principal part of every verb is the present active infinitive: **laudāre**, **monēre**, **dūcere**, **capere**, **audīre**; **esse**, **posse**, **velle**, **īre**. (See Section 20f.2.) In early Latin the ending was **-se** (still preserved in **esse** and **posse**; **velle** is an example of back-assimilation: *velse > velle).

All present passive infinitives end in **-ī**. To form them, change final **-e** to **-ī** in the first, second, and fourth conjugations; in the third conjugation, replace the stem vowel and the ending with **-ī**.

ACTIVE	PASSIVE	
laudāre	**laudārī**	('to praise/to be praised')
monēre	**monērī**	('to warn/to be warned')
dūcere	**dūcī**	('to lead/to be led')
capere	**capī**	('to take/to be taken')
audīre	**audīrī**	('to hear/to be heard')

> *Note:* The irregular verbs **sum**, **possum**, **volō**, and **eō** have no passive present infinitives.

153. Negative Direct Commands (or Requests)

Commands (or requests) in the negative may be expressed through a negative particle + an infinitive, a subjunctive, or an indicative.

a.* Nōlī/nōlīte *and Infinitive The isolated imperative forms **nōlī** (singular) and **nōlīte** (plural) 'be unwilling, do not' take a complementary infinitive.

Ō puer, nōlī flēre!
'O child, do not weep!'

Ō mulier, nōlī implērī odiō!
'O woman, do not be filled with hatred!'

Pāstōrēs, nōlīte timēre!
'Shepherds, do not be afraid!'

Meī discipulī, nōlīte ā malīs praecipī!
'My disciples, be unwilling to be taught by the wicked!'

b. Nē/nōn and Present or Perfect Subjunctive **Nē** or (less frequently) **nōn** may be used with the subjunctive tenses of primary sequence, the present or the perfect.

Nē tangās hoc!
'Do not touch this!'

Nōn dūcāris!
'Do not be led!'

Nē laudētis illum!
'Do not praise that man!'

Nē trādideris mē!
'Do not betray me!'

c. Nōn and Future Indicative The jussive future indicative (see Section 110c) uses **nōn** for the negative.

Nōn hīs maledīcēs!
'You shall not speak evil of these people!'

> *Note:* The negatives **numquam** 'never' and **nihil** 'not at all' may also occur in these three kinds of negative command.

154. Indirect Statements (3): Subject Accusative and Present Infinitive

An indirect statement may take the form of a **quod** (**quia**, **quoniam**) clause with either the indicative or the subjunctive (see Sections 43 and 135), or it may be cast into the subject accusative and infinitive construction. The introductory verb in either construction is a verb of saying, knowing, or thinking.

When the time of the indirect statement is simultaneous with that of the main verb, the present infinitive is used. The subject accusative is always expressed: if the direct statement does not have an expressed subject, a pronoun is supplied in the accusative; if the subjects of the main verb and of the quoted statement are the same, a reflexive pronoun in the accusative is supplied.

SIMULTANEOUS TIME IN THE PRESENT:

DIRECT STATEMENT: **Jēsūs in synagōgā praedicat.**
'Jesus is preaching in the synagogue.'

INDIRECT STATEMENT: **Dīcunt Jēs*ūm* in synagōgā praedicā*re*.**
'They *say* that Jesus *is preaching* in the synagogue.'

SIMULTANEOUS TIME IN THE PAST:

DIRECT STATEMENT: **Jēsūs in synagōgā praedicat.**
'Jesus is preaching in the synagogue.'

INDIRECT STATEMENT: **Dīcēbant Jēs*ūm* in synagōgā praedicā*re*.**
'They *were saying* that Jesus *was preaching* in the synagogue.'

SIMULTANEOUS TIME IN THE FUTURE:

DIRECT STATEMENT: **Jēsūs in synagōgā praedicat.**
'Jesus is preaching in the synagogue.'

INDIRECT STATEMENT: **Dīcent Jēs*ūm* in synagōgā praedicā*re*.**
'They *will say* that Jesus *is preaching* in the synagogue.'

Note that, in a future construction, English idiom also uses the present tense to express simultaneity: 'will say . . is preaching.'

DIRECT STATEMENT,
NO EXPRESSED SUBJECT: **In synagōgā praedicat.**
'He preaches in the synagogue.'

INDIRECT STATEMENT,
SUBJECT ACCUSATIVE SUPPLIED: **Dīcunt *eum* in synagōgā praedicā*re*.**
'They say that *he* preaches in the synagogue.'

DIRECT STATEMENT,	**In synagōgā praedicō.**
NO EXPRESSED SUBJECT:	'I preach in the synagogue.'

INDIRECT STATEMENT,	**Jēsūs dīxit *sē* in synagōgā praedicā*re*.**
REFLEXIVE SUBJECT	'Jesus said that *he* was preaching in
ACCUSATIVE SUPPLIED:	the synagogue.'

Vocabulary

cōgitō, cōgitāre, cōgitāvī, cōgitātus think; plan

commendō, commendāre, commendāvī, commendātus entrust

exīstimō, exīstimāre, exīstimāvī, exīstimātus think, judge

liquō, liquāre, liquāvī, liquātus melt

negō, negāre, negāvī, negātus deny, say . . . not

persevērō, persevērāre, persevērāvī, persevērātus continue

putō, putāre, putāvī, putātus think, reckon

    dēputō, dēputāre, dēputāvī, dēputātus appoint; reckon, count

sociō, sociāre, sociāvī, sociātus share in; ally

vetō, vetāre, vetuī (vetāvī), vetitus (vetātus) forbid

illūcēscō, illūcēscere, illūxī, — shine (upon), become light

dīvidō, dīvidere, dīvīsī, dīvīsus part, divide

premō, premere, pressī, pressus press (upon); oppress

    exprimō, exprimere, expressī, expressus represent, express

trahō, trahere, trāxī, trāctus draw, drag; lead

attrahō, attrahere, attrāxī, attrāctus draw toward

dētrahō, dētrahere, dētrāxī, dētrāctus draw from, take away

domina, dominae, f. mistress, lady

amīcus, amīcī, m. friend

inimīcus, inimīcī, m. enemy

somnus, somnī, m. sleep

lignum, lignī, n. wood; tree

monumentum, monumentī, n. tomb

hostis, hostis, hostium, m. & f. enemy, host

parēns, parentis, m. & f. parent

dīvīnitās, dīvīnitātis, f. divinity

sēdēs, sēdis, f. place, seat

vīcīnus, -a, -um neighboring

    vīcīnus, vīcīnī, m. neighbor

facilis, facile easy

    difficilis, difficile difficult

inaestimābilis, inaestimābile priceless

ineffābilis, ineffābile inexpressible, ineffable

nēmō [nūllīus, nēminī, nēminem, nūllō/nūllā]

(*pron./m. & f. adj.*)
nobody; no
nōlī/nōlīte (*imperative + inf.*)
be unwilling, do not
quisquam, quaequam, quid-

quam (*indef. pron.*) anyone,
anything [*used with
negative or implied
negative*]
vel (*coord. conj.*) or (if you
prefer)

Vocabulary Notes

Cōgitō may take an accusative ('plan something') or **dē** + ablative
('think about something').

Negō means 'deny.' When used to introduce an indirect statement,
it translates a negative in the quoted statement: **negō Petrum esse
hīc** 'I say that Peter is not here' [original statement: 'Peter is not here'].

Persevērō takes **in** + ablative: **persevērat in fidē** 'he continues in
the faith.' In imitation of the Greek idiom, it may take a present sup-
plementary participle (agreeing with the subject): **persevērat ōrāns**
'he continues praying.'

Sociō, the denominative of **socius** (Unit 9), takes an accusative + a
dative or ablative: 'share something with someone,' or 'ally something to something.' Personal nouns in this construction go into the
accusative: **Petrus domō nōs sociāvit** 'Peter shared his home with us.'

Vetō takes either indirect command construction—**ut** + subjunctive or accusative + infinitive (see Section 120). The latter is the
accusative of the person forbidden and the infinitive of the action
forbidden: **vetō tē exīre** 'I forbid you to leave.'

Somnus 'sleep' means 'dream' in the plural.

Lignum means 'tree' [Rev. xxii, 2] or '(piece of) wood' (and so a
'club' [Mk. xiv, 43, 48]).

Nēmō < **nē** + **homō** 'no man.' The genitive and ablative forms
nēminis and **nēmine** are usually supplanted by the equivalent forms
of **nūllus** (Unit 28).

The imperative forms **nōlī** and **nōlīte** come from a verb which is
seldom used in ecclesiastical Latin: **nōlō, nōlle, nōluī**, — 'be unwilling, wish not': **nōlō** < **nē** + **volō**.

Quisquam is an indefinite pronoun, declined like **quis, quid** (see
Section 140), except that the feminine nominative has its own form:
quaequam (not **quisquam**). There are no plural forms. It is used with
negatives. For example, **nec quisquam** (which always replaces **et
nēmō**).

Cōgitō, exīstimō, negō, putō, and any similar verbs of saying,

thinking, or knowing may take the newly presented indirect statement construction, the subject accusative + infinitive. Formal English requires the subordinating conjunction 'that' to introduce this
construction, even though there is no expressed equivalent in the
Latin. **Putās** may be used parenthetically to signal a question.

Derivatives:	LATIN	ENGLISH
	cōgitō	cogitate, cogitative
	commendō	commend, commendation
	exīstimō	estimate, esteem
	liquō	liquor, liquid, liquidate
	negō	negate, negative, renege
	persevērō	persevere, perseveration
	putō	putative, computer
	dēputō	depute, deputy
	sociō	associate
	vetō	veto
	dīvidō	division, divisor
	premō	pressure
	exprimō	expression
	trahō	tractor, traction
	attrahō	attraction, attractive
	dētrahō	detract, detraction
	domina	dame, donna
	amīcus	amicable, amity
	inimīcus	inimical
	somnus	somnolent, somnambulist
	lignum	lignum vitae, ligneous
	monumentum	monument
	sēdēs	Holy See
	vīcīnus	vicinage, vicinal, vicinity
	facilis	facile
	inaestimābilis	inestimable
	nōlī	noli-me-tangere

Drills

I. Negative direct commands (or requests).

1. Nē gerātis vōs in istō modō!
2. Nē calicem indīgnē sūmant!

3. Nōn interficiēs!
4. Nōlīte loquī!
5. Vāde, nōlī peccāre amplius!
6. Nē suscitāveris tuum patrem!
7. Nōlīte vestrōs in calicēs meum vīnum fundere!
8. Nē sīmus maestī!

II. Indirect statements: subject accusative and present infinitive.
a. Translate.
b. Reconstruct the original statement in Latin and in English.

1. Sciō meum Redēmptōrem vīvere.
2. Jēsūs dēmōnstrāvit eīs sē moritūrum esse.
3. Dīxērunt sē templum dēstruere posse.
4. Dīxērunt eōs templum dēstruere posse.
5. Dīxit eōs Petrum cognōscere.
6. Hospes crēdidit sē plūs vīnī habēre.
7. Scīvimus eum ā Paulō laudārī.
8. Mulierēs vīdērunt Jēsūm crucifīgī.
9. Dīcis fidem ōrandō crēscī?
10. Audierant Jēsūm esse in cīvitāte.
11. Vultis mihi dīcere maximum apostolōrum esse Petrum?

Exercises

I. 1. Nihil hōrum timeās, quae passūrus es. Rev. ii, 10.
2. Haec dīcit Sānctus, Vērus, quī habet *clāvem* ('key') *Dāvid, quī aperit et nēmō claudet, et claudit et nēmō aperit.* Rev. iii, 7.
3. At (= sed) ille negāvit cōram omnibus dīcēns: "Nesciō quid dīcis." Mt. xxvi, 70.
4. Nōlīte mīrārī hoc, quia venit hōra, in quā omnēs, quī in monumentīs sunt, audient vōcem ejus et prōcēdent, quī bona fēcērunt, in resurrēctiōnem vītae, quī vērō mala ēgērunt, in resurrēctiōnem jūdiciī. Jn. v, 28–29.
5. At (= sed) illī, ut vīdērunt eum ambulantem super mare, putāvērunt phantasma ('ghost') esse et exclāmāvērunt. Mk. vi, 49.
6. Omne gaudium exīstimāte, frātrēs meī, cum in tentātiōnibus variīs ('various') incideritis. James i, 2.
7. Et cōnfestim, adhūc eō loquente, venit Jūdās ūnus ex

Duodecim ('twelve'), et cum illō turba cum gladiīs et lignīs. Mk. xiv, 43.

8. Et ait illīs: "Trīstis est anima mea ūsque ad mortem." Mk. xiv, 34.

9. Haec autem eō cōgitante, ecce angelus Dominī in somnīs appāruit eī dīcēns: "Jōsēph fīlī Dāvid, nōlī timēre accipere Marīam conjugem ('wife') tuam. Quod enim in eā nātum est, dē Spīritū Sānctō est; pariet autem fīlium, et vocābis nōmen ejus Jēsūm: ipse enim salvum faciet populum suum ā peccātīs eōrum." Mt. i, 20–21.

10. Nēminī quidquam dēbeātis, nisi ut invicem dīligātis: quī enim dīligit proximum, lēgem implēvit. Rom. xiii, 8.

11. Nihil enim nōbīs nāscī prōfuit, nisī redimī prōfuisset . . . . Ō inaestimābilis dīlēctiō cāritātis!

12. Haec nox est, quae hodiē per ūniversum mundum in Chrīstō crēdentēs, ā vitiīs saeculī et cālīgine peccātōrum sēgregātōs, reddit grātiae, sociat sānctitātī.

13. Alitur enim liquantibus cērīs ('waxes').

14. Scrūtāminī ('you examine') Scrīptūrās, quia vōs putātis in ipsīs vītam aeternam habēre; et illae sunt, quae testimōnium perhibent dē mē. Et nōn vultis venīre ad mē, ut vītam habeātis. Jn. v, 39–40.

15. Nōlīte putāre quia ego accūsātūrus sim vōs apud Patrem; est quī accūset vōs: Mōysēs, in quō vōs spērātis. Jn. v, 45. [accūsō 'accuse']

16. Licet ignis in partēs dīvīsus sit, tamen dētrīmenta lūminis nōn nōvit.

17. Trādet autem frāter frātrem in mortem, et pater fīlium; et īnsurgent fīliī in parentēs et morte eōs afficient. Et eritis odiō omnibus propter nōmen meum; quī autem persevērāverit in fīnem, hic salvus erit. Mt. x, 21–22.

18. Ōrāmus ergō tē, Domine: ut Cēreus iste in honōrem tuī nōminis cōnsecrātus, ad noctis hujus cālīginem dēstruendam, indēficiēns persevēret.

19. Audīstis quia dictum est: "*Dīligēs proximum tuum* et odiō habēbis inimīcum tuum." Ego autem dīcō vobis: Dīligite inimīcōs vestrōs et ōrāte prō persequentibus vōs. Mt. v, 43–44.

20. Fīliae Jerūsalem, nōlīte flēre super mē, sed super vōs ipsās flēte et super fīliōs vestrōs. Lk. xxiii, 28.

21. Majōrem hāc dīlēctiōnem nēmō habet, ut animam suam quis pōnat prō amīcīs suīs. Vōs amīcī meī estis, sī fēceritis, quae ego praecipiō vōbīs. Jn. xv, 13–14.

22. Et nēmō poterat respondēre eī verbum, neque ausus fuit quisquam ex illā diē eum amplius interrogāre. Mt. xxii, 46.

23. Omnia ergō, quaecumque dīxerint vōbīs, facite et servāte; secundum opera vērō eōrum nōlīte facere: dīcunt enim et nōn faciunt. Mt. xxiii, 3.

24. Dīcit eī Jēsūs: Nōlī mē tangere, nōndum enim ascendī ad Patrem meum: vāde autem ad frātrēs meōs, et dīc eīs: Ascendō ad Patrem meum et Patrem vestrum, et Deum meum et Deum vestrum. Jn. xx, 17.

25. Et respondērunt sē nescīre unde esset. Lk. xx, 7.

26. Surgam et ībō ad patrem meum et dīcam illī: Pater, peccāvī in caelum et cōram tē et jam nōn sum dīgnus vocārī fīlius tuus. Lk. xv, 18–19.

27. Et cum vīdissent quōsdam ex discipulīs ejus commūnibus manibus, id est nōn lōtīs, mandūcāre pānēs[, vituperāvērunt ('scolded')]. Mk. vii, 2.

28. Sīve ergō mandūcātis sīve bibitis sīve aliud quid facitis, omnia in glōriam Deī facite. I Cor. x, 31.

29. Clāmāvit autem Paulus magnā vōce dīcēns: "Nihil fēceris tibi malī; ūniversī enim hīc sumus." Acts xvi, 28.

30. Frātrēs, nōlīte puerī efficī sēnsibus. I Cor. xiv, 20.

31. Ōrantēs autem nōlīte multum loquī. Mt. vi, 7.

32. Nōlīte putāre quoniam vēnī solvere Lēgem aut Prophētās; nōn vēnī solvere, sed adimplēre. Mt. v, 17.

33. Quō statim cognitō Jēsūs spīritū suō quia sīc cōgitārent intrā sē, dīcit illīs: "Quid ista cōgitātis in cordibus vestrīs?" Mk. ii, 8.

34. Nōlīte jūdicāre secundum faciem, sed jūstum jūdicium jūdicāte. Jn. vii, 24.

35. Et hoc scientēs tempus quia hōra est jam nōs dē somnō surgere, nunc enim propior est nōbīs salūs quam cum crēdidimus. Rom. xiii, 11.

36. Fīlius hominis trādendus est in manūs hominum. Mt. xvii, 22.

37. Et in viā interrogābat discipulōs suōs dīcēns eīs: "Quem mē dīcunt esse hominēs?" Mk. viii, 27.

38. Et ipse interrogābat eōs: "Vōs vērō quem mē dīcitis esse?" Respondēns Petrus ait eī: "Tū es Chrīstus." Mk. viii, 29.

39. Caelum et terra trānsībunt, verba autem mea nōn trānsībunt. Dē diē autem illō vel hōrā nēmō scit, neque angelī in caelō neque Fīlius nisi Pater. Mk. xiii, 31–32.

40. Et clāmāns vōce magnā Jēsūs ait: "Pater, *in manūs tuās commendō spīritum meum*"; et haec dīcēns exspīrāvit. Lk. xxiii, 46.

41. Ait autem: "Āmēn dīcō vōbīs: Nēmō prophēta acceptus est in patriā suā." Lk. iv, 24.

42. Ut cognōvit autem Jēsūs cōgitātiōnēs eōrum, respondēns dīxit ad illōs: "Quid cōgitātis in cordibus vestrīs? Quid est facilius, dīcere: 'Dīmittuntur tibi peccāta tua,' an dīcere: 'Surge, et ambulā'?" Lk. v, 22–23.
43. Et nōlīte jūdicāre et nōn jūdicābiminī. Lk. vi, 37.
44. Ō cor sacrātum Jēsū, trahe mē post tē!
45. Nostra Domina vocātur sēdēs sapientiae. Ineffābilis enim est Marīae sēnsus dīvīnitātis.
46. Cum diēs illūcēscēbat, Jēsūs circuībat ad vīcīna loca.
47. Nōnne Rōmānī mīlitēs Jūdaeōs premere vetābantur?
48. Erit nōbīscum grātia, misericordia, pāx ā Deō Patre et ā Jēsū Chrīstō, Fīliō Patris, in vēritāte et cāritāte. II Jn. 3.
49. Exībant autem daemonia ā multīs clāmantia et dīcentia: "Tū es fīlius Deī." Et increpāns ('rebuking') nōn sinēbat ('was allowing') ea loquī, quia sciēbant ipsum esse Chrīstum. Lk. iv, 41.
50. Nōn enim jūdicāvī scīre mē aliquid inter vōs nisi Jēsūm Chrīstum et hunc crucifīxum. I Cor. ii, 2.
51. Spīritālis autem jūdicat omnia, et ipse ā nēmine jūdicātur. I Cor. ii, 15.

II.   1. When asked, Peter said that he did not know Jesus.
   2. Do not try to drag the wood away alone!
   3. It is difficult to express our sorrow at the death of a friend.
   4. Do not think that you ought not to love your enemies.
   5. If you continue serving the Lord, joy and peace will be yours.
   6. Did our friends judge that it was difficult to forbid the enemy to enter the city?

Readings

1.   Lavabo, Ps. xxvi, 6–12.
   Lavābō inter innocentēs[1] manūs meās et circumdabō[2] altāre tuum, Domine,
   Ut audiam vōcem laudis et ēnārrem[3] ūniversa mīrābilia[4] tua.
   Domine, dīlēxī decōrem[5] domūs[6] tuae et locum habitātiōnis[7] glōriae tuae.

   [1] innocēns (gen., innocentis) innocent [2] circumdō, circumdare, circumdedī, circumdatus surround (here, go around) [3] ēnārrō, ēnārrāre, ēnārrāvī, ēnārrātus tell, narrate [4] mīrābilis, mīrābile wonderful [5] decor, decōris, m. beauty [6] domūs = domī [7] habitātiō, habitātiōnis, f. dwelling

Nē perdās cum impiīs, Deus, animam meam et cum virīs san-
guinum vītam meam,
In quōrum manibus inīquitātēs sunt: dextera eōrum replēta est
mūneribus.
Ego autem in innocentiā meā ingressus sum; redime mē et
miserēre meī.
Pēs meus stetit in dīrēctō;[8] in ecclēsiīs benedīcam tē, Domine.

[8]**dīrēctum, dīrēctī**, n. straight line, level surface

2. Expulsion of the Devils in Gerasa (I), Mk. v, 1–10.
Et vēnērunt trāns fretum[1] maris in regiōnem[2] Gerasēnōrum.[3] Et
exeunte eō dē nāvī,[4] statim occurrit eī dē monumentīs homō in
spīritū immundō, quī domicilium[5] habēbat in monumentīs;
et neque catēnīs[6] jam quisquam eum poterat ligāre,[7] quoniam
saepe compedibus[8] et catēnīs[6] vīnctus[9] dīrūpisset[10] catēnās[6] et
compedēs[8] comminuisset,[11] et nēmō poterat eum domāre;[12] et
semper nocte ac diē in monumentīs et in montibus erat clāmāns
et concīdēns[13] sē lapidibus.[14] Et vidēns Jēsūm ā longē[15] cucurrit
et adōrāvit eum et clāmāns vōce magnā dīcit: "Quid mihi et tibi,
Jēsū fīlī Deī Altissimī?[16] adjūrō[17] tē per Deum, nē mē torqueās."[18]
Dīcēbat enim illī: "Exī, spīritus immunde, ab homine." Et interrogābat eum: "Quod tibi nōmen est?" Et dīcit eī: "Legiō[19] nōmen
mihi est, quia multī sumus." Et dēprecābātur eum multum, nē
sē expelleret[20] extrā regiōnem.[2]

[1]**fretum, fretī**, n. strait [2]**regiō, regiōnis**, f. country, region [3]**Gerasēnī, Gerasēnōrum**, m. the Gerasenes [4]**nāvis, nāvis, nāvium**, f. ship, boat [5]**domicilium, domi-
ciliī**, n. dwelling [6]**catēna, catēnae**, f. chain [7]**ligō, ligāre, ligāvī, ligātus** bind, re-
strain [8]**compēs, compedis**, f. fetter, leg iron [9]**vinciō, vincīre, vīnxī, vīnctus** bind
[10]**dīrumpō, dīrumpere, dīrūpī, dīruptus** break in pieces, shatter [11]**comminuō,
comminuere, comminuī, comminūtus** break into small pieces [12]**domō, domāre,
domuī, domitus** tame, subdue [13]**concīdō, concīdere, concīdī, concīsus** cut up,
gash [14]**lapis, lapidis**, m. stone [15]**ā longē** (adv.) from afar, at a distance [16]**summus,
-a, -um** highest [17]**adjūrō, adjūrāre, adjūrāvī, adjūrātus** implore, adjure [18]**torqueō,
torquēre, torsī, tortus** twist, torture [19]**legiō, legiōnis**, f. legion, a division of the
Roman army (approx. 6,000 men) [20]**expellō, expellere, expulī, expulsus** drive out

Unit 31

155. Perfect Infinitives: Active and Passive

The perfect active infinitive is formed by adding **-isse** to the base of the third principal part.

> **laudāvī: laudāv- + -isse = laudāvisse**
> **monuī: monu- + -isse = monuisse**
> **dūxī: dūx- + -isse = dūxisse**
> **cēpī: cēp- + -isse = cēpisse**
> **audīvī: audīv- + -isse = audīvisse**
>
> **fuī: fu- + -isse = fuisse**
> **potuī: potu- + -isse = potuisse**
> **voluī: volu- + -isse = voluisse**
> **iī/īvī: i- + -isse = īsse**
>   **īv- + -isse = īvisse**

The perfect passive infinitive is a two-word compound; it is formed by using **esse** (the present infinitive of **sum**) with the fourth principal part.

> **laudātus, -a, -um esse**
> **monitus, -a, -um esse**
> **ductus, -a, -um esse**
> **captus, -a, -um esse**
> **audītus, -a, -um esse**

156. Indirect Statement (4): Subject Accusative and Perfect Infinitive

The perfect infinitive is used in the subject accusative and infinitive construction when the time of the indirect statement is prior to that of the main verb. Therefore, the translation of the perfect infinitive will vary according to the time of the main verb.

PRIOR TIME IN THE PRESENT:

DIRECT STATEMENT: **Jēsūs in synagōgā praedicāvit.**
'Jesus preached in the synagogue.'

INDIRECT STATEMENT: **Dīcunt Jēs*ūm* in synagōgā praedicā*visse*.**
'They *say* that Jesus *preached* in the synagogue.'

PRIOR TIME IN THE PAST:

DIRECT STATEMENT: **Jēsūs in synagōgā praedicāvit.**
'Jesus preached in the synagogue.'

INDIRECT STATEMENT: **Dīxērunt Jēs*ūm* in synagōgā praedicā*visse*.**
'They *said* that Jesus *had preached* in the synagogue.'

DIRECT STATEMENT: **Jēsūs trāditus est.**
'Jesus was betrayed.'

INDIRECT STATEMENT: **Dīxērunt Jēs*ūm* trādit*um* esse.**
'They *said* that Jesus *had been betrayed*.'

Note: As with other forms of **sum**, **esse** in the perfect passive infinitive may be omitted.

PRIOR TIME IN THE FUTURE:

DIRECT STATEMENT: **Jēsūs in synagōgā praedicāvit.**
'Jesus preached in the synagogue.'

INDIRECT STATEMENT: **Dīcent Jēs*ūm* in synagōgā praedicā*visse*.**
'They *will say* that Jesus *preached* in the synagogue.'

Note: This last may be translated 'that Jesus will have preached,' since the perfect infinitive indicates prior time either to a future or to a present.

---

157. Predicate Genitive

The genitive case may be used as a predicate as well as an attributive. This construction indicates a trait or an action which is characteristic of a certain type of person: a present infinitive or a noun is linked to the genitive by a form of **sum**.

Dīligere et Deum et vīcīnum est *bonī Chrīstiānī*.
['To love both God and neighbor is *of a good Christian*.']
'Loving both God and neighbor is *characteristic of a good Christian*.'

Petrus erat *magnae fideī*.
'Peter was (*a man*) *of great faith*.'

Jōannēs erat *episcopālis ōrdinis*.
'John was *of* (*belonged to*) *the episcopal rank*.'

158. Conditional Relative Clauses

A relative pronoun or adverb may be used in any conditional construction to express a general conditional idea. The relative word, which has no definite antecedent, replaces the introductory word **sī**.

Quodcumque minimīs fēceris, mihi faciēs.
'Whatever you do for the least, you will be doing for me.'

Quī vīcīnum dīligit, mē dīligit.
'He who loves his neighbor loves me.'

Quōcumque ieris, sequar.
'(To) wherever you go, I will follow.'

Vocabulary

appropinquō, appropinquāre, appropinquāvī, appropinquātus draw near, approach (+ *dat.*)

nārrō, nārrāre, nārrāvī, nārrātus tell, narrate

plōrō, plōrāre, plōrāvī, plōrātus bewail, lament, weep

maneō, manēre, mānsī, mānsus remain, wait, stay

permaneō, permanēre, permānsī, permānsus remain, continue

remaneō, remanēre, remānsī, remānsus be left, remain

paeniteor, paenitērī, —, — repent

taceō, tacēre, tacuī, tacitus be silent

legō:
  intellegō, intellegere, intel-
  lēxī, intellēctus perceive,
  understand; pay heed to
quaerō, quaerere, quaesīvī,
  quaesītus seek, ask for
  quaesō/quaesumus (parenthetical forms) I/we beg
requīrō, requīrere, requīsīvī,
  requīsītus seek, require
vertō, vertere, vertī, versus
  turn
  āvertō, āvertere, āvertī, āver-
  sus turn away, remove
  convertō, convertere, con-
  vertī, conversus
  or
  convertor, convertī, —, con-
  versus sum change,
  convert, turn around
  revertor, revertī, —, reversus
  sum return
sentiō, sentīre, sēnsī, sēnsus
  feel, perceive
magus, magī, m. wise man,
  magician, astrologer
daemonium, daemoniī, n.
  evil spirit, demon
sepulcrum, sepulcrī, n.
  sepulcher
sermō, sermōnis, m. talk,
  speech

victor, victōris, m. conqueror,
  victor
praeses, praesidis, m. & f.
  president, governor,
  procurator
majestās, majestātis, f.
  majesty
redēmptiō, redēmptiōnis, f.
  deliverance, redemption
urbs, urbis, urbium, f. city
vestis, vestis, vestium, f.
  garment; clothing
īnfernus, -a, -um of hell,
  infernal
īnferus, -a, -um of hell, below
octāvus, -a, -um eighth
pūrus, -a, -um clean, pure
pār (*gen.,* **paris**) equal, like
  (+ *dat.*)
  pariter (*adv.*) equally,
  together
  compār (*gen.,* **comparis**)
  equal, like
  dispār (*gen.,* **disparis**) unlike,
  different
at (*coord. conj.*) but,
  furthermore
īdem, eadem, idem (*pron. &*
  adj.) the same
itaque (*adv.*) therefore, and so

Vocabulary Notes

Intellegō may also be spelled with **-i-**: **intelligō**. Cf. **colligō, dīligō,**
ēligō (Unit 14).

Quaesō and **quaesumus** are used parenthetically: **Dōnā, Ō Domine,**
quaesumus, etc. 'grant, O Lord, we beg, etc.' They preserve archaic
spellings: **quaesō** > **quaerō; quaesumus** > **quaerimus.**

The deponent verb **convertor** is the intransitive form of **convertō**
(equivalent to the Greek middle voice): **convertor** 'I convert (myself).'
Likewise, **revertor** is intransitive: 'I turn (myself) back, I return.'

Magus is a Persian word for a priest of the Zoroastrian religion.
Īdem, eadem, idem 'the same' is the demonstrative **is, ea, id** (Unit
23) + the suffix **-dem**. The forms to note are these:

Nom. Masc. Sing.: *****isdem** > **īdem**
Nom./Acc. Neut. Sing.: *****iddem** > **idem**

any form of **is, ea, id** ending in **-m**: the **-m** is assimilated to **-n-**:
eundem, eandem, eōrundem, eārundem.

Derivatives:	LATIN	ENGLISH
	appropinquō	propinquity
	nārrō	narrative, narrator
	plōrō	deplore, explore
	maneō	manse, mansion, manor
	permaneō	permanent
	remaneō	remainder, remnant
	paeniteor	penitent, penitentiary
	taceō	tacit, taciturn, reticent
	intellegō	intelligent, intellect
	quaerō	query, quest, question
	requīrō	requisite, requisition
	vertō	verse, versus, versatile, version, verso, vertical, vertex, vertebra, vertigo
	convertō	conversion, conversation
	revertor	revert, reverse
	sentiō	sentient, sense, sensation, sensory, sensual, sensuous
	magus	magic
	daemonium	demoniac, demoniacal
	sepulcrum	sepulchral
	sermō	sermon
	urbs	urban, urbane, suburb, exurbia
	vestis	vest, vestry
	īnferus	inferior
	octāvus	octave, octavo
	pūrus	purblind, Puritan, purge, purgatory
	pār	par, peer, parity, nonpareil
	compār	compare, comparative
	dispār	disparage, disparity

Drills

I. Indirect statements: subject accusative and perfect infinitive.
   a. Translate.
   b. Reconstruct the original statement in Latin and in English.

   1. Diāconus crēdidit sē dēputātum esse. *Neuter nominative form*
   2. Tū crēdis Deum prō Hebraeīs mare dīvīsisse?
   3. Scīmus Lūciferum omnibus illūxisse.
   4. Dictum est turbam vetuisse Pīlātum Jēsūm dīmittere.
   5. Hī negant Jōannem fuisse Chrīstum.
   6. Marīa Magdalēna nōn vīdit Jēsūm resurrēxisse ā mortuīs.
   7. Vir vetitus est dīcere sē ā Jēsū sānātum.
   8. Nēminī quisquam dīcat Paulum baptizāvisse.
   9. Nōnne sciunt Marīam amplīs expressisse lacrimīs tālem dolōrem?
   10. Eum putāvit Jēsūm in viā vīdisse.

3rd Decl. Dative

II. Conditional relative clauses.

   1. Quī hoc dīcit, nimis humilis est.
   2. Quaecumque fēcērunt, prō amīcīs fēcērunt.
   3. Quī hoc faciant, eī sint Patrī grātī. *- pleasing*
   4. Quō vādere volēs, sequar.
   5. Quīcumque rogāvisset, accēpisset.

Exercises

Hist pres   *predicate genitive*

I. 1. Ait autem: "Quid enim malī fēcit?" At illī magis clāmābant dīcentēs: "Crucifīgātur!" Mt. xxvii, 23.
   2. Quī crēdit in Fīlium, habet vītam aeternam; quī autem incrēdulus ('unbelieving') est Fīliō, nōn vidēbit vītam, sed īra Deī manet super eum. Jn. iii, 36.
   3. "Putāsne intellegis, quae legis?" Quī ait: "Et quōmodo possum, sī nōn aliquis ostenderit mihi?" Acts viii, 30–31.
   4. Et omnis turba quaerēbant eum tangere, quia virtūs dē illō exībat et sānābat omnēs. Lk. vi, 19.
   5. Postquam autem trāditus est Jōannēs, vēnit Jēsūs in Galilaeam praedicāns evangelium Deī, et dīcēns: "Implētum est tempus, et appropinquāvit rēgnum Deī; paenitēminī et crēdite evangeliō." Mk. i, 14–15.
   6. Ille, reversus ab īnferīs, hūmānō generī serēnus illūxit.

7. Per eundem Dominum nostrum Jēsūm Chrīstum, Fīlium
   tuum: quī tēcum vīvit et rēgnat in ūnitāte Spīritūs Sānctī,
   Deus: per omnia saecula saeculōrum. Āmēn.

8. Sīcut sāncta concēpit virgō, Marīa virgō peperit, virgō
   permānsit.

9. Quōmodo potestis vōs crēdere, quī glōriam ab invicem
   accipitis, et glōriam, quae ā sōlō est Deō, nōn quaeritis?
   Jn. v, 44.

10. Dīcēbat ergō Jēsūs ad eōs, quī crēdidērunt eī, Jūdaeōs: "Sī
    vōs mānseritis in sermōne meō, vērē discipulī meī estis et
    cognōscētis vēritātem, et vēritās līberābit vōs." Jn. viii,
    31–32.

11. Tunc reversī sunt in Jerūsalem ā monte, quī vocātur
    Olīvētī. Acts i, 12.

12. Paenitēminī igitur et convertiminī, ut dēleantur vestra
    peccāta. Acts iii, 19.

13. Jēsūs itaque sciēns omnia, quae ventūra erant super eum,
    prōcessit, et dīcit eīs: "Quem quaeritis?" Jn. xviii, 4.

14. [Nescītis cujus spīritūs estis?] Lk. ix, 55.

15. Hīc jam quaeritur inter dispēnsātōrēs ('stewards'), ut
    fidēlis quis inveniātur. I Cor. iv, 2.

16. Nam et Pater tālēs quaerit, quī adōrent eum. Jn. iv, 23.

17. Vēnērunt dīcentēs sē etiam vīsiōnem ('vision') angelōrum
    vīdisse, quī dīcunt eum vīvere. Lk. xxiv, 23.

18. Omnis sermō malus ex ōre vestrō nōn prōcēdat.
    Eph. iv, 29.

19. Tunc ait illī Jēsūs: "Converte gladium tuum in locum
    suum. Omnēs enim, quī accēperint gladium, gladiō
    perībunt." Mt. xxvi, 52.

20. Ego autem nōn quaerō glōriam meam; est quī quaerit et
    jūdicat. Jn. viii, 50.

21. Jēsūs autem stetit ante praesidem; et interrogāvit eum
    praeses dīcēns: "Tū es Rēx Jūdaeōrum?" Dīcit eī Jēsūs:
    "Tū dīcis." Mt. xxvii, 11.

22. Servus autem nōn manet in domō in aeternum; fīlius
    manet in aeternum. Jn. viii, 35.

23. Iterum ergō locūtus est eīs Jēsūs dīcēns: "Ego sum lūx
    mundī; quī sequitur mē, nōn ambulābit in tenebrīs, sed
    habēbit lūcem vītae." Jn. viii, 12.

24. Āmēn, āmēn dīcō vōbīs: Venit hōra, et nunc est, quandō
    mortuī audient vōcem Fīliī Deī et, quī audierint, vīvent.
    Jn. v, 25.

25. Et stāns Jēsūs [praecipit illum vocārī]. Mk. x, 49.

26. Sī quis habet aurēs audiendī, audiat. Mk. iv, 23.

27. Et dīcēbat: "Quī habet aurēs audiendī, audiat." Mk. iv, 9.

28. Eōdem tempore nātus est Mōysēs et erat fōrmōsus ('handsome') cōram Deō. Acts vii, 20.

29. Tunc submīsērunt virōs, quī dīcerent [sē audīsse eum dīcentem verba blasphēmiae] in Mōsēn et Deum. Acts vi, 11.

30. Cum autem nātus esset Jēsūs in Bēthlehem Jūdaeae in diēbus Hērōdis rēgis, ecce magī ab oriente vēnērunt Hierosolymam dīcentēs: "Ubi est, quī nātus est, rēx Jūdaeōrum? Vīdimus enim stēllam ejus in oriente et vēnimus adōrāre eum." Mt. ii, 1−2.

31. Mulierēs in ecclēsiīs taceant, nōn enim permittitur eīs loquī; sed subditae ('submissive') sint, sīcut et lēx dīcit. I Cor. xiv, 34.

32. Pāpa in urbe Rōmae sēdem suam habet.

33. Et ait illī: "Propter hunc sermōnem vāde; exiit daemonium dē fīliā tuā." Mk. vii, 29.

34. Hīs, quī vīderant eum resuscitātum, nōn crēdiderant. Mk. xvi, 14.

35. Jubē ergō custōdīrī sepulcrum ūsque in diem tertium. Mt. xxvii, 64.

36. Et dīcunt eī illī: "Mulier, quid plōrās?" Jn. xx, 13.

37. Octāvō diē Jēsūs apostolīs appāruit.

38. Cumque intuērentur in caelum eunte illō, ecce duo ('two') virī astitērunt jūxtā ('near') illōs in vestibus albīs ('white'), quī et dīxērunt: "Virī Galilaeī, quid stātis aspicientēs in caelum? Hic Jēsūs, quī assūmptus est ā vōbīs in caelum, sīc veniet quemadmodum ('just as') vīdistis eum euntem in caelum." Acts i, 10−11.

39. Et cum complērētur diēs Pentēcostēs (*Greek gen. sing.*), erant omnēs pariter in eōdem locō. Acts ii, 1.

40. Fīlium Deus suscitāvit, solūtīs dolōribus īnfernī.

41. Ō vērē beāta nox, quae sōla meruit scīre tempus et hōram, in quā Chrīstus ab īnferīs resurrēxit!

42. Appropinquat redēmptiō vestra. Lk. xxi, 28.

43. Magister puerīs pūrīs et innocentibus dē majestāte Deī nārrābat.

44. At Jēsūs conversus et vidēns eam dīxit: "Cōnfīde, fīlia; fidēs tua tē salvam fēcit." Mt. ix, 22.

45. Nōnne discipulus sentit Chrīstum victōrem mortis resurrēxisse?

46. Contrītī hominis est exprimere dolōrem peccātōrum.

47. Vir populō nārrāvit quanta Jēsūs fēcerat.

48. Presbyter (= senior) ēlēctae dominae et fīliīs ejus, quōs ego dīligō in vēritāte, et nōn ego sōlus, sed et omnēs quī nōvērunt vēritātem, propter vēritātem, quae permanet in nōbīs et nōbīscum erit in sempiternum (= aeternum). II Jn. 1–2.

49. Quis enim scit hominum, quae sint hominis, nisi spīritus hominis, quī in ipsō est? Ita et, quae Deī sunt, nēmō cognōvit nisi Spīritus Deī. I Cor. ii, 11.

II. 1. Whoever, like the Magi, should follow the star would be able to find the King of the Jews.

2. When Paul was drawing near to the city, he suddenly heard a voice from the sky.

3. Whoever remains faithful will not die forever.

4. Having returned to the city, Jesus was sought by the crowd.

5. Paul says that it was the mark of a good woman to be silent in the assemblies.

Readings

1. Easter Sequence (Wipo, 1048).

Victimae[1] Paschālī laudēs
Immolent[2] Chrīstiānī.
Agnus redēmit ovēs:
Chrīstus innocēns Patrī
Reconciliāvit[3]
Peccātōrēs.
Mors et vīta duellō[4]
Cōnflīxēre[5] mīrandō:
Dux[6] vītae mortuus
Rēgnat vīvus.
Dīc nōbīs, Marīa,
Quid vīdistī in viā?
Sepulcrum Chrīstī vīventis,

Et glōriam vīdī resurgentis:
Angelicōs testēs,
Sūdārium[7] et vestēs.
Surrēxit Chrīstus
Spēs mea:
Praecēdet vōs
In Galilaeam.
Scīmus Chrīstum surrēxisse
Ā mortuīs vērē:
Tū nōbīs, victor Rēx,
Miserēre.
Āmēn. Allēlūjā.

[1] victima, victimae, f. victim, sacrifice [2] immolō, immolāre, immolāvī, immolātus sacrifice, offer [3] reconciliō, reconciliāre, reconciliāvī, reconciliātus restore, reunite, reconcile [4] duellum, duellī, n. war, battle [5] cōnflīgō, cōnflīgere, cōnflīxī, cōnflīctus (cōnflīxēre = cōnflīxērunt) struggle, contend [6] dux, ducis, m. leader [7] sūdārium, sūdāriī, n. shroud

2. Expulsion of the Devils in Gerasa (II), Mk. v, 11–20.

Erat autem ibi circā montem grex porcōrum[1] magnus pāscēns; et dēprecātī sunt eum dīcentēs: "Mitte nōs in porcōs,[1] ut in eōs introeāmus." Et concessit eīs. Et exeuntēs spīritūs immundī introiērunt in porcōs.[1] Et magnō impetū[2] grex ruit[3] per praecipitium[4] in mare, ad duo mīlia,[5] et suffōcābantur[6] in marī. Quī autem pāscēbant eōs, fūgērunt et nūntiāvērunt in cīvitātem et in agrōs; et ēgressī sunt vidēre quid esset factī.[7] Et veniunt ad Jēsūm; et vident illum, quī ā daemoniō vexābātur,[8] sedentem, vestītum et sānae mentis, eum quī legiōnem[9] habuerat, et timuērunt. Et quī vīderant, nārrāvērunt illīs quāliter[10] factum esset eī, quī daemonium habuerat, et dē porcīs.[1] Et rogāre eum coepērunt,[11] ut discēderet ā fīnibus eōrum. Cumque ascenderet nāvem,[12] quī daemoniō vexātus fuerat,[8] dēprecābātur eum, ut esset cum illō. Et nōn admīsit eum, sed ait illī: "Vāde in domum tuam ad tuōs, et annūntiā illīs quanta tibi Dominus fēcerit et misertus sit tuī." Et abiit et coepit[11] praedicāre in Decapolī[13] quanta sibi fēcisset Jēsūs, et omnēs mīrābantur.

[1]**porcus, porcī,** m. pig, hog [2]**impetus, impetūs,** m. rapid motion, rush [3]**ruō, ruere, ruī, rutus** fall, go to ruin, rush [4]**praecipitium, praecipitiī,** n. precipice [5]**duo mīlia** 'two thousand' [6]**suffōcō, suffōcāre, suffōcāvī, suffōcātus** choke, drown [7]**factum, factī,** n. thing done, deed, happening [8]**vexō, vexāre, vexāvī, vexātus** harass, vex [9]**legiō, legiōnis,** f. legion [10]**quāliter** (*adv.*) how [11]**—, —, coepī, coeptus** began [12]**nāvis, nāvis, nāvium,** f. ship, boat [13]**Decapolis, Decapoleōs,** f. Decapolis, the Ten Cities

Unit 32

159. Future Active Infinitive

The future active infinitive is a two-word compound; it is composed of the future active participle + **esse**.

> **laudātūrus, -a, -um esse**
> **monitūrus, -a, -um esse**
> **ductūrus, -a, -um esse**
> **captūrus, -a, -um esse**
> **audītūrus, -a, -um esse**

Notes: 1. The future active infinitive and the periphrastic present active infinitive (see Section 98a) are identical in form.
2. As with other forms of **sum**, **esse** may be omitted.
3. The future passive infinitive is quite rare, and so has been omitted from this text.

---

160. Indirect Statements (5): Subject Accusative and Future Infinitive

The future infinitive is used in the subject accusative and infinitive construction when the time of the indirect statement is subsequent to that of the main verb. The translation of the future infinitive will vary according to the time of the main verb.

SUBSEQUENT TIME IN THE PRESENT:

DIRECT STATEMENT: **Jēsūs in synagōgā praedicābit.**
'Jesus will preach in the synagogue.'

INDIRECT STATEMENT: **Dīcunt Jēs*um* in synagōgā praedicātūr*um* esse.**
'They *say* that Jesus *will preach* in the synagogue.'

SUBSEQUENT TIME IN THE PAST:

DIRECT STATEMENT: **Jēsūs in synagōgā praedicābit.**
'Jesus will preach in the synagogue.'

INDIRECT STATEMENT: **Dīxērunt Jēs*um* in synagōgā praedicātūr*um* esse.**
'They *said* that Jesus *would preach* in the synagogue.'

SUBSEQUENT TIME IN THE FUTURE:

DIRECT STATEMENT: **Jēsūs in synagōgā praedicābit.**
'Jesus will preach in the synagogue.'

INDIRECT STATEMENT: **Dīcent Jēs*um* in synagōgā praedicātūr*um* esse.**
'They *will* say that Jesus *will preach* in the synagogue.'

161. Indirect Reflexives

A reflexive pronoun used in a subordinate construction may some-times refer, not to the subject of its own clause, but to that of the main clause. Context will make such cases clear.

DIRECT REFLEXIVE: **Aliquī virī sibi cibum habuērunt.**
'Some men had food for themselves.'

INDIRECT REFLEXIVE: ***Paulus* subitō audīvit virum loquentem sibi.**
'*Paul* suddenly heard a man speaking to him.'

162. Summary of Ways to Express Purpose

Purpose or intention may be expressed by prepositional phrases, sub-junctive clauses, gerund or gerundive constructions, infinitives, par-ticiples, or the dative case.

(a) Prepositions: **in** or **ad** + accusative (Unit 1)
In remissiōnem peccātōrum.
   'For (the purpose of) the forgiveness of sins.'
Ad majōrem Deī glōriam.
   'For (the purpose of) the greater glory of God.'

(b) Subjunctive Clauses: **ut** (**nē**) or **quī**, etc. + present or imperfect (Section 118)
Jēsūs vēnit ut (quī) mundum salvum faceret.
   'Jesus came in order that he might save the world.'

(c) Gerund or Gerundive: **ad** or **causā** (Sections 129, 130)

Apostolī missī sunt ⎰ **ad īnfirmōs sānandōs.**
                 ⎱ **ad īnfirmōs sānandum.**
                 īnfirmōs sānandī causā.

   'The apostles were sent to heal the sick.'

(d) Infinitives: present (Section 119)
Iterum ventūrus est jūdicāre vīvōs et mortuōs.
   'He is going to come again to judge the living and the dead.'

(e) Participles: present or future (Section 87b, 96)
Vir vēnit audiēns dē Jēsū.
   'The man came to hear about Jesus.'

Vīsūrus Petrum, in domum introīvit.
   'He entered the house to see Peter.'

(f) Dative Case: abstract noun (Section 150)
Hoc sacrificium sit ūtilitātī nōbīs.
   'May this sacrifice be for our benefit.'
[**ūtilitās, ūtilitātis,** f. 'benefit, profit, good']

Vocabulary

coadūnō, coadūnāre,
   coadūnāvī, coadūnātus unite
spērō, spērāre, spērāvī,
   spērātus hope (for), wait
   (for); trust
verberō, verberāre, verberāvī,
   verberātus beat
pendeō, pendēre, pependī, —
   hang; depend

teneō, tenēre, tenuī, tentus
   hold, keep, possess, arrest
contineō, continēre,
   continuī, contentus
   hold together, contain
sustineō, sustinēre, sustinuī,
   sustentus hold up, uphold,
   sustain

occīdō, occīdere, occīdī,
  occīsus kill
sistō, sistere, stetī (stitī), status
  stand; be, become
  exsistō, exsistere, exstitī,
    exstitus step forth,
    come out
vincō, vincere, vīcī, victus
  overcome, conquer
  dēvincō, dēvincere, dēvīcī,
    dēvictus overcome
    (thoroughly), conquer
    (thoroughly)
cēra, cērae, f. wax
palma, palmae, f. palm (of the
  hand)
thronus, thronī, m. throne
piāculum, piāculī, n. sin,
  crime
flōs, flōris, m. flower
fōns, fontis, fontium, m.
  source, fountain
jūdex, jūdicis, m. judge
orbis, orbis, orbium, m.
  sphere, orb
  orbis (terrae/terrārum) world

apis, apis, apium, f. bee
illūminātiō, illūminātiōnis, f.
  light
ratiō, ratiōnis, f. reckoning,
  account; plan, rule, way;
  reason, reasoning
regiō, regiōnis, f. country,
  region
ūtilitās, ūtilitātis, f. benefit,
  profit, good
sīdus, sīderis, n. star,
  constellation
requiēs, requiēī, f. rest
speciēs, speciēī, f. appearance;
  kind, type; beauty
eucharisticus, -a, -um
  eucharistic
adversus (adversum) (*prep.* +
  acc.) against
fore = futūrus, -a, -um esse
  (*fut. inf.*) about to be
palam (*adv.*) openly, plainly
quisquis, quaequae, quidquid
  (*indef. rel. pron.*) whosoever,
  whatsoever

Vocabulary Notes

Coadūnō is a denominative verb compounded of two prefixes and
the base of ūnus 'one' (Unit 7).

Spērō (a denominative verb from spēs [Unit 19]) takes a present or
a future infinitive, an ut-clause, or a quod-clause.

Verberō is a denominative verb formed from verber (Unit 33).

Occīdō is a compound verb: ob + caedō 'cut.' (Caedō is not formally presented in this text.) Occīdō must be carefully distinguished
from occidō 'fall into; happen,' a compound of cadō 'fall (down)'
(Unit 19).

Sistō (the reduplicated form of stō [Unit 13]) is transitive ('[make]
stand') or intransitive ('stand, be, become').

Vincō 'conquer' yields victōria (Unit 7) and victor (Unit 31).

Jūdex 'judge' is the source of **jūdicō** (Unit 22) and **jūdicium** (Unit 29).

Note that **ratiō** has several related meanings grouped around the idea of some mental calculation.

Eucharisticus is a Greek word meaning 'thankful, grateful.'

Quisquis is another indefinite relative pronoun (see Section 149); both parts are declined (like **quis, quid** [Unit 26]).

Derivatives:	LATIN	ENGLISH
	spērō	desperate
	verberō	reverberation
	pendeō	pendant, dependent
	teneō	tenant, lieutenant
	contineō	continent, content
	sustineō	sustenance
	exsistō	exist
	cēra	ceraceous, cerated
	flōs	florist
	apis	apiary
	illūminātiō	illumination
	ratiō	rational, rationale, ratio studiorum (a 'plan' of studies)
	ūtilitās	utility
	requiēs	Requiem

Drills

I. Indirect statements: subject accusative and future infinitive. a. Translate. b. Reconstruct the original statement in Latin and in English.

  1. Scīvērunt apostolī Jēsūm moritūrum esse?
  2. Magī nōn vīdērunt rēgem interfectūrum puerōs.
  3. Intellegunt sē peritūrōs esse in marī.
  4. Sēnsimus Paulum Rōmae mānsūrum.
  5. Putāvit eam tacitūram esse.
  6. Nēmō sēnsit Spīritum Sānctum dēscēnsūrum esse super Jēsūm.

II. Indirect reflexives.

1. Jēsūs vīdit turbās sequentēs sē.

[handwritten: Jesus saw that the crowds followed him]

2. Petrus audīvit virum quī sē vocābat?

[handwritten: Peter heard the man who was calling him]

3. Paulus benedīxit virō quī sibi maledīxit.

[handwritten: Paul blest the man who cursed him]

4. Jēsūs rogāvit ut parvulī ad sē venīre admitterentur.

[handwritten: Jesus asked that the little ones might be allowed to come to him.]

Exercises

I.
1. Audiēns autem Jēsūs, mīrātus est et sequentibus sē dīxit: "Āmēn dīcō vōbīs: Apud nūllum invēnī tantam fidem in Israēl." Mt. viii, 10.

2. Vōbīs prīmum Deus suscitāns Puerum suum, mīsit eum benedīcentem vōbīs in avertendō ūnumquemque ('each one') ā nēquitiīs ('evil ways') vestrīs. Acts iii, 26.

3. Et palam verbum loquēbātur. Mk. viii, 32.

4. Dum ōrāret, speciēs vultūs mūtāta est.

5. Requiem aeternam dōnā eīs, Domine!

6. Ipse Jēsūs appropinquāns ībat cum illīs; oculī autem illōrum tenēbantur, nē eum agnōscerent. Lk. xxiv, 15–16.

7. Et cum audīssent suī, exiērunt tenēre eum. Mk. iii, 21.

8. Vēnit enim Jōannēs Baptista neque mandūcāns pānem neque bibēns vīnum, et dīcitis: "Daemonium habet!" Lk. vii, 33.

9. At ille intendēbat in eōs, spērāns sē aliquid acceptūrum ab eīs. Acts iii, 5.

10. Et volēns illum occīdere, timuit populum, quia sīcut prophētam eum habēbant. Mt. xiv, 5.

11. Mītis sum et humilis corde, et inveniētis requiem animābus vestrīs. Mt. xi, 29.

12. Audīstis quia dictum est antīquīs: "*Nōn occīdēs.*" Mt. v, 21.

13. Spēs autem, quae vidētur, nōn est spēs; nam, quod videt quis, spērat? Rom. viii, 24.

14. Quod dīcō vōbīs in tenebrīs, dīcite in lūmine; et quod in aure audītis, praedicāte super tēcta. Et nōlīte timēre eōs, quī occīdunt corpus, animam autem nōn possunt occīdere. Mt. x, 26–28.

15. Laudō autem vōs quod omnia meī memorēs estis et sīcut trādidī vōbīs, trāditiōnēs meās tenētis. I Cor. xi, 2.

16. Cōtīdiē sedēbam docēns in templō, et nōn mē tenuistis. Mt. xxvi, 55.

17. Cum introīssēmus autem Rōmam, permissum est Paulō
manēre sibimet cum custōdiente sē mīlite. Acts xxviii, 16.

18. Et sustulit illum et ostendit illī omnia rēgna orbis terrae.
Lk. iv, 5.

19. Aliī autem palmās in faciem eī dedērunt. Mt. xxvi, 67.

20. Et respōnsum accēperat ā Spīritū Sānctō nōn vīsūrum sē
mortem nisi prius vidēret Chrīstum Dominī. Lk. ii, 26.

21. Occīdit autem Jacōbum ('James') frātrem Jōannis gladiō.
Acts xii, 2.

22. Et respōnsō acceptō in somnīs, nē redīrent ad Hērōdem
('Herod'), per aliam viam reversī sunt in regiōnem suam.
Quī cum recessissent, ecce angelus Dominī appāret in
somnīs Jōsēph dīcēns: "Surge et accipe puerum et mātrem
ejus et fuge in Aegyptum ('Egypt') et estō ibi, ūsque dum
dīcam tibi; futūrum est enim ut Hērōdēs quaerat puerum
ad perdendum eum." Mt. ii, 12−13.

23. Alitur enim liquantibus cērīs, quās in substantiam
pretiōsae hujus lampadis apis māter ēdūxit.

24. Sīcut apēs vertunt flōrēs in cēram, et nōs omnia in bona
operārī dēbēmus.

25. Haec sunt enim fēsta paschālia, in quibus vērus ille Agnus
occīditur, cujus sanguine postēs fidēlium cōnsecrantur.
Haec igitur nox est, quae peccātōrum tenebrās columnae
illūminātiōne pūrgāvit.

26. Fore spērāmus, ut simul glōriā tuā perenniter satiēmur,
per Chrīstum Dominum nostrum, per quem mundō bona
cūncta largīris.

27. Ecclēsiam tuam secundum voluntātem tuam coadūnāre
dīgnēris!

28. Veteris piāculī cautiōnem piō cruōre dētersit.

29. In novissimō diē omnēs dūcentur ante thronum jūdicārī.

30. In illō librō tōtum continētur unde mundus jūdicētur.

31. Ō fōns pietātis, fac mē salvum!

32. Dōnum fac remissiōnis ante diem ratiōnis!

33. Quā clēmentiā victus es?

34. Tē ergō quaesumus, tuīs famulīs subvenī!

35. In tē, Domine, spērāvī: nōn cōnfundar in aeternum!

36. Jēsūs, jūdex omnium, ā mīlitibus verberātus est Rōmānīs.

37. Sānctus dē Jēsū pendente in cruce salūtiferā scrīpsit.

38. Suscipiat Dominus sacrificium dē manibus tuīs ad laudem
et glōriam nōminis suī, ad ūtilitātem quoque nostram
tōtīusque Ecclēsiae suae sānctae.

39. Quisquis adversus mē loquitur, loquitur adversus et Patrem, quī est in caelīs.

40. Sacerdōs eucharisticā lītūrgiā fungī incipit.

41. Multī, sīcut Jōannēs, putāvērunt Antichrīstum in novissimīs diēbus exstitūrum.

42. Dominus illūminātiō mea, et salūs mea, quem timēbō? Ps. xxvii, 1.

II. 1. Christ died in order to conquer death.

2. We believe that we will stand before the throne of God.

3. Some men were sent to arrest Jesus.

4. Jesus hoped that the apostles would sustain him.

5. Jesus knew beforehand that some men would arrest and beat him.

Readings

1. Tantum Ergo, by St. Thomas Aquinas (1225–1274).
Tantum ergō sacrāmentum
venerēmur cernuī;[1]
et antīquum documentum
novō cēdat rītuī;
praestet fidēs supplēmentum[2]
sēnsuum dēfectuī.[3]

Genitōrī,[4] genitōque
laus et jūbilātiō,[5]
salūs, honor, virtūs quoque
sit et benedictiō:
prōcēdentī ab utrōque[6]
compār sit laudātiō.[7]

[1]**cernuus, -a, -um** bowing [2]**supplēmentum, supplēmentī,** n. reinforcement [3]**dēfectus, dēfectūs,** m. failure, defect [4]**genitor, genitōris,** m. father [5]**jūbilātiō, jūbilātiōnis,** f. gladness, festal cry [6]**uterque, utraque, utrumque** each (of two), both [7]**laudātiō, laudātiōnis,** f. praise

2. Peter's Discourse in Caesarea (I), Acts x, 34–39.
Aperiēns autem Petrus ōs dīxit: "In vēritāte comperiō[1] quoniam nōn est persōnārum[2] acceptor[3] Deus, sed in omnī gente, quī

[1]**comperiō, comperīre, comperī, compertus** find out, discover [2]**persōna, persōnae,** f. person [3]**acceptor, acceptōris,** m. respecter, one who shows favoritism

timet eum et operātur jūstitiam, acceptus [4] est illī. Verbum mīsit [5] fīliīs Israēl evangelizāns pācem per Jēsūm Chrīstum; hic est omnium Dominus. Vōs scītis quod factum est verbum per ūniversam Jūdaeam incipiēns [5] ā Galilaeā post baptismum, [6] quod praedicāvit Jōannēs: Jēsūm ā Nazareth, quōmodo ūnxit [7] eum Deus Spīritū sānctō et virtūte, quī pertrānsīvit benefaciendō [8] et sānandō [9] omnēs oppressōs [10] ā Diabolō, quoniam Deus erat cum illō. Et nōs testēs sumus omnium, quae fēcit in regiōne Jūdaeōrum et Jerūsalem; quem et occīdērunt suspendentēs [11] in lignō."

[4] **acceptus, -a, -um** welcome, acceptable (+ *dat.*) [5] **incipiēns** modifies the understood subject of **mīsit** (i.e., **Deus**) [6] **baptismum = baptisma** [7] **ungō (unguō), ungere (unguere), ūnxī, ūnctus** anoint [8] **faciendō = faciēns** [9] **sānandō = sānāns** [10] **opprimō, opprimere, oppressī, oppressus** oppress, overpower [11] **suspendō, suspendere, suspendī, suspēnsus** hang up

3. Mary Magdalen sees the risen Lord, Jn. xx, 15 – 18.
   Dīcit eī Jēsūs: "Mulier, quid plōrās? Quem quaeris?" Illa, exīstimāns quia hortulānus [1] esset, dīcit eī: "Domine, sī tū sustulistī eum, dīcitō [2] mihi, ubi posuistī eum, et ego eum tollam." Dīcit eī Jēsūs: "Marīa!" Conversa illa dīcit eī Hebraicē: [3] "Rabbūnī!" quod dīcitur Magister. Dīcit eī Jēsūs: "Jam nōlī mē tenēre, nōndum enim ascendī ad Patrem; vāde autem ad frātrēs meōs et dīc eīs: Ascendō ad Patrem meum et Patrem vestrum, et Deum meum et Deum vestrum." Venit Marīa Magdalēnē annūntiāns discipulīs: "Vīdī Dominum!" et quia haec dīxit eī.

[1] **hortulānus, hortulānī,** m. gardener [2] **dīcitō = dīc** [3] **Hebraicē** (*adv.*) in Hebrew

Unit 33

163. The Irregular Verb ferō

The present indicative and the imperative of **ferō, ferre, tulī, lātus** 'bring, bear, carry' are slightly irregular. All other forms are constructed like those of a third conjugation verb.

PRESENT INDICATIVE

ACTIVE		PASSIVE	
ferō	ferimus	feror	ferimur
fers	fertis	ferris, ferre	feriminī
fert	ferunt	fertur	feruntur

IMPERATIVE

SINGULAR	PLURAL
fer!	ferte!

164. Ablative of Time When or Time within Which

The ablative case of a word denoting a measurement of time, with or without the preposition **in**, may be used to indicate the time when something occurs or the period within which it occurs.

(In) illō tempore Jēsūs in Galilaeā praedicābat.
'In that time/ at that time/ within that period of time Jesus was preaching in Galilee.'

Note: The extended use of the ablative of time within which leads to the ablative of duration of time (see Section 166).

165. *Accusative of Extent of Time or Space*

The accusative case of a word denoting measurement of time or space may be used to indicate extent of time or space.

Paulus mānsit ibi *diēs paucōs*.
'Paul stayed there *for a few days*.'

166. *Ablative of Duration of Time*

The ablative case of a word denoting measurement of time may be used to indicate duration of time.

Quīnque *diēbus* mulier fuerat īnfirma.
'The woman had been sick *for five days*.'

167. *Summary of Conditional Clauses*

Particular or general conditional clauses fall into three categories: simple, future, or contrafactual. Particular clauses are introduced by **sī**, **nisi**, or **sī . . nōn**; general clauses, by a relative pronoun or adverb (Section 158).

(a) Simple conditional clauses (Section 115a) take the present indicative or any past indicative tense. They express the idea of mere contingency; nothing else is implied.

Sī abit, . . 'If he leaves, . .'
Sī abībat, . . 'If he was leaving, . .'
Sī abiit, . . 'If he left, . .'
Sī abierat, . . 'If he had left, . .'
Quīcumque abiit, . . 'Whoever left, . .'

(b) Future conditional clauses (Section 115b) are of two kinds: more vivid and less vivid, depending on the firmness with which the contingency is viewed. The future more vivid conditional clause employs the future or future-perfect tense of the indicative.

Nisi vīcīnum tuum dīligis/dīlēxeris, . .
'Unless you love your neighbor, . .'

The future less vivid conditional clause employs the present subjunctive.

Quōcumque īre velīs, . .
'(To) wherever you should wish to go, . .'

Sī eum rogēs, . .
'If you should ask him, . .'

(c) Contrafactual conditional clauses (Sections 128, 132) are of two kinds: present and past. The present contrafactual conditional clause employs the imperfect subjunctive.

Sī hoc facerent, . .
'If they were doing this, . .'

The past contrafactual conditional clause employs the pluperfect subjunctive.

Sī hoc fēcissent, . .
'If they had done this, . .'

Note: The ablative absolute construction or a participle alone may be used to express a conditional idea (Sections 65, 68, 87c).

Vocabulary

dītō, dītāre, dītāvī, — enrich

mūtuor, mūtuārī, —, mūtuātus sum borrow

sīgnificō, sīgnificāre, sīgnificāvī, sīgnificātus signify

cōgō, cōgere, coēgī, coāctus lead, bring, assemble; force, compel

fallō, fallere, fefellī, falsus deceive

falsus, -a, -um false

pangō, pangere, pānxī (pēgī, pepigī), pānctus (pactus) make; compose; sing

pellō, pellere, pepulī, pulsus drive out

expellō, expellere, expulī, expulsus drive out

repellō, repellere, repulī, repulsus cast off, overcome

spargō, spargere, sparsī, sparsus sprinkle

aspergō, aspergere, aspersī, aspersus sprinkle

dispergō, dispergere, dispersī, dispersus scatter

ferō, ferre, tulī, lātus bring, bear, carry

auferō, auferre, abstulī, ablātus take away

cōnferō, cōnferre, contulī, collātus accompany;

grant; **cōnferre sē:**
take oneself (to), go
**dēferō, dēferre, dētulī, dē-
lātus** offer, bring
efferō, efferre, extulī, ēlātus
bring out; bear, lift up
īnferō, īnferre, intulī, illātus
bring in
**offerō, offerre, obtulī,
oblātus** offer
**perferō, perferre, pertulī,
perlātus** carry through,
carry up
**prōferō, prōferre, prōtulī,
prōlātus** bring forth, bring
forward
**referō, referre, rettulī, re-
lātus** bring back; yield,
render; report
vinciō, vincīre, vīnxī, vīnctus
bind
poena, poenae, f. pain, punishment, penalty
dāmnum, dāmnī, n. damage,
loss, punishment
flagellum, flagellī, n. scourge
medium, mediī, n. the middle,
midst

praecōnium, praecōniī, n.
praise, proclamation
fulgor, fulgōris, m. brightness
sodālis, sodālis, sodālium, m.
companion, associate
venter, ventris, m. belly;
womb
**commūnicātiō, commūnicā-
tiōnis,** f. partaking,
fellowship
nātiō, nātiōnis, f. nation; *pl.*,
gentiles, heathens
nātīvitās, nātīvitātis, f. birth
reconciliātiō, reconciliātiōnis,
f. restoration, reconciliation
verber, verberis, n. lash;
scourging
castus, -a, -um chaste
dēfūnctus, -a, -um deceased,
dead
jūcundus, -a, -um pleasing
tranquillus, -a, -um peaceful,
tranquil
perennis, perenne eternal
inquam (*defective verb*) I say
velut (*adv.*) as, like

Vocabulary Notes

As its third and fourth principal parts clearly reveal, **cōgō** is a compound of **agō** (Unit 6). It may take an object accusative + infinitive or
ut + subjunctive (the indirect command).

Pangō (the root of which is PAG) shows three types of the third
principal part: 1) **pānxī** (PAG palatalized + -s- = PANGS- = PĀNX-),
2) **pēgī** (PAG with vowel lengthened = PĒG-), 3) **pepigī** (PAG reduplicated = PEPIG-).

Ferō forms many compounds; others may be encountered, includ-
ing **afferō** (ad + ferō), **differō** (dis- + ferō), **sufferō** (sub + ferō), **cir-
cumferō, praeferō, superferō,** and **trānsferō.**

Nātiō and **nātīvitās** are nouns formed from the perfect participle of **nāscor** (Unit 20).

Inquam is a defective verb, used parenthetically after one or more words in its clause. It means 'I mean' as well as 'I say.' A third-person singular form—**inquit**—may also be found.

Derivatives:	LATIN	ENGLISH
	mūtuor	mutual, mutuel
	sīgnificō	significant, signification
	cōgō	cogent
	fallō	fallacy, fail, infallibility
	pangō	compact, pact, impinge
	pellō	pulse
	expellō	expel, expulsion
	repellō	repellent, repulse
	spargō	sparge, sparse
	aspergō	Asperges Me, aspergillum, aspersion, aspersorium
	dispergō	disperse, dispersion
	ferō	fertile, conifer
	auferō	ablative
	cōnferō	confer, conference, collation
	dēferō	defer, deference
	efferō	efferent, elation
	īnferō	infer, inference
	offerō	Oblation, Oblate
	prōferō	prolate
	referō	refer, referee, relate
	vinciō	vinculum
	poena	penal, subpoena
	dāmnum	damn, damage, condemn, damnable, damnation
	flagellum	flagellation
	medium	medium, mean
	sodālis	sodality, sodalist
	venter	ventral, ventrad
	commūnicātiō	communication
	nātīvitās	Nativity
	castus	castigate
	dēfūnctus	defunct

Derivatives: LATIN   ENGLISH
                jūcundus   jocund
                perennis   perennial

Drills

I. Ferō and its compounds.
    a. Translate. b. Change the number.

    1. auferētur   6. perferiminī
    2. cōnfers   7. prōferimus
    3. dēferris   8. refert
    4. efferēns   9. offeram
    5. īnferunt   10. referre

II. Time expressions.

    1. in illō diē   5. septem annīs
    2. per diēs   6. in illō tempore *both ablative*
    3. octāvā hōrā   7. in novissimā hōrā
    4. octō diēs

Exercises

I. 1. Avē, Marīa, grātiā plēna, Dominus tēcum; benedicta tū in
       mulieribus, et benedictus frūctus ventris tuī (Lk. i, 28, 42),
       Jēsūs. Sāncta Marīa, Māter Deī, ōrā prō nōbīs peccātōribus,
       nunc et in hōrā mortis nostrae. Āmēn.
    2. Sī linguīs hominum loquar et angelōrum, cāritātem
       autem nōn habeam, factus sum velut aes ('gong') sonāns.
       I Cor. xiii, 1.
    3. Ad fīnem lēctiōnis sīgnificandum, lēctor subdit: Verbum
       Dominī. R. Deō grātiās.
    4. In Sabbatō Sānctō diāconus Praecōnium Paschāle prō
       populō cantāvit.
    5. Pīlātus trādidit Jēsūm ut flagellīs verberātum
       crucifīgerent.
    6. Chrīstus rēx Israēl dēscendat nunc dē cruce, ut videāmus
       et crēdāmus. Mk. xv, 32.
    7. Pange, lingua, glōriōsī/ corporis mystērium,
       sanguinisque pretiōsī,/ quem in mundī pretium
       frūctus ventris generōsī ('noble')/ rēx effūdit gentium.
                                        St. Thomas Aquinas

8. Quī enim habet, dabitur illī; et quī nōn habet, etiam quod habet, auferētur ab illō. Mk. iv, 25.

9. Haec Hostia nostrae reconciliātiōnis prōficiat, quaesumus, Domine, ad tōtīus mundī pācem atque salūtem.

10. Grātia Dominī nostrī Jēsū Chrīstī et cāritās Deī et commūnicātiō Sānctī Spīritūs cum omnibus vōbīs. II Cor. xiii, 13.

11. In hīs autem diēbus supervēnērunt ab Hierosolymīs prophētae Antiochīam ('Antioch'); et surgēns ūnus ex eīs nōmine Agabus, sīgnificāvit per Spīritum famem ('famine') magnam futūram in ūniversō orbe terrārum. Acts xi, 27–28.

12. Afferēbant ad eum omnēs male habentēs et daemonia habentēs. Mk. i, 32.

13. Omnēs fīliōs tuōs ubīque dispersōs tibi, clēmēns Pater miserātus conjunge.

14. Vēnit Jēsūs et stetit in mediō et dīcit eīs: "Pāx vōbīs!" Jn. xx, 19.

15. Quī licet sit dīvīsus in partēs, mūtuātī tamen lūminis dētrīmenta nōn nōvit.

16. Quī nōn est mēcum, adversum mē est, et quī nōn colligit mēcum, dispergit. Lk. xi, 23.

17. Et obtulērunt eī omnēs male habentēs. Mt. iv, 24.

18. Quid hīc stātis tōtā diē ōtiōsī ('idle')? Mt. xx, 6.

19. In diēbus autem illīs venit Jōannēs Baptista, praedicāns in dēsertō Jūdaeae. Mt. iii, 1.

20. Inventīs frātribus rogātī sumus manēre apud eōs diēs septem. Acts xxviii, 14.

21. Et veniunt ferentēs ad eum paralyticum, quī ā quattuor portābātur. Mk. ii, 3.

22. Āmēn dīcō vōbīs: Ubicumque praedicātum fuerit hoc evangelium in tōtō mundō, dīcētur et quod haec fēcit in memoriam ejus. Mt. xxvi, 13.

23. Et nōn admīsit quemquam sequī sē nisi Petrum et Jacōbum et Jōannem frātrem Jacōbī. Mk. v, 37.

24. Cum autem esset Hierosolymīs in Pascha, in diē fēstō, multī crēdidērunt in nōmine ejus, videntēs sīgna ejus, quae faciēbat. Jn. ii, 23.

25. Tantō tempore vōbīscum sum, et nōn cognōvistī mē, Philippe? Quī vīdit mē, vīdit Patrem. Quōmodo tū dīcis: "Ostende nōbīs Patrem"? Jn. xiv, 9.

26. Dēfūnctō autem Hērōde, ecce appāret angelus Dominī in somnīs Jōsēph in Aegyptō. Mt. ii, 19.

27. Mīra enim quaedam īnfers auribus nostrīs. Acts xvii, 20.

28. Quisquis nōn recēperit rēgnum Deī velut parvulus, nōn intrābit in illud. Mk. x, 15.

29. Igitur quī dispersī erant, pertrānsiērunt evangelizantēs verbum. Acts viii, 4.

30. Sequentī autem diē introībat Paulus nōbīscum ad Jacōbum, omnēsque collēctī sunt presbyterī (= seniōrēs). Acts xxi, 18.

31. Et statim Spīritus expellit eum in dēsertum. Mk. i, 12.

32. Ō vērē beāta nox, quae dītāvit Hebraeōs!

33. Ō Deus, dōnā nōbīs tranquillum tempus pācis perpetuae!

34. Māter dolēbat, dum nātī poenās vulnerātī verberibus videt.

35. Laus nostra sit plēna et jūcunda!

36. Bone pāstor, fac nōs sodālēs sānctōrum!

37. Nōn falsum testimōnium dīcēs. Mt. xix, 18.

38. Chrīstus, Adam Secundus, in lignō pependit, ut dāmna lignī solveret.

39. Nūntiābō nōmen tuum frātribus meīs, in mediō ecclēsiae laudābō tē. Heb. ii, 12.

40. Ignis, inquam, erit perennis.

41. Cōnfestim cecidit ante pedēs eius et exspīrāvit; intrantēs autem juvenēs ('young men') invēnērunt illam mortuam: et extulērunt et sepeliērunt ad virum suum. Acts v, 10.

42. Marīa autem cōnservābat omnia verba haec cōnferēns in corde suō. Lk. ii, 19.

43. Et postquam implētī sunt diēs pūrgātiōnis ('purification') eōrum secundum Lēgem Mōysis, tulērunt illum in Hierosolymam, ut sisterent eum Dominō. Lk. ii, 22.

44. In Jēsū Nātīvitāte Magī fulgōrem in caelīs secūtī sunt.

45. Gladiō volēbat sē interficere, aestimāns ('thinking') fūgisse vīnctōs. Acts xvi, 27.

II. 1. At the time of the offering, the Levite will bring forward the gifts of the people.

2. When Paul was bound by the soldiers, he was forced to speak before the king.

3. To signify the purification of the people, the priest will sprinkle them with water.

4. The sick were brought to Jesus in order that they might be healed.

5. In the night the rich man came to Jesus to ask him about the kingdom of heaven.

Readings

1. Asperges Me (Ps. li, 9, 3).
Aspergēs mē, Domine, hyssōpō[1] et mundābor:[2] lavābis mē, et super nivem[3] dealbābor.[4] Miserēre meī, Deus, secundum magnam misericordiam tuam. Glōria Patrī, et Fīliō, et Spīrituī Sānctō. Sīcut erat in prīncipiō, et nunc, et semper, et in saecula saeculōrum. Āmēn.

[1]**hyssōpum, hyssōpī**, n. hyssop [2]**mundō, mundāre, mundāvī, mundātus** cleanse [3]**nix, nivis**, f. snow [4]**dealbō, dealbāre, dealbāvī, dealbātus** whiten, make white

2. Salutis Humanae, by St. Ambrose (340–397).

Salūtis hūmānae sator,[1]
Jēsū, voluptās[2] cordium,
orbis redēmptī conditor,[3]
et casta lūx amantium:

Quā victus es clēmentiā,
ut nostra ferrēs crīmina?
Mortem subīrēs innocēns,
ā morte nōs ut tollerēs?

Perrumpis[4] īnfernum chaos:[5]
vīnctīs catēnās[6] dētrahis;
victor triumphō nōbilī[7]
ad dexteram patris sedēs.

Tē cōgat indulgentia,
ut dāmna nostra sarciās,[8]
tuīque vultūs compotēs[9]
dītēs beātō lūmine.

Tū, dux[10] ad astra,[11] et sēmita,
sīs mēta[12] nostrīs cordibus,
sīs lacrimārum gaudium,
sīs dulce vītae praemium.

[1]**sator, satōris**, m. sower, causer [2]**voluptās, voluptātis**, f. pleasure, delight [3]**conditor, conditōris**, m. founder, author [4]**perrumpō, perrumpere, perrūpī, perruptus** burst through [5]**chaos, —**, n. chaos, the lower world [6]**catēna, catēnae**, f. chain [7]**nōbilis, nōbile** noble [8]**sarciō, sarcīre, sarsī, sartus** make good, mend [9]**compos** (gen., **compotis**) possessed of, sharing in (+ gen.) [10]**dux, ducis**, m. leader [11]**astrum, astrī**, n. star [12]**mēta, mētae**, f. turning post, goal

3. Peter's Discourse in Caesarea (II), Acts x, 40–48.
"Hunc Deus suscitāvit tertiā diē et dedit eum manifestum[1] fierī[2] nōn omnī populō, sed testibus praeōrdinātīs[3] ā Deō, nōbīs, quī mandūcāvimus et bibimus cum illō postquam resurrēxit ā mortuīs; et praecēpit nōbīs praedicāre populō et testificārī[4] quia ipse est, quī cōnstitūtus est ā Deō jūdex vīvōrum et mortuōrum.

[1]**manifestus, -a, -um** clear, evident, manifest [2]**fierī** 'be made' [3]**praeōrdinātus, -a, -um** preordained [4]**testificor, testificārī, —, testificātus sum** bear witness, testify, bring to light

Huic omnēs Prophētae testimōnium perhibent remissiōnem peccātōrum accipere per nōmen ejus omnēs, quī crēdunt in eum."

Adhūc loquente Petrō verba haec, cecidit Spīritus Sānctus super omnēs, quī audiēbant verbum. Et obstipuērunt,[5] quī ex circum-cīsiōne[6] fidēlēs, quī vēnerant cum Petrō, quia et in nātiōnēs grātia Spīritūs Sānctī effūsa est; audiēbant enim illōs loquentēs linguīs et magnificantēs Deum. Tunc respondit Petrus: "Num-quid aquam quis prohibēre[7] potest, ut nōn baptizentur hī, quī Spīritum Sānctum accēpērunt sīcut et nōs?" Et jussit eōs in nōmine Jēsū Chrīstī baptizārī. Tunc rogāvērunt eum, ut manēret aliquot[8] diēbus.

[5] **obstipēscō, obstipēscere, obstipuī,** — be astounded [6]**circumcīsiō, circumcīsiō-nis,** f. circumcision [7]**prohibeō, prohibēre, prohibuī, prohibitus** prohibit, stop, forbid [8]**aliquot** (*indecl. adj.*) some

Unit 34

168. The Irregular Verb fīō

Fīō; fierī, —, factus sum 'be made, be done; become, happen, be' is remarkable in three ways:

1. in the present-stem system (excluding only the present infinitive), it has active forms, but passive meanings,
2. the present stem, **fī-**, retains the length of its vowel in all forms of the present subjunctive, and of the present, imperfect, and future indicatives,
3. the present infinitive has the unique passive ending **-erī**. (Thus the infinitive is passive in form as well as in meaning.)

Like that of a deponent verb, the imperfect subjunctive is made from the hypothetical active infinitive (*__fiere__) with final **-e** lengthened (**fierē-**), to which the active personal endings are added.

Fīō serves as the passive present-stem system for **faciō, facere, fēcī, factus** 'do, make' (Unit 6). Note that these verbs are identical in the perfect passive system.

Fīō almost never forms compounds; **faciō**, when compounded, may form all passive tenses, including those of the present-stem system. For example:

	ACTIVE	PASSIVE
Simple verb:	**faciō** ('I make')	**fīō** ('I am made')
Compound verb:	**efficiō** ('I make')	**efficior** ('I am made')

INDICATIVES

PRESENT	IMPERFECT	FUTURE
fīō ('I am made')	**fīēbam** ('I was made')	**fīam** ('I will be made')
fīs	**fīēbās**	**fīēs**
fit	**fīēbat**	**fīet**
fīmus	**fīēbāmus**	**fīēmus**
fītis	**fīēbātis**	**fīētis**
fīunt	**fīēbant**	**fīent**

> *Note:* The stem vowel, by rule, shortens before **-t**.

SUBJUNCTIVE
PRESENT	IMPERFECT
fīam	fierem
fīās	fierēs
fīat	fieret
fīāmus	fierēmus
fīātis	fierētis
fīant	fierent

> *Note:* The stem vowels **-a-** and **-e-**, by rule, shorten before **-m**, **-t**, and **-nt**.

169. Some Cardinal and Ordinal Numerals

The cardinal numerals one, two, and three are declined; most others are not. All ordinal numerals are declined.

The number one—**ūnus, -a, -um**—has already been presented (Units 7 and 28). The number two is thus declined:

M.	F.	N.
duo	duae	duo
duōrum	duārum	duōrum
duōbus	duābus	duōbus
duōs, duo	duās	duo
duōbus	duābus	duōbus

The number three is thus declined:

M./F.	N.
trēs	tria
trium	trium
tribus	tribus
trēs	tria
tribus	tribus

Cardinal and ordinal numerals are adjectives: **trēs episcopī** 'three bishops'; **tertius episcopus** 'the third bishop.' Although the partitive idea with cardinal numerals may occasionally be conveyed by the partitive genitive, most often it is expressed through the use of **dē** or **ex** + the ablative: **trēs dē (ex) episcopīs** 'three of the bishops.'

NUMBER	CARDINAL	ORDINAL
1	ūnus, -a, -um	prīmus, -a, -um ('first')
2	duo, duae, duo	secundus, -a, -um ('second')
3	trēs, tria	tertius, -a, -um ('third')
4	quattuor	quārtus, -a, -um ('fourth')
5	quīnque	quīntus, -a, -um ('fifth')
6	sex	sextus, -a, -um ('sixth')
7	septem	septimus, -a, -um ('seventh')
8	octō	octāvus, -a, -um ('eighth')
9	novem	nōnus, -a, -um ('ninth')
10	decem	decimus, -a, -um ('tenth')
11	ūndecim	
12	duodecim	
13	trēdecim (decem [et] trēs)	
14	quattuordecim	
15	quīndecim	
16	sēdecim	
17	septendecim	
18	duodēvīgintī (octōdecim)	
19	ūndēvīgintī (novendecim)	
20	vīgintī	
21	vīgintī ūnus, -a, -um	
30	trīgintā	
40	quadrāgintā	
50	quīnquāgintā	
60	sexāgintā	
70	septuāgintā	
80	octōgintā	
90	nōnāgintā	
100	centum	
1000	mīlle; *pl.*, mīlia (*gen.*, mīlium)	

170. Impersonal Verbs

Impersonal verbs occur in the third-person singular only. Either no subject is immediately in mind or a clause or infinitive is the grammatical subject. In either case, the English expletive *it* is used in the translation. Some otherwise personal verbs may be used impersonally.

The following have a clause or an infinitive as subject:

audītur 'it is heard'
convenit 'it is fitting'
dīcitur 'it is said'
licet 'it is permitted'
placet 'it is pleasing'
vidētur 'it seems good'
oportet 'it is proper'
necesse est 'it is necessary'

Note: These present-tense forms are merely illustrative; all other tenses may also occur.

The following are impersonal passive forms which focus on the action itself and not on the agent:

cēnātum est
'it was dined' = 'there was dining,' 'people dined'

ventum est
'it was come' = 'there was coming,' 'people came'

Note: The perfect is here illustrated; other tenses may occur.

A curious survival of Hebraic idiom is **factum est** 'it happened (that),' 'it came to pass (that).' An introductory expression, it does not ordinarily affect the grammatical structure of what follows.

Factum est autem cum haec dīceret, . .
'And it happened that when he was saying these things, . .'

171. *Summary of Uses of the Genitive Case*

Although the genitive case is most often used to limit a noun, it may also depend on an adjective or a verb. Several uses of the genitive are distinguishable:

(a) Genitive of Possession (Section 10)
Librī puerōrum.
  'The books of the children.' 'The children's books.'

(b) Genitive of Description (Section 73)
Hominēs bonae voluntātis.
  'Persons of good will.'

(c) Subjective and Objective Genitive (Section 75)
Deī dīlēctiō hominum.
  'God's love of human beings.'

(d) Partitive (Section 81)
Satis cibī.
  'Enough (of) food.'

Pars cīvitātis.
  'Part of the city.'

(e) Predicate Genitive (Section 157)
Vir est sānae mentis.
  'The man is of sound mind.'

(f) Genitive after Certain Adjectives
Memor Petrī.
  'Mindful of Peter.'

Potēns daemoniōrum.
  'Having power over evil spirits.'

(g) Genitive after Certain Verbs
Misereor tuī.
  'I pity you.'

(h) Miscellaneous Uses
The genitive is used with **causā** (Unit 9), and after comparatives and superlatives (Section 142b). In imitation of a Hebraic idiom, a noun in the genitive case may follow a different case of itself (e.g., **in saecula saeculōrum** 'forever and ever').

172. Summary of Uses of the Dative Case

In general, the dative case is used to denote the person interested in or affected by the verbal action. Several uses may be distinguished:

(a) Dative of the Possessor (Section 14)
Quid est tibi nōmen?
'What is your name?' 'What name do you have?'

(b) Dative of Indirect Object (Section 26)
Petrus mihi hoc dedit.
'Peter gave me this.' 'Peter gave this to me.'

(c) Dative of Reference: Advantage or Disadvantage (Section 76)
Jēsūs eīs peccāta dīmīsit.
'Jesus forgave them their sins.'

Deō et hominibus peccāvit.
'He has sinned against God and men.'

(d) Dative of Personal Agency with Passive Periphrastics (Section 99)
Hymnus nōbīs cantandus est.
'A hymn ought to be sung by us.' 'We ought to sing a hymn.'

(e) Dative of Purpose (Section 150)
Eritis odiō eīs.
'You will be for the purpose of a hatred with reference to them.'
'They will hate you.'

Eīs is the dative of reference in the double dative construction (Section 150).

(f) Dative with Certain Adjectives (Section 82)
Fīlius Patrī similis est.
'The Son is like the Father.'

(g) Dative with Certain Verbs
1. Intransitive verbs:
Crēdunt Evangeliō.
'They believe in the Gospel.'

2. Impersonal verbs:
Nōn licet tibi abīre.
'It is not permitted for you to leave.'

3. Compounds (especially of **sum**):
Quid mihi prōdest?
'What does it profit me?'

Modīs antīquīs inhaerēbant.
'They were clinging to their ancient ways.'

Vocabulary

errō, errāre, errāvī, errātus
wander, go astray; err

**penetrō, penetrāre, penetrāvī,
penetrātus** pierce, penetrate

**rutilō, rutilāre, rutilāvī, ruti-
lātus** glow

noceō, nocēre, nocuī, nocitus
hurt, do harm to (+ *dat.*)

placeō, placēre, placuī, placitus
please, be pleasing to (+ *dat.*)

placet (*impersonal verb*)
it is pleasing (+ *dat.*)

**complaceō, complacēre,
complacuī (complacitus
sum)** please, be acceptable
to (+ *dat.*)

cadō:

**occidō, occidere, occidī, oc-
cāsus** go down, set [of the
sun]

occidēns (*gen.*, **occidentis**)
west

**prōcidō, prōcidere, prōcidī,
—** fall forward

**ēnītor, ēnītī, —, ēnīsus
(ēnīxus) sum** bring forth,
give birth to

**parcō, parcere, pepercī (parsī),
parsus** spare (+ *dat.*)

**oboediō, oboedīre, oboedīvī
(oboediī), oboedītus** obey,
listen to (+ *dat.*)

**serviō, servīre, servīvī (serviī),
servītus** serve, comply with
(+ *dat.*)

fīō; fierī, —, factus sum

be made, be done; become,
happen, be

concordia, concordiae, f.
union, peace

oboedentia, oboedentiae, f.
obedience

radius, radiī, m. ray

sōl, sōlis, m. sun

commūniō, commūniōnis, f.
communion

genetrīx, genetrīcis, f. mother

humilitās, humilitātis, f. lowliness, humility

īnstitūtiō, īnstitūtiōnis, f.
instruction

sānctitās, sānctitātis, f.
holiness

**lūmināre, lūmināris, lūmi-
nārium, n.** light, lamp,
heavenly body

pectus, pectoris, n. breast

occāsus, occāsūs, m. setting
[of the sun]

ortus, ortūs, m. rising
[of the sun]

lacrimōsus, -a, -um tearful

sincērus, -a, -um sincere

factum est (*Hebraic idiom*)
it happened (that), it came
to pass (that)

jūxtā (*prep.* + *acc.*) near, along;
according to

licet, licere, licuit (licitum est)
it is permitted (+ *dat. and
inf.*)

necesse est (*impersonal verb*)
  it is needful, it is necessary
  (+ *dat. or acc. and inf.*)

oportet, oportēre, oportuit, —
  it is proper, it is necessary
  (+ *acc. and inf.*)

Vocabulary Notes

Although the verbs 'harm, please, obey, and serve' in English are transitive and take a direct object, **noceō**, **placeō**, **complaceō**, **oboediō**, and **serviō** are intransitive and take the dative. In the passive, these verbs are used impersonally and the dative is retained: **rēgī servīmus** 'we serve the king'; **rēgī ā nōbīs servītur** ['it is served the king by us'] 'the king is served by us.'

The compound **complaceō** uses perfect active or passive forms with no difference in meaning: **complacuī/complacitus sum** 'I pleased.' The same is true of **licet: licuit/licitum est** 'it was permitted.'

Humilitās and **sānctitās** are the abstract nouns formed from **humilis** (Unit 29) and **sānctus** (Unit 5).

Occāsus and **ortus** are fourth declension nouns formed from the last principal part of **occidō** and **orior** (Unit 20).

Besides the infinitive construction, **licet** and **necesse est** may take an **ut** or **quod** clause.

Derivatives:	LATIN	ENGLISH
	errō	errata
	penetrō	penetration
	rutilō	rutilant
	noceō	nocent, innocent
	placeō	placebo, please
	complaceō	complacent, complaisant
	occidō	occident, occasion
	parcō	parsimonious
	oboediō	obedient
	serviō	servant
	fīō	fiat
	concordia	concord, Concorde
	radius	radius, radiator
	sōl	solar, solarium
	īnstitūtiō	institution
	sānctitās	sanctity
	lūmināre	luminary
	pectus	pectoral, expectorate

Derivatives: LATIN   ENGLISH
                  lacrimōsus   lachrymose
                  jūxtā   juxtaposition
                  licet   licit, leisure
                  numerals: unit, duo, triceps, Septuagint,
                                      decimate

Drills

I. The irregular verb fīō.

   1. Lūx fīat!
   2. Matthīās factus est apostolus.
   3. Vir rogāvit ut fieret sānus.
   4. Nocte factā, in domum reversī sumus.
   5. Sī verbum cōnservāverimus, salvī fīēmus.
   6. Factum est, apertum est caelum.

[Handwritten annotations: "Ablative absolute"; "deponent"; "Both Adj"; "home"; "Future passive meaning active form"]

II. Numerals.

   1. Ūndecim ex apostolīs erant in cēnāculō.
   2. Duōs (duo) pānēs habēbant.
   3. Nōnā hōrā ad eōs accessit.
   4. Decem mīlia mīlitum vīgintī mīlia vincere possunt?
   5. Post diēs sex Paulus abiit.

Exercises

I.   1. Aut quaerō hominibus placēre? Sī adhūc hominibus
      placērem, Chrīstī servus nōn essem! Gal. i, 10.
   2. Deinde post annōs trēs ascendī Hierosolymam vidēre
      Cēpham (= Petrum) et mānsī apud eum diēbus
      quīndecim; alium autem apostolōrum nōn vīdī nisi
      Jacōbum frātrem Dominī. Gal. i, 18–19.
   3. Erātis enim sīcut ovēs errantēs, sed conversī estis nunc ad
      pāstōrem et episcopum animārum vestrārum. I Pet. ii, 25.
   4. Ūndecim autem discipulī abiērunt in Galilaeam, in
      montem ubi cōnstituerat illīs Jēsūs. Mt. xxviii, 16.
   5. Ascendit ergō Simōn Petrus et trāxit rēte ('net') in terram,
      plēnum magnīs piscibus ('fish') centum quīnquāgintā
      tribus. Jn. xxi, 11.
   6. Quod cum vidēret Simōn Petrus, prōcidit ad genua Jēsū

dīcēns: "Exī ā mē, quia homō peccātor sum, Domine."
Lk. v, 8.

7. Gaudet chorus caelestium,/ et angelī canunt Deō;
palamque fit pāstōribus/ pāstor, creātor omnium.

8. Dīcēbat enim Jōannēs Hērōdī: "Nōn licet tibi habēre
uxōrem ('wife') frātris tuī." Mk. vi, 18.

9. Et nūntiātum est illī: "Māter tua et frātrēs tuī stant forīs
('outside') volentēs tē vidēre." Lk. viii, 20.

10. Jōannēs septem ecclēsiīs, quae sunt in Asiā: Grātia vōbīs
et pāx ab eō, quī est et quī erat et quī ventūrus est, et ā
septem spīritibus, quī in cōnspectū thronī ejus sunt.
Rev. i, 4.

11. Scrībe ergō, quae vīdistī et quae sunt et quae oportet fierī
post haec. Rev. i, 19.

12. Benedictus es, Domine, Deus ūniversī, quia dē tuā largi-
tāte accēpimus pānem, quem tibi offerimus, frūctum terrae
et operis manuum hominum, ex quō nōbīs fīet pānis vītae.

13. Ego, quae placita sunt eī, faciō semper. Jn. viii, 29.

14. Per hujus aquae et vīnī mystērium ejus efficiāmur dīvīnitātis cōnsortēs, quī hūmānitātis nostrae fierī dīgnātus
est particeps.

15. Sed et in lēge vestrā scrīptum est quia duōrum hominum
testimōnium vērum est. Jn. viii, 17.

16. Et vōx facta est dē caelīs: "Tū es Fīlius meus dīlēctus;
in tē complacuī." Mk. i, 11.

17. Et erat in dēsertō quadrāgintā diēbus[, et quadrāgintā
noctibus]. Mk. i, 13.

18. Dīxit autem Marīa: "Ecce ancilla Dominī; fīat mihi
secundum verbum tuum." Lk. i, 38.

19. Erat autem quīdam homō ibi trīgintā et octō annōs habēns
in īnfirmitāte suā. Jn. v, 5.

20. Diū ('for a long time') autem illīs exspectantibus et
videntibus nihil malī in eō fierī, convertentēs sē dīcēbant
eum esse deum. Acts xxviii, 6.

21. Ubi enim sunt duo vel trēs congregātī in nōmine meō, ibi
sum in mediō eōrum. Mt. xviii, 20.

22. Et nunc dīxī vōbīs, priusquam fīat, ut, cum factum fuerit,
crēdātis. Jn. xiv, 29.

23. Et alia cecidērunt in terram bonam et dabant frūctum:
ascendēbant et crēscēbant et afferēbant ūnum trīgintā et
ūnum sexāgintā et ūnum centum. Mk. iv, 8.

24. Nōnne haec oportuit patī Chrīstum et intrāre in glōriam
suam? Lk. xxiv, 26.

25. Tunc dīcit eī Jēsūs: "Vāde, Satanās! Scrīptum est enim:

"Dominum Deum tuum adōrābis et illī sōlī *serviēs."*
Mt. iv, 10.

26. Et dīcit eīs: "Licet sabbatīs bene facere an male? Animam salvam facere an perdere?" At illī tacēbant. Mk. iii, 4.

27. Dīcō autem vōbīs quod multī ab oriente et occidente venient et recumbent ('will recline') cum Abraham et Isaac et Jacob in rēgnō caelōrum. Mt. viii, 11.

28. Quem vultis vōbīs dē duōbus dīmittam? Mt. xxvii, 21.

29. Factum est autem in illīs diēbus, exiit in montem ōrāre. Lk. vi, 12.

30. Etenim Chrīstus nōn sibi placuit. Rom. xv, 3.

31. Dum vēnissent ergō ad illum Samarītānī, rogāvērunt eum, ut apud ipsōs manēret; et mānsit ibi duōs diēs. Jn. iv, 40.

32. Et exiēns sequēbātur et nesciēbat quia vērum est, quod fīēbat per angelum. Acts xii, 9.

33. Factum est autem in aliō sabbatō ut intrāret in synagōgam et docēret. Lk. vi, 6.

34. Vīdī aquam ēgredientem dē templō, ā latere dextrō, allēlūjā: et omnēs ad quōs pervēnit aqua ista, salvī factī sunt, et dīcent: Allēlūjā, allēlūjā.

35. Oportet enim fierī, sed nōndum est fīnis. Mt. xxiv, 6.

36. Nunc autem manet fidēs, spēs, cāritās, tria haec; major autem ex hīs est cāritās. I Cor. xiii, 13.

37. Placuit nōbīs, ut relinquerēmur Athēnīs sōlī. I Thess. iii, 1.

38. Nescīmus quid factum sit eī. Acts vii, 40.

39. Tunc jūstī fulgēbunt sīcut sōl in rēgnō Patris eōrum. Mt. xiii, 43.

40. Et dīcēbat eīs: "Sabbatum propter hominem factum est, et nōn homō propter sabbatum; itaque dominus est Fīlius hominis etiam sabbatī." Mk. ii, 27—28.

41. Sed in ecclēsiā volō quīnque verba sēnsū meō loquī, ut et aliōs īnstruam, quam decem mīlia verbōrum in linguā. I Cor. xiv, 19.

42. Et audītum est quod in domō esset. Mk. ii, 1.

43. Cum autem diēs factus esset, terram nōn agnōscēbant. Acts xxvii, 39.

44. Sed jam columnae hujus praecōnia nōvimus, quam in honōrem Deī rutilāns ignis accendit.

45. Fac ut ardeat cor meum/ in amandō Chrīstum Deum, ut sibi complaceam.

46. Latus Chrīstī gladiō mīlitis penetrātum est.

47. Marīa, ēnīsa Jēsūm, facta est Genetrīx Deī.

48. Peccātōrēs, tē rogāmus, audī nōs, ut nōbīs parcās.

49. Quis putās est iste, quia et ventus ('wind') et mare oboediunt eī? Mk. iv, 41.

50. Vēnērunt ergō et vīdērunt, ubi manēret, et apud eum mānsērunt diē illō; hōra erat quasi ('about') decima. Jn. i, 39.

51. Hic est Fīlius meus dīlēctus, in quō mihi bene complacuī; ipsum audīte. Mt. xvii, 5.

52. In oboedientiam cāritātis castae fiant animae vestrae.

53. Nē noceātis nocentibus vōbīs.

54. In spīritū humilitātis et in animō contrītō suscipiāmur ā tē, Domine; et sīc fīat sacrificium nostrum in cōnspectū tuō hodiē, ut placeat tibi, Domine Deus.

55. Populum tibi congregāre nōn dēsinis, ut ā sōlis ortū ūsque ad occāsum oblātiō munda offerātur nōminī tuō.

56. Sincērīs cum pectoribus, dīvīnā īnstitūtiōne fōrmātī, incipiāmus rītum Commūniōnis.

57. Et in odōrem suāvitātis acceptus, supernīs lūmināribus misceātur.

58. Ille, inquam, lūcifer quī nescit occāsum.

59. Stābat māter dolōrōsa/ jūxtā crucem lacrimōsa.

60. Concordiā sānctitāteque vīvāmus.

61. Sīcut radiī sōlis nōbīs illūcēscunt, et Deī dīlēctiō nōs illūstrat.

62. Nēmō servus potest duōbus dominīs servīre. Lk. xvi, 13.

63. Jēsūs dīcēbat necesse esse sibi morī et tertiā diē resurgere.

64. Dīxitque illī: "Accipe cautiōnem tuam et sedē cito ('quickly'), scrībe quīnquāgintā." Lk. xvi, 6.

II.   1. Twelve men were made apostles by Jesus.

2. Is it permitted to cure on the sabbath?

3. If we wish to please God, it is necessary for us to obey his commandments.

4. Falling forward, the man asked Jesus that he spare him.

5. The three deacons prayed that they be considered worthy to become priests.

Readings

1.   The Conversion of Saul (I), Acts ix, 1–12.

Saulus[1] autem, adhūc spīrāns minārum[2] et caedis[3] in discipulōs

---

[1] **Saulus, Saulī**, m. Saul, a rabbi (later known as Paul [Acts xiii, 9]) [2] **minae, minārum**, f. threats [3] **caedēs, caedis**, f. murder, slaughter

Dominī, accessit ad prīncipem sacerdōtum et petiit ab eō epistulās[4] in Damascum[5] ad synagōgās, ut sī quōs invēnisset hujus viae, virōs ac mulierēs, vīnctōs perdūceret in Jerūsalem. Et cum iter faceret, contigit[6] ut appropinquāret Damascō, et subitō circumfulsit eum lūx dē caelō, et cadēns in terram audīvit vōcem dīcentem sibi: "Saul, Saul, quid mē persequeris?" Quī dīxit: "Quis es, Domine?" Et ille: "Ego sum Jēsūs, quem tū persequeris! Sed surge et ingredere cīvitātem, et dīcētur tibi quid tē oporteat facere." Virī autem illī, quī comitābantur[7] cum eō, stābant stupefactī,[8] audientēs quidem vōcem, nēminem autem videntēs. Surrēxit autem Saulus dē terrā apertīsque oculīs nihil vidēbat; ad manūs[9] autem illum trahentēs intrōdūxērunt[10] Damascum. Et erat tribus diēbus nōn vidēns et nōn mandūcāvit, neque bibit.

Erat autem quīdam discipulus Damascī nōmine Ananīās, et dīxit ad illum in vīsū[11] Dominus: "Ananīā!" At ille ait: "Ecce ego, Domine!" Et Dominus ad illum: "Surgēns vāde in vīcum,[12] quī vocātur Rēctus,[13] et quaere in domō Jūdae Saulum nōmine Tarsēnsem;[14] ecce enim ōrat et vīdit virum Ananīam nōmine introeuntem et impōnentem sibi manūs, ut vīsum[11] recipiat."

[4]**epistula, epistulae,** f. letter [5]**Damascus, Damascī,** f. Damascus [6]**contigit** 'it happened' [7]**comitor, comitārī, —, comitātus sum** accompany, travel with [8]**stupefactus, -a, -um** astounded [9]**ad manūs** *here,* 'by the hand' [10]**intrōdūcō** < **intrō** + **dūcō** [11]**vīsus, vīsūs,** m. vision, sight [12]**vīcus, vīcī,** m. street [13]**rēctus, -a, -um** straight [14]**Tarsēnsis, Tarsēnse** of Tarsus

2. Christum Ducem, by St. Bonaventure (1221–1274).

Chrīstum ducem,[1]
quī per crucem
redēmit nōs ab hostibus,
laudet coetus[2]
noster laetus,
exsultet caelum laudibus.

Poena fortis
tuae mortis
et sanguinis effūsiō

corda terant,[3]
ut tē quaerant,
Jēsū, nostra redēmptiō.

Per fēlīcēs
cicātrīcēs,[4]
spūta,[5] flagella, verbera,
nōbīs grāta
sint collāta
aeterna Chrīstī mūnera.

[1]**dux, ducis,** m. leader [2]**coetus, coetūs,** m. assembly, company [3]**terō, terere, trīvī, trītus** rub, bruise, afflict [4]**cicātrīx, cicātrīcis,** f. scar [5]**spūtum, spūtī,** n. saliva, spit

May the blood of your wounds may touch our heart that it may mourn

Nostrum tangat
cor, ut plangat, *purpose*
tuōrum sanguis vulnerum,[6]
in quō tōtī *in which we may all be*
sīmus lōtī, *cleansed*
conditor[7] alme[8] sīderum. *nourishing founder of the stars*

Passiōnis
tuae dōnīs
salvātor, nōs inēbriā,[9]
quā fidēlis
dare velīs
beāta nōbīs gaudia.

[6] **vulnus, vulneris,** n. wound [7] **conditor, conditōris,** m. author, founder [8] **almus, -a, -um** nourishing [9] **inēbriō, inēbriāre, inēbriāvī, inēbriātus** soak, imbue

By the gifts of your Passion, Savior, make us drunk by which faithful to you wish to give you faithful by which desire to give us the blessed joys.

Unit 35

173. Greek Periphrastic Tenses

In imitation of Greek, the Latin of the Vulgate sometimes uses a present participle with **sum** to form periphrastic tenses equivalent to the English progressive. Since the participle modifies the subject, only the nominative is used. The most common tenses are the present, the imperfect, and the future.

a. Present The present Greek periphrastic is compounded of the present participle and the present tense of **sum**.

laudāns sum	**laudantēs sumus**
('I am praising')	('we are praising')
etc.	etc.

b. Imperfect The imperfect Greek periphrastic is compounded of the present participle and the imperfect tense of **sum**.

laudāns eram	**laudantēs erāmus**
('I was praising')	('we were praising')
etc.	etc.

c. Future The future Greek periphrastic is compounded of the present participle and the future tense of **sum**.

laudāns erō	**laudantēs erimus**
('I will be praising')	('we will be praising')
etc.	etc.

174. Syncopated and Shortened Perfect-Active System Forms

Forms of the perfect, pluperfect, and future-perfect active, and the perfect active infinitive may undergo syncopation, i.e., the loss of a medial syllable, when the sequence **-vi-** or **-ve-** occurs. For example:

laudāvistī > laudāstī
laudāvistis > laudāstis
laudāvissēmus > laudāssēmus
laudāvisse > laudāsse
etc.

Eō and fourth conjugation verbs whose perfect-active stems end in -īv- have collateral forms which end in -i-: audīvī (audiī); custōdīvī (custōdiī); īvī (iī).

> Notes: 1. The third plural of the perfect indicative active has an alternate ending used in poetry or highly colored prose: -ēre (< -ērunt).
> 2. Occasionally, other parts of speech may lose a medial syllable: ā dextrīs 'on the right' (for ā dexterīs); vinclum 'bond' (for vinculum).

175. Historical Present

As in English, lively narrative may use the present tense to represent a past tense. A subjunctive in a subordinate clause depending on a historical present takes a secondary tense (see Section 117).

Et ēdūcunt illum ut crucifīgerent eum. Mk. xv, 20.
'And they lead (led) him out in order that they might crucify him.'

176. Cognate Ablative

The verbal idea of a sentence may be reinforced by the ablative case of a noun which denotes the same action as that of the verb. Often the verb and the noun are etymologically related. The cognate ablative is a special form of either the ablative of means (Section 34) or of the ablative of manner (Section 35).

Gāvīsī sunt magnō gaudiō.
'They rejoiced with a great joy.'
'They were exceedingly joyful.'

Clāmāvit magnā vōce.
'He shouted with a great voice.'
'He shouted very loudly.'

177. Summary of Uses of the Accusative Case

The accusative case is used to express 1) various forms of the direct object, 2) motion toward or duration of time (with or without a preposition), 3) an adverbial idea.

I. FORMS OF DIRECT OBJECT

(a) Direct Object (Section 25)
Petrum vīdit Paulus.
'Paul saw Peter.'

(b) Predicate Accusative (Section 83)
Fēcērunt eum pāpam.
'They made him pope.'

(c) Cognate Accusative (Section 84)
Vītās nostrās vīvimus.
'We live our own lives.'

(d) Double Accusative (Section 105)
Nōs ōrātiōnem docuit.
'He taught us the prayer.'

(e) Subject Accusative and Infinitive (Sections 154, 156, 160)
The subject accusative and infinitive is a form of double object.
Putāvērunt Paulum esse deum.
'They thought that Paul was a god.'

(f) Anticipatory Accusative (Section 43n3)
Dīcimus Petrum quod hic est bonus.
['We say Peter that he is good.']
'We say that Peter is good.'

2. SPACE AND TIME (SECTIONS 92 AND 165)

(a) **In domum intrāvit.**
'He entered the house.'
Rōmam iit.
'He went to Rome.'

(b) **Quīnque diēs mānsit.**
'He stayed for five days.'

3. ADVERBIAL ACCUSATIVE (SECTION 141)
Quid plōrās?
['As to what are you weeping?']
'Why are you weeping?'

178. Summary of Uses of the Ablative Case

The ablative case is used to express a great variety of adverbial ideas.

(a) Ablative of Accompaniment (Section 4c)
Cum Petrō vēnit.
'He came with Peter.'

(b) Ablative of Separation (Section 27)
Līberā nōs (ā) malō.
'Deliver us from evil.'

(c) Ablative of Means (Section 34)
Gladiō occīsus est.
'He was killed with a sword.'

(d) Ablative of Manner (Section 35)
Magnō (cum) dolōre locūtus est.
'He spoke with great sorrow.'

(e) Ablative of Personal Agency (Section 37)
Missa ab episcopō celebrābitur.
'Mass will be celebrated by the bishop.'

(f) Ablative with Certain Adjectives (Section 38)
Avē, Marīa, grātiā plēna.
'Hail, Mary, full of grace.'

(g) Ablative of Respect or Specification (Section 50)
Beātī pauperēs spīritū.
'Blessed are the poor in spirit.'

(h) Ablative of Cause (Section 58)
(Prae) gaudiō clāmāvērunt.
'They shouted for joy.'

(i) Ablative Absolute (Section 68)
Hōc factō, abiit.
'With this having been done, he went away.'
'This done, he went away.'
'When he had done this, he went away.'

(j) Ablative of Description (Section 74)

Petrus erat magnā vir fidē.

  'Peter was a man of great faith.'

(k) Ablative of Place Where (Section 93)

In domō Petrī manēbant.

  'They were staying in Peter's house.'

(l) Ablative of Place from Which/out of Which (Section 94)

Ē domō vēnērunt.

  'They came from the house.'

(m) Ablative of Comparison (Section 143)

Quis est major illō?

  'Who is greater than that man?'

(n) Ablative of Degree of Difference (Section 144)

Petrus erat multō senior quam Jōannēs?

  'Was Peter much older than John?'

(o) Ablative of Time When/Time within Which (Section 164)

(In) illō tempore Jōannēs baptizābat in dēsertō.

  'At that time John was baptizing in the desert.'

Quīnque annīs hoc strūxērunt.

  'They built this in five years.'

(p) Ablative of Duration of Time (Section 166)

Duodecim annīs īnfirma fuerat.

  'She had been sick for twelve years.'

(q) Cognate Ablative (Section 176)

Magnō timōre timuērunt.

  'They feared with a great fear.'

  'They were exceedingly afraid.'

(r) Ablative with Certain Verbs

Certain verbs take a form of ablative of means rather than an accusative as direct object.

Sacerdōs rītū fungitur.

  'The priest is performing the ceremony.'

Vocabulary

accommodō, accommodāre, accommodāvī, accommodā-tus apply, fit; grant

cōnfortō, cōnfortāre, —, — strengthen; *pass.*, grow strong

exspoliō, exspoliāre,
exspoliāvī, exspoliātus
despoil, rob
irradiō, irradiāre, irradiāvī,
irradiātus shine, illumine
ōrnō, ōrnāre, ōrnāvī, ōrnātus
adorn, garnish, trim
adōrnō, adōrnāre, adōrnāvī,
adōrnātus adorn
pācificō, pācificāre, pācificāvī,
pācificātus make peace,
grant peace
revēlō, revēlāre, revēlāvī,
revēlātus show, reveal
jaceō, jacēre, jacuī, — lie,
be situated; sleep
cernō, cernere, crēvī, crētus
see, discern
discō, discere, didicī, — learn
tremō, tremere, tremuī, —
tremble (at), quake (at)
jaciō, jacere, jēcī, jactus throw
ējiciō, ējicere, ējēcī, ējectus
throw out
prōjiciō, prōjicere, prōjēcī,
prōjectus cast forth, throw
down
ēsuriō, ēsurīre, ēsurīvī (ēsuriī),
ēsurītus desire food, be
hungry

—, —, coepī, coeptus began,
started
—, —, ōdī, — hate
paenitentia, paenitentiae, f.
repentance
ruīna, ruīnae, f. fall,
destruction
baptismus, baptismī, m.
baptism
splendor, splendōris, m.
brilliance, splendor
dīgnātiō, dīgnātiōnis, f.
condescension, graciousness
hērēditās, hērēditātis, f.
generation; inheritance
immolātiō, immolātiōnis, f.
offering
multitūdō, multitūdinis, f.
great number, multitude
ops, opis, f. help
mātūtīnus, -a, -um (of) morning, early
propitius, -a, -um kind, favorable, propitious
mīrābilis, mīrābile wonderful
domus, domūs, f. house, home
necnōn (coord. conj.) and also,
and indeed

Vocabulary Notes

The verb —, —, coepī, coeptus 'began, started' has no present system; this lack is made up for by the use of the present system of incipiō (Unit 12). Coepī + infinitive is a common Greek periphrasis for
an imperfect: coepit discere 'he began to learn' = 'he was in the pro-
cess of learning,' 'he was learning.'

The verb —, —, ōdī, — 'hate' is a perfect used as a present. The
Vulgate also has ōdiō, ōdīre, ōdī, ōsus. The passive is conveyed by
the idiom ōdiō esse 'to be for the purpose of a hatred,' i.e., 'to be
hated.'

Baptismus and domus are heteroclites, i.e., nouns which use the

endings of two declensions. Cf. **baptisma, baptismatis**, n. (Unit 14)
and **domus, domī**, f. (Unit 6).

Derivatives:	LATIN	ENGLISH
	accommodō	accommodate
	cōnfortō	comfort
	exspoliō	spoil
	irradiō	irradiate
	ōrnō	ornament
	adōrnō	adornment
	pācificō	pacification
	revēlō	revelation
	jaceō	adjacent
	cernō	discrete, discreet
	discō	discipline, disciple
	tremō	tremor, tremendous
	ējiciō	eject
	prōjiciō	project
	ēsuriō	esurient
	paenitentia	penitence
	ruīna	ruin
	hērēditās	heredity
	immolātiō	immolation
	ops	opulent
	mātūtīnus	Matins, matinee, matutinal

Drills

I. Greek periphrastic tenses.
1. Apostolī erant in cēnāculō ōrantēs.
2. Jēsūs erat in monte ōrāns.
3. Diēbus tribus nōn erat vidēns.
4. Erimus in ecclēsiā cantantēs.
5. Sedentēs sunt in silentiō.

II. Syncopated and shortened forms. a. Identify. b. Give the full form.

1. audīsse	4. cūrāssent	7. fīniit
2. dēlērunt	5. laudārim	8. nescierat
3. amāstis	6. abiērunt	9. exiimus

Exercises

I.   1. Tunc Hērōdēs, clam ('secretly') vocātīs Magīs, dīligenter
         didicit ab eīs tempus stēllae, quae appāruit eīs, et mittēns
         illōs in Bēthlehem dīxit: "Īte et interrogāte dīligenter
         dē puerō; et cum invēneritis renūntiāte mihi, ut et ego
         veniēns adōrem eum." Mt. ii, 7–8.

      2. Tunc surrēxērunt omnēs virginēs illae et ōrnāvērunt lam-
         padēs suās. Mt. xxv, 7.

      3. Ecce sum vīvēns in saecula saeculōrum. Rev. i, 18.

      4. Et alterā diē cum exīrent ā Bēthaniā, ēsuriit. Mk. xi, 12.

      5. Et ait ad Simōnem Jēsūs: "Nōlī timēre; ex hōc jam homi-
         nēs eris capiēns." Lk. v, 10.

      6. Ēsurīvī enim, et dedistis mihi mandūcāre. Mt. xxv, 35.

      7. Et iterum coepit docēre ad mare. Mk. iv, 1.

      8. Avē, Rēx noster, Fīlī Dāvid, Redēmptor mundī, quem
         prophētae praedīxērunt Salvātōrem domuī Israēl esse
         ventūrum.

      9. Salvum fac populum tuum, Domine, et benedīc hērēditātī
         tuae, et rege eōs et extolle illōs ūsque in aeternum.

     10. Placuit Deō . . ut revēlāret Fīlium suum in mē. Gal. i,
         15–16.

     11. Venīte, occīdāmus eum et habēbimus hērēditātem ejus.
         Mt. xxi, 38.

     12. Nōn potest mundus ōdisse vōs, mē autem ōdit, quia ego
         testimōnium perhibeō dē illō quia opera ejus mala sunt.
         Jn. vii, 7.

     13. Ipse vērō, ējectīs omnibus, assūmit patrem puellae ('girl')
         et mātrem et, quī sēcum erant, et ingreditur, ubi erat puella
         [jacēns]. Mk. v, 40.

     14. Hērōdēs autem, vīsō Jēsū, gāvīsus est valdē: erat enim
         cupiēns ('desiring') ex multō tempore vidēre eum, eō quod
         audīret dē illō et spērābat sīgnum aliquod vidēre ab eō
         fierī. Lk. xxiii, 8.

     15. Oportet ergō ex hīs virīs, quī nōbīscum congregātī erant
         in omnī tempore, quō intrāvit et exīvit inter nōs Dominus
         Jēsūs, incipiēns ā baptismate Jōannis ūsque in diem, quā
         assūmptus est ā nōbīs, testem resurrēctiōnis ejus nōbīs-
         cum fierī ūnum ex istīs. Acts i, 21–22.

     16. Laetētur et māter Ecclēsia, tantī lūminis adōrnāta
         fulgōribus.

     17. Gaudeat et tellūs tantīs irradiāta fulgōribus: et aeternī
         Rēgis splendōre illūstrāta, tōtīus orbis sē sentiat āmīsisse
         cālīginem.

18. Ō vērē beāta nox, quae exspoliāvit Aegyptiōs, dītāvit Hebraeōs!

19. Tranquillum perpetuae pācis accommodā!

20. Flammās ejus lūcifer mātūtīnus inveniat!

21. Ō mīra circā nōs tuae pietātis dīgnātiō!

22. Fugat odia, concordiam parat et curvat imperia.

23. Sī quis dīxerit: [quoniam] "Dīligō Deum," et frātrem suum ōderit, mendāx ('liar') est. I Jn. iv, 20.

24. Et ecce: eris tacēns et nōn poteris loquī ūsque in diem, quō haec fīant. Lk. i, 20.

25. Tunc Paulus, extentā manū, coepit rationem reddere. Acts xxvi, 1.

26. Et vēnit praedicāns in synagōgis eōrum per omnem Galilaeam et daemonia ējiciēns. Mk. i, 39.

27. Exinde (= deinde) coepit Jēsūs ostendere discipulīs suīs quia oportēret eum īre Hierosolymam et multa patī ā seniōribus et prīncipibus sacerdōtum et scrībīs ('scribes') et occīdī et tertiā diē resurgere. Mt. xvi, 21.

28. Gaudiō gaudet propter vōcem spōnsī ('bridegroom'). Jn. iii, 29.

29. Fuit Jōannēs Baptista in dēsertō praedicāns baptismum paenitentiae in remissiōnem peccātōrum. Mk. i, 4.

30. Propitius estō, parce nōbīs, Domine!

31. Mulier autem timēns et tremēns, sciēns quod factum esset in sē, vēnit et prōcidit ante eum et dīxit eī omnem vēritātem. Mk. v, 33.

32. Hunc cum vīdisset Jēsūs jacentem, et cognōvisset quia multum jam tempus habet, dīcit eī: "Vīs sānus fierī?" Jn. v, 6.

33. Et replētī sunt timōre dīcentēs: "Vīdimus mīrābilia hodiē." Lk. v, 26.

34. Ait autem quīdam eī dē turbā: "Magister, dīc frātrī meō, ut dīvidat mēcum hērēditātem." Lk. xii, 13.

35. Dīxit eīs Jēsūs: "Ego sum pānis vītae. Quī venit ad mē, nōn ēsuriet." Jn. vi, 35.

36. Et exeuntēs praedicābant, ut paenitentiam agerent; et daemonia multa ējiciēbant. Mk. vi, 12–13.

37. Et quidem cum esset Fīlius, didicit ex hīs, quae passus est, oboedientiam. Heb. v, 8.

38. Et ait illīs: "Dēsīderiō dēsīderāvī hoc Pascha mandūcāre vōbīscum, antequam patiar. Dīcō enim vōbīs: Nōn mandūcābō illud, dōnec impleātur in rēgnō Deī." Lk. xxii, 15–16.

39. Nōnne praecipiendō praecēpimus vōbīs, nē docērētis in

nōmine istō? Et ecce replēstis Jerūsalem doctrīnā vestrā et vultis indūcere super nōs sanguinem hominis istīus. Acts v, 28.

40. Tū ergō, fīlī mī, cōnfortāre in grātiā, quae est in Chrīstō Jēsū, et, quae audīstī ā mē per multōs testēs, haec commendā fidēlibus hominibus, quī idōneī (= aptī) erunt et aliōs docēre. II Tim. ii, 1–2.

II. 1. Jesus was revealing many things to the apostles about the ruin of Jerusalem.
2. We are strengthened by God's help.
3. The multitude began to be hungry.
4. The women were exceedingly afraid until the angel spoke to them.
5. And Jesus told them to sit down in order that they might eat.
6. The apostles were going around in Galilee, and preaching the Gospel and casting out evil spirits.

Readings

1. The Conversion of Saul (II), Acts ix, 13–22.

Respondit autem Ananīās: "Domine, audīvī ā multīs dē virō hōc, quanta mala sānctīs tuīs fēcerit in Jerūsalem; et hic habet potestātem ā prīncipibus sacerdōtum alligandī[1] omnēs, quī invocant nōmen tuum." Dīxit autem ad eum Dominus: "Vāde, quoniam vās[2] ēlēctiōnis[3] est mihi iste, ut portet nōmen meum cōram gentibus et rēgibus et fīliīs Israēl; ego enim ostendam illī quanta oporteat eum prō nōmine meō patī." Et abiit Ananīās et introīvit in domum et impōnēns eī manūs dīxit: "Saul frāter, Dominus mīsit mē, Jēsūs quī appāruit tibi in viā, quā veniēbās, ut videās et impleāris Spīritū Sānctō." Et cōnfestim cecidērunt ab oculīs ejus tamquam[4] squāmae,[5] et vīsum[6] recēpit. Et surgēns baptizātus est et, cum accēpisset cibum, cōnfortātus est.

Fuit autem cum discipulīs, quī erant Damascī, per diēs aliquot[7] et continuō[8] in synagōgīs praedicābat Jēsūm, quoniam hic est Fīlius Deī. Stupēbant[9] autem omnēs, quī audiēbant et dīcēbant:

[1] **alligō, alligāre, alligāvī, alligātus** arrest [2] **vās, vāsis,** n. vessel [3] **ēlēctiō, ēlēctiōnis,** f. choice [4] **tamquam** (*adv.*) as it were [5] **squāma, squāmae,** f. scale, flake [6] **vīsus, vīsūs,** m. vision, sight [7] **aliquot** (*indecl. adj.*) some [8] **continuō** (*adv.*) at once [9] **stupeō, stupēre, stupuī,** — be stunned

"Nōnne hic est, quī expugnābat[10] in Jerūsalem eōs, quī invo-
cābant nōmen istud, et hūc[11] ad hoc vēnerat, ut vīnctōs illōs
dūceret ad prīncipēs sacerdōtum?" Saulus autem magis conva-
lēscēbat[12] et cōnfundēbat Jūdaeōs, quī habitābant[13] Damascī, af-
firmāns quoniam hic est Chrīstus.

[10]**expugnō, expugnāre, expugnāvī, expugnātus** attack [11]**hūc** (*adv.*) (to) here [12]**con-
valēscō, convalēscere, convaluī,** — become strong [13]**habitō, habitāre, habitāvī,
habitātus** dwell, live

2.   The Lord's Prayer.
      (a) Mt. vi, 9–13.
          Sīc ergō vōs ōrābitis:[1]
          Pater noster, quī es in caelīs,
          sānctificētur nōmen tuum,
          adveniat rēgnum tuum,
          fīat voluntās tua
             sīcut in caelō et in terrā.
          Pānem nostrum supersubstantiālem dā nōbīs hodiē;
          et dīmitte nōbīs dēbita nostra,
          sīcut et nōs dīmittimus dēbitōribus nostrīs;
          et nē nōs indūcās in tentātiōnem,
          sed līberā nōs ā Malō.

[1]Note the use of the plural; the singular is the norm in the future jussive
construction.

      (b) Lk. xi, 2–4.
          Et ait illīs: "Cum ōrātis, dīcite:
          Pater,
          sānctificētur nōmen tuum,
          adveniat rēgnum tuum;
          pānem nostrum cōtīdiānum dā nōbīs cōtīdiē,
          et dīmitte nōbīs peccāta nostra,
          sīquidem[1] et ipsī dīmittimus omnī dēbentī nōbīs,
          et nē nōs indūcās in tentātiōnem."

[1]**sīquidem** (*coord. conj.*) for indeed

Further Readings

1. The Ordinary of the Mass

℣. In nomine Patris, et Filii, et Spiritus Sancti.

R. Amen.

℣. Gratia Domini nostri Jesu Christi, et caritas Dei, et communicatio Sancti Spiritus sit cum omnibus vobis.

R. Et cum spiritu tuo.

℣. Fratres, agnoscamus peccata nostra, ut apti simus ad sacra mysteria celebranda.

Confiteor Deo omnipotenti, et vobis, fratres, quia peccavi nimis cogitatione, verbo, opere, et omissione: mea culpa, mea culpa, mea maxima culpa. Ideo precor beatam Mariam semper Virginem, omnes Angelos, et Sanctos, et vos, fratres, orare pro me ad Dominum Deum nostrum.

℣. Misereatur nostri omnipotens Deus, et, dimissis peccatis nostris, perducat nos ad vitam aeternam.

R. Amen.

℣. Kyrie eleison.

R. Kyrie eleison.

℣. Christe eleison.

R. Christe eleison.

℣. Kyrie eleison.

R. Kyrie eleison.

Gloria in excelsis Deo et in terra pax hominibus bonae voluntatis. Laudamus te, benedicimus te, adoramus te, glorificamus te, gratias agimus tibi propter magnam gloriam tuam, Domine Deus, Rex caelestis, Deus Pater omnipotens. Domine Fili unigenite, Jesu Christe, Domine Deus, Agnus Dei, Filius Patris, qui tollis peccata mundi, miserere nobis; qui tollis peccata mundi, suscipe deprecationem nostram. Qui sedes ad dexteram Patris, miserere nobis. Quoniam tu solus Sanctus, tu solus Dominus, tu solus Altissimus, Jesu Christe, cum Sancto Spiritu: in gloria Dei Patris. Amen.

Oremus.

[Et omnes una cum sacerdote per aliquod temporis spatium in silentio orant. Tunc sacerdos, manibus extensis, dicit orationem; qua finita, populus acclamat:]

R. Amen.

LITURGIA VERBI

[Lector ad ambonem legit primam lectionem. Ad finem lectionis significandam, lector subdit:]

Verbum Domini.
R. Deo gratias.

[Psalmista seu cantor psalmum dicit, populo responsum proferente. Postea, si habenda sit, legitur secunda lectio. Ad finem lectionis significandam, lector subdit:]

Verbum Domini.
R. Deo gratias.

[Sequitur Alleluja, vel alter cantus.]

℣. Dominus vobiscum.
R. Et cum spiritu tuo.
℣. Lectio sancti Evangelii secundum N.
R. Gloria tibi, Domine.

[Finito Evangelio, diaconus vel sacerdos dicit:]

Verbum Domini.
R. Laus tibi, Christe.

Credo in unum Deum Patrem omnipotentem, factorem caeli et terrae, visibilium omnium et invisibilium. Et in unum Dominum Jesum Christum, Filium Dei unigenitum, et ex Patre natum ante omnia saecula. Deum de Deo, lumen de lumine, Deum verum de Deo vero, genitum, non factum, consubstantialem Patri: per quem omnia facta sunt. Qui propter nos homines et propter nostram salutem descendit de caelis. [Ad verba quae sequuntur, usque ad *factus est*, omnes se inclinant.] Et incarnatus est de Spiritu Sancto ex Maria Virgine, et homo factus est. Crucifixus etiam pro nobis sub Pontio Pilato; passus et sepultus est, et resurrexit tertia die, secundum Scripturas, et ascendit in caelum, sedet ad dexteram Patris. Et iterum venturus est cum gloria judicare vivos et mortuos, cujus regni non erit finis. Et in Spiritum Sanctum, Dominum et vivificantem; qui ex Patre Filioque procedit. Qui cum Patre et Filio simul adoratur et conglorificatur; qui locutus est per prophetas. Et unam sanctam, catholicam et apostolicam Ecclesiam. Confiteor unum baptisma in remissionem peccatorum. Et exspecto resurrectionem mortuorum, et vitam venturi saeculi.

LITURGIA EUCHARISTICA

℣. Benedictus es, Domine, Deus universi, quia de tua largitate accepimus panem, quem tibi offerimus, fructum terrae et operis manuum hominum, ex quo nobis fiet panis vitae.

R. Benedictus Deus in saecula.

℣. Per hujus aquae et vini mysterium ejus efficiamur divinitatis consortes, qui humanitatis nostrae fieri dignatus est particeps. Benedictus es, Domine, Deus universi, quia de tua largitate accepimus vinum, quod tibi offerimus, fructum vitis et operis manuum hominum, ex quo nobis fiet potus spiritualis.

R. Benedictus Deus in saecula.

In spiritu humilitatis et in animo contrito suscipiamur a te, Domine; et sic fiat sacrificium nostrum in conspectu tuo hodie, ut placeat tibi, Domine Deus.

Lava me, Domine, ab iniquitate mea, et a peccato meo munda me.

℣. Orate, fratres: ut meum ac vestrum sacrificium acceptabile fiat apud Deum Patrem omnipotentem.

R. Suscipiat Dominus sacrificium de manibus tuis ad laudem et gloriam nominis sui, ad utilitatem quoque nostram totiusque Ecclesiae suae sanctae.

[In fine orationis super oblata, populus acclamat:]

R. Amen.

℣. Dominus vobiscum.
R. Et cum spiritu tuo.

℣. Sursum corda.
R. Habemus ad Dominum.
℣. Gratias agamus Domino Deo nostro.
R. Dignum et justum est.

[Sacerdos prosequitur praefationem. In fine praefationis, una cum populo, ipsam praefationem concludit, cantans vel clara voce dicens:]

Sanctus, Sanctus, Sanctus Dominus Deus Sabaoth. Pleni sunt caeli et terra gloria tua. Hosanna in excelsis. Benedictus qui venit in nomine Domini. Hosanna in excelsis.

Prex Eucharistica III

Vere Sanctus es, Domine, et merito te laudat omnis a te condita creatura, quia per Filium tuum, Dominum nostrum Jesum Christum, Spiritus Sancti operante virtute, vivificas et sanctificas universa, et populum tibi congregare non desinis, ut a solis ortu usque ad occasum oblatio munda offeratur nomini tuo.

Supplices ergo te, Domine, deprecamur, ut haec munera, quae tibi sacranda detulimus, eodem Spiritu sanctificare digneris, ut Corpus et Sanguis fiant Filii tui Domini nostri Jesu Christi, cujus mandato haec mysteria celebramus.

Ipse enim in qua nocte tradebatur accepit panem et tibi gratias agens benedixit, fregit, deditque discipulis suis, dicens:
Accipite et manducate ex hoc omnes: hoc est enim Corpus meum, quod pro vobis tradetur.

Simili modo, postquam cenatum est, accipiens calicem, et tibi gratias agens benedixit, deditque discipulis suis, dicens:
Accipite et bibite ex eo omnes: hic est enim calix Sanguinis mei novi et aeterni testamenti qui pro vobis et pro multis effundetur in remissionem peccatorum. Hoc facite in meam commemorationem.

Mysterium fidei:
R. Mortem tuam annuntiamus, Domine, et tuam resurrectionem confitemur, donec venias.

Memores igitur, Domine, ejusdem Filii tui salutiferae passionis necnon mirabilis resurrectionis et ascensionis in caelum, sed et praestolantes alterum ejus adventum, offerimus tibi, gratias referentes, hoc sacrificium vivum et sanctum.

Respice, quaesumus, in oblationem Ecclesiae tuae et, agnoscens

Hostiam, cujus voluisti immolatione placari, concede, ut, qui Corpore et Sanguine Filii tui reficimur, Spiritu ejus Sancto repleti, unum corpus et unus spiritus inveniamur in Christo.

Ipse nos tibi perficiat munus aeternum, ut cum electis tuis hereditatem consequi valeamus, in primis cum beatissima Virgine, Dei Genetrice, Maria, cum beatis Apostolis tuis et gloriosis Martyribus (cum Sancto N.: Sancto diei vel patrono) et omnibus Sanctis, quorum intercessione perpetuo apud te confidimus adjuvari.

Haec Hostia nostrae reconciliationis proficiat, quaesumus, Domine, ad totius mundi pacem atque salutem. Ecclesiam tuam, peregrinantem in terra, in fide et caritate firmare digneris cum famulo tuo Papa nostro N. et Episcopo nostro N., cum episcopali ordine et universo clero et omni populo acquisitionis tuae. Votis hujus familiae, quam tibi astare voluisti, adesto propitius. Omnes filios tuos ubique dispersos tibi, clemens Pater, miseratus conjunge.

Fratres nostros defunctos et omnes qui, tibi placentes, ex hoc saeculo transierunt in regnum tuum benignus admitte, ubi fore speramus, ut simul gloria tua perenniter satiemur, per Christum Dominum nostrum, per quem mundo bona cuncta largiris.

Per ipsum, et cum ipso, et in ipso, est tibi Deo Patri omnipotenti, in unitate Spiritus Sancti, omnis honor et gloria per omnia saecula saeculorum.

R. Amen.

RITUS COMMUNIONIS

℣. Praeceptis salutaribus moniti, et divina institutione formati, audemus dicere:

Pater noster, qui es in caelis, sanctificetur nomen tuum; adveniat regnum tuum; fiat voluntas tua, sicut in caelo et in terra. Panem nostrum cotidianum da nobis hodie; et dimitte nobis debita nostra, sicut et nos dimittimus debitoribus nostris; et ne nos inducas in tentationem; sed libera nos a malo.

℣. Libera nos, quaesumus, Domine, ab omnibus malis, da propitius pacem in diebus nostris, ut, ope misericordiae tuae adjuti, et a peccato simus semper liberi et ab omni perturbatione securi: exspectantes beatam spem et adventum Salvatoris nostri Jesu Christi.

R. Quia tuum est regnum, et potestas, et gloria in saecula.

℣. Domine, Jesu Christe, qui dixisti Apostolis tuis: Pacem relinquo vobis, pacem meam do vobis: ne respicias peccata nostra, sed fidem Ecclesiae tuae; eamque secundum voluntatem tuam pacificare et coadunare digneris. Qui vivis et regnas in saecula saeculorum.

R. Amen.

℣. Pax Domini sit semper vobiscum.

R. Et cum spiritu tuo.

℣. Offerte vobis pacem.

Haec commixtio Corporis et Sanguinis Domini nostri Jesu Christi fiat accipientibus nobis in vitam aeternam.

Agnus Dei, qui tollis peccata mundi: miserere nobis.
Agnus Dei, qui tollis peccata mundi: miserere nobis.
Agnus Dei, qui tollis peccata mundi: dona nobis pacem.

Domine Jesu Christe, Fili Dei vivi, qui ex voluntate Patris, cooperante Spiritu Sancto, per mortem tuam mundum vivificasti: libera me per hoc sacrosanctum Corpus et Sanguinem tuum ab omnibus iniquitatibus meis et universis malis: et fac me tuis semper inhaerere mandatis, et a te numquam separari permittas.

Ecce Agnus Dei, ecce qui tollit peccata mundi. Beati qui ad cenam Agni vocati sunt.

Domine, non sum dignus, ut intres sub tectum meum, sed tantum dic verbo, et sanabitur anima mea.

Corpus Christi custodiat me in vitam aeternam.
Sanguis Christi custodiat me in vitam aeternam.

℣. Corpus Christi.

R. Amen.

Quod ore sumpsimus, Domine, pura mente capiamus, et de munere temporali fiat nobis remedium sempiternum.

Oremus.

[Et omnes una cum Praeside per aliquod temporis spatium in silentio orant, nisi silentium jam praecesserit. Deinde Praeses, manibus extensis, dicit orationem post Communionem. Populus in fine acclamat:]

R. Amen.

RITUS CONCLUSIONIS

℣. Dominus vobiscum.

R. Et cum spiritu tuo.

℣. Benedicat vos omnipotens Deus, Pater, et Filius, et Spiritus Sanctus.

R. Amen.

℣. Ite, missa est.

R. Deo gratias.

2. The Exsultet (Ambrose, d. 397)

Sabbato Sancto: Praeconium Paschale

Exsultet jam angelica turba caelorum: exsultent divina mysteria: et pro tanti Regis victoria tuba insonet salutaris. Gaudeat et tellus tantis irradiata fulgoribus: et aeterni Regis splendore illustrata, totius orbis se sentiat amisisse caliginem. Laetetur et mater Ecclesia, tanti luminis adornata fulgoribus: et magnis populorum vocibus haec aula resultet. Quapropter astantes vos, fratres carissimi, ad tam miram hujus sancti luminis claritatem, una mecum, quaeso, Dei omnipotentis misericordiam invocate. Ut, qui me non meis meritis intra Levitarum numerum dignatus est aggregare: luminis sui claritatem infundens, cerei hujus laudem implere perficiat.

℣. Dominus vobiscum.

R. Et cum spiritu tuo.

℣. Sursum corda.

R. Habemus ad Dominum.

℣. Gratias agamus Domino Deo nostro.

R. Dignum et justum est.

Vere dignum et justum est, invisibilem Deum Patrem omnipotentem Filiumque ejus unigenitum, Dominum nostrum Jesum Christum, toto cordis ac mentis affectu et vocis ministerio personare. Qui pro nobis aeterno Patri Adae debitum solvit: et veteris piaculi cautionem pio cruore detersit. Haec sunt enim festa paschalia, in quibus verus ille Agnus occiditur, cujus sanguine postes fidelium consecrantur. Haec nox est, in qua primum patres nostros, filios Israel eductos de Aegypto, Mare Rubrum sicco vestigio transire fecisti. Haec igitur nox est, quae peccatorum tenebras columnae illuminatione purgavit. Haec nox est, quae hodie per universum mundum in Christo credentes, a vitiis saeculi et caligine peccatorum segregatos, reddit gratiae, sociat sanctitati. Haec nox est, in qua, destructis vinculis mortis, Christus ab inferis victor ascendit. Nihil enim nobis nasci profuit, nisi redimi profuisset. O mira circa nos tuae pietatis dignatio! O inaestimabilis dilectio caritatis: ut servum redimeres, Filium tradidisti! O certe necessarium Adae peccatum, quod Christi morte deletum est. O felix culpa, quae talem ac tantum meruit habere Redemptorem! O vere beata nox, quae sola meruit scire tempus et horam, in qua Christus ab inferis resurrexit! Haec nox est, de qua scriptum est: Et nox sicut dies illuminabitur: Et nox illuminatio mea in deliciis meis. Hujus igitur sanctificatio noctis fugat scelera, culpas lavat: et reddit innocentiam lapsis et maestis laetitiam. Fugat odia, concordiam parat et curvat imperia. In hujus igitur noctis gratia, suscipe, sancte Pater, incensi hujus sacrificium vespertinum: quod tibi in hac Cerei oblatione sollemni, per ministrorum manus de operibus apum, sacrosancta reddit Ecclesia. Sed jam columnae hujus praeconia novimus, quam in honorem Dei rutilans ignis accendit. Qui licet sit divisus in partes, mutuati tamen luminis detrimenta non novit. Alitur enim liquantibus ceris, quas in substantiam pretiosae hujus lampadis apis mater eduxit.

O vere beata nox, quae exspoliavit Aegyptios, ditavit Hebraeos! Nox, in qua terrenis caelestia, humanis divina junguntur. Oramus ergo te, Domine: ut Cereus iste in honorem tui nominis consecratus, ad noctis hujus caliginem destruendam, indeficiens perseveret. Et in odorem suavitatis acceptus, supernis luminaribus misceatur. Flammas ejus lucifer matutinus inveniat. Ille, inquam, lucifer qui nescit occasum. Ille, qui regressus ab inferis, humano generi serenus illuxit. Precamur ergo te, Domine: ut nos famulos tuos, omnemque clerum, et devotissimum populum: una cum beatissimo Papa nostro et Antistite nostro, quiete temporum concessa, in his paschalibus gaudiis, assidua protectione regere, gubernare et conservare digneris. Respice etiam ad devotissimum Imperatorem nostrum, cujus tu, Deus, desideri vota praenoscens, ineffabili pietatis et misericordiae tuae munere, tranquillum perpetuae pacis accommoda: et caelestem victoriam cum omni populo suo.

Per eundem Dominum nostrum Jesum Christum, Filium tuum: qui tecum vivit et regnat in unitate Spiritus Sancti, Deus: per omnia saecula saeculorum. Amen.

3. Luke's Gospel, cc. 1 & 2

Quoniam quidem multi conati sunt ordinare[1] narrationem,[2] quae in nobis completae sunt, rerum, sicut tradiderunt nobis, qui ab initio[3] ipsi viderunt et ministri fuerunt verbi, visum est et mihi, adsecuto a principio omnia, diligenter ex ordine tibi scribere, optime Theophile, ut cognoscas eorum verborum, de quibus eruditus[4] es, firmitatem.[5]

Fuit in diebus Herodis regis Judaeae sacerdos quidam nomine Zacharias de vice[6] Abiae et uxor[7] illi de filiabus Aaron, et nomen ejus Elisabeth. Erant autem justi ambo[8] ante Deum, incedentes in omnibus mandatis et justificationibus[9] Domini, irreprehensibiles.[10] Et non erat illis filius eo quod esset Elisabeth sterilis,[11] et ambo processissent in diebus suis.

Factum est autem cum sacerdotio[12] fungeretur in ordine vicis suae ante Deum, secundum consuetudinem sacerdotii sorte[13] exiit, ut incensum poneret ingressus in templum Domini; et omnis multitudo erat populi orans foris[14] hora incensi. Apparuit autem illi angelus Domini stans a dextris altaris incensi; et Zacharias turbatus est[15] videns, et timor irruit[16] super eum. Ait autem ad illum angelus: "Ne timeas, Zacharia, quoniam exaudita est deprecatio tua, et uxor tua Elisabeth pariet tibi filium, et vocabis nomen ejus Joannem. Et erit gaudium tibi et exsultatio, et multi in nativitate ejus gaudebunt: erit enim magnus coram Domino et vinum et siceram[17] non bibet et Spiritu Sancto replebitur adhuc ex utero[18] matris suae et multos filiorum Israel convertet ad Dominum Deum ipsorum. Et ipse prae-

[1] ōrdinō, ōrdināre, ōrdināvī, ōrdinātus arrange, compile
[2] nārrātiō, nārrātiōnis, f. account, narrative
[3] initium, initiī, n. beginning
[4] ērudītus, -a, -um learned, versed
[5] firmitās, firmitātis, f. firmness, certainty
[6] —, vicis, f. turn, duty. Priestly classes rotated their service.
[7] uxor, uxōris, f. wife
[8] ambō, ambae, ambō both
[9] jūstificātiō, jūstificātiōnis, f. formality, ordinance
[10] irreprehēnsibilis, -e blameless
[11] sterilis, -e sterile, barren
[12] sacerdōtium, sacerdōtiī, n. priesthood, priestly duties
[13] sors, sortis, f. lot
[14] forīs (adv.) outside, outdoors
[15] turbō, turbāre, turbāvī, turbātus disturb, throw into confusion
[16] irruō, irruere, irruī, — rush into, rush upon, take hold of
[17] sīcera, sīcerae, f. an intoxicating drink, hard liquor
[18] uterus, uterī, m. belly, womb

cedet ante illum in spiritu et virtute Eliae, *ut convertat corda pa-trum in filios* et incredibiles[19] ad prudentiam[20] justorum, parare Domino plebem[21] perfectam." Et dixit Zacharias ad angelum: "Unde hoc sciam? Ego enim sum senex et uxor mea processit in diebus suis." Et respondens angelus dixit ei: "Ego sum Gabriel, qui adsto ante Deum, et missus sum loqui ad te et haec tibi evangelizare. Et ecce: eris tacens et non poteris loqui usque in diem, quo haec fiant, pro eo quod[22] non credidisti verbis meis, quae implebuntur in tem-pore suo."

Et erat plebs exspectans Zachariam, et mirabantur quod tardaret[23] ipse in templo. Egressus autem non poterat loqui ad illos, et cog-noverunt quod visionem[24] vidisset in templo; et ipse erat innuens[25] illis et permansit mutus.[26]

Et factum est ut impleti sunt dies officii[27] ejus, abiit in domum suam. Post hos autem dies concepit Elisabeth uxor ejus et occul-tabat[28] se mensibus[29] quinque dicens: "Sic mihi fecit Dominus in diebus, quibus respexit auferre opprobrium[30] meum inter homines."

In mense autem sexto missus est angelus Gabriel a Deo in civita-tem Galilaeae, cui nomen Nazareth, ad virginem desponsatam[31] viro, cui nomen erat Joseph de domo David, et nomen virginis Maria. Et ingressus ad eam dixit: "Ave, gratia plena, Dominus tecum." Ipsa autem turbata est in sermone ejus et cogitabat qualis esset ista sa-lutatio.[32] Et ait angelus ei: "Ne timeas, Maria; invenisti enim gra-tiam apud Deum. Et ecce concipies in utero et paries filium, et vocabis nomen ejus Jesum. Hic erit magnus et Filius Altissimi vo-cabitur, et dabit illi Dominus Deus sedem David patris ejus, et reg-nabit super domum Jacob in aeternum, et regni ejus non erit finis."

Dixit autem Maria ad angelum: "Quomodo fiet istud, quoniam virum non cognosco?" Et respondens angelus dixit ei: "Spiritus

[19] **incrēdibilis, -e** disobedient, rebellious
[20] **prūdentia, prūdentiae**, f. insight, wisdom, way of thinking
[21] **plēbs, plēbis**, f. people
[22] **prō eō quod** 'because'
[23] **tardō, tardāre, tardāvī, tardātus** delay, loiter
[24] **vīsiō, vīsiōnis**, f. vision
[25] **innuō, innuere, innuī**, — give a nod to, make signals to
[26] **mūtus, -a, -um** speechless, dumb
[27] **officium, officiī**, n. service
[28] **occultō, occultāre, occultāvī, occultātus** hide, conceal
[29] **mēnsis, mēnsis, mēnsium**, m. month
[30] **opprobrium, opprobriī**, n. reproach, disgrace
[31] **dēspōnsātus, -a, -um** engaged
[32] **salūtātiō, salūtātiōnis**, f. greeting

Sanctus superveniet in te, et virtus Altissimi obumbrabit[33] tibi: ideoque et, quod nascetur, sanctum vocabitur, Filius Dei. Et ecce Elisabeth cognata[34] tua et ipsa concepit filium in senecta[35] sua, et hic mensis est sextus illi, quae vocatur sterilis, quia *non erit impossibile*[36] *apud Deum omne verbum."* Dixit autem Maria: "Ecce ancilla Domini; fiat mihi secundum verbum tuum." Et discessit ab illa angelus.

Exsurgens[37] autem Maria in diebus illis abiit in montana[38] cum festinatione[39] in civitatem Judae et intravit in domum Zachariae et salutavit[40] Elisabeth. Et factum est ut audivit salutationem Mariae Elisabeth, exsultavit[41] infans[42] in utero ejus, et repleta est Spiritu Sancto Elisabeth et exclamavit voce magna et dixit: "Benedicta tu inter mulieres, et benedictus fructus ventris tui. Et unde hoc mihi, ut veniat mater Domini mei ad me? Ecce enim ut facta est vox salutationis tuae in auribus meis, exsultavit in gaudio infans in utero meo. Et beata, quae credidit, quoniam perficientur ea, quae dicta sunt ei a Domino."
Et ait Maria:

"Magnificat *anima mea Dominum,*
et *exsultavit* spiritus meus *in Deo salvatore meo,*
quia *respexit humilitatem ancillae* suae.
Ecce enim ex hoc[43] beatam me dicent omnes generationes,[44]
quia fecit mihi magna, qui potens est,
et sanctum nomen ejus,
et misericordia ejus in progenies[45] et progenies
timentibus eum.
Fecit potentiam in brachio suo,
dispersit superbos[46] mente cordis sui;
deposuit potentes de sede

[33] **obumbrō, obumbrāre, obumbrāvī, obumbrātus** overshadow
[34] **cognāta, cognātae,** f. kinswoman, female relative
[35] **senecta, senectae,** f. old age
[36] **impossibilis, -e** impossible
[37] **exsurgō** = **ex** + **surgō** rise up, depart
[38] **montāna, montānōrum,** n. mountainous districts, hill country
[39] **festīnātiō, festīnātiōnis,** f. haste, speed
[40] **salūtō, salūtāre, salūtāvī, salūtātus** greet
[41] **exsultāvit** *here,* 'leapt, stirred'
[42] **īnfāns, īnfantis,** m. & f. baby, infant
[43] **ex hōc** 'from this (time), from now on'
[44] **generātiō, generātiōnis,** f. generation, age
[45] **prōgeniēs, prōgeniēī,** f. generation, age
[46] **superbus, -a, -um** proud, haughty

et exaltavit humiles;
esurientes implevit bonis
et divites dimisit inanes.[47]
Suscepit Israel puerum suum,
recordatus[48] misericordiae,
sicut locutus est ad patres nostros,
Abraham et semini[49] ejus in saecula."

Mansit autem Maria cum illa quasi[50] mensibus tribus et reversa est in domum suam. Elisabeth autem impletum est tempus pariendi, et peperit filium. Et audierunt vicini et cognati[51] ejus quia magnificavit Dominus misericordiam suam cum illa, et congratulabantur[52] ei. Et factum est in die octavo venerunt circumcidere[53] puerum et vocabant eum nomine patris ejus Zachariam. Et respondens mater ejus dixit: "Nequaquam,[54] sed vocabitur Joannes." Et dixerunt ad illam: "Nemo est in cognatione[55] tua, qui vocetur hoc nomine." Innuebant autem patri ejus quem vellet vocari eum. Et postulans pugillarem[56] scripsit dicens: "Joannes est nomen ejus." Et mirati sunt universi. Apertum est autem ilico[57] os ejus et lingua ejus, et loquebatur benedicens Deum. Et factus est timor super omnes vicinos eorum, et super omnia montana Judaeae divulgabantur[58] omnia verba haec. Et posuerunt omnes, qui audierant, in corde suo dicentes: "Quid putas puer iste erit?" Etenim[59] manus Domini erat cum illo.

Et Zacharias pater ejus impletus est Spiritu Sancto et prophetavit[60] dicens:

"*Benedictus Dominus Deus Israel*,
quia visitavit[61] et fecit redemptionem plebi suae

---

[47] **inānis, -e** empty
[48] **recordor, recordārī, —, recordātus sum** remember (+ *gen.*)
[49] **sēmen, sēminis**, n. seed, offspring
[50] **quasi** (*adv.*) as if, as it were; about
[51] **cognātī, cognātōrum**, m. relatives
[52] **congrātulor, congrātulārī, —, congrātulātus sum** wish joy, congratulate (+ *dat.*)
[53] **circumcīdō, circumcīdere, circumcīdī, circumcīsus** circumcise
[54] **nēquāquam** (*adv.*) by no means, not at all
[55] **cognātiō, cognātiōnis**, f. relatives, family
[56] **pugillārēs, pugillārium**, m. writing-tablets; *here, in sing.*
[57] **īlico** (*adv.*) on the spot, immediately
[58] **dīvulgō, dīvulgāre, dīvulgāvī, dīvulgātus** make common, talk about
[59] **etenim** (*coord. conj.*) and indeed, for indeed
[60] **prophētō, prophētāre, prophētāvī, prophētātus** prophesy, foretell
[61] **vīsitō, vīsitāre, vīsitāvī, vīsitātus** visit

et erexit cornu salutis nobis
in domo David pueri sui,
sicut locutus est per os sanctorum,
qui a saeculo sunt, prophetarum ejus,
salutem ex inimicis nostris
et de manu omnium, qui oderunt nos;
ad faciendam misericordiam cum patribus nostris
et memorari testamenti sui sancti,
jusjurandum,[62] quod juravit[63] ad Abraham patrem nostrum,
daturum se nobis,
ut sine timore, de manu inimicorum liberati,
serviamus illi
in sanctitate et justitia coram ipso
omnibus diebus nostris.
Et tu, puer, propheta Altissimi vocaberis:
praeibis enim *ante faciem Domini parare vias ejus,*
ad dandam scientiam[64] salutis plebi ejus
in remissionem peccatorum eorum,
per viscera misericordiae[65] Dei nostri,
in quibus visitabit nos oriens ex alto,
illuminare his, qui in tenebris et in umbra mortis sedent,
ad dirigendos pedes nostros in viam pacis."

Puer autem crescebat et confortabatur spiritu et erat in deserto usque in diem ostensionis[66] suae ad Israel.

Factum est autem in diebus illis exiit edictum[67] a Caesare Augusto, ut describeretur universus orbis. Haec descriptio[68] prima facta est praeside Syriae Quirino. Et ibant omnes, ut profiterentur,[69] singuli[70] in suam civitatem. Ascendit autem et Joseph a Galilaea de civitate Nazareth in Judaeam in civitatem David, quae vocatur Bethlehem, eo quod esset de domo et familia David, ut profiteretur cum Maria desponsata sibi, uxore praegnante.[71] Factum est autem cum essent ibi, impleti sunt dies, ut pareret, et peperit filium suum pri-

---

[62] **jūsjūrandum, jūrisjūrandī**, n. oath
[63] **jūrō, jūrāre, jūrāvī, jūrātus** swear
[64] **scientia, scientiae**, f. knowledge
[65] **viscera misericordiae** 'bowels of compassion,' a Hebraism
[66] **ostēnsiō, ostēnsiōnis**, f. public appearance
[67] **ēdictum, ēdictī**, n. decree
[68] **dēscrīptiō, dēscrīptiōnis**, f. registration, census
[69] **profitērī** *here*, 'to make a public statement'
[70] **singulī, -ae, -a** each one
[71] **praegnāns** (*gen.*, **praegnantis**) pregnant

mogenitum; [72] et pannis [73] eum involvit [74] et reclinavit eum in praesepio,[75] quia non erat eis locus in deversorio.[76]

Et pastores erant in regione eadem vigilantes [77] et custodientes vigilias [78] noctis supra [79] gregem suum. Et angelus Domini stetit juxta illos, et claritas Domini circumfulsit illos, et timuerunt timore magno. Et dixit illis angelus: "Nolite timere; ecce enim evangelizo vobis gaudium magnum, quod erit omni populo, quia natus est vobis hodie Salvator, qui est Christus Dominus, in civitate David. Et hoc vobis signum: invenietis infantem pannis involutum et positum in praesepio." Et subito facta est cum angelo multitudo militiae [80] caelestis laudantium Deum et dicentium:

"Gloria in altissimis Deo,
et super terram pax in hominibus bonae voluntatis." [81]

Et factum est ut discesserunt ab eis angeli in caelum, pastores loquebantur ad invicem: 'Transeamus usque Bethlehem et videamus hoc verbum,[82] quod factum est, quod Dominus ostendit nobis." Et venerunt festinantes [83] et invenerunt Mariam et Joseph et infantem positum in praesepio. Videntes autem notum fecerunt verbum, quod dictum erat illis de puero hoc. Et omnes, qui audierunt, mirati sunt de his, quae dicta erant a pastoribus ad ipsos. Maria autem conservabat omnia verba haec conferens in corde suo.

Et reversi sunt pastores glorificantes et laudantes Deum in omnibus, quae audierant et viderant, sicut dictum est ad illos. Et postquam consummati [84] sunt dies octo, ut circumcideretur, vocatum est nomen ejus Jesus, quod vocatum est ab angelo, priusquam in utero conciperetur.

Et postquam impleti sunt dies purgationis [85] eorum secundum

[72] **prīmogenitus, -a, -um** first-born
[73] **pannus, pannī,** m. cloth, piece of cloth; *pl.*, baby clothes
[74] **involvō, involvere, involvī, involūtus** wrap up
[75] **praesēpium, praesēpiī,** n. manger, feeding-trough
[76] **dēversōrium, dēversōriī,** n. inn, lodging-place
[77] **vigilō, vigilāre, vigilāvī, vigilātus** stay awake
[78] **vigilia, vigiliae,** f. a watch
[79] **suprā** (*prep.* + *acc.*) over
[80] **mīlitia, mīlitiae,** f. army, host
[81] **bonae voluntātis** 'of His good pleasure'
[82] **verbum** *here*, 'event'
[83] **festīnō, festīnāre, festīnāvī, festīnātus** hasten, hurry
[84] **cōnsummō, cōnsummāre, cōnsummāvī, cōnsummātus** finish, complete
[85] **pūrgātiō, pūrgātiōnis,** f. purification

Legem Moysis, tulerunt illum in Hierosolymam, ut sisterent Domino, sicut scriptum est in lege Domini: "*Omne masculinum*[86] *adaperiens*[87] *vulvam*[88] *sanctum Domino vocabitur,*" et ut darent hostiam secundum quod dictum est in lege Domini: *par*[89] *turturum*[90] *aut duos pullos*[91] *columbarum.*[92]

Et ecce homo erat in Jerusalem, cui nomen Simeon, et homo iste justus et timoratus, exspectans consolationem[93] Israel, et Spiritus Sanctus erat super eum, et responsum acceperat ab Spiritu Sancto non visurum se mortem nisi prius videret Christum Domini. Et venit in Spiritu in templum. Et cum inducerent puerum Jesum parentes ejus, ut facerent secundum consuetudinem legis pro eo, et ipse accepit eum in ulnas[94] suas et benedixit Deum et dixit:

> "Nunc dimittis servum tuum, Domine,
> secundum verbum tuum in pace,
> quia viderunt oculi mei
> salutare tuum,
> quod parasti
> ante faciem omnium populorum,
> lumen ad revelationem gentium
> et gloriam plebis tuae Israel."

Et erat pater ejus et mater mirantes super his, quae dicebantur de illo. Et benedixit illis Simeon et dixit ad Mariam matrem ejus: "Ecce positus est hic in ruinam et resurrectionem multorum in Israel et in signum, cui contradicetur—et tuam ipsius[95] animam pertransiet[96] gladius—ut revelentur ex multis cordibus cogitationes."

Et erat Anna prophetissa,[97] filia Phanuel, de tribu[98] Aser. Haec processerat in diebus multis et vixerat cum viro suo annis septem a virginitate sua; et haec vidua[99] usque ad annos octoginta quattuor,

---

[86] **masculīnus, -a, -um** male
[87] **adaperiō = ad + aperiō**
[88] **vulva, vulvae**, f. womb
[89] **pār** *here*, 'pair'
[90] **turtur, turturis**, m. turtle-dove
[91] **pullus, pullī**, m. young (of a bird)
[92] **columba, columbae**, f. dove, pigeon
[93] **cōnsōlātiō, cōnsōlātiōnis**, f. consolation, help, rescue
[94] **ulna, ulnae**, f. arm
[95] **tuam ipsīus** 'your own'
[96] **pertrānsiet = pertrānsībit**
[97] **prophētissa, prophētissae**, f. prophetess
[98] **tribus, tribūs**, f. tribe
[99] **vidua, viduae**, f. widow

quae non discedebat de templo, jejuniis [100] et obsecrationibus [101] serviens nocte ac die. Et haec ipsa hora superveniens confitebatur Deo et loquebatur de illo omnibus, qui exspectabant redemptionem Jerusalem.

Et ut perfecerunt omnia secundum legem Domini, reversi sunt in Galilaeam in civitatem suam Nazareth. Puer autem crescebat et confortabatur plenus sapientia; et gratia Dei erat super illum.

Et ibant parentes ejus per omnes annos in Jerusalem in die festo Paschae. Et cum factus esset annorum duodecim, ascendentibus illis secundum consuetudinem diei festi, consummatisque diebus, cum redirent, remansit puer Jesus in Jerusalem, et non cognoverunt parentes ejus. Existimantes autem illum esse in comitatu, [102] venerunt iter diei et requirebant eum inter cognatos et notos [103] et non invenientes regressi sunt in Jerusalem requirentes eum. Et factum est post triduum [104] invenerunt illum in templo sedentem in medio doctorum, audientem illos et interrogantem eos; stupebant [105] autem omnes, qui eum audiebant, super prudentia et responsis ejus. Et videntes eum admirati sunt, et dixit Mater ejus ad illum: "Fili, quid fecisti nobis sic? Ecce pater tuus et ego dolentes quaerebamus te." Et ait ad illos: "Quid est quod me quaerebatis? Nesciebatis quia in his, quae Patris mei sunt, oportet me esse?" Et ipsi non intellexerunt verbum, quod locutus est ad illos.

Et descendit cum eis et venit Nazareth et erat subditus illis. Et mater ejus conservabat omnia verba in corde suo. Et Jesus *proficiebat* sapientia et aetate [106] *et gratia apud Deum et homines.*

[100] **jējūnium, jējūniī,** n. fast
[101] **obsecrātiō, obsecrātiōnis,** f. prayer
[102] **comitātus, comitātūs,** m. company of travelers, traveling party
[103] **nōtī, nōtōrum,** m. friends, acquaintances
[104] **trīduum, trīduī,** n. a three-day period
[105] **stupeō, stupēre, stupuī,** — be stunned, be astonished
[106] **aetās, aetātis,** f. time of life, age

4. Mark's Passion, xiv, 26–xv, 47

Et hymno dicto, exierunt in montem Olivarum.[1] Et ait eis Jesus: "Omnes scandalizabimini,[2] quia scriptum est:

'Percutiam[3] pastorem, et dispergentur oves.'

[1] **olīva, olīvae,** f. olive (tree)
[2] **scandalizō** (1) make stumble
[3] **percutiō, percutere, percussī, percussus** strike

Sed posteaquam[4] resurrexero, praecedam vos in Galilaeam." Petrus autem ait ei: "Et si omnes scandalizati fuerint, sed non ego." Et ait illi Jesus: "Amen dico tibi: Tu hodie, in nocte hac, priusquam bis[5] gallus[6] vocem dederit, ter[7] me es negaturus." At ille amplius loquebatur: "Et si oportuerit me commori[8] tibi, non te negabo." Similiter autem et omnes dicebant.

Et veniunt in praedium,[9] cui nomen Gethsemani, et ait discipulis suis: "Sedete hic, donec orem." Et assumit Petrum et Jacobum et Joannem secum et coepit pavere[10] et taedere[11] et ait illis: "Tristis est anima mea usque ad mortem; sustinete hic et vigilate." Et cum processisset paululum,[12] procidebat super terram et orabat, ut, si fieri posset, transiret ab eo hora, et dicebat: "Abba, Pater! Omnia tibi possibilia sunt. Transfer calicem hunc a me; sed non quod ego volo, sed tu." Et venit et invenit eos dormientes[13] et ait Petro: "Simon, dormis? Non potuisti una hora vigilare? Vigilate et orate, ut non intretis in tentationem; spiritus quidem promptus,[14] caro vero infirma." Et iterum abiens oravit, eundem sermonem[15] dicens. Et veniens denuo[16] invenit eos dormientes; erant enim oculi illorum ingravati,[17] et ignorabant[18] quid responderent ei. Et venit tertio et ait illis: "Dormite jam et requiescite?[19] Sufficit, venit hora: ecce traditur Filius hominis in manus peccatorum. Surgite, eamus; ecce, qui me tradit, prope[20] est."

Et confestim, adhuc eo loquente, venit Judas unus ex Duodecim, et cum illo turba cum gladiis et lignis a summis[21] sacerdotibus et scribis[22] et senioribus. Dederat autem traditor[23] ejus signum eis di-

---

[4] posteāquam = postquam
[5] bis (adv.) twice
[6] gallus, gallī, m. cock
[7] ter (adv.) three times, thrice
[8] commorior = com + morior die with (+ dat.)
[9] praedium, praediī, n. piece of land, estate
[10] paveō, pavēre, pavī, — tremble with fear
[11] taedeō, taedēre, taeduī, taesus be distressed
[12] paululum (adv.) a little, a short distance
[13] dormiō (4) sleep
[14] prōmptus, -a, -um willing, ready, eager
[15] sermō, sermōnis, m. word, speech
[16] dēnuō (adv.) again
[17] ingravō (1) weigh down
[18] ignōrō (1) not to know
[19] requiēscō, requiēscere, requiēvī, requiētus rest oneself
[20] prope (adv.) near
[21] summus, -a, -um highest; here, 'chief'
[22] scrība, scrībae, m. scribe (i.e., one versed in Jewish law)
[23] trāditor, trāditōris, m. betrayer

cens: "Quemcumque osculatus fuero,[24] ipse est; tenete eum et du-
cite caute."[25] Et cum venisset, statim accedens ad eum ait: "Rabbi,"
et osculatus est eum. At illi manus injecerunt[26] in eum et tenuerunt
eum. Unus autem quidam de circumstantibus educens gladium per-
cussit servum summi sacerdotis et amputavit[27] illi auriculam.[28] Et
respondens Jesus ait illis: "Tamquam[29] ad latronem[30] existis cum
gladiis et lignis comprehendere[31] me? Cotidie eram apud vos in templo docens et non me tenuistis; sed adimpleantur Scripturae." Et re-
linquentes eum omnes fugerunt. Et adulescens[32] quidam sequebatur
eum amictus[33] sindone[34] super nudo,[35] et tenent eum; at ille, re-
jecta[36] sindone, nudus profugit.[37]

Et adduxerunt[38] Jesum ad summum sacerdotem, et conveniunt
omnes summi sacerdotes et seniores et scribae. Et Petrus a longe[39]
secutus est eum usque intro[40] in atrium[41] summi sacerdotis, et sede-
bat cum ministris et calefaciebat[42] se ad ignem. Summi vero sacerdotes et omne concilium[43] quaerebant adversus Jesum testimonium,
ut eum morte afficerent, nec inveniebant. Multi enim testimonium
falsum dicebant adversus eum, et convenientia testimonia non erant.
Et quidam surgentes falsum testimonium ferebant adversus eum dicentes: "Nos audivimus eum dicentem: 'Ego dissolvam[44] templum
hoc manu factum et intra triduum aliud non manu factum aedifi-
cabo.'"[45] Et ne ita quidem[46] conveniens erat testimonium illorum.

---

[24] ōsculor (1) kiss
[25] cautē (adv.) under close watch
[26] injiciō = in + jaciō
[27] amputō (1) lop off
[28] auricula, auriculae, f. ear
[29] tamquam (adv.) just as
[30] lātrō, lātrōnis, m. brigand, bandit
[31] comprehendō, comprehendere, comprehendī, comprehēnsus arrest
[32] adulēscēns (gen., adulēscentis) young; subst., young man, youth
[33] amiciō, amicīre, amicuī/amixī, amictus clothe, cover
[34] sindōn, sindonis, f. linen cloth
[35] nūdus, -a, -um naked
[36] rejiciō = re + jaciō
[37] profugiō = prō + fugiō
[38] addūcō = ad + dūcō
[39] ā longē (adv.) from afar, at a distance
[40] intrō (adv.) within, inside
[41] ātrium, ātriī, n. courtyard
[42] calefaciō (< faciō) make warm, warm
[43] concilium, conciliī, n. Sanhedrin
[44] dissolvō = dis + solvō
[45] aedificō (1) build
[46] nē . . quidem 'not even'

Et exsurgens summus sacerdos in medium interrogavit Jesum dicens: "Non respondes quidquam ad ea, quae isti testantur[47] adversum te?" Ille autem tacebat et nihil respondit. Rursum[48] summus sacerdos interrogabat eum et dicit ei: "Tu es Christus filius Benedicti?" Jesus autem dixit: "Ego sum, et *videbitis Filium hominis a dextris sedentem Virtutis* et *venientem cum nubibus*[49] *caeli.*"

Summus autem sacerdos scindens[50] vestimenta[51] sua ait: "Quid adhuc necessarii sunt nobis testes? Audistis blasphemiam; quid vobis videtur?" Qui omnes condemnaverunt[52] eum esse reum mortis.[53]

Et coeperunt quidam conspuere[54] eum et velare[55] faciem ejus et colaphis[56] eum caedere[57] et dicere ei: "Prophetiza";[58] et ministri alapis[59] eum caedebant.

Et cum esset Petrus in atrio deorsum,[60] venit una ex ancillis summi sacerdotis et, cum vidisset Petrum calefacientem se, aspiciens illum ait: "Et tu cum hoc Nazareno, Jesu, eras." At ille negavit dicens: "Neque scio neque novi quid tu dicas." Et exiit foras[61] ante atrium, et gallus cantavit. Et ancilla, cum vidisset illum, rursus[62] coepit dicere circumstantibus: "Hic ex illis est." At ille iterum negabat. Et post pusillum[63] rursus, qui astabant, dicebant Petro: "Vere ex illis es, nam et Galilaeus es." Ille autem coepit anathematizare[64] et jurare:[65] "Nescio hominem istum, quem dicitis." Et statim iterum gallus cantavit. Et recordatus est[66] Petrus verbi, sicut dixerat ei Jesus: "Priusquam gallus cantet bis, ter me negabis," et coepit flere.

---

[47] **testor** (1) bear witness, give evidence of
[48] **rūrsum** (*adv.*) again
[49] **nūbēs, nūbis, nūbium,** f. cloud
[50] **scindō, scindere, scidī, scissus** tear, rend
[51] **vestīmentum, vestīmentī,** n. garment; *pl.,* clothes
[52] **condemnō** (1) condemn, pass judgment
[53] **reum mortis** 'deserving of death'
[54] **cōnspuō, cōnspuere, cōnspuī, cōnspūtus** spit on
[55] **vēlō** (1) cover
[56] **colaphus, colaphī,** m. punch (sharp blow with the fist)
[57] **caedō, caedere, cecīdī, caesus** cut, strike
[58] **prophētizō** (1) be a prophet, play the prophet
[59] **alapa, alapae,** f. slap
[60] **deorsum** (*adv.*) down, below
[61] **forās** (*adv.*) outside
[62] **rūrsus** = **rūrsum**
[63] **pusillum, pusillī,** n. a little (while)
[64] **anathematizō** (1) curse
[65] **jūrō** (1) swear
[66] **recordor** (1) remember (+ *gen.*)

Et confestim mane[67] consilium[68] facientes summi sacerdotes cum senioribus et scribis, id est universum concilium, vincientes Jesum duxerunt et tradiderunt Pilato. Et interrogavit eum Pilatus: "Tu es rex Judaeorum?" At ille respondens ait illi: "Tu dicis." Et accusabant[69] eum summi sacerdotes in multis. Pilatus autem rursum interrogabat eum dicens: "Non respondes quidquam? Vide in quantis te accusant." Jesus autem amplius nihil respondit, ita ut miraretur Pilatus.

Per diem autem festum dimittere solebat[70] illis unum ex vinctis, quem peterent. Erat autem qui dicebatur Barabbas, vinctus cum seditiosis,[71] qui in seditione[72] fecerant homicidium.[73] Et cum ascendisset turba, coepit rogare, sicut faciebat illis. Pilatus autem respondit eis et dixit: "Vultis dimittam vobis regem Judaeorum?" Sciebat enim quod per invidiam[74] tradidissent eum summi sacerdotes. Pontifices[75] autem concitaverunt[76] turbam, ut magis Barabbam dimitteret eis. Pilatus autem iterum respondens aiebat[77] illis: "Quid ergo vultis faciam regi Judaeorum?" At illi iterum[78] clamaverunt: "Crucifige eum." Pilatus vero dicebat eis: "Quid enim mali fecit?" At illi magis clamaverunt: "Crucifige eum." Pilatus autem, volens populo satisfacere,[79] dimisit illis Barabbam et tradidit Jesum flagellis caesum, ut crucifigeretur.

Milites autem duxerunt eum intro in atrium, quod est praetorium,[80] et convocant[81] totam cohortem.[82] Et induunt[83] eum purpuram[84] et imponunt ei plectentes[85] spineam[86] coronam, et coeperunt

[67] **māne** (*adv.*) in the morning
[68] **cōnsilium, cōnsiliī**, n. counsel, plans
[69] **accūsō** (1) accuse
[70] **soleō, solēre; —, solitus sum** be accustomed (+ *inf.*)
[71] **sēditiōsus, -a, -um** seditious; *subst.*, rebel
[72] **sēditiō, sēditiōnis**, f. revolt, uprising
[73] **homicīdium, homicīdiī**, n. murder
[74] **invidia, invidiae**, f. jealousy
[75] **pontifex, pontificis**, m. chief priest
[76] **concitō** (1) incite, stir up
[77] **aiēbat = dīcēbat**
[78] **iterum** *here*, 'back'
[79] **satisfaciō = satis + faciō**
[80] **praetōrium, praetōriī**, n. praetorium (Roman headquarters)
[81] **convocō = com + vocō**
[82] **cohors, cohortis**, f. cohort (a body of 600 Roman soldiers)
[83] **induō, induere, induī, indūtus** put on, clothe
[84] **purpura, purpurae**, f. purple, purple cloth
[85] **plectō, plectere, plexī/plexuī, plexus** braid, weave
[86] **spīneus, -a, -um** of thorns

salutare eum: "Ave, rex Judaeorum," et percutiebant caput ejus arundine[87] et conspuebant eum et ponentes genua adorabant eum. Et postquam illuserunt[88] ei, exuerunt[89] illum purpuram et induerunt eum vestimentis suis. Et educunt illum, ut crucifigerent eum.

Et angariant[90] praetereuntem quempiam[91] Simonem Cyrenaeum venientem de villa,[92] patrem Alexandri et Rufi, ut tolleret crucem ejus. Et perducunt illum in Golgotha locum, quod est interpretatum[93] Calvariae[94] locus. Et dabant ei myrrhatum[95] vinum, ille autem non accepit.

Et crucifigunt eum et *dividunt vestimenta* ejus, *mittentes sortem super eis* quis quid tolleret. Erat autem hora tertia, et crucifixerunt eum. Et erat titulus[96] causae[97] ejus inscriptus:[98] "Rex Judaeorum." Et cum eo crucifigunt duos latrones, unum a dextris et alium a sinistris[99] ejus.

Et praetereuntes blasphemabant[100] eum *moventes capita* sua et dicentes: "Vah,[101] qui destruit templum et in tribus diebus aedificat; salvum fac temetipsum descendens de cruce." Similiter et summi sacerdotes ludentes[102] ad alterutrum[103] cum scribis dicebant: "Alios salvos fecit, seipsum non potest salvum facere. Christus rex Israel descendat nunc de cruce, ut videamus et credamus." Etiam qui cum eo crucifixi erant, conviciabantur[104] ei.

Et, facta hora sexta, tenebrae factae sunt per totam terram usque in horam nonam. Et hora nona exclamavit Jesus voce magna: *"Heloi, Heloi, lema sabacthani?"* quod est interpretatum: *"Deus meus, Deus meus, ut quid dereliquisti[105] me?"* Et quidam de circumstan-

---

[87] **arundō, arundinis,** f. reed, cane
[88] **illūdō, illūdere, illūsī, illūsus** mock, make fun of
[89] **exuō, exuere, exuī, exūtus** strip
[90] **angariō** (1) press into service
[91] **quispiam, quaepiam, quodpiam** some, a certain
[92] **vīlla, vīllae,** f. farm
[93] **interpretātus, -a, -um** translated
[94] **calvāria, calvāriae,** f. skull
[95] **myrrhātus, -a, -um** laced with myrrh
[96] **titulus, titulī,** m. inscription, public notice
[97] **causa** *here,* 'wrong, offense'
[98] **īnscrībō = in + scrībō**
[99] **ā sinistrīs** 'on the left'
[100] **blasphēmō** (1) blaspheme; revile, insult
[101] **vah** (*interj.*) ha!
[102] **lūdō, lūdere, lūsī, lūsus** joke
[103] **alteruter, alterutra, alterutrum** one another, each other
[104] **convīcior** (1) reproach, insult (+ *dat.*)
[105] **dērelinquō = dē + relinquō**

tibus audientes dicebant: "Ecce Eliam vocat." Currens autem unus et implens spongiam[106] *aceto*[107] circumponensque[108] calamo[109] *potum dabat* ei dicens: "Sinite,[110] videamus, si veniat Elias ad deponendum eum." Jesus autem, emissa voce magna, exspiravit.

Et velum[111] templi scissum est in duo a sursum usque deorsum.[112]

Videns autem centurio, qui ex adverso[113] stabat, quia sic clamans exspirasset, ait: "Vere homo hic Filius Dei erat."

Erant autem et mulieres de longe aspicientes, inter quas et Maria Magdalene et Maria Jacobi minoris et Josetis mater et Salome, quae, cum esset in Galilaea, sequebantur eum et ministrabant[114] ei, et aliae multae, quae simul cum eo ascenderant Hierosolymam.

Et cum jam sero[115] esset factum, quia erat Parasceve,[116] quod est ante sabbatum, venit Joseph ab Arimathea nobilis[117] decurio,[118] qui et ipse erat exspectans regnum Dei, et audacter[119] introivit ad Pilatum et petiit corpus Jesu. Pilatus autem miratus est si jam obisset, et, accersito[120] centurione, interrogavit eum si jam mortuus esset, et, cum cognovisset a centurione, donavit corpus Joseph. Is autem mercatus[121] sindonem et deponens eum involvit sindone[122] et posuit eum in monumento, quod erat excisum[123] de petra,[124] et advolvit[125] lapidem[126] ad ostium[127] monumenti. Maria autem Magdalene et Maria Josetis aspiciebant, ubi positus esset.

[106] **spongia, spongiae,** f. sponge
[107] **acētum, acētī,** n. sour wine
[108] **circumpōnō = circum + pōnō**
[109] **calamus, calamī,** m. reed
[110] **sinite** *here,* 'wait!'
[111] **vēlum, vēlī,** n. curtain
[112] **ā sūrsum ūsque deorsum** 'from top to bottom'
[113] **ex adversō** 'opposite'
[114] **ministrō** (1) serve, take care of (+ *dat.*)
[115] **sērō** (*adv.*) late
[116] **Parasceve** (Day of) Preparation
[117] **nōbilis, -e** noble, respected
[118] **decuriō, decuriōnis,** m. member of the Sanhedrin
[119] **audācter** (*adv.*) boldly
[120] **accersō = arcessō, arcessere, arcessīvī, arcessītus** summon
[121] **mercor** (1) buy
[122] **sindōn, sindonis,** f. muslin
[123] **excīdō = ex + caedō** hew out, cut out
[124] **petra, petrae,** f. rock
[125] **advolvō, advolvere, advolvī, advolūtus** roll to, roll across
[126] **lapis, lapis, lapium,** m. stone
[127] **ōstium, ōstiī,** n. entrance

5. *Stabat Mater (Jacopone da Todi, d. 1306)*

Stabat mater dolorosa
juxta crucem lacrimosa,
   dum pendebat filius,
cujus animam gementem,[1]
contristatam[2] et dolentem
   pertransivit gladius.

O quam tristis et afflicta[3]
fuit illa benedicta
   mater unigeniti,
quae maerebat[4] et dolebat,
et tremebat, dum videbat
   nati poenas incliti.[5]

Quis est homo, qui non fleret,
matrem Christi si videret
   in tanto supplicio?[6]
Quis non posset contristari,
piam matrem contemplari[7]
   dolentem cum filio?

Pro peccatis suae gentis
vidit Jesum in tormentis[8]
   et flagellis subditum,[9]
vidit suum dulcem natum
morientem, desolatum,[10]
   dum emisit spiritum.

Pia mater, fons amoris,[11]
me sentire vim[12] doloris
   fac, ut tecum lugeam,[13]
fac ut ardeat cor meum
in amando Christum Deum,
   ut sibi complaceam.

Sancta mater, istud agas,
crucifixi fige plagas[14]
   cordi meo valide,[15]
tui nati vulnerati,
tam dignati pro me pati,
   poenas mecum divide.

Fac me vere tecum flere,
crucifixi fige plagas[14]
   cordi meo valide;[15]
juxta crucem tecum stare
et me tibi sociare
   in planctu desidero.

Virgo virginum praeclara,[16]
mihi jam non sis amara,[17]
   fac me tecum plangere;
fac ut portem Christi mortem,
passionis fac consortem
   et plagas recolere.[18]

[1] **gemō, gemere, gemuī, gemitus** sigh, groan, lament
[2] **contrīstō** (1) make sad, afflict
[3] **afflictus, -a, -um** miserable, downcast
[4] **maereō, maerēre, —, —** be sad, grieve, mourn
[5] **inclitus, -a, -um** famous, glorious
[6] **supplicium, suppliciī,** n. torture, pain
[7] **contemplor** (1) look at, consider carefully
[8] **tormentum, tormentī,** n. torture, torment
[9] **subditus, -a, -um** subject, submissive
[10] **dēsōlātus, -a, -um** forsaken
[11] **amor, amōris,** m. love
[12] **vīs, —;** *pl.,* **vīrēs, vīrium,** f. force, power; *pl.,* strength
[13] **lūgeō, lūgēre, lūxī, lūctus** mourn, cry out in grief
[14] **plāga, plāgae,** f. blow, stroke
[15] **validē = valdē**
[16] **praeclārus, -a, -um** very beautiful, splendid, illustrious
[17] **amārus, -a, -um** bitter
[18] **recolō, recolere, recoluī, recultus** call to mind, contemplate

Fac me plagis vulnerari,
cruce fac inebriari[19]
 et cruore filii;
inflammatus[20] et accensus
per te, virgo, sim defensus
 in die judicii.

Fac me cruce custodiri,
morte Christi praemuniri,[21]
 confoveri[22] gratia;
quando corpus morietur,
fac ut animae donetur
 Paradisi gloria.

[19] inēbriō (1) saturate, steep
[20] īnflammō (1) kindle, set afire
[21] praemūniō, praemūnīre, praemūnīvī, praemūnītus fortify, make safe
[22] cōnfoveō, cōnfovēre, —, — cherish assiduously

6. *The Cockcrow Hymn: Aeterne Rerum Conditor* (Ambrose, d. 397)

Aeterne rerum Conditor[1]
noctem diemque qui regis,
et temporum das tempora
ut alleves[2] fastidium.[3]

Nocturna[4] lux viantibus[5]
a nocte noctem segregans,
praeco[6] diei jam sonat,
jubarque[7] solis evocat.

Hoc excitatus[8] lucifer
solvit polum[9] caligine:
hoc omnis erronum[10] cohors[11]
viam nocendi deserit.[12]

Hoc nauta vires[13] colligit,
pontique[14] mitescunt[15] freta:[16]
hoc, ipsa petra[17] Ecclesiae,
canente, culpam diluit.[18]

[1] conditor, conditōris, m. (< condō) founder, creator
[2] allevō (1) lighten, alleviate
[3] fastīdium, fastīdiī, n. pride; weariness
[4] nocturnus, -a, -um nightly, by night
[5] viantēs, viantium, m. travelers
[6] praecō, praecōnis, m. proclaimer, herald
[7] jubar, jubāris, n. radiance, light
[8] excitō (1) rouse forth, arouse from sleep
[9] polus, polī, m. sky
[10] errō, errōnis, m. vagabond
[11] cohors here, 'band'
[12] dēserō, dēserere, dēseruī, dēsertus desert, leave
[13] vīs, —; pl., vīrēs, vīrium, f. force, power; pl., strength
[14] pontus, pontī, n. the deep sea
[15] mītēscō, mītēscere, —, — become mild
[16] fretum, fretī, n. channel; raging, swelling
[17] petra, petrae, f. rock (cf. Mt. xvi, 18)
[18] dīluō, dīluere, dīluī, dīlūtus wash away

Surgamus ergo strenue: [19]
gallus [20] jacentes excitat,
et somnolentos [21] increpat [22]
gallus, negantes arguit. [23]

Gallo canente spes redit,
aegris [24] salus refunditur,
mucro [25] latronis [26] conditur,
lapsis fides revertitur.

Jesu, labantes [27] respice,
et nos videndo corrige:
si respicis, labes [28] cadunt
fletuque culpa solvitur.

Tu, lux, refulge sensibus,
mentisque somnum discute: [29]
te nostra vox primum sonet
et vota solvamus tibi.

[19] **strēnuē** (*adv.*) briskly, promptly
[20] **gallus, gallī,** m. cock
[21] **somnolentus, -a, -um** given to sleep, sleepy
[22] **increpō** (1) chide, rebuke
[23] **arguō, arguere, arguī, argūtus** put in a clear light, convict, expose
[24] **aeger, aegra, aegrum** sick
[25] **mūcrō, mūcrōnis,** m. sword-point, sword
[26] **lātrō, lātrōnis,** m. brigand, bandit
[27] **labō** (1) totter, waver
[28] **lābēs, lābis, lābium,** f. a falling in; failing, disgrace
[29] **discutiō, discutere, discussī, discussus** shatter; scatter

7. *Te Deum (Nicetas of Remesiana, d. 414)*

Te Deum laudamus, te Dominum confitemur.
Te aeternum Patrem omnis terra veneratur.
Tibi omnes angeli, tibi caeli et universae potestates,
tibi cherubim et seraphim [1] incessabili [2] voce proclamant: [3]
Sanctus, sanctus, sanctus Dominus Deus Sabaoth!
Pleni [4] sunt caeli et terra majestatis [4] gloriae tuae.
Te gloriosus apostolorum chorus, te prophetarum laudabilis [5]
   numerus,
te martyrum candidatus [6] laudat exercitus, [7]
te per orbem terrarum sancta confitetur ecclesia,
Patrem immensae [8] majestatis, venerandum tuum verum et unicum
   Filium,
Sanctum quoque Paraclitum [9] Spiritum.
Tu rex gloriae, Christe,

[1] **cherubim et seraphim** Hebrew: indecl. pl. nouns
[2] **incessābilis, incessābile** unceasing
[3] **prōclāmō** = prō + clāmō
[4] **plēnī . . majestātis: plēnus, -a, -um** may also take the gen.
[5] **laudābilis, laudābile** praiseworthy
[6] **candidātus, -a, -um** clothed in white
[7] **exercitus, exercitūs,** m. army, multitude
[8] **immēnsus, -a, -um** immeasurable, boundless
[9] **Paraclitus, Paraclitī,** m. Paraclete, Helper

tu Patris sempiternus[10] es Filius.
Tu ad liberandum suscepturus hominem
non horruisti[11] virginis uterum.
Tu, devicto mortis aculeo,[12]
aperuisti credentibus regna caelorum.
Tu ad dexteram Dei sedes in gloria Patris.
Judex crederis esse venturus.
Te ergo quaesumus, tuis famulis subveni,
quos pretioso sanguine redemisti.
Aeterna fac cum sanctis tuis in gloria numerari.
Salvum fac populum tuum, Domine, et benedic hereditati tuae,
et rege eos et extolle illos usque in aeternum.
Per singulos[13] dies benedicimus te,
et laudamus nomen tuum in saeculum et in saeculum saeculi.
Dignare, Domine, die isto sine peccato nos custodire.
Miserere nostri, Domine, miserere nostri;
fiat misericordia tua, Domine, super nos,
quemadmodum[14] speravimus in te.
In te, Domine, speravi: non confundar in aeternum.

[10] **sempiternus, -a, -um** perpetual, everlasting
[11] **horreō, horrēre, horruī,** — shudder at, loathe
[12] **aculeus, aculeī,** m. sting
[13] **singulī, -ae, -a** every single, each one
[14] **quemadmodum** (*subord. conj.*) in what manner, just as

8. *Vexilla Regis (Venantius Fortunatus, 569)*

Vexilla[1] Regis prodeunt:
fulget Crucis mysterium,
qua vita mortem pertulit,
et morte vitam protulit.

Quae vulnerata lanceae[2]
mucrone[3] diro,[4] criminum
ut nos lavaret sordibus,[5]
manavit[6] unda, et sanguine,

Impleta sunt quae concinit
David fideli carmine,[7]
dicendō nationibus:
Regnavit a ligno Deus.

[1] **vexillum, vexillī,** n. flag, standard, banner
[2] **lancea, lanceae,** f. spear, lance
[3] **mūcrō, mūcrōnis,** m. sharp point
[4] **dīrus, -a, -um** horrible, cruel
[5] **sordēs, sordium,** f. filth
[6] **mānō** (I) flow, drip
[7] **carmen, carminis,** n. song, prophetic song

Arbor decora[8] et fulgida,[9]
ornata regis purpura,[10]
electa digno stipite[11]
tam sancta membra tangere.

Beata, cujus brachiis
pretium pependit saeculi,
statera[12] facta corporis,
tulitque praedam[13] Tartari.[14]

O Crux, ave, spes unica,
hoc passionis tempore
piis adauge[15] gratiam,
reisque[16] dele crimina.

Te, fons salutis Trinitas,
collaudet omnis spiritus:
quibus Crucis victoriam
largiris, adde praemium.

[8] **decōrus, -a, -um** fitting, beautiful
[9] **fulgidus, -a, -um** gleaming
[10] **purpura, purpurae,** f. purple
[11] **stīpes, stīpitis,** m. log, post
[12] **statēra, statērae,** f. a balance, scales
[13] **praeda, praedae,** f. spoils, booty
[14] **Tartarus, Tartarī,** m. the Underworld, Hell
[15] **adaugeō, adaugēre, audauxī, adauctus** increase
[16] **reus, reī,** m. one liable for punishment

9. *Pange Lingua (Venantius Fortunatus, 569)*

Pange, lingua, gloriosi lauream[1] certaminis,[2]
et super Crucis tropaeo[3] dic triumphum[4] nobilem:[5]
qualiter[6] Redemptor orbis immolatus[7] vicerit.

De parentis protoplasti[8] fraude[9] Factor condolens,
quando pomi[10] noxialis[11] in necem[12] morsu[13] ruit:[14]
ipse lignum tunc notavit,[15] damna ligni ut solveret.

Hoc opus nostrae salutis ordo depoposcerat;

[1] **laurea, laureae,** f. laurel; victory
[2] **certāmen, certāminis,** n. contest, contention, struggle
[3] **tropaeum, tropaeī,** n. trophy, victory
[4] **triumphus, triumphī,** m. triumph, victory
[5] **nōbilis, nōbile** noble
[6] **quāliter** (*rel. & interrog. adv.*) (< **quālis, -e**) how
[7] **immolō** (1) sacrifice, offer
[8] **prōtoplastus, -a, -um** first-formed
[9] **fraus, fraudis,** f. self-deception, error
[10] **pōmum, pōmī,** n. fruit (of any kind)
[11] **noxiālis, noxiāle** injurious
[12] **nex, necis,** f. death
[13] **morsus, morsūs,** m. a bite, eating
[14] **ruō, ruere, ruī, rutus** rush, fall, go to ruin
[15] **notō** (1) mark (for censure)

multiformis [16] proditoris [17] ars ut artem falleret,
et medelam [18] ferret inde,/ hostis unde laeserat. [19]

Quando venit ergo sacri plenitudo [20] temporis,
missus est ab arce [21] patris natus, orbis conditor; [22]
atque ventre virginali [23] carne amictus [24] prodiit.

Vagit [25] infans inter arcta [26] conditus praesepia: [27]
membra pannis involuta virgo mater alligat: [28]
et Dei manus pedesque stricta [29] cingit [30] fascia. [31]

Lustra [32] sex qui jam peregit, [33] tempus implens corporis,
sponte [34] libera Redemptor passioni deditus, [35]
Agnus in Crucis levatur [36] immolandus stipite. [37]

Felle [38] potus [39] ecce languet: [40] spina, [41] clavi, [42] lancea
mite [43] corpus perforarunt: [44] unda [45] manat, [46] et cruor:
terra, pontus, astra, mundus, quo [47] lavantur flumine! [48]

[16] multiformis, multiforme many-shaped
[17] prōditor, prōditōris, m. betrayer
[18] medēla, medēlae, f. cure, remedy
[19] laedō, laedere, laesī, laesus injure, do harm
[20] plēnitūdō, plēnitūdinis, f. fullness
[21] arx, arcis, f. stronghold, citadel, summit
[22] conditor, conditōris, m. founder, creator
[23] virginālis, virgināle virginal, of a virgin
[24] amictus, -a, -um clothed
[25] vāgiō, vāgīre, vāgīvī, — cry [said of an infant]
[26] arctus, -a, -um narrow, confined
[27] praesēpium, praesēpiī, n. feeding-trough, manger
[28] alligō (1) bind up, bind round
[29] strictus, -a, -um drawn together, tight
[30] cingō, cingere, cīnxī, cīnctus gird, surround
[31] fascia, fasciae, f. band, wrapping
[32] lustrum, lustrī, n. a period of five years
[33] peragō, peragere, perēgī, perāctus complete
[34] spōns, spontis, f. free will
[35] dēdō (dē + -dō) dedicate, devote
[36] levō (1) raise, lift up
[37] stīpes, stīpitis, f. log, post
[38] fel, fellis, n. gall
[39] pōtus, -a, -um drunk
[40] langueō, languēre, languī, — be faint, be weak
[41] spīna, spīnae, f. thorn
[42] clāvus, clāvī, m. nail
[43] mītis, mīte mild, gentle
[44] perforō (1) pierce
[45] unda, undae, f. wave, water
[46] mānō (1) flow, drip
[47] quō = et hōc
[48] flūmen, flūminis, n. stream, flow

Crux fidelis, inter omnes arbor una nobilis:
silva[49] talem nulla profert fronde,[50] flore, germine:[51]
dulce ferrum,[52] dulce lignum, dulce pondus[53] sustinent.

Flecte ramos,[54] arbor alta, tensa laxa[55] viscera,[56]
et rigor[57] lentescat[58] ille, quem dedit nativitas;[59]
et superni membra Regis tende miti stipite.

Sola digna tu fuisti ferre mundi victimam;[60]
atque portum[61] praeparare/ arca[62] mundo naufrago,[63]
quam sacer cruor perunxit,[64] fusus Agni corpore.

Sempiterna[65] sit beatae Trinitati[66] gloria:
aequa[67] Patri, Filioque; par decus[68] Paraclito:[69]
unius Trinique[70] nomen laudet universitas.[71]

[49] silva, silvae, f. forest
[50] fröns, frondis, f. branch
[51] germen, germinis, n. bud
[52] ferrum, ferrī, n. iron: the nails, collectively
[53] pondus, ponderis, n. weight, burden
[54] rāmus, rāmī, m. branch, bough
[55] laxō (1) loosen, relax
[56] viscera, viscerum, n. entrails, insides
[57] rigor, rigōris, m. stiffness
[58] lentēscō, lentēscere, —, — become pliant, become soft
[59] nātīvitās here = nātūra
[60] victima, victimae, f. sacrificial offering, victim
[61] portus, portūs, m. haven, harbor
[62] arca, arcae, f. ark, boat
[63] naufragus, -a, -um shipwrecked
[64] perungō, perungere, perūnxī, perūnctus smear
[65] sempiternus, -a, -um perpetual, everlasting
[66] Trīnitās, Trīnitātis, f. Trinity
[67] aequus, -a, -um equal
[68] decus, decoris, n. honor, glory
[69] Paraclitus, Paraclitī, m. Paraclete, Helper: Holy Spirit
[70] trīnī, -ae, -a three together
[71] ūniversitās, ūniversitātis, f. the whole: the world

10. Veni Creator Spiritus (Rabanus Maurus?, d. 856)

Veni, Creator Spiritus,
mentes tuorum visita:[1]
imple superna gratia
quae tu creasti pectora.

Qui diceris Paraclitus,
altissimi donum Dei,
fons vivus, ignis, caritas,
et spiritalis unctio.[2]

[1] vīsitō (1) visit
[2] ūnctiō, ūnctiōnis, f. ointment, balm

Tu septiformis[3] munere,
digitus paternae dexterae,
tu rite[4] promissum[5] Patris,
sermone ditans guttura.[6]

Accende lumen sensibus,
infunde amorem cordibus,
infirma[7] nostri corporis
virtute firmans perpeti.[8]

Hostem repellas longius,[9]
pacemque dones protinus:[10]
ductore[11] sic te praevio[12]
vitemus[13] omne noxium.[14]

Per te sciamus, da, Patrem,
noscamus atque Filium,
teque utriusque[15] Spiritum
credamus omni tempore.

Deo Patri sit gloria,
et Filio, qui a mortuis
surrexit, ac Paraclito,
in saeculorum saecula. Amen.

[3] **septiformis, septiforme** sevenfold
[4] **rīte** (*adv.*) duly, properly
[5] **prōmissum, prōmissī**, n. something promised, a promise
[6] **guttur, gutturis**, n. throat
[7] **īnfirma** *neut. pl., subst.*: weaknesses
[8] **perpes** (*gen.*, **perpetis**) = **perpetuus, -a, -um**
[9] **longius** (*comp. adj.*) at some distance
[10] **prōtinus** (*adv.*) immediately
[11] **ductor, ductōris**, m. leader
[12] **praevius, -a, -um** leading the way
[13] **vītō** (1) avoid
[14] **noxius, -a, -um** harmful, injurious
[15] **uterque, utraque, utrumque** each (of two), both

11. *Ave Maris Stella (Paul the Deacon?, d. 799?)*

Ave, maris stella,
Dei Mater alma[1]
atque semper Virgo,
felix caeli porta.[2]

Sumens illud Ave
Gabrielis ore,
funda nos in pace,
mutans Hevae[3] nomen.

Solve vincla reis,
profer lumen caecis,[4]
mala nostra pelle,
bona cuncta posce.

Monstra te esse matrem:
sumat per te preces,
qui pro nobis natus,
tulit[5] esse tuus.[6]

[1] **almus, -a, -um** nourishing
[2] **porta, portae**, f. gate
[3] **Hēvae** = **Ēvae** (AVE ↔ EVA)
[4] **caecus, -a, -um** blind
[5] **tulit** *here*, endured (+ *inf.*)
[6] **tuus**: *sc.* 'son'

Virgo singularis,[7]
inter omnes mitis,[8]
culpis nos solutos,
mites[8] fac et castos.

Vitam praesta puram,
iter para tutum,[9]
ut videntes Jesum,
semper collaetemur.

Sit laus Deo Patri,
summo[10] Christo decus,[11]
Spiritui Sancto,
tribus honor unus.

[7] singulāris, singulāre singular, unique, extraordinary
[8] mītis, mīte mild, gentle
[9] tūtus, -a, -um safe
[10] summus, -a, -um highest
[11] decus, decoris, n. glory

12. Gloria Laus (Theodulf, d. 821)

Gloria, laus, et honor, tibi sit Rex Christe Redemptor:
  cui puerile[1] decus[2] prompsit[3] Hosanna pium.
Israel es tu Rex, Davidis et inclita[4] proles:[5]
  nomine qui in Domini, Rex benedicte, venis.
Coetus[6] in excelsis te laudat caelicus[7] omnis
  et mortalis homo, et cuncta creata simul.
Plebs[8] Hebraea tibi cum palmis obvia[9] venit:
  cum prece, voto, hymnis, adsumus ecce tibi.
Hi tibi passuro solvebant munia[10] laudis:
  nos tibi regnanti pangimus ecce melos.[11]
Hi placuere tibi, placeat devotio[12] nostra:
  Rex bone, Rex clemens, cui bona cuncta placent.

[1] puerīlis, puerīle youthful
[2] decus, decoris, n. glory, beauty
[3] prōmō, prōmere, prōmpsī, prōmptus bring forth
[4] inclitus, -a, -um famous, glorious
[5] prōlēs, prōlis, f. offspring
[6] coetus, coetūs, m. assembly
[7] caelicus, -a, -um celestial
[8] plēbs, plēbis, f. people
[9] obvius, -a, -um to meet (+ dat.)
[10] mūnia, mūnium, n. duty
[11] melos, melī, n. song
[12] dēvōtiō, dēvōtiōnis, f. devotion

13. *Veni Sancte Spiritus (Stephen Langton, d. 1228)*

Veni, Sancte Spiritus,
et emitte caelitus[1]
lucis tuae radium.

Veni, pater pauperum,
veni, dator[2] munerum,
veni, lumen cordium.

Consolator[3] optime,
dulcis hospes animae,
dulce refrigerium.[4]

In labore requies,
in aestu[5] temperies,[6]
in fletu solatium.[7]

O lux beatissima,
reple cordis intima[8]
tuorum fidelium.

Sine tuo numine,[9]
nihil est in homine,
nihil est innoxium.[10]

Lava quod est sordidum,[11]
riga[12] quod est aridum,[13]
sana quod est saucium.[14]

Flecte quod est rigidum,[15]
fove[16] quod est frigidum,[17]
rege quod est devium.[18]

Da tuis fidelibus,
in te confidentibus,
sacrum septenarium.[19]

Da virtutis meritum,
da salutis exitum,[20]
da perenne gaudium.
Amen. Alleluja.

[1] **caelitus** (*adv.*) from heaven
[2] **dator, datōris**, m. giver
[3] **cōnsōlātor, cōnsōlātōris**, m. consoler
[4] **refrīgerium, refrīgeriī**, n. consolation
[5] **aestus, aestūs**, m. heat
[6] **temperiēs, temperiēī**, f. tempering
[7] **sōlātium, sōlātiī**, n. solace, comfort
[8] **intima, intimōrum**, n. inmost parts
[9] **nūmen, nūminis**, n. divinity
[10] **innoxius, -a, -um** without harm, innocent
[11] **sordidus, -a, -um** filthy
[12] **rigō** (1) wet, water
[13] **āridus, -a, -um** dry
[14] **saucius, -a, -um** wounded
[15] **rigidus, -a, -um** stiff
[16] **foveō, fovēre, fōvi, fōtus** warm
[17] **frīgidus, -a, -um** cold
[18] **dēvius, -a, -um** off the road, astray
[19] **septēnārius, -a, -um** containing seven
[20] **exitus, exitūs**, m. outcome

14. *Dies Irae (Thomas of Celano?, c. 1230)*

Dies irae, dies illa,
solvet saeclum in favilla,[1]
teste David cum Sibylla.

Quantus tremor[2] est futurus,
quando judex est venturus,
cuncta stricte[3] discussurus.[4]

Tuba, mirum spargens sonum[5]
per sepulcra regionum,
coget omnes ante thronum.

Mors stupebit[6] et natura,
cum resurget creatura,
judicanti responsura.

Liber scriptus proferetur,
in quo totum continetur,
unde mundus judicetur.

Judex ergo cum sedebit,
quidquid latet[7] apparebit:
nil inultum[8] remanebit.

Quid sum miser tunc dicturus?
Quem patronum rogaturus?—
cum vix[9] justus sit securus.[10]

Rex tremendae majestatis,
qui salvandos[11] salvas[11] gratis,[12]
salva[11] me, fons pietatis.

Recordare,[13] Jesu pie,
quod sum causa tuae viae:
ne me perdas illa die.

Quaerens me sedisti lassus:[14]
redemisti crucem passus:
tantus labor non sit cassus.[15]

Juste judex ultionis,[16]
donum fac remissionis
ante diem rationis.

Ingemisco[17] tamquam[18] reus,
culpa rubet[19] vultus meus:
supplicanti parce, Deus.

Qui Mariam absolvisti,
et latronem exaudisti,
mihi quoque spem dedisti.

Preces meae non sunt dignae,
sed tu bonus fac benigne,
ne perenni cremer[20] igne.

[1] **favilla, favillae,** f. ashes (of the dead)
[2] **tremor, tremōris,** m. trembling
[3] **strictus, -a, -um** severe, strict
[4] **discutiō, discutere, discussī, discussus** shatter, knock apart
[5] **sonus, sonī,** m. sound
[6] **stupeō, stupēre, stupuī,** — be stunned, be astonished
[7] **lateō, latēre, latuī,** — be hidden
[8] **inultus, -a, -um** unpunished
[9] **vix** (*adv.*) scarcely
[10] **sēcūrus, -a, -um** free from worry, safe
[11] **salvō** (1) save
[12] **grātīs** (*adv.*) for nothing, gratis
[13] **recordor** (1) remember
[14] **lassus, -a, -um** weary, exhausted
[15] **cassus, -a, -um** useless, futile
[16] **ultiō, ultiōnis,** f. punishing, avenging
[17] **ingemīscō, ingemīscere, ingemuī,** — sigh, groan
[18] **tamquam** (*adv.*) just as
[19] **rubeō, rubēre,** —, — be red, blush
[20] **cremō** (1) burn

Inter oves locum praesta,
et ab haedis[21] me sequestra,[22]
statuens in parte dextra.

Confutatis[23] maledictis,
flammis acribus addictis,
voca me cum benedictis.

Oro supplex et acclinis,[24]
cor contritum quasi[25] cinis:[26]
gere curam mei finis.

Lacrimosa dies illa,
qua resurget ex favilla

judicandus homo reus:
huïc ergo parce, Deus.

Pie Jesu Domine,
dona eos requie. Amen.

[21] **haedus, haedī**, m. kid, young goat
[22] **sequestrō** (1) remove, separate
[23] **cōnfūtō** (1) check, suppress
[24] **acclīnis, acclīne** bowing
[25] **quasi** (*adv.*) as if
[26] **cinis, cineris**, m. ashes

15. *Lauda Sion (Thomas Aquinas, c. 1264)*

Lauda, Sion, salvatorem,
lauda ducem[1] et pastorem
  in hymnis et canticis.
Quantum potes, tantum aude:
quia major omni laude,
  nec laudare sufficis.

Laudis thema[2] specialis,[3]
panis vivus et vitalis[4]
  hodie proponitur.
Quem in sacrae mensa cenae,
turbae fratrum duodenae[5]
  datum non ambigitur.[6]

Sit laus plena, sit sonora,[7]
sit jucunda, sit decora[8]
  mentis jubilatio.[9]
Dies enim solemnis agitur,
in qua mensae prima recolitur[10]
  hujus institutio.

In hac mensa novi regis
novum Pascha novae legis,
  Phase[11] vetus terminat.
Vetustatem[12] novitas,[13]
umbram fugat veritas,
  noctem lux eliminat.[14]

[1] **dux, ducis**, m. leader
[2] **thema, thematis**, n. subject, theme
[3] **speciālis, speciāle** special
[4] **vītālis, vītāle** life-giving
[5] **duodēnus, -a, -um** twelve each; **turbae frātrum d.** = 'to his twelve apostles'
[6] **ambigō, ambigere, —, —** doubt (+ *acc. & inf.*)
[7] **sonōrus, -a, -um** loud, resounding
[8] **dēcōrus, -a, -um** fitting, proper
[9] **jūbilātiō, jūbilātiōnis**, f. shout of joy
[10] **recolō, recolere, recoluī, recultus** recall
[11] **Phase** (*indecl. noun*) Passover
[12] **vetustās, vestustātis**, f. old age, antiquity
[13] **novitās, novitātis**, f. newness
[14] **ēlīminō** (1) banish

Quod in cena Christus gessit,
faciendum hoc expressit
   in sui memoriam.
Docti [15] sacris institutis,[16]
panem, vinum in salutis
   consecramus hostiam.

Dogma datur Christianis,
quod in carnem transit panis,
   et vinum in sanguinem.
Quod non capis, quod non vides,
animosa [17] firmat fides
   praeter rerum ordinem.

Sub diversis [18] speciebus,
signis tantum, et non rebus,
   latent [19] res eximiae: [20]
caro cibus, sanguis potus,
manet tamen Christus totus,
   sub utraque [21] specie.

A sumente non concisus,[22]
non confractus, non divisus:
   integer accipitur.
Sumit unus, sumunt mille:
quantum isti, tantum ille:
   nec sumptus consumitur.[23]

Sumunt boni, sumunt mali:
sorte [24] tamen inaequali,[25]
   vitae, vel interitus.[26]
Mors est malis, vita bonis:
vide paris sumptionis [27]
   quam sit dispar exitus.[28]

Fracto demum [29] sacramento,
ne vacilles,[30] sed memento,[31]
tantum esse sub fragmento [32]
   quantum toto tegitur.[33]
Nulla rei fit scissura: [34]
signi tantum fit fractura: [35]
qua nec status [36] nec statura [37]
   signati [38] minuitur.[39]

---

[15] **doctus, -a, -um** taught
[16] **īnstitūtum, īnstitūtī,** n. regulation, instruction
[17] **animōsus, -a, -um** living, lively
[18] **dīversus, -a, -um** different
[19] **lateō, latēre, latuī,** — be hidden
[20] **eximius, -a, -um** extraordinary
[21] **uterque, utraque, utrumque** each (of two), both
[22] **concīdō, concīdere, concīdī, concīsus** cut to pieces, destroy
[23] **cōnsūmō = con + sūmō** consume, use up
[24] **sors, sortis,** f. lot
[25] **inaequālis, inaequāle** unequal, different
[26] **interitus, interitūs,** m. ruin, destruction
[27] **sūmptiō, sūmptiōnis,** f. taking
[28] **exitus, exitūs,** m. outcome, result
[29] **dēmum** (*adv.*) finally; only
[30] **vacillō** (1) waver, doubt
[31] **mementō** (*imperative*) remember!
[32] **frāgmentum, frāgmentī,** n. fragment, piece, part
[33] **tegō, tegere, tēxī, tēctus** cover
[34] **scissūra, scissūrae,** f. tearing, rending
[35] **frāctūra, frāctūrae,** f. fracture, breaking
[36] **status, statūs,** m. state, condition
[37] **statūra, statūrae,** f. stature
[38] **sīgnō** (1) signify
[39] **minuō, minuere, minuī, minūtus** diminish

Ecce panis angelorum,
factus cibus viatorum: [40]
vere panis filiorum,
    non mittendus canibus.[41]
In figuris praesignatur: [42]
cum Isaäc immolatur,
agnus paschae deputatur,
    datur manna [43] patribus.

Bone pastor, panis vere,
Jesu, nostri miserere:
tu nos pasce, nos tuere:
tu nos bona fac videre
    in terra viventium.
Tu, qui cuncta scis et vales,
qui nos pascis hic mortales:
tuos ibi commensales,[44]
coheredes [45] et sodales
    fac sanctorum civium.[46]

[40] **viātor, viātōris**, m. traveler
[41] **canis, canis**, m. & f. dog
[42] **praesīgnō** (1) foreshadow, prefigure
[43] **manna, mannae**, f. the manna of the Hebrews
[44] **commēnsālis, commēnsālis**, m. table companion
[45] **cohērēs, cohērēdis**, m. coheir
[46] **cīvis, cīvis, cīvium**, m. & f. citizen

16. *Pange Lingua (Thomas Aquinas, c. 1264)*

Pange, lingua, gloriosi
    corporis mysterium,
sanguinisque pretiosi,
    quem in mundi pretium
fructus ventris generosi [1]
    rex effudit gentium.

Nobis datus, nobis natus,
    ex intacta [2] virgine,
et in mundo conversatus,[3]
    sparso verbi semine,[4]
sui moras [5] incolatus [6]
    miro clausit ordine.

In supremae nocte cenae,
    recumbens [7] cum fratribus,
observata lege plene
    cibis in legalibus,[8]
cibum turbae duodenae[9]
    se dat suis manibus.

Verbum caro panem verum
    verbo carnem efficit,
fitque sanguis Christi merum,[10]
    et si sensus deficit,
ad firmandum cor sincerum
    sola fides sufficit.

[1] **generōsus, -a, -um** noble
[2] **intāctus, -a, -um** untouched, chaste
[3] **conversor** (1) live (a certain lifestyle)
[4] **sēmen, sēminis**, n. seed
[5] **mora, morae**, f. delay; period of time
[6] **incolātus, incolātūs**, m. residing, dwelling
[7] **recumbō, recumbere, recubuī**, — recline at table
[8] **lēgālis, lēgāle** prescribed in the Torah
[9] **turbae duodēnae** = 'to the twelve'
[10] **merum, merī**, n. wine

Tantum ergo sacramentum
  veneremur cernui;[11]
et antiquum documentum
  novo cedat ritui;
praestet fides supplementum[12]
  sensuum defectui.[13]

Genitori[14] genitoque
  laus et jubilatio,
salus, honor, virtus quoque
  sit et benedictio:
procedenti ab utroque
  compar sit laudatio.

[11] cernuus, -a, -um bowing
[12] supplēmentum, supplēmentī, n. reinforcement
[13] dēfectus, dēfectūs, m. lack, failure, defect
[14] genitor, genitōris, m. begetter, father

17. *Verbum Supernum (Thomas Aquinas, c. 1264)*

Verbum supernum prodiens,
  nec Patris linquens[1] dexteram,
ad opus suum exiens,
  venit ad vitae vesperam.[2]

In mortem a discipulo
  suis tradendus aemulis,[3]
prius[4] in vitae ferculo[5]
  se tradidit discipulis.

Quibus sub bina[6] specie
  carnem dedit et sanguinem,
ut duplicis[7] substantiae
  totum cibaret[8] hominem.

Se nascens dedit socium,
  convescens[9] in edulium[10]
se, moriens in pretium,
  se regnans dat in praemium.

O salutaris Hostia,
  quae caeli pandis[11] ostium,[12]
bella premunt hostilia:[13]
  da robur,[14] fer auxilium.[15]

Uni trinoque Domino,
  sit sempiterna gloria:
qui vitam sine termino
  nobis donet in patria.

[1] linquō, linquere, līquī, — leave
[2] vespera, vesperae, f. evening
[3] aemulus, aemulī, m. rival
[4] prius (*adv.*) before that, first [of two actions]
[5] ferculum, ferculī, n. dish (of food)
[6] bīnī, -ae, -a two apiece, two
[7] duplex (*gen.*, duplicis) double
[8] cibō (1) feed
[9] convescor, convescī, —, — eat (with others)
[10] edulium, edulii, n. food
[11] pandō, pandere, pandī, pānsus (passus) throw open
[12] ōstium, ōstii, n. door
[13] hostīlis, hostīle hostile, caused by the enemy
[14] rōbur, rōboris, n. strength
[15] auxilium, auxilii, n. help

18. Creator Alme Siderum (Anon., 7' c., rewritten 1632)

Creator alme[1] siderum,
aeterna lux credentium,
Jesu, Redemptor omnium,
intende votis supplicum.

Qui—daemonis[2] ne fraudibus[3]
periret orbis—impetu[4]
amoris actus, languidi[5]
mundi medela[6] factus es.

Commune qui mundi nefas[7]
ut expiares,[8] ad crucem
e Virginis sacrario[9]
intacta prodis[10] victima.

Cujus potestas gloriae,
nomenque cum primum sonat,
et caelites[11] et inferi
tremente curvantur genu.

Te deprecamur, ultimae
magnum diei judicem:
armis[12] supernae gratiae
defende nos ab hostibus.

Virtus, honor, laus, gloria
Deo Patri cum Filio,
Sancto simul Paraclito
In saeculorum saecula.

[1] **almus, -a, -um** nourishing
[2] **daemōn, daemonis**, m. devil
[3] **fraus, fraudis**, f. deceit, deception
[4] **impetus, impetūs**, m. impulse, force
[5] **languidus, -a, -um** faint, weak
[6] **medēla, medēlae**, f. remedy, cure
[7] **nefās** (*indecl. noun*) sin
[8] **expiō** (1) expiate, atone for
[9] **sacrārium, sacrāriī**, n. sacred place, sanctuary
[10] **prōdis = prōdīstī**
[11] **caeles** (*gen.*, **caelitis**) heavenly
[12] **arma, armōrum**, n. weapons

19. A Solis Ortus (Sedulius, d. 450?)

A solis ortus cardine[1]
ad usque terrae limitem,[2]
Christum canamus principem,
natum Maria virgine.

Beatus auctor[3] saeculi
servile[4] corpus induit:[5]
ut carne carnem liberans,
ne perderet quos condidit.

[1] **cardō, cardinis**, m. hinge; line, limit
[2] **līmes, līmitis**, m. boundary, limit
[3] **auctor, auctōris**, m. creator, author
[4] **servīlis, servīle** of a slave or servant
[5] **induō, induere, induī, indūtus** put on

Castae parentis viscera
caelestis intrat gratia:
venter puellae bajulat[6]
secreta[7] quae non noverat.

Domus pudici[8] pectoris
templum repente[9] fit Dei:
intacta nesciens virum,
concepit alvo[10] filium.

Enititur puerpera[11]
quem Gabriel praedixerat,
quem ventre matris gestiens,[12]
baptista clausum senserat.

Faeno[13] jacere pertulit:
praesepe non abhorruit:
et lacte[14] modico[15] pastus est,
per quem nec ales[16] esurit.

Gaudet chorus caelestium,
et angeli canunt Deo;
palamque fit pastoribus
pastor, creator omnium.

Jesu, tibi sit gloria,
qui natus es de virgine,
cum Patre, et almo Spiritu,
in sempiterna saecula.

[6] bājulō, bājulāre, —, — bear, carry
[7] sēcrētum, sēcrētī, n. secret, mystery
[8] pudīcus, -a, -um modest, chaste
[9] repente (adv.) suddenly
[10] alvus, alvī, f. belly, womb
[11] puerpera, puerperae, f. a woman in labor
[12] gestiō, gestīre, gestīvī, gestītus exult, be joyful
[13] faenum, faenī, n. hay
[14] lac, lactis, n. milk
[15] modicus, -a, -um a little
[16] āles (gen., ālitis) winged; subst.: bird

20. *Veni Carthaginem (Augustine,* Confessiones, *III, i)*

Veni Carthaginem[1] et circumstrepebat[2] me undique[3] sartago[4] flagi-
tiosorum[5] amorum. Nondum amabam et amare amabam et secre-
tiore[6] indigentia[7] oderam me minus[8] indigentem.[9] Quaerebam quod
amarem, amans amare, et oderam securitatem[10] et viam sine mus-
cipulis[11] quoniam fames[12] mihi erat intus[13] ab interiore[14] cibo, te

[1] Carthāgō, Carthāginis, f. Carthage
[2] circumstrepō, circumstrepere, circumstrepuī, circumstrepitus roar: crackle, sizzle
[3] undique (adv.) on all sides
[4] sartāgō, sartāginis, f. frying pan
[5] flāgitiōsus, -a, -um shameful
[6] sēcrētus, -a, -um secret
[7] indigentia, indigentiae, f. want, desire
[8] minus = nōn
[9] indigeō, indigēre, indiguī, — want, desire
[10] sēcūritās, sēcūritātis, f. security, safety
[11] mūscipula, mūscipulae, f. mousetrap: snare
[12] famēs, famis, famium, f. hunger
[13] intus (adv.) within
[14] interior, interius inner

ipso, Deus meus, et ea fame non esuriebam, sed eram sine desiderio alimentorum[15] incorruptibilium,[16] non quia plenus eis eram, sed quo[17] inanior[18] eo[17] fastidiosior.[19] Et ideo non valebat anima mea et ulcerosa[20] projiciebat se foras,[21] miserabiliter[22] scalpi[23] avida[24] contactu[25] sensibilium.[26] Sed si non haberent animam, non utique amarentur. Amare et amari dulce mihi erat magis.

[15] alimenta, alimentōrum, n. food
[16] incorruptibilis, incorruptibile imperishable
[17] quō . . eō 'the (more) . . the (more)'
[18] inānis, ināne empty
[19] fastīdiōsus, -a, -um full of loathing
[20] ulcerōsus, -a, -um full of sores
[21] forās (adv.) outdoors, outward
[22] miserābiliter (adv.) wretchedly
[23] scalpō, scalpere, scalpsī, scalptus scrape, scratch
[24] avidus, -a, -um greatly desiring, greedy
[25] contāctus, contāctūs, m. contact, touch
[26] sēnsibilis, sēnsibile that can be perceived by the senses

21. Eucharistic Prayer of Hippolytus (d. 235)

℣. Dominus vobiscum.
R. Et cum spiritu tuo.
℣. Sursum corda.
R. Habemus ad Dominum.
℣. Gratias agamus Domino.
R. Dignum et justum est.

Gratias tibi referimus,[1] Deus, per dilectum puerum tuum Jesum Christum, quem in ultimis[2] temporibus misisti nobis salvatorem et redemptorem et angelum voluntatis tuae, qui est verbum tuum inseparabile,[3] per quem omnia fecisti et bene placitum tibi fuit, misisti de caelo in matricem[4] virginis, quique in utero[5] habitus incarnatus est et filius tibi ostensus est, ex Spiritu Sancto et virgine natus.

Qui voluntatem tuam complens et populum sanctum tibi acquirens[6] extendit manus cum pateretur, ut a passione liberaret eos qui in te crediderunt.

[1] re + ferō bring back, return
[2] ultimus, -a, -um last, final
[3] īnsēparābilis, -e inseparable
[4] mātrīx, mātrīcis, f. womb, matrix
[5] uterus, uterī, m. belly, womb
[6] acquīrō = ad + quaerō acquire, get

Qui cumque traderetur voluntariae[7] passioni, ut mortem solvat et vincula diaboli dirumpat,[8] et infernum calcet[9] et justos illuminet, et terminum[10] figat et resurrectionem manifestet,[11] accipiens panem gratias tibi agens dixit: Accipite, manducate, hoc est corpus meum quod pro vobis confringetur.

Similiter et calicem dicens: Hic est sanguis meus qui pro vobis effunditur. Quando hoc facitis, meam commemorationem facitis.

Memores igitur mortis et resurrectionis ejus, offerimus tibi panem et calicem, gratias tibi agentes quia nos dignos habuisti astare coram te et tibi ministrare.

Et petimus ut mittas Spiritum tuum Sanctum in oblationem sanctae ecclesiae: in unum congregans des[12] omnibus qui percipiunt[13] sanctis[14] in repletionem[15] Spiritus Sancti ad confirmationem[16] fidei in veritate, ut te laudemus et glorificemus per puerum tuum Jesum Christum, per quem tibi gloria et honor Patri et Filio cum Sancto Spiritu in sancta ecclesia tua et nunc et in saecula saeculorum. Amen.

[7] **voluntārius, -a, -um** voluntary
[8] **dīrumpō, dīrumpere, dīrūpī, dīruptus** break apart, shatter
[9] **calcō, calcāre, calcāvī, calcātus** trample underfoot, conquer
[10] **terminus, terminī,** m. limit, boundary
[11] **manifestō, manifestāre, manifestāvī, manifestātus** make clear, reveal
[12] **dēs:** *sc.* **percipere** as object
[13] **percipiō, percipere, percēpī, perceptus** *here,* partake in
[14] **sānctīs:** *sc.* **mystēriīs**
[15] **replētiō, replētiōnis,** f. filling up
[16] **cōnfirmātiō, cōnfirmātiōnis,** f. strengthening, confirmation

22. *Unam Sanctam, excerpted (Boniface VIII, Nov. 18, 1302)*

Denz 870.   Unam sanctam Ecclesiam catholicam et ipsam apostolicam urgente[1] fide credere cogimur et tenere, nosque hanc firmiter[2] credimus et simpliciter[3] confitemur, extra quam nec salus est nec remissio peccatorum . . . ; quae unum corpus mysticum[4] repraesentat,[5] cujus corporis caput Christus, Christi vero Deus. In qua 'unus

[1] **urgeō, urgēre, ursī,** — urge
[2] **firmiter = firmē**
[3] **simpliciter** (*adv.*) plainly
[4] **mysticus, -a, -um** mystical
[5] **repraesentō** (1) represent

Dominus, una fides, unum baptisma.' Una nempe[6] fuit diluvii[7] tempore arca[8] Noe, unam Ecclesiam praefigurans,[9] quae in uno cubito[10] consummata[11] unum, Noe videlicet,[12] gubernatorem[13] habuit et rectorem,[14] extra quam omnia subsistentia[15] super terram legimus fuisse deleta.

Denz 871.   Hanc[16] autem veneramur et unicam,[17] dicente Domino in Propheta: 'Erue[18] a framea,[19] Deus, animam meam, et de manu canis[20] unicam[17] meam.' Pro anima enim, id est pro se ipso, capite simul oravit et corpore, quod corpus unicam[17] scl.[21] Ecclesiam nominavit,[22] propter sponsi, fidei, sacramentorum et caritatis Ecclesiae unitatem. Haec est 'tunica'[23] illa Domini 'inconsutilis,'[24] quae scissa[25] non fuit, sed sorte[26] provenit.[27]

Denz 872.   Igitur Ecclesiae unius et unicae[17] unum corpus, unum caput, non duo capita quasi[28] monstrum,[29] Christus videlicet[12] et Christi vicarius[30] Petrus Petrique successor[31] dicente Domino ipsi Petro: 'Pasce oves meas.' 'Meas,' inquit, et generaliter,[32] non singula-

---

[6] **nempe** (*adv.*) truly, to be sure
[7] **dīluvium, dīluviī,** n. flood
[8] **arca, arcae,** f. ark
[9] **praefigūrō** (1) prefigure
[10] **cubitum, cubitī,** n. cubit
[11] **cōnsummō** (1) complete
[12] **vidēlicet** (*adv.*) of course
[13] **gubernātor, gubernātōris,** m. pilot
[14] **rēctor, rēctōris,** m. captain
[15] **subsistō** (**sub + sistō**) *here,* exist
[16] **hanc:** *sc.* **ecclēsiam**
[17] **ūnicus, -a, -um** only, sole
[18] **ēruō, ēruere, ēruī, ērutus** tear out; rescue
[19] **framea, frameae,** f. sword
[20] **canis, canis,** m. & f. dog
[21] **scl. = scīlicet** (*adv.*) of course
[22] **nōminō** (1) name, call
[23] **tunica, tunicae,** f. tunic, robe
[24] **incōnsūtilis, -e** not sewn together, seamless
[25] **scindō, scindere, scidī, scissus** tear, rend
[26] **sors, sortis,** f. lot
[27] **prōveniō** (**prō + veniō**) come forth, pass on
[28] **quasi** (*adv.*) as if, like
[29] **mōnstrum, mōnstrī,** n. monster
[30] **vīcārius, vīcāriī,** m. vicar
[31] **successor, successōris,** m. successor
[32] **generāliter** (*adv.*) generally, universally

riter[33] has vel illas: per quod commisisse[34] sibi intelligitur universas. Sive ergo Graeci[35] sive alii se dicant Petro ejusque successoribus[31] non esse commissos:[34] fateantur necesse est[36] se de ovibus Christi non esse, dicente Domino in Joanne, 'unum ovile,[37] unum et unicum[17] esse pastorem.'

Denz 873.   In hac[38] ejusque potestate duos esse gladios, spiritualem videlicet[12] et temporalem,[39] evangelicis[40] dictis instruimur . . . Uterque[41] ergo est in potestate Ecclesiae, spiritualis scilicet[21] gladius et materialis.[42] Sed is quidem *pro* Ecclesia, ille vero *ab* Ecclesia exercendus.[43] Ille sacerdotis, is manu regum et militum, sed ad nutum[44] et patientiam[45] sacerdotis. Oportet autem gladium esse sub gladio, et temporalem[39] auctoritatem[46] spirituali subjici[47] potestati . . . . Spiritualem et dignitate[48] et nobilitate[49] terrenam quamlibet[50] praecellere[51] potestatem, oportet tanto[52] clarius nos fateri, quanto[52] spiritualia[39] antecellunt.[53] . . . Nam Veritate testante,[54] spiritualis potestas terrenam potestatem instituere[55] habet,[56] et judicare, si bona non fuerit. . . . Ergo si deviat[57] terrena potestas, judicabitur a potestate spirituali; sed, si deviat[57] spiritualis minor, a suo superiore; si vero suprema, a solo Deo, non ab homine poterit judicari, testante[54]

---

[33] **singulāriter** (*adv.*) singly, particularly
[34] **committō** (**con** + **mittō**) commit, entrust
[35] **Graecus, -a, -um** Greek
[36] **necesse est**: parenthetical
[37] **ovīle, ovīlis, ovīlium**, n. sheepfold
[38] **hāc**: *sc.* **ecclēsiā**
[39] **temporālis, -e** temporal
[40] **evangelicus, -a, -um** of the Gospel
[41] **uterque, utraque, utrumque** each (of two), both
[42] **māteriālis, -e** material, temporal
[43] **exerceō, exercēre, exercuī, exercitus** work out, wield
[44] **nūtus, nūtūs**, m. nod, assent
[45] **patientia, patientiae**, f. permission
[46] **auctōritās, auctōritātis**, f. authority
[47] **subjiciō** (**sub** + **jaciō**) subjugate, subordinate
[48] **dīgnitās, dīgnitātis**, f. dignity
[49] **nōbilitās, nōbilitātis**, f. nobility
[50] **quīlibet, quaelibet, quodlibet** any at all
[51] **praecellō, praecellere, —, —** excel, surpass
[52] **tantō . . quantō**: 'the (more) . . the more'
[53] **antecellō, antecellere, —, —** excel
[54] **testor, testārī, —, testātus sum** call to witness, witness
[55] **īnstituō** (**in** + **statuō**) appoint, establish
[56] **habet** = **potest**
[57] **dēviō** (1) go astray

Apostolo:[58] 'Spiritualis homo judicat omnia, ipse autem a nemine judicatur.'

[58] i.e., Paul

23. *Prooemium,* General Instruction of the Roman Missal *(1970), excerpted*

10. Novum igitur Missale, dum testificatur[1] legem orandi Ecclesiae Romanae, fideique depositum[2] a Conciliis recentioribus[3] traditum tutatur,[4] ipsum vicissim[5] magni momenti[6] gradum[7] designat[8] in liturgica traditione.

Cum enim Patres Concilii Vaticani II asseverationes dogmaticas Concilii Tridentini iterarunt,[9] in longe[10] alia mundi aetate sunt locuti; qua de causa in re pastorali valuerunt afferre proposita et consilia,[11] quae ante quattuor saecula[12] ne[13] praevideri quidem[13] potuerunt.

11. Agnoverat jam Tridentinum Concilium magnam utilitatem catecheticam, quae in Missae celebratione contineretur . . . A multis reapse[14] flagitabatur,[15] ut sermonem vulgarem in Sacrificio eucharistico peragendo[16] usurpari[17] liceret. Ad talem quidem postulationem, Concilium . . . sui officii esse arbitrabatur doctrinam Ecclesiae tralaticiam[18] denuo[19] inculcare,[20] secundum quam Sacrificium eu-

[1] **testificor** (1) testify (to)
[2] **dēpositum, dēpositī,** n. deposit
[3] **recēns** (*gen.,* **recentis**) new, recent
[4] **tūtor** (1) protect, preserve
[5] **vicissim** (*adv.*) in turn
[6] **mōmentum, mōmentī,** n. importance
[7] **gradus, gradūs,** m. step
[8] **dēsīgnō** (1) mark
[9] **iterō** (1) repeat
[10] **longē** (*adv.*) far, by far
[11] **cōnsilium, cōnsiliī,** n. suggestion
[12] **saecula:** *here,* 'centuries'
[13] **nē . . quidem:** 'not even'
[14] **rēapse** (*adv.*) indeed
[15] **flāgitō** (1) demand
[16] **peragō** (**per** + **agō**) accomplish, perform
[17] **ūsurpō** (1) use, make use of
[18] **trālātīcius, -a, -um** traditional
[19] **dēnuō** (*adv.*) anew, again
[20] **inculcō** (1) inculcate, stress, emphasize

charisticum imprimis Christi ipsius est actio, cujus proinde[21] effica-
citas propria eo modo non afficitur, quo fideles ejusdem fiunt parti-
cipes. Idcirco[22] firmis hisce simulque moderatis verbis edictum est:
'Etsi Missa magnam continet populi fidelis eruditionem,[23] non tamen
expedire[24] visum est Patribus, ut vulgari passim[25] lingua celebraretur.' Atque condemnandum esse pronuntiavit eum, qui censeret[26]
'Ecclesiae Romanae ritum, quo submissa voce pars Canonis et verba
consecrationis proferuntur, damnandum esse; aut lingua vulgari
Missam celebrari debere.' Nihilominus,[27] dum hinc[28] vetuit in Missa
linguae vernaculae usum, illinc[28] animarum pastores ejus in locum
congruentem[29] substituere catechesim jussit: 'Ne oves Christi esu-
riant . . . mandat[30] sancta Synodus pastoribus et singulis curam animarum gerentibus, ut frequenter inter[31] Missarum celebrationem
vel per se vel per alios, ex his, quae in Missa leguntur, aliquid expo-
nant[32] atque inter cetera sanctissimi hujus sacrificii mysterium aliquod declarent,[33] diebus praesertim[34] dominicis et festis.'

12. Propterea congregatum, ut Ecclesiam aptaret ad proprii mune-
ris apostolici necessitates hisce ipsis temporibus, Concilium Vatica-
num II funditus[35] perspexit, quemadmodum[36] Tridentinum, didas-
calicam et pastoralem indolem[37] sacrae Liturgiae. Et, cum nemo
catholicorum esset, qui legitimum efficacemque ritum sacrum ne-
garet lingua Latina peractum,[16] concedere etiam valuit: 'Haud[38] raro
linguae vernaculae usurpatio[39] valde utilis apud populum exsistere

---

[21] **proinde** (*adv.*) accordingly
[22] **idcircō** (*adv.*) therefore
[23] **ērudītiō, ērudītiōnis,** f. teaching
[24] **expedīre**: *impersonal*, 'be advantageous'
[25] **passim** (*adv.*) far and wide
[26] **cēnseō, cēnsēre, cēnsuī, cēnsus** have an opinion
[27] **nihilōminus** (*adv.*) nevertheless
[28] **hinc . . illinc**: *here*, 'on the one hand . . on the other hand'
[29] **congruēns** (*gen.*, **congruentis**) appropriate
[30] **mandō** (1) order
[31] **inter**: *here*, 'during'
[32] **expōnō** (**ex** + **pōnō**) explain
[33] **dēclārō** (1) make clear, explain
[34] **praesertim** (*adv.*) especially
[35] **funditus** (*adv.*) completely
[36] **quemadmodum** (*adv.*) just as
[37] **indolēs, indolis,** f. quality, nature
[38] **haud** (*adv.*) not
[39] **ūsurpātiō, ūsurpātiōnis,** f. use

possit,' ejusque adhibendae[40] facultatem[41] dedit. Flagrans[42] illud studium,[43] quo hoc consultum ubivis[44] est susceptum, profecto[45] effecit ut, ducibus Episcopis atque ipsa Apostolica Sede, universae liturgicae celebrationes quas populus participaret, exsequi liceret vulgari sermone, quo plenius intellegeretur mysterium, quod celebraretur.

[40] **adhibeō** (**ad** + **habeō**) apply, employ
[41] **facultās, facultātis**, f. possibility, opportunity
[42] **flagrāns** (*gen.*, **flagrantis**) flaming, eager
[43] **studium, studiī**, n. enthusiasm, zeal
[44] **ubivīs** (*adv.*) everywhere
[45] **profectō** (*adv.*) indeed

Metrical Notes

The metrical patterns found in the verse readings are either quantitative or accentual. In a quantitative measure length of syllable is counted: vowels are long or short (by nature or by position). Long vowels and diphthongs are long; short vowels followed by two or more consonants are long by position; short vowels followed by a mute and a liquid consonant are short or long, depending on the demand of the meter. In an accentual meter the loud or soft stress on a syllable is counted, and the quantity is ignored—as it is in English verse. In quantitative measures two iambs or two trochees count as *one* metrum; in accentual measures two iambs or two trochees count as *two* metra. For example, in the quantitative line of an Ambrosian hymn, there are eight syllables, four iambs, *two* metra: hence, iambic dimeter; in the accentual line of the Verbum Supernum, there are eight syllables, four iambs, *four* metra: hence, iambic tetrameter. In quantitative measures, a final vowel is elided before an initial vowel: e.g., petra͜ Ecclesiae; thus it is not counted in the meter. A line may be either catalectic—missing a beginning or ending short or unaccented syllable—or acatalectic, i.e., complete.

5) Stabat Mater: accentual.
Six-line stanzas:
trochaic tetrameter acatalectic (lines 1, 2, 4, 5): /◡|/◡|/◡|/◡
trochaic tetrameter catalectic (lines 3, 6): /◡|/◡|/◡|/∧
Rime scheme: AABCCB, with occasional internal rime.

6) The Cockcrow Hymn: quantitative.
Iambic dimeter: x−◡−|x−◡x
Aētērně rḗrūm Cōndĭtŏr

Note: Syllables 1, 5, and 8 may be either long or short; syllables 3 and 7 must always be short; syllables 2, 4, and 6 must always be long.

8) Vexilla Regis: quantitative.

Iambic dimeter. See 6).

Note the scansion of dicendŏ (line 11) and cūjus (line 17); see vocabulary note on major (Unit 22). Pretium (line 18) is scanned as two syllables: -i- here counts as a consonant (pretⱼum).

9) Pange Lingua [Fortunatus]: quantitative.

Each 3-line stanza is in reality a 6-line stanza: each line is composed of a trochaic dimeter acatalectic ($-\cup-x|-\cup-x$) and a trochaic dimeter catalectic ($-\cup-x|-\cup x\wedge$). Quando (lines 5 and 10) is scanned quandŏ; the -o may count as either long or short. The final long o of ordo (line 7), ergo (line 10), and virgo (line 14) is artificially shortened: ordŏ, ergŏ, virgŏ; this is a common metrical liberty. The -i- in unius (line 33) is common in quantity: -ĭ-.

10) Veni Creator Spiritus: quantitative.

Iambic dimeter. See 6).

Line 10 begins with a rare anapestic substitution: dĭgĭtūs paternae.

11) Ave Maris Stella: accentual.

Trochaic trimeter:

Occasionally, accentual poems make use of elision, as in line 13: te‿esse.

12) Gloria Laus: quantitative.

Elegiac couplet: $-\cup\cup|-\cup\cup|-\cup\cup|-\cup\cup|-\cup\cup|-x$

$$-\cup\cup|-\cup\cup|-||-\cup\cup|-\cup\cup|x$$

The quantities of names and foreign words often vary: e.g., Israēl is here scanned Israĕl. Final o of dēvōtiō is artificially shortened: devotiŏ. Final -i of tibi may count as long or short.

13) Veni Sancte Spiritus: accentual.

Trochaic tetrameter catalectic: /$\cup$|/$\cup$|/$\cup$|/$\wedge$

All ten stanzas end with the same rime.

14) Dies Irae: accentual.

Trochaic tetrameter: /$\cup$|/$\cup$|/$\cup$|/$\cup$

Each stanza is triply rimed (except the last three shorter stanzas, which are later additions).

15) Lauda Sion: accentual.

Trochaic tetrameter acatalectic and catalectic. See 5).

The first nine stanzas have the same metrical and riming pattern as
   that of the Stabat Mater. Stanzas 10 and 11 add two more lines;
   stanza 12 adds four more lines, all acatalectic. Note the final rime
   scheme: AAAABCCCCB.

16) Pange Lingua [Aquinas]: accentual.
The metrical pattern copies accentually the quantitative pattern of
   Fortunatus's Pange Lingua. See 9). But Aquinas's poem rimes, as
   accentual poems most often do.

17) Verbum Supernum: accentual.
Iambic tetrameter: ᴗ/|ᴗ/|ᴗ/|ᴗ/
An accentual version of the Ambrosian quantitative measure.
   See 6). Rime has been added to the form: ABAB.

18) Creator Alme Siderum: quantitative.
Iambic dimeter. See 6).

19) A Solis Ortus: quantitative.
Iambic dimeter. See 6).

Morphology

Regular Verbs

The Four Conjugations

The stem vowel of the second principal part reveals the conjugation of a Latin verb.

1: -*ā*re   2: -*ē*re   3: -*ere*   4: -*ī*re
  -*ā*rī   -*ē*rī   -ī   -*ī*rī

(Note: In the passive, the third conjugation has -ī.)

1: cantō, cant*ā*re, cantāvī, cantātus; cōnor, cōn*ā*rī, —, cōnātus sum
2: appāreō, appār*ē*re, appāruī, appāritus; fateor, fat*ē*rī, —, fassus sum
3: agō, ag*ere*, ēgī, āctus; fugiō, fug*ere*, fūgī, fugitus; amplector, amplectī, —, amplexus sum; gradior, gradī, —, gressus sum
4: aperiō, aperīre, aperuī, apertus; largior, largīrī, —, largītus sum

The Personal Endings

	ACTIVE	PASSIVE		PERFECT ACTIVE
	Sing.	*Sing.*		*Sing.*
1:	-ō (-m)	-or (-r)	1:	-ī
2:	-s	-ris, -re	2:	-istī
3:	-t	-tur	3:	-it
	Pl.	*Pl.*		*Pl.*
1:	-mus	-mur	1:	-imus
2:	-tis	-minī	2:	-istis
3:	-nt	-ntur	3:	-ērunt (-ēre)

First Conjugation: laudō, laudāre, laudāvī, laudātus

Indicative

	ACTIVE	PASSIVE
Present	laudō	laudor
	laudās	laudāris, laudāre

Indicative

	ACTIVE	PASSIVE
	laudat	laudātur
	laudāmus	laudāmur
	laudātis	laudāminī
	laudant	laudantur
Imperfect	laudābam	laudābar
	laudābās	laudābāris, laudābāre
	laudābat	laudābātur
	laudābāmus	laudābāmur
	laudābātis	laudābāminī
	laudābant	laudābantur
Future	laudābō	laudābor
	laudābis	laudāberis, laudābere
	laudābit	laudābitur
	laudābimus	laudābimur
	laudābitis	laudābiminī
	laudābunt	laudābuntur
Perfect	laudāvī	laudātus (-a, -um) sum
	laudāvistī	laudātus (-a, -um) es
	laudāvit	laudātus (-a, -um) est
	laudāvimus	laudātī (-ae, -a) sumus
	laudāvistis	laudātī (-ae, -a) estis
	laudāvērunt (-ēre)	laudātī (-ae, -a) sunt
Pluperfect	laudāveram	laudātus (-a, -um) eram
	laudāverās	laudātus (-a, -um) erās
	laudāverat	laudātus (-a, -um) erat
	laudāverāmus	laudātī (-ae, -a) erāmus
	laudāverātis	laudātī (-ae, -a) erātis
	laudāverant	laudātī (-ae, -a) erant
Future-Perfect	laudāverō	laudātus (-a, -um) erō
	laudāveris	laudātus (-a, -um) eris
	laudāverit	laudātus (-a, -um) erit
	laudāverimus	laudātī (-ae, -a) erimus
	laudāveritis	laudātī (-ae, -a) eritis
	laudāverint	laudātī (-ae, -a) erunt

Subjunctive

	ACTIVE	PASSIVE
Present	laudem	lauder
	laudēs	laudēris, laudēre

Subjunctive

	laudet	laudētur
	laudēmus	laudēmur
	laudētis	laudēinī ~~—~~ *laudemini*
	laudent	laudentur
Imperfect	laudārem	laudārer
	laudārēs	laudārēris, laudārēre
	laudāret	laudārētur
	laudārēmus	laudārēmur
	laudārētis	laudārēminī
	laudārent	laudārentur
Perfect	laudāverim	laudātus (-a, -um) sim
	laudāveris	laudātus (-a, -um) sīs
	laudāverit	laudātus (-a, -um) sit
	laudāverimus	laudātī (-ae, -a) sīmus
	laudāveritis	laudātī (-ae, -a) sītis
	laudāverint	laudātī (-ae, -a) sint
Pluperfect	laudāvissem	laudātus (-a, -um) essem
	laudāvissēs	laudātus (-a, -um) essēs
	laudāvisset	laudātus (-a, -um) esset
	laudāvissēmus	laudātī (-ae, -a) essēmus
	laudāvissētis	laudātī (-ae, -a) essētis
	laudāvissent	laudātī (-ae, -a) essent

Participles

	ACTIVE	PASSIVE
Present	laudāns (*gen.*, laudantis)	none
Perfect	none	laudātus, -a, -um
Future	laudātūrus, -a, -um	laudandus, -a, -um

Infinitives

	ACTIVE	PASSIVE
Present	laudāre	laudārī
Perfect	laudāvisse	laudātus, -a, -um esse
Future	laudātūrus, -a, -um esse	rare

Imperatives

ACTIVE		PASSIVE	
Singular	*Plural*	*Singular*	*Plural*
laudā	laudāte	laudāre	laudāminī

Second Conjugation: moneō, monēre, monuī, monitus

Indicative

	ACTIVE	PASSIVE
Present	moneō	moneor
	monēs	monēris, monēre
	monet	monētur
	monēmus	monēmur
	monētis	monēminī
	* monent	monentur
Imperfect	monēbam	monēbar
	monēbās	monēbāris, monēbāre
	monēbat	monēbātur
	monēbāmus	monēbāmur
	monēbātis	monēbāminī
	monēbant	monēbantur
Future	monēbō	monēbor
	monēbis	*monēberis, monēbere
	monēbit	monēbitur
	monēbimus	monēbimur
	monēbitis	monēbiminī
	monēbunt	monēbuntur
Perfect	monuī	monitus (-a, -um) sum
	monuistī	monitus (-a, -um) es
	monuit	monitus (-a, -um) est
	monuimus	monitī (-ae, -a) sumus
	monuistis	monitī (-ae, -a) estis
	*monuērunt (-ēre)	monitī (-ae, -a) sunt
Pluperfect	monueram	monitus (-a, -um) eram
	monuerās	monitus (-a, -um) erās
	monuerat	monitus, (-a, -um) erat
	monuerāmus	monitī (-ae, -a) erāmus
	monuerātis	monitī (-ae, -a) erātis
	monuerant	monitī (-ae, -a) erant
Future-Perfect	monuerō	monitus (-a, -um) erō
	monueris	monitus (-a, -um) eris
	monuerit	monitus (-a, -um) erit
	monuerimus	monitī (-ae, -a) erimus
	monueritis	monitī (-ae, -a) eritis
	* monuerint	monitī (-ae, -a) erunt

Subjunctive

	ACTIVE	PASSIVE
Present	moneam	monear
	moneās	moneāris, moneāre
	moneat	moneātur
	moneāmus	moneāmur
	moneātis	moneāminī
	moneant	moneantur
Imperfect	monērem	monērer
	monērēs	monērēris, monērēre
	monēret	monērētur
	monērēmus	monērēmur
	monērētis	monērēminī
	monērent	monērentur
Perfect	monuerim	monitus (-a, -um) sim
	monueris	monitus (-a, -um) sīs
	monuerit	monitus (-a, -um) sit
	monuerimus	monitī (-ae, -a) sīmus
	monueritis	monitī (-ae, -a) sītis
	monuerint	monitī (-ae, -a) sint
Pluperfect	monuissem	monitus (-a, -um) essem
	monuissēs	monitus (-a, -um) essēs
	monuisset	monitus (-a, -um) esset
	monuissēmus	monitī (-ae, -a) essēmus
	monuissētis	monitī (-ae, -a) essētis
	monuissent	monitī (-ae, -a) essent

Participles

	ACTIVE	PASSIVE
Present	monēns (*gen.*, monentis)	none
Perfect	none	monitus, -a, -um
Future	monitūrus, -a, -um	monendus, -a, -um

Infinitives

	ACTIVE	PASSIVE
Present	monēre	monērī
Perfect	monuisse	monitus, -a, -um esse
Future	monitūrus, -a, -um esse	rare

Imperatives

ACTIVE		PASSIVE	
Singular	*Plural*	*Singular*	*Plural*
monē	monēte	monēre	monēminī

Third Conjugation ('-ō' type): dūcō, dūcere, dūxī, ductus

Indicative

	ACTIVE	PASSIVE
Present	dūcō	dūcor
	dūcis	dūceris, dūcere
	dūcit	dūcitur
	dūcimus	dūcimur
	dūcitis	dūciminī
	dūcunt	dūcuntur
Imperfect	dūcēbam	dūcēbar
	dūcēbās	dūcēbāris, dūcēbāre
	dūcēbat	dūcēbātur
	dūcēbāmus	dūcēbāmur
	dūcēbātis	dūcēbāminī
	dūcēbant	dūcēbantur
Future	dūcam	dūcar
	dūcēs	dūcēris, dūcēre
	dūcet	dūcētur
	dūcēmus	dūcēmur
	dūcētis	dūcēminī
	dūcent	dūcentur
Perfect	dūxī	ductus (-a, -um) sum
	dūxistī	ductus (-a, -um) es
	dūxit	ductus (-a, -um) est
	dūximus	ductī (-ae, -a) sumus
	dūxistis	ductī (-ae, -a) estis
	dūxērunt (-ēre)	ductī (-ae, -a) sunt
Pluperfect	dūxeram	ductus (-a, -um) eram
	dūxerās	ductus (-a, -um) erās
	dūxerat	ductus (-a, -um) erat
	dūxerāmus	ductī (-ae, -a) erāmus
	dūxerātis	ductī (-ae, -a) erātis
	dūxerant	ductī (-ae, -a) erant
Future-Perfect	dūxerō	ductus (-a, -um) erō
	dūxeris	ductus (-a, -um) eris

Indicative

ACTIVE	PASSIVE
dūxerit	ductus (-a, -um) erit
dūxerimus	ductī (-ae, -a) erimus
dūxeritis	ductī (-ae, -a) eritis
dūxerint	ductī (-ae, -a) erunt

Subjunctive

	ACTIVE	PASSIVE
Present	dūcam	dūcar
	dūcās	dūcāris, dūcāre
	dūcat	dūcātur
	dūcāmus	dūcāmur
	dūcātis	dūcāminī
	dūcant	dūcantur
Imperfect	dūcerem	dūcerer
	dūcerēs	dūcerēris, dūcerēre
	dūceret	dūcerētur
	dūcerēmus	dūcerēmur
	dūcerētis	dūcerēminī
	dūcerent	dūcerentur
Perfect	dūxerim	ductus (-a, -um) sim
	dūxeris	ductus (-a, -um) sīs
	dūxerit	ductus (-a, -um) sit
	dūxerimus	ductī (-ae, -a) sīmus
	dūxeritis	ductī (-ae, -a) sītis
	dūxerint	ductī (-ae, -a) sint
Pluperfect	dūxissem	ductus (-a, -um) essem
	dūxissēs	ductus (-a, -um) essēs
	dūxisset	ductus (-a, -um) esset
	dūxissēmus	ductī (-ae, -a) essēmus
	dūxissētis	ductī (-ae, -a) essētis
	dūxissent	ductī (-ae, -a) essent

Participles

	ACTIVE	PASSIVE
Present	dūcēns (*gen.*, dūcentis)	none
Perfect	none	ductus, -a, -um
Future	ductūrus, -a, -um	dūcendus, -a, -um

Infinitives

	ACTIVE	PASSIVE
Present	dūcere	dūcī
Perfect	dūxisse	ductus, -a, -um esse
Future	ductūrus, -a, -um esse	rare

Imperatives

ACTIVE		PASSIVE	
Singular	Plural	Singular	Plural
dūc*	dūcite	dūcere	dūciminī

*dūcō, dīcō, faciō, and ferō drop the final -e.

Third Conjugation ('-iō' type): capiō, capere, cēpī, captus

Indicative

	ACTIVE	PASSIVE
Present	capiō	capior
	capis	*caperis, capere
	capit	capitur
	capimus	capimur
	capitis	capiminī
	*capiunt	*capiuntur
Imperfect	capiēbam	capiēbar
	capiēbās	capiēbāris, capiēbāre
	capiēbat	capiēbātur
	capiēbāmus	capiēbāmur
	capiēbātis	capiēbāminī
	capiēbant	capiēbantur
Future	capiam	capiar
	capiēs	capiēris, capiēre
	capiet	capiētur
	capiēmus	capiēmur
	capiētis	capiēminī
	capient	capientur
Perfect	cēpī	captus (-a, -um) sum
	cēpistī	captus (-a, -um) es
	cēpit	captus (-a, -um) est
	cēpimus	captī (-ae, -a) sumus
	cēpistis	captī (-ae, -a) estis
	cēpērunt (-ēre)	captī (-ae, -a) sunt

Indicative

	ACTIVE	PASSIVE
Pluperfect	cēperam	captus (-a, -um) eram
	cēperās	captus (-a, -um) erās
	cēperat	captus (-a, -um) erat
	cēperāmus	captī (-ae, -a) erāmus
	cēperātis	captī (-ae, -a) erātis
	cēperant	captī (-ae, -a) erant
Future-Perfect	cēperō	captus (-a, -um) erō
	cēperis	captus (-a, -um) eris
	cēperit	captus (-a, -um) erit
	cēperimus	captī (-ae, -a) erimus
	cēperitis	captī (-ae, -a) eritis
	✕cēperint	captī (-ae, -a) erunt

Subjunctive

	ACTIVE	PASSIVE
Present	capiam	capiar
	capiās	capiāris, capiāre
	capiat	capiātur
	capiāmus	capiāmur
	capiātis	capiāminī
	capiant	capiantur
Imperfect	caperem	caperer
	caperēs	caperēris, caperēre
	caperet	caperētur
	caperēmus	caperēmur
	caperētis	caperēminī
	caperent	caperentur
Perfect	cēperim	captus (-a, -um) sim
	cēperis	captus (-a, -um) sīs
	cēperit	captus (-a, -um) sit
	cēperimus	captī (-ae, -a) sīmus
	cēperitis	captī (-ae, -a) sītis
	cēperint	captī (-ae, -a) sint
Pluperfect	cēpissem	captus (-a, -um) essem
	cēpissēs	captus (-a, -um) essēs
	cēpisset	captus (-a, -um) esset
	cēpissēmus	captī (-ae, -a) essēmus
	cēpissētis	captī (-ae, -a) essētis
	cēpissent	captī (-ae, -a) essent

Participles

	ACTIVE	PASSIVE
Present	capiēns (*gen.*, capientis)	none
Perfect	none	captus, -a, -um
Future	captūrus, -a, -um	capiendus, -a, -um

Infinitives

	ACTIVE	PASSIVE
Present	capere	capī
Perfect	cēpisse	captus, -a, -um esse
Future	captūrus, -a, -um esse	rare

Imperatives

ACTIVE		PASSIVE	
Singular	*Plural*	*Singular*	*Plural*
cape	capite	capere	capiminī

Fourth Conjugation: audiō, audīre, audīvī, audītus

Indicative

	ACTIVE	PASSIVE
Present	audiō	audior
	audīs	audīris, audīre
	audit	audītur
	audīmus	audīmur
	audītis	audīminī
	✶audiunt	✶ audiuntur
Imperfect	audiēbam	audiēbar
	audiēbās	audiēbāris, audiēbāre
	audiēbat	audiēbātur
	audiēbāmus	audiēbāmur
	audiēbātis	audiēbāminī
	audiēbant	audiēbantur
Future	Λ ✶ audiam	Λ ✶audiar
	audiēs	audiēris, audiēre
	audiet	audiētur
	audiēmus	audiēmur
	audiētis	audiēminī
	audient	audientur

(Handwritten annotations in margins: "IE" braces beside the Imperfect and Future forms; "NO 'B'" beside the Future active.)

Indicative

	ACTIVE	PASSIVE
Perfect	audīvī	audītus (-a, -um) sum
	audīvistī	audītus (-a, -um) es
	audīvit	audītus (-a, -um) est
	audīvimus	audītī (-ae, -a) sumus
	audīvistis	audītī (-ae, -a) estis
	audīvērunt (-ēre)	audītī (-ae, -a) sunt
Pluperfect	audīveram	audītus (-a, -um) eram
	audīverās	audītus (-a, -um) erās
	audīverat	audītus (-a, -um) erat
	audīverāmus	audītī (-ae, -a) erāmus
	audīverātis	audītī (-ae, -a) erātis
	audīverant	audītī (-ae, -a) erant
Future-Perfect	audīverō	audītus (-a, -um) erō
	audīveris	audītus (-a, -um) eris
	audīverit	audītus (-a, -um) erit
	audīverimus	audītī (-ae, -a) erimus
	audīveritis	audītī (-ae, -a) eritis
	audīverint	audītī (-ae, -a) erunt

Subjunctive

	ACTIVE	PASSIVE
Present	audiam	audiar
	audiās	audiāris, audiāre
	audiat	audiātur
	audiāmus	audiāmur
	audiātis	audiāminī
	audiant	audiantur
Imperfect	audīrem	audīrer
	audīrēs	audīrēris, audīrēre
	audīret	audīrētur
	audīrēmus	audīrēmur
	audīrētis	audīrēminī
	audīrent	audīrentur
Perfect	audīverim	audītus (-a, -um) sim
	audīveris	audītus (-a, -um) sīs
	audīverit	audītus (-a, -um) sit
	audīverimus	audītī (-ae, -a) sīmus
	audīveritis	audītī (-ae, -a) sītis
	audīverint	audītī (-ae, -a) sint

Subjunctive

	ACTIVE	PASSIVE
Pluperfect	audīvissem	audītus (-a, -um) essem
	audīvissēs	audītus (-a, -um) essēs
	audīvisset	audītus (-a, -um) esset
	audīvissēmus	audītī (-ae, -a) essēmus
	audīvissētis	audītī (-ae, -a) essētis
	audīvissent	audītī (-ae, -a) essent

Participles

	ACTIVE	PASSIVE
Present	audiēns (gen., audientis)	none
Perfect	none	audītus, -a, -um
Future	audītūrus, -a, -um	audiendus, -a, -um

Infinitives

	ACTIVE	PASSIVE
Present	audīre	audīrī
Perfect	audīvisse	audītus, -a, -um esse
Future	audītūrus, -a, -um esse	rare

Imperatives

ACTIVE		PASSIVE	
Singular	Plural	Singular	Plural
audī	audīte	audīre	audīminī

Deponent Verbs

First Conjugation: mīror, mīrārī, —, mīrātus sum

Indicative

Present	Imperfect
mīror	mīrābar
mīrāris, mīrāre	mīrābāris, mīrābāre
mīrātur	mīrābātur
mīrāmur	mīrābāmur
mīrāminī	mīrābāminī
mīrantur	mīrābantur
Future	Perfect
mīrābor	mīrātus (-a, -um) sum
mīrāberis, mīrābere	mīrātus (-a, -um) es

Indicative

Future	Perfect
mīrābitur	mīrātus (-a, -um) est
mīrābimur	mīrātī (-ae, -a) sumus
mīrābiminī	mīrātī (-ae, -a) estis
mīrābuntur	mīrātī (-ae, -a) sunt

Pluperfect	Future-Perfect
mīrātus (-a, -um) eram	mīrātus (-a, -um) erō
mīrātus (-a, -um) erās	mīrātus (-a, -um) eris
mīrātus (-a, -um) erat	mīrātus (-a, -um) erit
mīrātī (-ae, -a) erāmus	mīrātī (-ae, -a) erimus
mīrātī (-ae, -a) erātis	mīrātī (-ae, -a) eritis
mīrātī (-ae, -a) erant	mīrātī (-ae, -a) erunt

Subjunctive

Present	Imperfect
mīrer	mīrārer
mīrēris, mīrēre	mīrārēris, mīrārēre
mīrētur	mīrārētur
mīrēmur	mīrārēmur
mīrēminī	mīrārēminī
mīrentur	mīrārentur

Perfect	Pluperfect
mīrātus (-a, -um) sim	mīrātus (-a, -um) essem
mīrātus (-a, -um) sīs	mīrātus (-a, -um) essēs
mīrātus (-a, -um) sit	mīrātus (-a, -um) esset
mīrātī (-ae, -a) sīmus	mīrātī (-ae, -a) essēmus
mīrātī (-ae, -a) sītis	mīrātī (-ae, -a) essētis
mīrātī (-ae, -a) sint	mīrātī (-ae, -a) essent

Participles

Present	Perfect
mīrāns (gen., mīrantis)	mīrātus, -a, -um
Future Active	Future Passive
mīrātūrus, -a, -um	mīrandus, -a, -um

Infinitives

Present	Perfect
mīrārī	mīrātus, -a, -um esse
Future	
mīrātūrus, -a, -um esse	

Imperatives

Singular	Plural
mīrāre	mīrāminī

Second Conjugation: misereor, miserērī, —, misertus sum

Indicative

Present
misereor
miserēris, miserēre
miserētur
miserēmur
miserēminī
miserentur

Imperfect
miserēbar
miserēbāris, miserēbāre
miserēbātur
miserēbāmur
miserēbāminī
miserēbantur

Future
miserēbor
miserēberis, miserēbere
miserēbitur
miserēbimur
miserēbiminī
miserēbuntur

Perfect
misertus (-a, -um) sum
misertus (-a, -um) es
misertus (-a, -um) est
misertī (-ae, -a) sumus
misertī (-ae, -a) estis
misertī (-ae, -a) sunt

Pluperfect
misertus (-a, -um) eram
misertus (-a, -um) erās
misertus (-a, -um) erat
misertī (-ae, -a) erāmus
misertī (-ae, -a) erātis
misertī (-ae, -a) erant

Future-Perfect
misertus (-a, -um) erō
misertus (-a, -um) eris
misertus (-a, -um) erit
misertī (-ae, -a) erimus
misertī (-ae, -a) eritis
misertī (-ae, -a) erunt

Subjunctive

Present
miserear
misereāris, misereāre
misereātur
misereāmur
misereāminī
misereantur

Imperfect
miserērer
miserērēris, miserērēre
miserērētur
miserērēmur
miserērēminī
miserērentur

Perfect
misertus (-a, -um) sim
misertus (-a, -um) sīs
misertus (-a, -um) sit

Pluperfect
misertus (-a, -um) essem
misertus (-a, -um) essēs
misertus (-a, -um) esset

Subjunctive

Perfect

misertī (-ae, -a) sīmus
misertī (-ae, -a) sītis
misertī (-ae, -a) sint

Pluperfect

misertī (-ae, -a) essēmus
misertī (-ae, -a) essētis
misertī (-ae, -a) essent

Participles

Present

miserēns (*gen.*, miserentis)

Future Active

misertūrus, -a, -um

Perfect

misertus, -a, -um

Future Passive

miserendus, -a, -um

Infinitives

Present

miserērī

Future

misertūrus, -a, -um esse

Perfect

misertus, -a, -um esse

Imperatives

Singular

miserēre

Plural

miserēminī

Third Conjugation ('-ō' type): nāscor, nāscī, —, nātus sum

Indicative

Present

nāscor
nāsceris, nāscere
nāscitur
nāscimur
nāsciminī
nāscuntur

Imperfect

nāscēbar
nāscēbāris, nāscēbāre
nāscēbatur
nāscēbāmur
nāscēbāminī
nāscēbantur

Future

nāscar
nāscēris, nāscēre
nāscētur
nāscēmur
nāscēminī
nāscentur

Perfect

nātus (-a, -um) sum
nātus (-a, -um) es
nātus (-a, -um) est
nātī (-ae, -a) sumus
nātī (-ae, -a) estis
nātī (-ae, -a) sunt

Indicative

Pluperfect	*Future-Perfect*
nātus (-a, -um) eram	nātus (-a, -um) erō
nātus (-a, -um) erās	nātus (-a, -um) eris
nātus (-a, -um) erat	nātus (-a, -um) erit
nātī (-ae, -a) erāmus	nātī (-ae, -a) erimus
nātī (-ae, -a) erātis	nātī (-ae, -a) eritis
nātī (-ae, -a) erant	nātī (-ae, -a) erunt

Subjunctive

Present	*Imperfect*
nāscar	nāscerer
nāscāris, nāscāre	nāscerēris, nāscerēre
nāscātur	nāscerētur
nāscāmur	nāscerēmur
nāscāminī	nāscerēminī
nāscantur	nāscerentur

Perfect	*Pluperfect*
nātus (-a, -um) sim	nātus (-a, -um) essem
nātus (-a, -um) sīs	nātus (-a, -um) essēs
nātus (-a, -um) sit	nātus (-a, -um) esset
nātī (-ae, -a) sīmus	nātī (-ae, -a) essēmus
nātī (-ae, -a) sītis	nātī (-ae, -a) essētis
nātī (-ae, -a) sint	nātī (-ae, -a) essent

Participles

Present	*Perfect*
nāscēns (*gen.*, nāscentis)	nātus, -a, -um
Future Active	*Future Passive*
nātūrus, -a, -um	nāscendus, -a, -um

Infinitives

Present	*Perfect*
nāscī	nātus, -a, -um esse
Future	
nātūrus, -a, -um esse	

Imperatives

Singular	*Plural*
nāscere	nāsciminī

Third Conjugation ('-iō' type): patior, patī, —, passus sum

Indicative

Present

patior
pateris, patere
patitur
patimur
patiminī
patiuntur

Imperfect

patiēbar
patiēbāris, patiēbāre
patiēbātur
patiēbāmur
patiēbāminī
patiēbantur

Future

patiar
patiēris, patiēre
patiētur
patiēmur
patiēminī
patientur

Perfect

passus (-a, -um) sum
passus (-a, -um) es
passus (-a, -um) est
passī (-ae, -a) sumus
passī (-ae, -a) estis
passī (-ae, -a) sunt

Pluperfect

passus (-a, -um) eram
passus (-a, -um) erās
passus (-a, -um) erat
passī (-ae, -a) erāmus
passī (-ae, -a) erātis
passī (-ae, -a) erant

Future-Perfect

passus (-a, -um) erō
passus (-a, -um) eris
passus (-a, -um) erit
passī (-ae, -a) erimus
passī (-ae, -a) eritis
passī (-ae, -a) erunt

Subjunctive

Present

patiar
patiāris, patiāre
patiātur
patiāmur
patiāminī
patiantur

Imperfect

paterer
paterēris, paterēre
paterētur
paterēmur
paterēminī
paterentur

Perfect

passus (-a, -um) sim
passus (-a, -um) sīs
passus (-a, -um) sit
passī (-ae, -a) sīmus
passī (-ae, -a) sītis
passī (-ae, -a) sint

Pluperfect

passus (-a, -um) essem
passus (-a, -um) essēs
passus (-a, -um) esset
passī (-ae, -a) essēmus
passī (-ae, -a) essētis
passī (-ae, -a) essent

Participles

Present	*Perfect*
patiēns (*gen.*, patientis)	passus, -a, -um
Future Active	*Future Passive*
passūrus, -a, -um	patiendus, -a, -um

Infinitives

Present	*Perfect*
patī	passus, -a, -um esse
Future	
passūrus, -a, -um esse	

Imperatives

Singular	*Plural*
patere	patiminī

Fourth Conjugation: experior, experīrī, —, expertus sum

Indicative

Present	*Imperfect*
experior	experiēbar
experīris, experīre	experiēbāris, experiēbāre
experītur	experiēbātur
experīmur	experiēbāmur
experīminī	experiēbāminī
experiuntur	experiēbantur
Future	*Perfect*
experiar	expertus (-a, -um) sum
experiēris, experiēre	expertus (-a, -um) es
experiētur	expertus (-a, -um) est
experiēmur	expertī (-ae, -a) sumus
experiēminī	expertī (-ae, -a) estis
experientur	expertī (-ae, -a) sunt
Pluperfect	*Future-Perfect*
expertus (-a, -um) eram	expertus (-a, -um) erō
expertus (-a, -um) erās	expertus (-a, -um) eris
expertus (-a, -um) erat	expertus (-a, -um) erit
expertī (-ae, -a) erāmus	expertī (-ae, -a) erimus
expertī (-ae, -a) erātis	expertī (-ae, -a) eritis
expertī (-ae, -a) erant	expertī (-ae, -a) erunt

Subjunctive

Present	Imperfect
experiar	experīrer
experiāris, experiāre	experīrēris, experīrēre
experiātur	experīrētur
experiāmur	experīrēmur
experiāminī	experīrēminī
experiantur	experīrentur

Perfect	Pluperfect
expertus (-a, -um) sim	expertus (-a, -um) essem
expertus (-a, -um) sīs	expertus (-a, -um) essēs
expertus (-a, -um) sit	expertus (-a, -um) esset
expertī (-ae, -a) sīmus	expertī (-ae, -a) essēmus
expertī (-ae, -a) sītis	expertī (-ae, -a) essētis
expertī (-ae, -a) sint	expertī (-ae, -a) essent

Participles

Present	Perfect
experiēns (gen., experientis)	expertus, -a, -um

Future Active	Future Passive
expertūrus, -a, -um	experiendus, -a, -um

Infinitives

Present	Perfect
experīrī	expertus, -a, -um esse

Future
expertūrus, -a, -um esse

Imperatives

Singular	Plural
experīre	experīminī

Irregular Verbs

sum, esse, fuī, futūrus
possum, posse, potuī, —

Indicative

Present	sum	possum
	es	potes
	est	potest
	sumus	possumus
	estis	potestis
	sunt	possunt
Imperfect	eram	poteram
	erās	poterās
	erat	poterat
	erāmus	poterāmus
	erātis	poterātis
	erant	poterant
Future	erō	poterō
	eris	poteris
	erit	poterit
	erimus	poterimus
	eritis	poteritis
	erunt	poterunt
Perfect	fuī	potuī
	fuistī	potuistī
	fuit	potuit
	fuimus	potuimus
	fuistis	potuistis
	fuērunt (-ēre)	potuērunt (-ēre)
Pluperfect	fueram	potueram
	fuerās	potuerās
	fuerat	potuerat
	fuerāmus	potuerāmus
	fuerātis	potuerātis
	fuerant	potuerant
Future-Perfect	fuerō	potuerō
	fueris	potueris
	fuerit	potuerit
	fuerimus	potuerimus
	fueritis	potueritis
	fuerint	potuerint

Subjunctive

Present		
	sim	possim
	sīs	possīs
	sit	possit
	sīmus	possīmus
	sītis	possītis
	sint	possint
Imperfect	essem	possem
	essēs	possēs
	esset	posset
	essēmus	posēmus
	essētis	possētis
	essent	possent
Perfect	fuerim	potuerim
	fueris	poteris
	fuerit	potuerit
	fuerimus	potuerimus
	fueritis	potueritis
	fuerint	potuerint
Pluperfect	fuissem	potuissem
	fuissēs	potuissēs
	fuisset	potuisset
	fuissēmus	potuissēmus
	fuissētis	potuissētis
	fuissent	potuissent

Participles

Present	none	potēns (*gen.*, potentis)
Perfect	none	none
Future	futūrus, -a, -um	none

Infinitives

Present	esse	posse
Perfect	fuisse	potuisse
Future	futūrus, -a, -um esse	none

Imperatives

	Singular	Plural	Singular	Plural
Present	es	este	none	none
	Singular	Plural	Singular	Plural
Future	estō	estōte	none	none

eō, īre, īvī (iī), itus

Indicative

Present	Imperfect	Future
eō	ībam	ībō
īs	ībās	ībis
it	ībat	ībit
īmus	ībāmus	ībimus
ītis	ībātis	ībitis
eunt	ībant	ībunt

Perfect	Pluperfect	Future-Perfect
īvī (iī)	īveram (ieram)	īverō (ierō)
īvistī (īstī)	īverās (ierās)	īveris (ieris)
īvit (iit)	īverat (ierat)	īverit (ierit)
īvimus (iimus)	īverāmus (ierāmus)	īverimus (ierimus)
īvistis (īstis)	īverātis (ierātis)	īveritis (ieritis)
īvērunt, īvēre (iērunt, iēre)	īverant (ierant)	īverint (ierint)

Subjunctive

Present	Imperfect	Perfect	Pluperfect
eam	īrem	īverim (ierim)	īvissem (īssem)
eās	īrēs	īveris (ieris)	īvissēs (īssēs)
eat	īret	īverit (ierit)	īvisset (īsset)
eāmus	īrēmus	īverimus (ierimus)	īvissēmus (īssēmus)
eātis	īrētis	īveritis (ieritis)	īvissētis (īssētis)
eant	īrent	īverint (ierint)	īvissent (īssent)

Participles

	ACTIVE	PASSIVE
Present	iēns (gen., euntis)	none
Perfect	none	itum
Future	itūrus, -a, -um	eundum

Infinitives

	ACTIVE	PASSIVE
Present	īre	none
Perfect	īvisse (īsse)	none
Future	itūrus, -a, -um esse	none

Imperatives

Singular	Plural
ī	īte

ferō, ferre, tulī, lātus

Indicative

	ACTIVE	PASSIVE
Present	ferō	feror
	fers	ferris, ferre
	fert	fertur
	ferimus	ferimur
	fertis	feriminī
	ferunt	feruntur
Imperfect	ferēbam	ferēbar
	ferēbās	ferēbāris, ferēbāre
	ferēbat	ferēbātur
	ferēbāmus	ferēbāmur
	ferēbātis	ferēbāminī
	ferēbant	ferēbantur
Future	feram	ferar
	ferēs	ferēris, ferēre
	feret	ferētur
	ferēmus	ferēmur
	ferētis	ferēminī
	ferent	ferentur
Perfect	tulī	lātus (-a, -um) sum
	tulistī	lātus (-a, -um) es
	tulit	lātus (-a, -um) est
	tulimus	lātī (-ae, -a) sumus
	tulistis	lātī (-ae, -a) estis
	tulērunt (-ēre)	lātī (-ae, -a) sunt
Pluperfect	tuleram	lātus (-a, -um) eram
	tulerās	lātus (-a, -um) erās
	tulerat	lātus (-a, -um) erat
	tulerāmus	lātī (-ae, -a) erāmus
	tulerātis	lātī (-ae, -a) erātis
	tulerant	lātī (-ae, -a) erant
Future-Perfect	tulerō	lātus (-a, -um) erō
	tuleris	lātus (-a, -um) eris
	tulerit	lātus (-a, -um) erit
	tulerimus	lātī (-ae, -a) erimus
	tuleritis	lātī (-ae, -a) eritis
	tulerint	lātī (-ae, -a) erunt

Subjunctive

	ACTIVE	PASSIVE
Present	feram	ferar
	ferās	ferāris, ferāre
	ferat	ferātur
	ferāmus	ferāmur
	ferātis	ferāminī
	ferant	ferantur
Imperfect	ferrem	ferrer
	ferrēs	ferrēris, ferrēre
	ferret	ferrētur
	ferrēmus	ferrēmur
	ferrētis	ferrēminī
	ferrent	ferrentur
Perfect	tulerim	lātus (-a, -um) sim
	tuleris	lātus (-a, -um) sīs
	tulerit	lātus (-a, -um) sit
	tulerimus	lātī (-ae, -a) sīmus
	tuleritis	lātī (-ae, -a) sītis
	tulerint	lātī (-ae, -a) sint
Pluperfect	tulissem	lātus (-a, -um) essem
	tulissēs	lātus (-a, -um) essēs
	tulisset	lātus (-a, -um) esset
	tulissēmus	lātī (-ae, -a) essēmus
	tulissētis	lātī (-ae, -a) essētis
	tulissent	lātī (-ae, -a) essent

Participles

	ACTIVE	PASSIVE
Present	ferēns (gen., ferentis)	none
Perfect	none	lātus, -a, -um
Future	lātūrus, -a, -um	ferendus, -a, -um

Infinitives

	ACTIVE	PASSIVE
Present	ferre	ferrī
Perfect	tulisse	lātus, -a, -um esse
Future	lātūrus, -a, -um esse	rare

Imperatives

ACTIVE		PASSIVE	
Singular	*Plural*	*Singular*	*Plural*
fer	ferte	ferre	feriminī

volō, velle, voluī, —

Indicative

Present	*Imperfect*	*Future*
volō	volēbam	volam
vīs	volēbās	volēs
vult	volēbat	volet
volumus	volēbāmus	volēmus
vultis	volēbātis	volētis
volunt	volēbant	volent
Perfect	*Pluperfect*	*Future-Perfect*
voluī	volueram	voluerō
voluistī	voluerās	volueris
voluit	voluerat	voluerit
voluimus	voluerāmus	voluerimus
voluistis	voluerātis	volueritis
voluērunt (-ēre)	voluerant	voluerint

Subjunctive

Present	*Imperfect*	*Perfect*	*Pluperfect*
velim	vellem	voluerim	voluissem
velīs	vellēs	volueris	voluissēs
velit	vellet	voluerit	voluisset
velīmus	vellēmus	voluerimus	voluissēmus
velītis	vellētis	volueritis	voluissētis
velint	vellent	voluerint	voluissent

Participles

Present
volēns (*gen.*, volentis)

Infinitives

Present	*Perfect*
velle	voluisse

fīō, fierī, —, factus sum

Indicative

Present	Imperfect	Future
fīō	fīēbam	fīam
fīs	fīēbās	fīēs
fit	fīēbat	fīet
fīmus	fīēbāmus	fīēmus
fītis	fīēbātis	fīētis
fīunt	fīēbant	fīent

Perfect	Pluperfect	Future-Perfect
factus (-a, -um) sum	factus (-a, -um) eram	factus (-a, -um) erō
factus (-a, -um) es	factus (-a, -um) erās	factus (-a, -um) eris
factus (-a, -um) est	factus (-a, -um) erat	factus (-a, -um) erit
factī (-ae, -a) sumus	factī (-ae, -a) erāmus	factī (-ae, -a) erimus
factī (-ae, -a) estis	factī (-ae, -a) erātis	factī (-ae, -a) eritis
factī (-ae, -a) sunt	factī (-ae, -a) erant	factī (-ae, -a) erunt

Subjunctive

Present	Imperfect	Perfect	Pluperfect
fīam	fierem	factus (-a, -um) sim	factus (-a, -um) essem
fīās	fierēs	factus (-a, -um) sīs	factus (-a, -um) essēs
fīat	fieret	factus (-a, -um) sit	factus (-a, -um) esset
fīāmus	fierēmus	factī (-ae, -a) sīmus	factī (-ae, -a) essēmus
fīātis	fierētis	factī (-ae, -a) sītis	factī (-ae, -a) essētis
fīant	fierent	factī (-ae, -a) sint	factī (-ae, -a) essent

Participles

Perfect	Future
factus, -a, -um	faciendus, -a, -um

Infinitives

Present	Perfect
fierī	factus, -a, -um esse

Imperatives

Singular	Plural
fī	fīte

Nouns

The Five Declensions

The ending of the genitive singular reveals the declension of a Latin noun.

1: -ae   2: -ī   3: -is   4: -ūs   5: -eī (-ēī)

1: ancilla, ancill*ae*, f. baptista, baptist*ae*, m.
2: agnus, agn*ī*, m. ager, agr*ī*, m. aurum, aur*ī*, n.
3: calix, calic*is*, m. cāritās, cāritāt*is*, f. tempus, tempor*is*, n. mōns, mont*is*, montium, m. ars, art*is*, artium, f. altāre, altār*is*, altārium, n.
4: adventus, advent*ūs*, m. manus, man*ūs*, f. genū, gen*ūs*, n.
5: fidēs, fid*eī*, f. diēs, di*ēī*, m. & f.

		First F. (M.)	Second M.	N.	Third M./F.	N.
SING	Nom.	-a	-us (—)	-um	—	—
	Gen.	-ae	-ī	-ī	-is	-is
	Dat.	-ae	-ō	-ō	-ī	-ī
	Acc.	-am	-um	-um	-em	—
	Abl.	-ā	-ō	-ō	-e	-e (-ī)
PLURAL	Nom.	-ae	-ī	-a	-ēs	-a (-ia)
	Gen.	-ārum	-ōrum	-ōrum	-um (-ium)	-um (-ium)
	Dat.	-īs	-īs	-īs	-ibus	-ibus
	Acc.	-ās	-ōs	-a	-ēs	-a (-ia)
	Abl.	-īs	-īs	-īs	-ibus	-ibus

		Fourth M. (F.)	N.	Fifth F. (M.)
SING	Nom.	-us	-ū	-ēs
	Gen.	-ūs	-ūs	-eī (-ēī)
	Dat.	-uī	-ū	-eī (-ēī)
	Acc.	-um	-ū	-em
	Abl.	-ū	-ū	-ē
PLURAL	Nom.	-ūs	-ua	-ēs
	Gen.	-uum	-uum	-ērum
	Dat.	-ibus	-ibus	-ēbus
	Acc.	-ūs	-ua	-ēs
	Abl.	-ibus	-ibus	-ēbus

First Declension

	Singular	Plural	Singular	Plural
Nom.	ancilla	ancillae	baptista	baptistae
Gen.	ancillae	ancillārum	baptistae	baptistārum
Dat.	ancillae	ancillīs	bapistae	baptistīs
Acc.	ancillam	ancillās	baptistam	baptistās
Abl.	ancillā	ancillīs	baptistā	baptistīs

Second Declension

	Singular M.	M.	N.	Plural M.	M.	N.
Nom.	agnus	ager	aurum	agnī	agrī	aura
Gen.	agnī	agrī	aurī	agnōrum	agrōrum	aurōrum
Dat.	agnō	agrō	aurō	agnīs	agrīs	aurīs
Acc.	agnum	agrum	aurum	agnōs	agrōs	aura
Abl.	agnō	agrō	aurō	agnīs	agrīs	aurīs

Third Declension

	Singular M.	F.	N.	Plural M.	F.	N.
Nom.	calix	cāritās	tempus	calicēs	cāritātēs	tempora
Gen.	calicis	cāritātis	temporis	calicum	cāritātum	temporum
Dat.	calicī	cāritātī	temporī	calicibus	cāritātibus	temporibus
Acc.	calicem	cāritātem	tempus	calicēs	cāritātēs	tempora
Abl.	calice	cāritāte	tempore	calicibus	cāritātibus	temporibus

Third Declension: i-Stems

	Singular M.	F.	N.	Plural M.	F.	N.
Nom.	mōns	ars	altāre	montēs	artēs	altāria
Gen.	montis	artis	altāris	montium	artium	altārium
Dat.	montī	artī	altārī	montibus	artibus	altāribus
Acc.	montem	artem	altāre	montēs	artēs	altāria
Abl.	monte	arte	altārī	montibus	artibus	altāribus

Fourth Declension

	Singular			Plural		
	M.	F.	N.	M.	F.	N.
Nom.	adventus	manus	genū	adventūs	manūs	genua
Gen.	adventūs	manūs	genūs	adventuum	manuum	genuum
Dat.	adventuī	manuī	genū	adventibus	manibus	genibus
Acc.	adventum	manum	genū	adventūs	manūs	genua
Abl.	adventū	manū	genū	adventibus	manibus	genibus

Fifth Declension

	Singular		Plural	
	F.	M. & F.	F.	M. & F.
Nom.	fidēs	diēs	fidēs	diēs
Gen.	fideī	diēī	fidērum	diērum
Dat.	fideī	diēī	fidēbus	diēbus
Acc.	fidem	diem	fidēs	diēs
Abl.	fidē	diē	fidēbus	diēbus

Adjectives

First/Second Declension Adjectives

	Singular			Plural		
	M.	F.	N.	M.	F.	N.
Nom.	bonus	bona	bonum	bonī	bonae	bona
Gen.	bonī	bonae	bonī	bonōrum	bonārum	bonōrun
Dat.	bonō	bonae	bonō	bonīs	bonīs	bonīs
Acc.	bonum	bonam	bonum	bonōs	bonās	bona
Abl.	bonō	bonā	bonō	bonīs	bonīs	bonīs

	Singular			Plural		
	M.	F.	N.	M.	F.	N.
Nom.	miser	misera	miserum	miserī	miserae	misera
Gen.	miserī	miserae	miserī	miserōrum	miserārum	miserōrum
Dat.	miserō	miserae	miserō	miserīs	miserīs	miserīs
Acc.	miserum	miseram	miserum	miserōs	miserās	misera
Abl.	miserō	miserā	miserō	miserīs	miserīs	miserīs

Third Declension Adjectives

THREE ENDINGS

	Singular			Plural		
	M.	F.	N.	M.	F.	N.
Nom.	ācer	ācris	ācre	ācrēs	ācrēs	ācria
Gen.	ācris	ācris	ācris	ācrium	ācrium	ācrium
Dat.	ācrī	ācrī	ācrī	ācribus	ācribus	ācribus
Acc.	ācrem	ācrem	ācre	ācrēs	ācrēs	ācria
Abl.	ācrī	ācrī	ācrī	ācribus	ācribus	ācribus

TWO ENDINGS

	Singular		Plural	
	M. & F.	N.	M. & F.	N.
Nom.	omnis	omne	omnēs	omnia
Gen.	omnis	omnis	omnium	omnium
Dat.	omnī	omnī	omnibus	omnibus
Acc.	omnem	omne	omnēs	omnia
Abl.	omnī	omnī	omnibus	omnibus

ONE ENDING

	Singular		Plural	
	M. & F.	N.	M. & F.	N.
Nom.	fēlīx		fēlīcēs	fēlīcia
Gen.	fēlīcis		fēlīcium	
Dat.	fēlīcī		fēlīcibus	
Acc.	fēlīcem	fēlīx	fēlīcēs	fēlīcia
Abl.	fēlīcī		fēlīcibus	

Pronouns

Emphatic Demonstrative Pronouns/Adjectives

	Singular			Plural		
	M.	F.	N.	M.	F.	N.
Nom.	hic	haec	hoc	hī	hae	haec
Gen.	hujus	hujus	hujus	hōrum	hārum	hōrum
Dat.	huic	huic	huic	hīs	hīs	hīs
Acc.	hunc	hanc	hoc	hōs	hās	haec
Abl.	hōc	hāc	hōc	hīs	hīs	hīs

Emphatic Demonstrative Pronouns/Adjectives

	Singular			Plural		
	M.	F.	N.	M.	F.	N.
Nom.	ille	illa	illud	illī	illae	illa
Gen.	illīus	illīus	illīus	illōrum	illārum	illōrum
Dat.	illī	illī	illī	illīs	illīs	illīs
Acc.	illum	illam	illud	illōs	illās	illa
Abl.	illō	illā	illō	illīs	illīs	illīs

Unemphatic Demonstrative Pronouns/Adjectives

	Singular			Plural		
	M.	F.	N.	M.	F.	N.
Nom.	is	ea	id	eī, iī	eae	ea
Gen.	ejus	ejus	ejus	eōrum	eārum	eōrum
Dat.	eī	eī	eī	eīs, iīs	eīs, iīs	eīs, iīs
Acc.	eum	eam	id	eōs	eās	ea
Abl.	eō	eā	eō	eīs, iīs	eīs, iīs	eīs, iīs

	Singular			Plural		
	M.	F.	N.	M.	F.	N.
Nom.	iste	ista	istud	istī	istae	ista
Gen.	istīus	istīus	istīus	istōrum	istārum	istōrum
Dat.	istī	istī	istī	istīs	istīs	istīs
Acc.	istum	istam	istud	istōs	istās	ista
Abl.	istō	istā	istō	istīs	istīs	istīs

Intensive Pronoun/Adjective

	Singular			Plural		
	M.	F.	N.	M.	F.	N.
Nom.	ipse	ipsa	ipsum	ipsī	ipsae	ipsa
Gen.	ipsīus	ipsīus	ipsīus	ipsōrum	ipsārum	ipsōrum
Dat.	ipsī	ipsī	ipsī	ipsīs	ipsīs	ipsīs
Acc.	ipsum	ipsam	ipsum	ipsōs	ipsās	ipsa
Abl.	ipsō	ipsā	ipsō	ipsīs	ipsīs	ipsīs

Relative Pronoun/Interrogative Adjective

	Singular			Plural		
	M.	F.	N.	M.	F.	N.
Nom.	quī	quae	quod	quī	quae	quae
Gen.	cujus	cujus	cujus	quōrum	quārum	quōrum
Dat.	cui	cui	cui	quibus	quibus	quibus
Acc.	quem	quam	quod	quōs	quās	quae
Abl.	quō .	quā	quō	quibus	quibus	quibus

Interrogative Pronoun

	Singular			Plural		
	M. & F.	N.		M.	F.	N.
Nom.	quis	quid		quī	quae	quae
Gen.	cujus	cujus		quōrum	quārum	quōrum
Dat.	cui	˙cui		quibus	quibus	quibus
Acc.	quem	quid		quōs	quās	quae
Abl.	quō	quō		quibus	quibus	quibus

Verb Synopsis Form

(See Section 70)

1 2 3 person   singular plural of: _____

_____

	ACTIVE	PASSIVE
INDICATIVE		
Present	_____	_____
Imperfect	_____	_____
Future	_____	_____
Perfect	_____	_____
Pluperfect	_____	_____
Future-Perfect	_____	_____
SUBJUNCTIVE		
Present	_____	_____
Imperfect	_____	_____
Perfect	_____	_____
Pluperfect	_____	_____
PARTICIPLES		
Present	_____	NONE
Future	_____	_____
Perfect	NONE	_____
INFINITIVES		
Present	_____	_____
Future	_____	RARE
Perfect	_____	_____
IMPERATIVES		
Present	_____	_____

Latin-English Vocabulary

A number in parentheses after an entry indicates the unit in which the word or phrase was first presented. Words glossed in exercises only (E), except for names, are here given in full. Compound verbs, where the simple verb has been formally presented, are listed under the simple verb: e.g., reficiō will be found under faciō.

ā (ab, abs) (*prep.* + *abl.*) from, away from (1); by (the agency of) (7)

accendō, accendere, accendī, accēnsus kindle, set on fire (24)

acceptābilis, acceptābile acceptable (17)

accommodō, accommodāre, accommodāvī, accommodātus apply, fit; grant (35)

accūsō, accūsāre, accūsāvī, accusātus accuse (E30)

ācer, ācris, ācre sharp, bitter, ardent (16)

acquīsītiō, acquīsītiōnis, f. purchase, acquisition (26)

ad (*prep.* + *acc.*) to, toward; for (the purpose of); at (1)

Adam, Adae, m. Adam (11)

adhūc (*adv.*) so far, till now, still (6)

adjuvō, adjuvāre, adjūvī, adjūtus help (27)

adventus, adventūs, m. coming, advent (17)

adversus (adversum) (*prep.* + *acc.*) against (32)

Aegyptius, -a, -um Egyptian (6)

aes, aeris, n. bronze: gong (E33)

aestimō, aestimāre, aestimāvī, aestimātus think, judge (E33)

aetās, aetātis, f. time of life, age (E29)

aeternus, -a, -um eternal (4)
in aeternum forever (4)

affectus, affectūs, m. devotion, affection; sense (21)

ager, agrī, m. field; *pl.*, country (2)

agnus, agnī, m. lamb (2)

agō, agere, ēgī, āctus do, drive, conduct (6)
grātiās agere = give thanks (to), thank (+ *dat.*) (6)

ait; aiunt (*defective verb*) he says; they say (27)

albus, -a, -um white (E31)

aliquī, aliqua, aliquod (*indef. pronominal adj.*) some, any (29)

aliquis, aliquid (*indef. pron.*) someone, something; anyone, anything (29)

alius, alia, aliud other, another (28)

allēlūjā (*Hebrew: interj.*) alleluia (*cry of joy and praise*) (10)

alō, alere, aluī, altus nourish (19)

altāre, altāris, altārium, n.
altar (18)

alter, altera, alterum the other
(of two), the second (28)

altus, -a, -um high, deep (9)

ambō, ambōnis, m. lectern,
ambo (15)

**ambulō, ambulāre, ambulāvī,
ambulātus** walk, take a walk;
'live' (5)

āmēn (*Hebrew*: 1. *indecl. adj.*;
2. *adv.*) 1. amen, true! (*word of
affirmation*) 2. truly (12)

amīcus, amīcī, m. friend (30)
inimīcus, inimīcī, m. enemy
(30)

amō, amāre, amāvī, amātus
love (23)

amor, amōris, m. love (E28)

**amplector, amplectī, —, amplexus
sum** embrace (21)

amplus, -a, -um abundant,
ample (28)
amplius (*comp. adv.*) (any) more
(28)

an (1. *coord. or subord. conj.,
introducing the second of two
[in]direct questions*; 2. *interrog.
adv.*) 1. or 2. can it be that? (26)

ancilla, ancillae, f. maid, (female)
servant (2)

angelicus, -a, -um angelic (8)

angelus, angelī, m. messenger,
angel (2)
archangelus, archangelī, m.
archangel (2)

angulus, angulī, m. angle, corner
(E23)

anima, animae, f. (*dat./abl. pl.,*
animābus) soul, life (7)

animus, animī, m. heart, mind,
spirit (4)

annus, annī, m. year (10)

ante (*prep. + acc.*) before (10)

antequam (*subord. conj.*) before
(12)

antīquus, -a, -um old, ancient;
subst. pl., ancients, forefathers (4)

antistes, antistitis, m. bishop (22)

aperiō, aperīre, aperuī, apertus
open; explain (11)

apis, apis, apium, f. bee (32)

apostolicus, -a, -um apostolic (9)

apostolus, apostolī, m. apostle (2)

**appāreō, appārēre, appāruī, appāri-
tus** show forth, appear (19)

**appropinquō, appropinquāre, ap-
propinquāvī, appropinquātus**
draw near, approach (+ *dat.*)
(31)

aptus, -a, -um (+ *dat.*) fitting,
suitable, apt (15)

apud (*prep. + acc.*) in the presence
of, among, at the house of (11)

aqua, aquae, f. water (1)

arbor, arboris, f. tree (20)

ardeō, ardēre, arsī, arsus burn (28)

ars, artis, artium, f. (practical)
knowledge, art (18)

ascēnsiō, ascēnsiōnis, f. going up,
ascension (18)

assiduus, -a, -um constant,
unceasing (21)

at (*coord. conj.*) but, furthermore
(31)

atque (**ac**) (*coord. conj.*) and (also),
and (even) (12)

audeō, audēre; —, ausus sum dare,
have the courage (20)

**audiō, audīre, audīvī (audiī),
audītus** hear (6)
**exaudiō, exaudīre, exaudīvī
(exaudiī), exaudītus** hear
(favorably) (6)

aula, aulae, f. hall, church (11)

auris, auris, aurium, f. (*abl. sing.,*
aure *or* **aurī**) ear (19)

aurum, aurī, n. gold (4)

aut (*coord. conj.*) or (6)
aut . . aut either . . or (6)

autem (*postpos. coord. conj.*) but, and (9)

avē! (*imperative;* pl., **avēte**) hail! farewell! hello! goodbye! greetings! (25)

baptisma, baptismatis, n. baptism (14)

baptismus, baptismī, m. baptism (35)

baptista, baptistae, m. baptizer, baptist (13)

baptizō, baptizāre, baptizāvī, baptizātus immerse, baptize (18)

beātus, -a, -um blessed, happy (4)

bene (*adv.*) well (7)

benedictiō, benedictiōnis, f. blessing, benediction (20)

benedictus, -a, -um blessed, blest (5)

benīgnus, -a, -um kindly (18)

bibō, bibere, bibī, bibitus drink (6)

blasphēmia, blasphēmiae, f. blasphemy (E31)

blasphēmō, blasphēmāre, blasphēmāvī, blasphēmātus blaspheme (E28)

bonus, -a, -um good (4)

brāchium, brāchiī, n. arm (13)

cadō, cadere, cecidī, cāsus fall (down) (19)

    incidō, incidere, incidī, — fall into; happen (19)

    occidō, occidere, occidī, occāsus go down, set [of the sun] *pres. part.*: 'west' (34)

    prōcidō, prōcidere, prōcidī, — fall forward (34)

caelestis, caeleste heavenly, divine (24)

caelicola, caelicolae, m. heaven-dweller (21)

caelum, caelī, n. (*nom. pl.,* **caelī**) heaven, sky (3)

cālīgō, cālīginis, f. mist, gloom (15)

calix, calicis, m. cup, chalice (16)

canō, canere, cecinī, cantus sing; prophesy (24)

    concinō, concinere, concinuī, concentus sing (24)

canticum, canticī, n. song, canticle (3)

cantō, cantāre, cantāvī, cantātus sing, chant (5)

cantor, cantōris, m. singer, cantor (15)

cantus, cantūs, m. chant (22)

capiō, capere, cēpī, captus take, receive; understand (6)

    accipiō, accipere, accēpī, acceptus take, get, receive (6)

    concipiō, concipere, concēpī, conceptus conceive (12)

    excipiō, excipere, excēpī, exceptus welcome (12)

    incipiō, incipere, incēpī, inceptus begin (+ *inf.*) (12)

    praecipiō, praecipere, praecēpī, praeceptus command; instruct, teach (24)

    recipiō, recipere, recēpī, receptus take back, receive (6)

    suscipiō, suscipere, suscēpī, susceptus take up, pick up; accept (14)

caput, capitis, n. head (19)

cāritās, cāritātis, f. love, charity (16)

carō, carnis, f. flesh (19)

cārus, -a, -um (+ *dat.*) dear, beloved (7)

castus, -a, -um chaste (33)

catholicus, -a, -um universal, catholic (9)

causa, causae, f. purpose, reason (9)

    causā (*improper prep.* + *gen.*) for the sake of (9)

cautiō, cautiōnis, f. bill, bail (29)

cēdō, cēdere, cessī, cessus go; yield (18)

accēdō, accēdere, accessī,
accessus go to, approach (18)
concēdō, concēdere, concessī,
concessus yield; grant (18)
discēdō, discēdere, discessī,
discessus depart (18)
incēdō, incēdere, incessī,
incessus go, walk (18)
praecēdō, praecēdere, praecessī,
praecessus go before, lead the
way (18)
prōcēdō, prōcēdere, prōcessī,
prōcessus go forth, proceed
(18)
recēdō, recēdere, recessī,
recessus go back, depart (18)
celebrō, celebrāre, celebrāvī,
celebrātus celebrate (7)
concelebrō, concelebrāre,
concelebrāvī, concelebrātus
celebrate together (7)
cēna, cēnae, f. supper, dinner (1)
cēnāculum, cēnāculī, n. dining
room, upper room, upstairs
room (4)
cēnō, cēnāre, cēnāvī, cēnātus
dine, eat supper (13)
centuriō, centuriōnis, m. centurion (E27)
cēra, cērae, f. wax (32)
cēreus, cēreī, m. candle (9)
cernō, cernere, crēvī, crētus see,
discern (35)
certāmen, certāminis, n. contest,
foot-race (E28)
certē (adv.) surely, certainly; at
least (9)
certus, -a, -um fixed, sure, certain
(12)
chorus, chorī, m. choir (3)
Chrīstiānus, -a, -um Christian (6)
Chrīstus, Chrīstī, m. Anointed
One, Messiah, Christ (2)
cibus, cibī, m. food (11)
circā (prep. + acc.) around, about
(25)

circum (prep. + acc.) around,
about (18)
cito (adv.) quickly (E34)
cīvitās, cīvitātis, f. city (22)
clam (adv.) secretly, privately
(E35)
clāmō, clāmāre, clāmāvī, clāmātus cry out, shout; call upon
(12)
  acclāmō, acclāmāre, acclāmāvī,
  acclāmātus cry out, exclaim
  (12)
  exclāmō, exclāmāre, exclāmāvī,
  exclāmātus cry aloud, exclaim (12)
clāritās, clāritātis, f. light, brightness; glory, fame (22)
clārus, -a, -um clear, bright;
glorious, famous (4)
claudō, claudere, clausī, clausus
shut, close (18)
  conclūdō, conclūdere, conclūsī,
  conclūsus shut up; conclude
  (18)
clāvis, clāvis, clāvium, f. key
(E30)
clēmēns (gen., clēmentis) merciful (17)
clēmentia, clēmentiae, f. mercy,
clemency (18)
clērus, clērī, m. clergy (10)
-clīnō, -clīnāre, -clīnāvī, -clīnātus
bend (11)
  inclīnō, inclīnāre, inclīnāvī,
  inclīnātus bow, lean forward
  (11)
  reclīnō, reclīnāre, reclīnāvī,
  reclīnātus lean back, recline
  (11)
coadūnō, coadūnāre, coadūnāvī,
coadūnātus unite (32)
—, —, coepī, coeptus began,
started (35)
cōgitātiō, cōgitātiōnis, f. thought
(23)

cōgitō, cōgitāre, cōgitāvī, cōgitātus think; plan (30)

cōgō, cōgere, coēgī, coāctus lead, bring, assemble; force, compel (33)

collēcta, collēctae, f. collect; collection (12)

columna, columnae, f. pillar, column (11)

commemorātiō, commemorātiōnis, f. remembrance, commemoration (23)

commendō, commendāre, commendāvī, commendātus entrust (30)

commixtiō, commixtiōnis, f. mingling (24)

commūnicātiō, commūnicātiōnis, f. partaking, fellowship (33)

commūnicō, commūnicāre, commūnicāvī, commūnicātus share (E24)

commūniō, commūniōnis, f. communion (34)

commūnis, commūne common; unclean (22)

conclūsiō, conclūsiōnis, f. conclusion (29)

concordia, concordiae, f. union, peace (34)

cōnfestim (adv.) immediately, at once (24)

cōnfīdō, cōnfīdere; —, cōnfīsus sum (+ dat.) trust (in); confide (in), hope (in) (20)

cōnfortō, cōnfortāre, —, — strengthen; pass., grow strong (35)

conjūnx, conjugis, m. or f. spouse, husband, wife (E30)

cōnor, cōnārī, —, cōnātus sum (+ inf.) try, strive (21)

cōnsors, cōnsortis, cōnsortium, m. or f. sharer (24)

cōnspectus, cōnspectūs, m. sight, presence (21)

cōnsubstantiālis, cōnsubstantiāle (+ dat.) of the same nature (as), consubstantial (with) (20)

cōnsuētūdō, cōnsuētūdinis, f. custom (26)

contrā (prep. + acc.) against, opposite (to) (28)

contrītus, -a, -um contrite (8)

cor, cordis, cordium, n. (abl. sing., corde) heart (15)

cōram (prep. + abl.) in the presence of (1)

cornū, cornūs, n. horn; mountaintop (16)

corōna, corōnae, f. wreath, crown (21)

corōnō, corōnāre, corōnāvī, corōnātus crown (29)

corpus, corporis, n. body, corpse (14)

cōtīdiānus, -a, -um daily (18)

cōtīdiē (adv.) daily (18)

crās (adv.) tomorrow (E26)

creātor, creātōris, m. maker, creator (24)

creātūra, creātūrae, f. creation, creature (11)

crēdō, crēdere, crēdidī, crēditus believe (in), trust (in) (6)

creō, creāre, creāvī, creātus create (13)

crēsco, crēscere, crēvī, crētus grow, increase (29)

crīmen, crīminis, n. guilt, sin (24)

cruor, cruōris, m. blood (from a wound) (15)

crux, crucis, f. cross (16)

culpa, culpae, f. blame, fault (1)

cum (prep. + abl.) with (1)

cum (subord. conj.) when, after (+ ind.) (13); (under the circumstances) when, since, although (+ subj.) (28)

cūnctus, -a, -um all (8)

cupiō, cupere, cupīvī (cupiī), cupītus desire, want (E35)

cūra, cūrae, f. care, concern (22)

cūria, cūriae, f. court, curia (29)

cūrō, cūrāre, cūrāvī, cūrātus heal, cure; care for (19)

currō, currere, cucurrī, cursus run, hasten (25)

   occurrō, occurrere, occurrī, occursus run up to, meet up with (+ *dat.*) (25)

   succurrō, succurrere, succurrī, succursus run to the aid of, aid, succor (+ *dat.*) (25)

curvō, curvāre, curvāvī, curvātus bend; humble (28)

custōdiō, custōdīre, custōdīvī (custōdiī), custōdītus guard, watch over (18)

daemonium, daemoniī, n. evil spirit, demon (31)

dāmnum, dāmnī, n. damage, loss, punishment (33)

dē (*prep.* + *abl.*) from, down from; about, concerning (1)

dēbeō, dēbēre, dēbuī, dēbitus owe; ought (+ *inf.*) (12)

dēbitor, dēbitōris, m. debtor (26)

dēbitum, dēbitī, n. debt (10)

dēfendō, dēfendere, dēfendī, dēfēnsus defend (25)

dēfūnctus, -a, -um deceased, dead (33)

deinde (*adv.*) then, next, thereupon (19)

dēleō, dēlēre, dēlēvī, dēlētus destroy, wipe out (6)

dēlicia, dēliciae, f. pleasure, delight (23)

dēprecātiō, dēprecātiōnis, f. earnest prayer, supplication (14)

dēsertus, -a, -um forsaken, deserted (13)

   dēsertum, dēsertī, n. desert (13)

dēsīderium, dēsīderiī, n. want, need, desire (10)

dēsīderō, dēsīderāre, dēsīderāvī, dēsīderātus desire (19)

dēsinō, dēsinere, dēsiī, dēsitus (+ *inf.*) cease (12)

dētergeō, dētergēre, dētersī, dētersus wipe away, cancel (14)

dētrīmentum, dētrīmentī, n. loss (10)

Deus, Deī, m. (*nom. pl.*, diī) God (2)

dēvōtus, -a, -um devout, devoted (18)

dexter, dextera, dexterum right (24)

dextera, dexterae, f. right hand (13)

diabolus, diabolī, m. devil (25)

diāconus, diāconī, m. deacon (7)

dīcō, dīcere, dīxī, dictus say, tell; *pass., also*, be called (7)

   addīcō, addīcere, addīxī, addictus adjudge, condemn (25)

   benedīcō, benedīcere, benedīxī, benedictus speak well (of), bless (7)

   contrādīcō, contrādīcere, contrādīxī, contrādictus dispute, contradict (+ *dat.*) (25)

   maledīcō, maledīcere, maledīxī, maledictus speak evil (of), curse (7)

   praedīcō, praedīcere, praedīxī, praedictus say earlier, foretell, predict (25)

diēs, diēī, m. & f. day (19)

digitus, digitī, m. finger, toe (13)

dīgnātiō, dīgnātiōnis, f. condescension, graciousness (35)

dīgnor, dīgnārī, —, dīgnātus sum consider worthwhile, deign (22)

   dēdīgnor, dēdīgnārī, —, dēdīgnātus sum scorn, disdain (22)

dīgnus, -a, -um (+ *abl.*) worthy (of) (7)

   indīgnus, -a, -um (+ *abl.*) unworthy (of) (7)

dīlēctiō, dīlēctiōnis, f. love (17)

dīlēctus, -a, -um beloved (19)
dīligenter (*adv.*) diligently (9)
discipulus, discipulī, m. disciple, student (2)
discō, discere, didicī, — learn (35)
discumbō, discumbere, discubuī, discubitus sit (down to eat) (E19)
dispēnsātor, dispēnsātōris, m. steward (E31)
dītō, dītāre, dītāvī, — enrich (33)
dīves (*gen.*, dīvitis) rich, wealthy (25)
dīvidō, dīvidere, dīvīsī, dīvīsus part, divide (30)
dīvīnitās, dīvīnitātis, f. divinity (30)
dīvīnus, -a, -um divine (5)
diū (*adv.*) for a long time (E34)
dō, dare, dedī, datus give (5)
___ addō, addere, addidī, additus give to, add (13)
perdō, perdere, perdidī, perditus lose; destroy (13)
reddō, reddere, reddidī, redditus give back, render (6)
trādō, trādere, trādidī, trāditus give over, hand over, betray (6)
-dō, -dere, -didī, -ditus put (13)
condō, condere, condidī, conditus found; hide (13)
subdō, subdere, subdidī, subditus put under, put after, subject (13)
doceō, docēre, docuī, doctus teach (19)
doctrīna, doctrīnae, f. teaching, doctrine (1)
doctor, doctōris, m. teacher (26)
documentum, documentī, n. example (5)
dogma, dogmatis, n. decision, dogma (26)
doleō, dolēre, doluī, dolitus grieve, suffer, feel pain (28)

condoleō, condolēre, —, — feel severe pain, suffer greatly; feel another's pain, empathize with (28)
dolor, dolōris, m. sorrow, pain (25)
dolōrōsus, -a, -um sorrowful (11)
domina, dominae, f. mistress, lady (30)
dominus, dominī, m. lord, master (2)
domus, domī, f. home, house (6)
domus, domūs, f. home, house (35)
dōnec (*subord. conj.*) while, as long as; till, until (13, 26)
dōnō, dōnāre, dōnāvī, dōnātus give, grant; forgive (5)
dōnum, dōnī, n. gift (3)
dūcō, dūcere, dūxī, ductus lead (6)
ēdūcō, ēdūcere, ēdūxī, ēductus lead out (6)
indūcō, indūcere, indūxī, inductus lead into, bring into (6)
perdūcō, perdūcere, perdūxī, perductus lead through, bring to (6)
sēdūcō, sēdūcere, sēdūxī, sēductus deceive (6)
dulcis, dulce sweet; kind (19)
dum (*subord. conj.*) while, as long as; till, until (13, 26)
ē (ex) (*prep.* + *abl.*) from, out of (1)
ecce (*interj.*) look! here! (10)
ecclēsia, ecclēsiae, f. church; assembly (1)
effūsiō, effūsiōnis, f. outpouring (25)
ego, meī (*pron.*) I (19)
ēlēctus, -a, -um chosen, elect (6)
eléīson (*Greek: imperative*) have mercy! (10)
ēlevātiō, ēlevātiōnis, f. a lifting up, raising (E29)
emō, emere, ēmī, ēmptus buy (27)

redimō, redimere, redēmī, redēmptus buy back, redeem
(27)

enim (postpos. coord. conj.) for;
indeed (5)

ēnītor, ēnītī, —, ēnīsus (ēnīxus)
sum bring forth, give birth to
(34)

eō, īre, īvī (iī), itus go (17)

abeō, abīre, abīvī (abiī), abitus
go away, leave (17)

adeō, adīre, adīvī (adiī), aditus
go to, approach (17)

circumeō, circumīre, circumīvī
(circumiī), circumitus go
about (17)

exeō, exīre, exīvī (exiī), exitus
go out, leave (17)

ineō, inīre, inīvī (iniī), initus
go in, enter (upon) (17)

intereō, interīre, interīvī (in-
teriī), interitus perish, die (17)

introeō, introīre, introīvī (introiī), introitus go within,
enter (17)

obeō, obīre, obīvī (obiī), obitus
go to meet; die (17)

pereō, perīre, perīvī (periī), peritus perish, die, be lost (17)

pertrānseō, pertrānsīre, per-
trānsīvī (pertrānsiī), pertrān-
situs go all about, go away;
pierce (17)

praeeō, praeīre, praeīvī (praeiī),
praeitus go before (17)

prōdeō, prōdīre, prōdīvī (prōdiī),
prōditus go forth (17)

redeō, redīre, redīvī (rediī),
reditus go back, return (17)

subeō, subīre, subīvī (subiī),
subitus go under, submit to;
climb (17)

trānseō, trānsīre, trānsīvī
(trānsiī), trānsitus go across,
pass through; pass away (17)

episcopālis, episcopāle of a
bishop, episcopal (17)

episcopus, episcopī, m. overseer,
bishop (2)

ergō (coord. conj.) therefore (14)

errō, errāre, errāvī, errātus wander, go astray; err (34)

ēsuriō, ēsurīre, ēsurīvī (ēsuriī),
ēsuritus desire food, be hungry
(35)

et (1. coord. conj.; 2. intens. adv.)
1. and 2. even, too

et . . et both . . and (1)

etiam (intensifying adv.) also;
even . . (8)

etsī (subord. conj.) although, even
if (13)

eucharisticus, -a, -um eucharistic
(32)

Ēva, Ēvae, f. Eve (12)

Evangelium, Evangeliī, n. Good
News, Gospel (3)

evangelizō, evangelizāre, evangelizāvī, evangelizātus preach
the Gospel (18)

excelsus, -a, -um high, lofty,
exalted (10)

exemplum, exemplī, n. example
(5)

exinde (adv.) from then on (E35)

exīstimō, exīstimāre, exīstimāvī,
exīstimātus think, judge (30)

exspectō, exspectāre, exspectāvī,
exspectātus look for, wait for
(21)

exspoliō, exspoliāre, exspoliāvī,
exspoliātus despoil, rob (35)

exsultō, exsultāre, exsultāvī,
exsultātus rejoice, exult (11)

extrā (prep. + acc.) beyond, outside (25)

faciēs, faciēī, f. face [i.e., appear-
ance] (27)

facilis, facile easy (30)

difficilis, difficile difficult (30)

faciō, facere, fēcī, factus do,
make (6)

afficiō, afficere, affēcī, affectus
affect (6)

dēficiō, dēficere, dēfēcī, dēfectus
fail, waste, vanish (6)

efficiō, efficere, effēcī, effectus
make, effect; *pass.*, become (6)

īnficiō, īnficere, īnfēcī, īnfectus
infect, pollute (28)

**interficiō, interficere, interfēcī,
interfectus** do away with,
kill (18)

**perficiō, perficere, perfēcī, per-
fectus** do completely, finish,
accomplish (18)

**prōficiō, prōficere, prōfēcī, prō-
fectus** avail; prevail (28)

reficiō, reficere, refēcī, refectus
refresh; repair (28)

**sufficiō, sufficere, suffēcī, suffec-
tus** be enough, be sufficient
(18)

factor, factōris, m. maker, doer
(23)

factum est (*Hebraic idiom*) it happened (that), it came to pass
(that) (34)

fallō, fallere, fefellī, falsus deceive
(33)

falsus, -a, -um false (33)

fāma, fāmae, f. report, news (E28)

familia, familiae, f. household,
family (1)

famēs, famis, famium, f. hunger,
famine (E33)

famulus, famulī, m. servant (5)

fateor, fatērī, —, fassus sum
acknowledge, confess (+ *acc.*);
praise (+ *dat.*) (22)

**cōnfiteor, cōnfitērī, —, cōn-
fessus sum** confess (+ *acc.*);
praise (+ *dat.*) (22)

**profiteor, profitērī, —, professus
sum** profess (22)

fēlīx (*gen.*, **fēlīcis**) happy, blessed
(16)

ferō, ferre, tulī, lātus bring, bear,
carry (33)

auferō, auferre, abstulī, ablātus
take away (33)

**cōnferō, cōnferre, contulī, col-
lātus** accompany; grant;
cōnferre sē: take oneself (to),
go (33)

dēferō, dēferre, dētulī, dēlātus
offer, bring (33)

efferō, efferre, extulī, ēlātus
bring out; bear; lift up (33)

īnferō, īnferre, intulī, illātus
bring in (33)

offerō, offerre, obtulī, oblātus
offer (33)

**perferō, perferre, pertulī, per-
lātus** carry through, carry
up (33)

**prōferō, prōferre, prōtulī, prō-
lātus** bring forth, bring forward (33)

referō, referre, rettulī, relātus
bring back; yield, render;
report (33)

fēstum, fēstī, n. feast, feast-day (3)

fēstus, -a, -um festal (18)

fidēlis, fidēle faithful, believing
(19)

fidēs, fideī, f. faith, faithfulness
(19)

fīgō, fīgere, fīxī, fīxus pierce, fix,
fasten (16)

**crucifīgō, crucifīgere, crucifīxī,
crucifīxus** fix to a cross, crucify (16)

figūra, figūrae, f. fashion, figure
(29)

fīlia, fīliae, f. daughter (25)

fīlius, fīliī, m. son (2)

fīniō, fīnīre, fīnīvī (fīniī), fīnītus
end, finish (10)

fīnis, fīnis, fīnium, m. & f. end,

boundary; *pl.*, territory, district
(15)

fīō; fierī, —, factus sum be made,
be done; become, happen, be
(34)

firmō, firmāre, firmāvī, firmātus
strengthen, make steady (7)

**affirmō, affirmāre, affirmāvī,
affirmātus** prove, assert (7)

**cōnfirmō, cōnfirmāre, cōn-
firmāvī, cōnfirmātus**
strengthen, uphold (7)

firmus, -a, -um steadfast, firm (7)

īnfirmitās, īnfirmitātis, f. sick-
ness, infirmity (E34)

īnfirmus, -a, -um weak, sick (7)

flagellum, flagellī, n. scourge (33)

flamma, flammae, f. flame (11)

flectō, flectere, flexī, flexus bend,
bow (16)

**genūflectō, genūflectere, genū-
flexī, genūflexus** bend the
knee, genuflect, kneel (down)
(16)

fleō, flēre, flēvī, flētus weep, lament (25)

flētus, flētūs, m. weeping (21)

flōs, flōris, m. flower (32)

fōns, fontis, fontium, m. source,
fountain (32)

fore = **futūrus, -a, -um esse** (*fut.
inf.*) about to be (32)

forīs (*adv.*) outside, outdoors (E34)

fōrmō, fōrmāre, fōrmāvī, fōrmātus
train, guide; fashion, form (9)

fōrmōsus, -a, -um beautiful, handsome (E20, 31)

forsitan (*adv.*) perhaps (*used in
apodosis with subj.*) (E24, 25)

fortis, forte strong (26)

frangō, frangere, frēgī, frāctus
break (16)

**cōnfringō, cōnfringere, cōnfrēgī,
cōnfrāctus** break in two,
break in pieces (16)

frāter, frātris, m. brother (19)

frūctus, frūctūs, m. fruit (17)

fugiō, fugere, fūgī, fugitus flee
(from) (25)

fugō, fugāre, fugāvī, fugātus put to
flight, chase away (6)

fulgeō, fulgēre, fulsī, — shine,
glow (27)

**circumfulgeō, circumfulgēre,
circumfulsī, —** shine around
(27)

refulgeō, refulgēre, refulsī, —
shine brightly, gleam (27)

fulgor, fulgōris, m. brightness (33)

fundō, fundāre, fundāvī, fundātus
establish, found (28)

fundō, fundere, fūdī, fūsus pour
(16)

**cōnfundō, cōnfundere, cōnfūdī,
cōnfūsus** confound, confuse;
put to shame (16)

**effundō, effundere, effūdī,
effūsus** pour out, shed, spill
(16)

**īnfundō, īnfundere, īnfūdī,
īnfūsus** pour, infuse (16)

**refundō, refundere, refūdī,
refūsus** pour back, restore,
pay back (16)

fungor, fungī, —, fūnctus sum
perform (+ *abl.*) (21)

Galilaea, Galilaeae, f. Galilee (10)

Galilaeus, -a, -um Galilean (13)

gaudeō, gaudēre; —, gāvīsus sum
rejoice, be glad (20)

gaudium, gaudiī, n. joy (3)

generōsus, -a, -um noble (E33)

genetrīx, genetrīcis, f. mother (34)

genitus, -a, -um begotten, engendered (27)

gēns, gentis, gentium, f. nation;
pl., nations, Gentiles (27)

genū, genūs, n. knee (16)

genus, generis, n. kind; race;
nation (14)

gerō, gerere, gessī, gestus bear, manage, conduct (29)

gladius, gladiī, m. sword (4)

glōria, glōriae, f. glory (1)

glōrificō, glōrificāre, glōrificāvī, glōrificātus glorify (11)

   conglōrificō, conglōrificāre, conglōrificāvī, conglōrificātus glorify (exceedingly) (11)

glōrior, glōriārī, —, glōriātus sum boast, vaunt oneself (E28)

glōriōsus, -a, -um glorious (8)

grabātus, grabātī, m. cot (E24)

gradior, gradī, —, gressus sum walk, step (21)

   aggredior, aggredī, —, aggressus sum approach (21)

   ēgredior, ēgredī, —, ēgressus sum come out, go out (21)

   ingredior, ingredī, —, ingressus sum walk along; come in (21)

   regredior, regredī, —, regressus sum go back, return (21)

grātia, grātiae, f. grace; favor, credit; *pl.,* thanks (1)

grātus, -a, -um (+ *dat.*) pleasing, agreeable (8)

gravis, grave heavy; serious, grievous (28)

gregō, gregāre, gregāvī, gregātus gather, assemble (11)

   aggregō, aggregāre, aggregāvī, aggregātus add to; join with (11)

   congregō, congregāre, congregāvī, congregātus gather together, assemble (11)

   sēgregō, sēgregāre, sēgregāvī, sēgregātus separate (11)

grex, gregis, m. flock (18)

gubernō, gubernāre, gubernāvī, gubernātus govern (12)

habeō, habēre, habuī, habitus have, hold; consider (6)

   perhibeō, perhibēre, perhibuī,

perhibitus hold out, produce, afford (9)

Hebraeus, Hebraeī, m. Hebrew (6)

hērēditās, hērēditātis, f. generation; inheritance (35)

hic, haec, hoc (*demon. pron./adj.*) this (23)

hīc (*adv.*) here, in this place (3)

hinc (*adv.*) from here (11)

hodiē (*adv.*) today (2)

homō, hominis, m. human being, person (14)

honor, honōris, m. honor (25)

honōrō, honōrāre, honōrāvī, honōrātus respect, honor (E21)

hōra, hōrae, f. hour (1)

hōsānnā (*Hebrew: interj.*) hosanna (*cry of praise*) (10)

hospes, hospitis, m. & f. host; guest (29)

hostia, hostiae, f. sacrificial offering, host (11)

hostis, hostis, hostium, m. & f. enemy, host (30)

hūmānitās, hūmānitātis, f. humanity (18)

hūmānus, -a, -um human (15)

humilis, humile lowly, humble (29)

humilitās, humilitātis, f. lowliness, humility (34)

hymnus, hymnī, m. hymn (3)

hypocrita, hypocritae, m. hypocrite (E23)

ibi (*adv.*) there, in that place; then (3)

īdem, eadem, idem (*pron. & adj.*) the same (32)

ideō (*adv.*) therefore, on that account (14)

idōneus, -a, -um suitable, capable, qualified (E35)

igitur (*conj.*) therefore, then (12)

ignis, ignis, ignium, m. (*abl. sing.,* **igne** or **ignī**) fire (20)

ille, illa, illud (*demon. pron./adj.*)
    that (23)
illūcēscō, illūcēscere, illūxī, —
    shine (upon), become light (30)
illūminātiō, illūminātiōnis, f.
    light (32)
illūminō, illūmināre, illūmināvī,
    illūminātus make shine, illumi-
    nate; enlighten (23)
illūstrō, illūstrāre, illūstrāvī, illūs-
    trātus illuminate; enlighten,
    explain (24)
imāgō, imāginis, f. likeness,
    image (E24)
immolātiō, immolātiōnis, f.
    offering (35)
imperātor, imperātōris, m. gen-
    eral, emperor (25)
imperium, imperiī, n. dominion,
    empire; recept, command (10)
in (*prep.*: 1. + *acc.*; 2. + *abl.*)
    1. into, onto; against; for (the
    purpose of) 2. in, on; among;
    by means of, with (1)
inaestimābilis, inaestimābile
    priceless (30)
incarnō, incarnāre, incarnāvī,
    incarnātus make into flesh,
    make incarnate (13)
incēnsum, incēnsī, n. incense (8)
incrēdulus, -a, -um unbelieving,
    disobedient (E31)
increpō, increpāre, increpuī,
    increpitus rebuke, chide (E30)
inde (*adv.*) from there; from then
    (18)
indēficiēns (*gen.*, indēficientis)
    unfailing (18)
indulgentia, indulgentiae, f. for-
    giveness, pardon, concession
    (26)
ineffābilis, ineffābile inexpres-
    sible, ineffable (30)
īnfernus, -a, -um of hell, infernal
    (31)

īnferus, -a, -um of hell, below (31)
inhaereō, inhaerēre, inhaesī,
    inhaesus cling to, adhere to
    (+ *dat.*) (14)
inīquitās, inīquitātis, f. wicked-
    ness (15)
innocēns (*gen.*, innocentis) clean,
    pure, innocent (20)
innocentia, innocentiae, f. inno-
    cence (11)
inquam (*defective verb*) I say (33)
īnstitūtiō, īnstitūtiōnis, f. instruc-
    tion (34)
inter (*prep.* + *acc.*) between,
    among (9)
intercessiō, intercessiōnis, f.
    intercession (22)
intermissiō, intermissiōnis, f.
    interruption (E27)
intrā (*prep.* + *acc.*) within, among
    (16)
intrō, intrāre, intrāvī, intrātus
    enter (9)
introitus, introitūs, m. a going in,
    introit (22)
invicem (1. *adv.*; 2. *indecl. re-
    ciprocal reflexive pron.*) 1. in
    turn 2. one another (28)
invīsibilis, invīsibile spiritual,
    invisible (17)
ipse, ipsa, ipsum (*intensive pron.
    & adj.*) -self, [*he, she, it*] (24)
īra, īrae, f. anger, wrath (27)
irradiō, irradiāre, irradiāvī, irra-
    diātus shine, illumine (35)
is, ea, id (*unemphatic demon.
    pron./adj.*) this, that, [= *he, she,
    it*] (23)
iste, ista, istud (*unemphatic
    demon. pron. & adj.*) this, that
    (of yours) (23)
ita (*adv.*) so, thus, in this way (23)
itaque (*adv.*) therefore, and so (31)
iter, itineris, n. journey (26)
iterum (*adv.*) again (8)

jaceō, jacēre, jacuī, — lie, be situated; sleep (35)

jaciō, jacere, jēcī, jactus throw (35)

  ējiciō, ējicere, ējēcī, ējectus throw out (35)

  prōjiciō, prōjicere, prōjēcī, prōjectus cast forth, throw down (35)

jam (*adv.*) already; now; soon (8)

Jerūsalem (*Hebrew: indecl. n.;* also, **Hierosolyma, Hierosolymae,** f., & **Hierosolyma, Hiersolymōrum,** n.) Jerusalem (17)

Jēsūs, Jēsū, Jēsū, Jēsūm, Jēsū, m. (*voc.,* Jēsū) Jesus, Joshua (7)

Jōannēs, Jōannis, m. John (14)

jubeō, jubēre, jussī, jussus command, ask, bid (22)

jūcundus, -a, -um pleasing (33)

Jūdaea, Jūdaeae, f. Judea (2)

Jūdaeus, -a, -um Jewish (13)

jūdex, jūdicis, m. judge (32)

jūdicium, jūdiciī, n. judgment (29)

jūdicō, jūdicāre, jūdicāvī, jūdicātus judge (22)

  dījūdicō, dījūdicāre, dījūdicāvī, dījūdicātus discern, distinguish (22)

jugum, jugī, n. yoke (E27)

jungō, jungere, jūnxī, jūnctus join, unite (6)

  conjungō, conjungere, conjūnxī, conjūnctus join, unite (6)

jūstitia, jūstitiae, f. righteousness, justice (2)

jūstus, -a, -um righteous, just (5)

juvenis, juvenis, m. or f. young adult (E33)

jūxtā (*prep. + acc.*) near, along; according to (34)

Kȳrie (*Greek: vocative*) O Lord! (10)

lābor, lābī, —, lāpsus sum slide, (slip and) fall (23)

labor, labōris, m. work, labor (27)

labōrō, labōrāre, labōrāvī, labōrātus work, labor (26)

lacrima, lacrimae, f. tear (20)

lacrimor, lacrimārī, —, lacrimātus sum weep (21)

lacrimōsus, -a, -um tearful (34)

laetitia, laetitiae, f. gladness, joy (7)

laetor, laetārī, —, laetātus sum rejoice, be glad (21)

  collaetor, collaetārī, —, collaetātus sum rejoice together (21)

laetus, -a, -um joyful (11)

lampas, lampadis, f. lamp, torch; flame (29)

largior, largīrī, —, largītus sum grant, bestow (23)

largitās, largitātis, f. bounty, abundance (15)

latus, lateris, n. side (19)

laudō, laudāre, laudāvī, laudātus praise (5)

  collaudō, collaudāre, collaudāvī, collaudātus praise exceedingly; praise together (5)

laus, laudis, f. praise (17)

lavō, lavāre, lāvī, lautus (lōtus) wash; *pass.,* be washed, bathe (27)

lēctiō, lēctiōnis, f. reading (15)

lēctor, lēctōris, m. reader, lector (15)

legō, legere, lēgī, lēctus choose, select; read (14)

  colligō, colligere, collēgī, collēctus gather up, take in, collect (14)

  dīligō, dīligere, dīlēxī, dīlēctus love (14)

  ēligō, ēligere, ēlēgī, ēlēctus choose, elect (14)

intellegō, intellegere, intellēxī,
intellēctus perceive, understand; pay heed to (31)

Lēvīta (Lēvītēs), Lēvītae, m.
deacon, Levite (18)

lēx, lēgis, f. law, Torah (18)

liber, librī, m. book (3)

līber, lībera, līberum free (21)

līberō, līberāre, līberāvī, līberātus
free (5)

licet, licēre, licuit (licitum est) it
is permitted (+ dat. & inf.) (34)

licet (subord. conj.) although (29)

lignum, lignī, n. wood; tree (30)

lingua, linguae, f. tongue; language (28)

liquō, liquāre, liquāvī, liquātus
melt (30)

lītūrgia, lītūrgiae, f. (divine) service, liturgy (7)

locus, locī, m. (pl., loca) place (17)

loquor, loquī, —, locūtus sum
speak (22)

alloquor, alloquī, —, allocūtus
sum speak to, address (+ acc.)
(22)

Lūcās, Lūcae, m. Luke (18)

lūcifer, lūciferī, m. daystar, morning star (26)

lucror, lucrārī, —, lucrātus sum
gain (E28)

lūmen, lūminis, n. light; pl., also,
eyes (14)

lūmināre, lūmināris, lūminārium,
n. light, lamp, heavenly body
(34)

lūx, lūcis, f. light (24)

maestus, -a, -um sad (7)

Magdalēna, Magdalēnae, f.
Magdalen (29)

magis (adv.) more (27)

magister, magistrī, m. teacher,
master, rabbi (4)

magnificō, magnificāre, magnificāvī, magnificātus extol,
praise, glorify (28)

magnus, -a, -um great, large,
big (4)

magus, magī, m. wise man, magician, astrologer (31)

majestās, majestātis, f. majesty
(31)

major, majus (gen., majōris)
greater, older (22)

male (adv.) badly, poorly (7)
male habēre = be sick (7)

malefactor, malefactōris, m. evil-
doer, criminal (E25)

malus, -a, -um bad, evil, wicked
(4)

mandātum, mandātī, n. order,
commandment (9)

mandūcō, mandūcāre, mandūcāvī,
mandūcātus eat (15)

maneō, manēre, mānsī, mānsus
remain, wait, stay (31)

permaneō, permanēre, per-
mānsī, permānsus remain,
continue (31)

remaneō, remanēre, remānsī, remānsus be left, remain (31)

manifestus, -a, -um obvious, evident, clear (E26)

manus, manūs, f. hand (16)

mare, maris, marium, n. sea (15)

Marīa, Marīae, f. Mary (2)

martyr, martyris, m. witness,
martyr (26)

māter, mātris, f. mother (14)

mātūtīnus, -a, -um (of) morning,
early (35)

maximus, -a, -um greatest, very
great (12)

medium, mediī, n. the middle,
midst (33)

memor (gen., memoris) mindful
of (+ gen.) (16)

memoria, memoriae, f. remembrance, memory (20)

memoror, memorārī, —, memorātus sum (+ gen. or acc.) be
mindful of, remember (22)

mendāx (*gen.*, **mendācis**) lying;
subst., liar (E35)

mēns, mentis, mentium, f. mind,
intention (15)

mēnsa, mēnsae, f. table; banquet
(12)

mereō, merēre, meruī, meritus
be worthy, deserve (27)

meritō (*adv.*) rightly, deservedly
(5)

meritum, meritī, n. merit (8)

metō, metere, messuī, messus
reap (E28)

meus, -a, -um my, mine (4)

mīles, mīlitis, m. soldier (24)

minister, ministrī, m. servant,
minister (2)

ministerium, ministeriī, n. ministry, service (10)

mīrābilis, mīrābile wonderful (35)

mīror, mīrārī, —, mīrātus sum
wonder (at), be amazed (at) (20)

   **admīror, admīrārī, —, admīrātus
sum** wonder at, be amazed at
(20)

mīrus, -a, -um wonderful (8)

misceō, miscēre, miscuī, mixtus
mix, mingle (6)

miser, misera, miserum wretched,
pitiable (20)

**misereor, miserērī, —, misertus
sum** (+ *gen. or dat.*) have pity
(on) (20)

misericordia, misericordiae, f.
mercy, kindness, pity (7)

**miseror, miserārī, —, miserātus
sum** bewail; pity (21)

missa, missae, f. Mass (1)

mītis, mīte mild, meek (24)

mittō, mittere, mīsī, missus send;
cast; put (12)

   **admittō, admittere, admīsī,
admissus** join, admit; allow,
permit (17)

   āmittō, āmittere, āmīsī, āmissus
send off; lose (17)

**dīmittō, dīmittere, dīmīsī,
dīmissus** send away, release;
forgive, permit (12)

ēmittō, ēmittere, ēmīsī, ēmissus
send out (17)

**permittō, permittere, permīsī,
permissus** allow, permit
(+ *dat. & inf.*) (12)

**remittō, remittere, remīsī, re-
missus** send back; forgive (17)

**submittō, submittere, submīsī,
submissus** lower; suborn,
bribe (12)

modo (*adv.*) (just) now (E27)

modus, modī, m. manner, way (4)

moneō, monēre, monuī, monitus
warn, advise; teach (6)

mōns, montis, montium, m.
mountain, hill (24)

**mōnstrō, mōnstrāre, mōnstrāvī,
mōnstrātus** show; command
(29)

   **dēmōnstrō, dēmōnstrāre, dē-
mōnstrāvī, dēmōnstrātus**
show, reveal (29)

monumentum, monumentī, n.
tomb (30)

morior, morī, —, mortuus sum
die (20)

mors, mortis, mortium, f. death
(15)

mortuus, -a, -um dead (4)

moveō, movēre, mōvī, mōtus
move; affect (28)

mulier, mulieris, f. woman, wife
(19)

multitūdō, multitūdinis, f. great
number, multitude (35)

multus, -a, -um much, many (4)

mundus, mundī, m. world (4)

mundus, -a, -um pure, clean (8)

   immundus, -a, -um impure,
unclean (8)

mūnus, mūneris, n. gift, offering;
task, duty; *pl., also,* bribes (14)

mūtō, mūtāre, mūtāvī, mūtātus
change, exchange (13)
**immūtō, immūtāre, immūtāvī,
immūtātus** transform (13)
**mūtuor, mūtuārī, —, mūtuātus
sum** borrow (33)
mystērium, mystēriī, n. mystery
(3)
nam (*coord. conj.*) for (2)
nārrō, nārrāre, nārrāvī, nārrātus
tell, narrate (31)
nāscor, nāscī, —, nātus sum be
born (20)
nātiō, nātiōnis, f. nation; *pl.*,
gentiles, heathens (33)
nātīvitās, nātīvitātis, f. birth (33)
nātūra, nātūrae, f. nature (1)
nātus, nātī, m. son, child (6)
nāvis, nāvis, nāvium, f. ship,
boat (E28)
Nazarēnus, -a, -um of Nazareth,
Nazarene, Nazorean (7)
nē (*subord. conj.*) in order that . .
not (*introducing negative purpose clause + subj.*); that . . not
(*introducing direct command +
subj.*) (22); that (*introducing affirmative clause of fear + subj.*)
(25)
-ne (*enclitic interrog. particle*)
used in sentence questions (6)
necessārius, -a, -um needful, fateful; needed (+ *dat.*) (25)
necesse est (*impersonal verb*) it is
needful, it is necessary (+ *dat.
or acc. & inf.*) (34)
necnōn (*coord. conj.*) and also,
and indeed (35)
negō, negāre, negāvī, negātus
deny, say . . not (30)
**nēmō, nūllīus, nēminī, nēminem,
nūllō/nūllā** (*pron. & m./f. adj.*)
nobody; no (30)
neque (**nec**) (*coord. conj.*) and not,
nor

neque (**nec**) . . **neque** (**nec**)
neither . . nor (21)
nēquitia, nēquitiae, f. wickedness,
evil ways (E32)
nesciō, nescīre, nescīvī (**nesciī**),
nescītus not to know, be
ignorant (26)
nihil (**nīl**) (1. *indecl. n.*; 2. *adv.*)
1. nothing 2. not at all (20)
nimis (*adv.*) too (much) (12)
nisi (*subord. conj.*) unless, if . .
not; except, but (13)
noceō, nocēre, nocuī, nocitus
hurt, do harm to (+ *dat.*) (34)
nōlī/nōlīte (*imperative + inf.*)
be unwilling, do not (30)
nōmen, nōminis, n. name (14)
nōn (*adv.*) not (2)
nōndum (*adv.*) not yet (27)
nōscō, nōscere, nōvī, nōtus
present-stem system: get
acquainted with, get to know
perfect system: know (21)
   **agnōscō, agnōscere, agnōvī,
   agnitus** know, recognize,
   acknowledge (21)
   **cognōscō, cognōscere, cognōvī,
   cognitus** *present-stem system*: get acquainted with, get
   to know *perfect system*:
   know (21)
   **praenōscō, praenōscere, prae-
   nōvī, praenōtus** know
   beforehand, foreknow (21)
noster, nostra, nostrum our,
ours (4)
novus, -a, -um new, recent (4)
nox, noctis, noctium, f. night (20)
nūbēs, nūbis, nūbium, f. cloud;
multitude (E28)
nūllus, -a, -um not any, no (28)
numerus, numerī, m. number,
multitude (4)
numquam (*adv.*) never (5)
numquid (*interrog. adv.*) intro-

*duces a question expecting
a negative reply* (26)
nunc (*adv.*) now (5)
nūntiō, nūntiāre, nūntiāvī, nūntiātus declare, announce (17)
 annūntiō, annūntiāre, annūntiāvī, annūntiātus announce (17)
ob (*prep.* + *acc.*) because of (11)
oblātiō, oblātiōnis, f. offering (25)
oboedentia, oboedentiae, f. obedience (34)
oboediō, oboedīre, oboedīvī (oboediī), oboedītus obey, listen to (+ *dat.*) (34)
occāsus, occāsūs, m. setting [of the sun] (34)
occīdō, occīdere, occīdī, occīsus kill (32)
octāvus, -a, -um eighth (31)
octō (*indecl. adj.*) eight (24)
octōgintā (*indecl. adj.*) eighty (24)
oculus, oculī, m. eye (13)
—, —, ōdī, — hate (35)
odium, odiī, n. hatred (3)
odor, odōris, m. aroma, odor (27)
olīva, olīvae, f. olive (tree) (E26)
Olīvētum, Olīvētī, n. Olivet [a hill east of Jerusalem] (24)
omissiō, omissiōnis, f. omission (29)
omnipotēns (*gen.*, **omnipotentis**) all-powerful (16)
omnis, omne every, all (16)
operō, operāre, operāvī, operātus work (5)
operor, operārī, —, operātus sum work, perform (23)
 cooperor, cooperārī, —, cooperātus sum work with, cooperate (with) (23)
oportet, oportēre, oportuit, — it is proper, it is necessary (+ *acc. & inf.*) (34)
ops, opis, f. help (35)

optimus, -a, -um best, very good (12)
opus, operis, n. work, deed (20)
 opus est = it is necessary, there is a need (+ *inf. or abl.*) (20)
ōrātiō, ōrātiōnis, f. prayer; speech (14)
orbis, orbis, orbium, m. sphere, orb (32)
 orbis (terrae / terrārum) world (32)
ōrdō, ōrdinis, m. rank, order (23)
orior, orīrī, —, ortus sum spring up, arise, appear (20)
ōrnō, ōrnāre, ōrnāvī, ōrnātus adorn, garnish, trim (35)
 adōrnō, adōrnāre, adōrnāvī, adōrnātus adorn (35)
ōrō, ōrāre, ōrāvī, ōrātus pray (5)
 adōrō, adōrāre, adōrāvī, adōrātus worship, adore (5)
 exōrō, exōrāre, exōrāvī, exōrātus beseech (5)
ortus, ortūs, m. rising [of the sun]
ōs, ōris, n. mouth (19)
ōsculor, ōsculārī, —, ōsculātus sum kiss (E29)
otiōsus, -a, -um idle, unemployed (E33)
ovis, ovis, ovium, f. sheep (21)
pācificō, pācificāre, pācificāvī, pācificātus make peace, grant peace (35)
paenitentia, paenitentiae, f. repentance (35)
paeniteor, paenitērī, —, — repent (31)
palam (*adv.*) openly, plainly (32)
palma, palmae, f. palm (of the hand) (32)
pangō, pangere, pānxī (pēgī, pepigī), pānctus (pactus) make; compose; sing (33)
pānis, pānis, pānium, m. bread, loaf of bread (15)
pāpa, pāpae, m. pope (1)

pār (*gen.*, **paris**) equal, like (+ *dat.*) (31)
pariter (*adv.*) equally, together
compār (*gen.*, **comparis**) equal, like (31)
dispār (*gen.*, **disparis**) unlike, different (31)
parcō, parcere, pepercī (**parsī**), **parsus** spare (+ *dat.*) (34)
parēns, parentis, m. & f. parent (30)
pariō, parere, peperī, partus beget, produce, bear (13)
parō, parāre, parāvī, parātus provide, prepare (11)
praeparō, praeparāre, praeparāvī, praeparātus prepare (11)
pars, partis, partium, f. part, some (15)
particeps, participis, m. & f. partaker, sharer (15)
parvus, -a, -um little, small (11)
parvulus, -a, -um little, small (11)
Pascha, Paschae, f. Passover, Pesach, Pasch; Easter (11)
Pascha, Paschatis, n. Passover, Pesach, Pasch; Easter (16)
paschālis, paschāle of Easter, Paschal (16)
pāscō, pāscere, pāvī, pāstus feed (27)
passer, passeris, m. sparrow (E27)
passiō, passiōnis, f. suffering, passion (16)
pāstor, pāstōris, m. shepherd; pastor (18)
pater, patris, m. father (14)
paternus, -a, -um of a father, paternal (20)
patior, patī, —, passus sum suffer; allow (20)
patria, patriae, f. native land, country (25)
patrōnus, patrōnī, m. defender, advocate (26)

paucī, -ae, -a few, a few (24)
Paulus, Paulī, m. Paul (11)
pauper (*gen.*, **pauperis**) poor, not wealthy (25)
pāx, pācis, f. harmony, peace (14)
peccātor, peccātōris, m. sinner (20)
peccātum, peccātī, n. sin (3)
peccō, peccāre, peccāvī, peccātus sin (20)
pectus, pectoris, n. breast (34)
pellō, pellere, pepulī, pulsus drive out (33)
expellō, expellere, expulī, expulsus drive out (33)
repellō, repellere, repulī, repulsus cast off, overcome (33)
pendeō, pendēre, pependī, — hang; depend (32)
penetrō, penetrāre, penetrāvī, penetrātus pierce, penetrate (34)
per (*prep.* + *acc.*) through (8)
peregrīnāns (*gen.*, **peregrīnantis**) traveling; *subst.*, (foreign) traveler, pilgrim (26)
perenniter (*adv.*) constantly, perennially (10)
perennis, perenne eternal (33)
perfectus, -a, -um perfect (28)
perpetuō (*adv.*) uninterruptedly, perpetually (25)
perpetuus, -a, -um everlasting, perpetual (10)
persevērō, persevērāre, persevērāvī, persevērātus continue (30)
pēs, pedis, m. foot (19)
petō, petere, petīvī (**petiī**), **petītus** ask (for), entreat (22)
Petrus, Petrī, m. Peter (2)
phantasma, phantasmatis, n. ghost, phantom (E30)
piāculum, piāculī, n. sin, crime (32)
pietās, pietātis, f. goodness; tenderness, pity (17)

piscis, piscis, piscium, m.
fish (E34)

pius, -a, -um holy; loving,
tender (4)

impius, -a, -um wicked, god-
less (4)

placeō, placēre, placuī, placitus
please, be pleasing to
(+ dat.) (34)

placet (impersonal verb) it is
pleasing (+ dat.) (34)

complaceō, complacēre, complacuī (complacitus sum)
please, be acceptable to
(+ dat.) (34)

plācō, plācāre, plācāvī, plācātus
appease; reconcile (17)

plānctus, plānctūs, (m.) mourning (22)

plangō, plangere, plānxī, plānctus
bewail, mourn (24)

platēa, platēae, f. (wide) street
(E23)

plēnitūdō, plēnitūdinis, f. fullness (E29)

plēnus, -a, -um (+ abl.) full (of) (7)

-pleō, -plēre, -plēvī, -plētus fill,
complete (8)

adimpleō, adimplēre, adimplēvī,
adimplētus fulfill (8)

compleō, complēre, complēvī,
complētus fulfill, accom-
plish (8)

impleō, implēre, implēvī, implētus fill, accomplish (8)

repleō, replēre, replēvī, replētus
fill, complete (8)

plōrō, plōrāre, plōrāvī, plōrātus
bewail, lament, weep (31)

poena, poenae, f. pain, punishment, penalty (33)

pondus, ponderis, n. burden, im-
pediment (E28)

pōnō, pōnere, posuī, positus put,
place, set (24)

dēpōnō, dēpōnere, dēposuī, dēpositus set down, lay down;
remove (24)

impōnō, impōnere, imposuī,
impositus put upon (24)

prōpōnō, prōpōnere, prōposuī,
prōpositus set before; propose (24)

repōnō, repōnere, reposuī,
repositus put back, replace;
lay aside; bury (24)

Pontius Pīlātus, Pontiī Pīlātī, m.
Pontius Pilatus, Pilate (27)

populus, populī, m. people (2)

portō, portāre, portāvī, portātus
carry (24)

poscō, poscere, poposcī, — ask,
beseech (25)

dēposcō, dēposcere, dēpoposcī,
— beseech, demand (25)

possideō, possidēre, possēdī, pos-
sessus inherit, gain possession
of (E24)

possum, posse, potuī, — be able,
can (+ inf.) (12)

post (prep. + acc.) after, behind (8)

posteā (adv.) afterward, later
on (10)

postis, postis, postium, m. doorpost (15)

postquam (subord. conj.) after (12)

postulō, postulāre, postulāvī,
postulātus ask (for), pray for;
require (22)

potēns (gen., potentis) powerful
(in), having power (over) (20)

potentia, potentiae, f. power (2)

potestās, potestātis, f. power,
authority (20)

pōtus, pōtūs, m. drink (16)

prae (prep. + abl.) before, in preference to; in comparison with;
in consequence of, because
of (15)

praeceptum, praeceptī, n. lesson,
precept; command (3)

praecōnium, praecōniī, n. praise,
proclamation (33)

praedicō, praedicāre, praedicāvī,
praedicātus preach, pro-
claim (22)

praefātiō, praefātiōnis, f. preface
(28)

praemium, praemiī, n. reward (3)

praeses, praesidis, m. & f. president, governor, procurator (31)

praestōlor, praestōlārī, —,
praestōlātus sum wait for
(+ dat. or acc.) (26)

praeter (prep. + acc.) except;
beyond, past (15)

praeterquam (prep. + acc.)
beyond, contrary to (E29)

precor, precārī, —, precātus sum
ask, pray (20)
    dēprecor, dēprecārī, —, dē-
    precātus sum beseech (20)

premō, premere, pressī, pressus
press (upon); oppress (30)
    exprimō, exprimere, expressī,
    expressus represent,
    express (30)

presbyter, presbyterī, m. elder
(E31, 33)

pretiōsus, -a, -um precious (29)

pretium, pretiī, n. price; ransom (27)

prex, precis, f. entreaty, prayer (19)

prīmus, -a, -um first (7)
    in prīmīs at first, in the first
    place (7)

prīmum (adv.) (at) first (13)

prīnceps, prīncipis, m. chief,
prince (14)

prīncipium, prīncipiī, n. beginning (5)

priusquam (subord. conj.) before (29)

prō (prep. + abl.) in front of; in
behalf of, for; instead of, on
behalf of (1)

prōmptus, -a, -um willing, ready,
eager (E24)

prope (adv.) near (E24)

prophēta, prophētae, m. prophet
(11)

prophētō, prophētāre, prophētāvī,
prophētātus prophesy, foretell (E28)

propitius, -a, -um kind, favorable,
propitious (35)

prōpositum, prōpositī, n. decree,
purpose, plan (E23)

propter (prep. + acc.) on account
of, because of (7)

proptereā (adv.) therefore (E29)

prōtēctiō, prōtēctiōnis, f. protection (28)

proximus, -a, -um nearest (+
dat.); subst., neighbor (15)

psalmista, psalmistae, m.
psalmist (29)

psalmus, psalmī, m. psalm (2)

puella, puellae, f. girl (E35)

puer, puerī, m. boy, child;
servant (2)

pūrgātiō, pūrgātiōnis, f. purification (E33)

pūrgō, pūrgāre, pūrgāvī, pūrgātus
purify, purge (17)

pūrus, -a, -um clean, pure (31)

putō, putāre, putāvī, putātus
think, reckon (30)
    dēputō, dēputāre, dēputāvī,
    dēputātus appoint; reckon,
    count (30)

quaerō, quaerere, quaesīvī,
quaesītus seek, ask for (31)
    quaesō/quaesumus (paren-
    thetical forms) I/we beg (31)
    requīrō, requīrere, requīsīvī,
    requīsītus seek, require (31)

quālis, quāle (of) what kind
(of) (23)

quam (1. adv.; 2. coord. conj.)
    1. how, how much; as . . as

possible (*with positive or superlative*) 2. than (*in comparisons*) (27)

quamquam (*subord. conj.*) although (14)

quandō (1. *interrog. adv.*; 2. *subord. conj.*) 1. when? (8) 2. when (26)

quantus, -a, -um how much, how great (23)

quāpropter (*coord. conj.*) wherefore, and therefore (16)

quārē (*interrog. adv.*) for what reason? why? (6)

quasi (*adv.*) as if, as it were; about (E34)

quattuor (*indecl. adj.*) four (21)

-que (*enclitic coord. conj.*) and (1)

quemadmodum (*conj.*) how, just as, to the extent that (E24, 31)

quī, quae, quod (1. *interrog. adj.*; 2. *rel. pron.*) 1. which? what? 2. who, which, that (10)

quia (*subord. conj.*) that; because (8)

quid (*interrog. adv.*) why? how? wherefore? (26)

  ut quid (*interrog. adv.*) as to what? to what purpose? why? (26)

quīdam, quaedam, quiddam (*indef. pron.*) a certain one, a certain thing (12)

quīdam, quaedam, quoddam (*indef. adj.*) a certain (12)

quidem (*intensifying adv.*) indeed, at any rate (24)

quiēs, quiētis, f. peace, rest, quiet (28)

quīnque (*indecl. adj.*) five (24)

quis, quid (1. *interrog. pron.*; 2. *indef. pron., after* **sī, nisī, numquid, nē**) 1. who? what? 2. someone, something; anyone, anything (26)

quisquam, quaequam, quidquam (*indef. pron.*) anyone, anything [*used with negative or implied negative*] (30)

quisquis, quaequae, quidquid (*indef. rel. pron.*) whosoever, whatsoever (32)

quō (*interrog. & rel. adv.*) (to) where (27)

quod (*subord. conj.*) that; because (8)

quōmodo (*interrog. adv.*) in what manner? how? (26)

quoniam (*subord. conj.*) that; because (8)

quoque (*intensifying adv.*) too, also (5)

radius, radiī, m. ray (34)

ratiō, ratiōnis, f. reckoning, account; plan, rule, way; reason, reasoning (32)

reconciliātiō, reconciliātiōnis, f. restoration, reconciliation (33)

recumbō, recumbere, recubuī, — recline at table (E34)

redēmptiō, redēmptiōnis, f. deliverance, redemption (31)

redēmptor, redēmptōris, m. one who buys back: redeemer (14)

rēgīna, rēgīnae, f. queen (3)

regiō, regiōnis, f. country, region (32)

rēgnō, rēgnāre, rēgnāvī, rēgnātus rule, reign (5)

rēgnum, rēgnī, n. kingdom, rule (3)

regō, regere, rēxī, rēctus rule, guide, govern (8)

  corrigō, corrigere, corrēxī, corrēctus correct (8)

  dīrigō, dīrigere, dīrēxī, dīrēctus direct (8)

  ērigō, ērigere, ērēxī, ērēctus raise up, erect (8)

  —surgō, surgere, surrēxī, surrēctus rise up, arise (12)

īnsurgō, īnsurgere, īnsurrēxī, īnsurrectus rise up (12)

resurgō, resurgere, resurrēxī, resurrēctus rise up again (12)

relinquō, relinquere, relīquī, relictus leave (behind), abandon (12)

remissiō, remissiōnis, f. forgiveness, remission (17)

requiēs, requiēī, f. rest (32)

rēs, reī, f. thing (19)

respondeō, respondēre, respondī, respōnsus answer, respond (to) (+ dat.) (22)

respōnsum, respōnsī, n. answer, response (7)

resultō, resultāre, resultāvī, resultātus resound, rebound (11)

resurrēctiō, resurrēctiōnis, f. rising again, resurrection (15)

rēte, rētis, rētium, n. net (E28, 34)

revēlō, revēlāre, revēlāvī, revēlātus show, reveal (35)

rēx, rēgis, m. king (14)

rītus, rītūs, m. ceremony, rite (16)

rogō, rogāre, rogāvī, rogātus ask (for), pray, beseech (22)

interrogō, interrogāre, interrogāvī, interrogātus ask, inquire (22)

Rōma, Rōmae, f. Rome (17)

Rōmānus, -a, -um Roman (13)

ruber, rubra, rubrum red (14)

ruīna, ruīnae, f. fall, destruction (35)

rūrsus (adv.) again (E24)

rutilō, rutilāre, rutilāvī, rutilātus glow (34)

Sabaōth (Hebrew: indecl. pl. noun) armies, hosts (4)

sabbatum, sabbatī, n. Sabbath (3)

sacer, sacra, sacrum holy, sacred (4)

sacerdōs, sacerdōtis, m. priest (14)

sacrāmentum, sacrāmentī, n. sacrament (4)

sacrificium, sacrificiī, n. sacrifice (3)

sacrō, sacrāre, sacrāvī, sacrātus make holy, consecrate (5)

cōnsecrō, cōnsecrāre, cōnsecrāvī, cōnsecrātus make holy, consecrate (5)

sacrōsānctus, -a, -um most holy, venerable (8)

saeculum, saeculī, n. age, world (3) in saecula (saeculōrum) forever (and ever) (3)

saepe (adv.) often (9)

salūs, salūtis, f. safety, health, salvation (15)

salūtāre, salūtāris, salūtārium, n. salvation (27)

salūtāris, salūtāre saving, of salvation (16)

salūtifer, salūtifera, salūtiferum salutary, saving (8)

salvātor, salvātōris, m. savior (17)

salvē! (imperative; pl., salvēte!) hail! farewell! hello! goodbye! greetings! (25)

salvus, -a, -um safe, saved; sound (15)

sānctificātiō, sānctificātiōnis, f. holiness; holy mystery (29)

sānctificō, sānctificāre, sānctificāvī, sānctificātus make holy, sanctify (11)

sānctitās, sānctitātis, f. holiness (34)

sānctus, -a, -um hallowed, holy; subst., saint (5)

sanguis, sanguinis, m. blood (15)

sānō, sānāre, sānāvī, sānātus heal (7)

sapientia, sapientiae, f. wisdom (18)

satiō, satiāre, satiāvī, satiātus nourish, satisfy (9)

satis (1. indecl. n.; 2. indecl. adj.; 3. adv.) 1. enough (of) (+ par-

titive gen.) 2. enough 3. enough,
sufficiently (15)

scandō, scandere, scandī, scānsus
climb, mount (16)

  **ascendō, ascendere, ascendī,
ascēnsus** go up, come up,
ascend (16)

  **dēscendō, dēscendere, dēscendī,
dēscēnsus** go down, come
down, descend (16)

scelus, sceleris, n. crime, sin (20)

sciō, scīre, scīvī, scītus know (9)

scrība, scrībae, m. scribe (i.e., one
versed in Jewish law) (E35)

scrībō, scrībere, scrīpsī, scrīptus
write (14)

  **dēscrībō, dēscrībere, dēscrīpsī,
dēscrīptus** describe; enroll (14)

scrīptūra, scrīptūrae, f. writing,
scripture (11)

**scrūtor, scrūtārī, —, scrūtātus
sum** examine thoroughly, pore
over (E30)

secundum (*prep. + acc.*) according
to (10)

secundus, -a, -um next, second (10)

sed (*coord. conj.*) but, yet (8)

sedeō, sedēre, sēdī, sessus sit
(down), be seated (23)

sēdēs, sēdis, f. place, seat (30)

sēmita, sēmitae, f. path (21)

semper (*adv.*) always (5)

senex (*gen.,* **senis**) old; *subst.,* old
man (21)

sēnsus, sēnsūs, m. feeling, sense;
understanding, mind (23)

sentiō, sentīre, sēnsī, sēnsus feel,
perceive (31)

**sēparō, sēparāre, sēparāvī, sēpa-
rātus** separate (9)

**sepeliō, sepelīre, sepelīvī (sepeliī),
sepultus** bury (21)

septem (*indecl. adj.*) seven (21)

sepulcrum, sepulcrī, n. sepulcher (31)

sequor, sequī, —, secūtus sum
follow (22)

  **assequor, assequī, —, assecūtus
sum** follow (22)

  **cōnsequor, cōnsequī, —,
cōnsecūtus sum** follow;
obtain (22)

  **persequor, persequī, —,
persecūtus sum** pursue,
track down; persecute (22)

  **prōsequor, prōsequī, —,
prōsecūtus sum** proceed
(with), go through (with) (22)

serēnus, -a, -um bright, serene (22)

sermō, sermōnis, m. talk,
speech (31)

**serviō, servīre, servīvī (serviī),
servītus** serve, comply with
(*+ dat.*) (34)

servō, servāre, servāvī, servātus
keep, preserve (5)

  **cōnservō, cōnservāre, cōn-
servāvī, cōnservātus** keep,
preserve (5)

  **observō, observāre, observāvī,
observātus** watch, observe (5)

servus, servī, m. slave, servant (2)

sextus, -a, -um sixth (23)

sī (*subord. conj.*) if; whether (13)

sīc (*adv.*) so, thus (23)

siccus, -a, -um dry (14)

sīcut (1. *adv.;* 2. *subord. conj.*)
1. like 2. (just) as (23)

  sīcut . . et (just) as . . (so)
too (23)

sīdus, sīderis, n. star, constellation (32)

**sīgnificō, sīgnificāre, sīgnificāvī,
sīgnificātus** signify (33)

sīgnum, sīgnī, n. sign; miracle (27)

silentium, silentiī, n. silence (8)

similis, simile (*+ dat.*) like,
similar (to) (16)

  dissimilis, dissimile (*+ dat.*)
dissimilar, unlike (16)

simul (*adv.*) together, at the same
time (24)
   simul ac *or* atque (*subord.*
   conj.) as soon as (24)
sincērus, -a, -um sincere (34)
sine (*prep.* + *abl.*) without (1)
sinō, sinere, sīvī, situs allow,
   permit (E30)
sistō, sistere, stetī (stitī), status
   stand; be, become (32)
   exsistō, exsistere, exstitī,
      exstitus step forth, come
      out (32)
sīve (seu) (*subord. conj.*) or if (25)
   sīve (seu) . . sīve (seu) if . . or if;
      whether . . or (25)
sociō, sociāre, sociāvī, sociātus
   share in; ally (30)
socius, sociī, m. companion,
   ally (9)
sodālis, sodālis, sodālium, m.
   companion, associate (33)
sōl, sōlis, m. sun (34)
sōlemnis, sōlemne annual,
   solemn, customary (25)
sōlor, sōlārī, —, sōlātus sum
   console, comfort (21)
   cōnsōlor, cōnsōlārī, —,
      cōnsōlātus sum
      or
   cōnsōlō, cōnsōlāre, cōnsōlāvī,
      cōnsōlātus console, com-
      fort (21)
sōlus, -a, -um only, alone (28)
   sōlum (*adv.*) only, alone (28)
solvō, solvere, solvī, solūtus set
   free; break up; pay back (10)
   absolvō, absolvere, absolvī,
      absolūtus set free (from),
      absolve; finish (10)
somnus, somnī, m. sleep (30)
sonō, sonāre, sonuī, sonitus
   (make a) sound (15)
   īnsonō, īnsonāre, īnsonuī, —
      resound (15)

personō, personāre, personuī,
   personitus proclaim; resound (15)
spargō, spargere, sparsī, sparsus
   sprinkle (33)
   aspergō, aspergere, aspersī,
      aspersus sprinkle (33)
   dispergō, dispergere, dispersī,
      dispersus scatter (33)
spatium, spatiī, n. space (10)
speciēs, speciēī, f. appearance;
   kind, type; beauty (32)
speciō, specere, spexī, spectus
   look (at) (13)
   aspiciō, aspicere, aspexī,
      aspectus look (at) (13)
   circumspiciō, circumspicere,
      circumspexī, circumspectus
      look around (13)
   dēspiciō, dēspicere, dēspexī,
      dēspectus look down on,
      despise (13)
   respiciō, respicere, respexī,
      respectus look at, regard,
      watch (13)
spērō, spērāre, spērāvī, spērātus
   hope (for), wait (for); trust (32)
spēs, speī, f. hope (19)
spīna, spīnae, f. thorn (22)
spīrituālis, spīrituāle spiritual,
   of the spirit (26)
spīritus, spīritūs, m. breath;
   spirit (16)
spīrō, spīrāre, spīrāvī, spīrātus
   breathe (26)
   exspīrō, exspīrāre, exspīrāvī,
      exspīrātus die, expire (26)
splendor, splendōris, m. brilliance, splendor (35)
spōnsus, spōnsī, m. bridegroom (E35)
statim (*adv.*) immediately, at
   once (9)
statuō, statuere, statuī, statū-
   tus establish, appoint, determine (27)

cōnstituō, cōnstituere, cōn-
stituī, cōnstitūtus decree,
ordain (27)

stēlla, stēllae, f. star (5)

stō, stāre, stetī, status stand (still)
(13)

astō, astāre, astitī, — stand by,
stand near (13)

circumstō, circumstāre, circumstetī, — stand around,
encircle (13)

īnstō, īnstāre, īnstitī, — urge;
threaten (+ dat.) (13)

praestō, praestāre, praestitī
(praestāvī), praestātus
(praestitus) bestow; accomplish (13)

restō, restāre, restitī, — remain
(behind) (13)

struō, struere, strūxī, strūctus
build (29)

dēstruō, dēstruere, dēstrūxī,
dēstrūctus destroy (29)

īnstruō, īnstruere, īnstrūxī,
īnstrūctus instruct (29)

suāvis, suāve sweet (27)

suāvitās, suāvitātis, f. sweetness (16)

sub (prep.: 1. + acc.; 2. + abl.)
1. (to a place) under 2. (in or at
a place) under (9)

subditus, -a, -um submissive,
subordinate (E31)

subitō (adv.) suddenly (10)

substantia, substantiae, f. nature,
substance (21)

—, suī (reflexive pron.) oneself
(i.e., himself, herself, itself,
themselves) (28)

sum, esse, fuī, futūrus be, exist (2)

adsum (assum), adesse, affuī, —
be present (17)

prōsum, prōdesse, prōfuī, —
avail, profit, be advantageous
(to) (+ dat.) (17)

sūmō, sūmere, sūmpsī, sūmptus
take, obtain (29)

assūmō, assūmere, assūmpsī,
assūmptus take up (29)

super (prep.: 1. + acc.; 2. + abl.)
1. above, upon; over 2. about,
concerning (1)

supernus, -a, -um heavenly, celestial (8)

supersubstantiālis, supersubstantiāle life-sustaining (19)

supplex (gen., supplicis) suppliant (17)

supplicō, supplicāre, supplicāvī,
supplicātus (humbly) be-
seech (29)

sūrsum (adv.) on high, upward (19)

suscitō, suscitāre, suscitāvī, suscitātus awaken, raise up (29)

resuscitō, resuscitāre, resuscitāvī, resuscitātus reawaken, raise up again (29)

suus, -a, -um (third-person refl.
pron. adj.) one's [own] (i.e.,
his/her/its/their [own]) (28)

synagōga, synagōgae, f. congregation, synagogue (27)

taceō, tacēre, tacuī, tacitus be
silent (31)

tālis, tāle such, of such a sort (23)

tam (adv.) so, to such a degree (23)

tamen (adv.) nevertheless (12)

tangō, tangere, tetigī, tāctus
touch (21)

tantum (adv.) only (27)

tantus, -a, -um so much, so
great (23)

tardus, -a, -um slow (E27)

tēctum, tēctī, n. roof, house (9)

tellūs, tellūris, f. earth (17)

templum, templī, n. temple,
church (6)

tempus, temporis, n. time (27)

tendō, tendere, tetendī, tentus
(tēnsus) stretch, extend (18)

extendō, extendere, extendī,
extentus (extēnsus) stretch
out (18)
intendō, intendere, intendī,
intentus (intēnsus) aim (at),
look at intently (18)
ostendō, ostendere, ostendī,
ostentus (ostēnsus) show;
explain (18)
tenebrae, tenebrārum, f. *pl.* darkness, gloom (18)
teneō, tenēre, tenuī, tentus hold,
keep, possess, arrest (32)
contineō, continēre, continuī,
contentus hold together,
contain (32)
sustineō, sustinēre, sustinuī,
sustentus hold up, uphold,
sustain (32)
tentātiō, tentātiōnis, f. temptation, trial (28)
terra, terrae, f. earth, land,
ground (1)
terrēnus, -a, -um earthly (8)
tertius, -a, -um third (11)
testāmentum, testāmentī, n.
covenant, testament (3)
testimōnium, testimōniī, n.
witness, testimony (9)
testis, testis, testium, m. witness (28)
thronus, thronī, m. throne (32)
timeō, timēre, timuī, — fear,
be afraid (of) (25)
timor, timōris, m. fear (29)
timōrātus, -a, -um God-fearing,
devout, reverent (29)
tollō, tollere, sustulī, sublātus
take away, lift up, take up (10)
extollō, extollere, extulī, —
lift up, extol (10)
tōtus, -a, -um all, the whole (28)
trāditiō, trāditiōnis, f. tradi-
tion (E32)

trahō, trahere, trāxī, trāctus draw,
drag; lead (30)
attrahō, attrahere, attrāxī,
attrāctus draw toward (30)
dētrahō, dētrahere, dētrāxī,
dētrāctus draw from, take
away (30)
tranquillus, -a, -um peaceful,
tranquil (33)
trāns (*prep.* + *acc.*) across (2)
tremō, tremere, tremuī, —
tremble (at), quake (at) (35)
trīstis, trīste sad, sorrowful,
gloomy (28)
triumphus, triumphī, m. triumph
(26)
tū, tuī (*pron.*) you (19)
tuba, tubae, f. trumpet (13)
tueor, tuērī, —, tuitus sum watch,
protect, uphold (23)
tunc (*adv.*) then, at that time (8)
turba, turbae, f. crowd, multitude (7)
tuus, -a, -um your, yours (*sing.*) (4)
ubi (1. *interrog. adv.*; 2. *subord.*
conj.; 3. *rel. adv.*) 1. where? (4)
2. when, as soon as (13)
3. where, in which place (13)
ubīque (*adv.*) everywhere, anywhere (13)
umbra, umbrae, f. shadow,
shade (28)
unde (*interrog. & rel. adv.*) from
where (27)
ūnigenitus, -a, -um only begotten,
only (10)
ūnitās, ūnitātis, f. unity (25)
ūniversum, ūniversī, n. universe (3)
ūniversus, -a, -um all, the whole (7)
ūnus, -a, -um one; a, an (7)
ūnā (*adv.*) together (7)
urbs, urbis, urbium, f. city (31)
ūsque (*adv.*) as far as, all the
way (17)

ūsque ad (+ *acc.*) even to, up to, all the way to (17)

ut (*subord. conj.*) when, as (+ *ind.*) (13); in order that (*introducing purpose clause + subj.*) (22); that (*introducing indirect command + subj.*) (22) (*or result clause + subj.*) (23); that . . not (*introducing negative clause of fearing + subj.*) (25)

ūtilitās, ūtilitātis, f. benefit, profit, good (32)

utīque (*adv.*) certainly, by all means, at any rate (29)

ūtor, ūtī, —, ūsus sum (+ *abl.*) use, enjoy, be friends with (22)

  coūtor, coūtī, —, coūsus sum (*abl.*) associate on friendly terms with, have dealings with (E22)

uxor, uxōris, f. wife (E34)

vādō, vādere, —, — go, walk, hurry (24)

valdē (*adv.*) greatly, very (much) (20)

valeō, valēre, valuī, — be well, be strong; be able (+ *inf.*) (12)

varius, -a, -um various, diverse (E30)

vel (*coord. conj.*) or (if you prefer) (30)

vēlox (*gen.*, **velōcis**) quick, swift (E27)

velut (*adv.*) as, like (33)

vendō, vendere, vendidī, venditus sell (E28)

venerō, venerāre, venerāvī, venerātus
  or
veneror, venerārī, —, venerātus sum worship, venerate (28)

venia, veniae, f. indulgence, kindness (25)

veniō, venīre, vēnī, ventus come (6)

  adveniō, advenīre, advēnī, adventus come, arrive (6)

conveniō, convenīre, convēnī, conventus come together; be fitting (6)

inveniō, invenīre, invēnī, inventus come upon, find (6)

perveniō, pervenīre, pervēnī, perventus arrive; attain (18)

subveniō, subvenīre, subvēnī, subventus come upon; assist, come to help (+ *dat.*) (18)

superveniō, supervenīre, supervēnī, superventus come upon, overtake (+ *dat.*); come up, arrive (18)

venter, ventris, m. belly; womb (33)

ventus, ventī, m. wind (E34)

verber, verberis, n. lash; scourging (33)

verberō, verberāre, verberāvī, verberātus beat (32)

verbum, verbī, n. word (3)

vērē (*adv.*) truly (9)

vēritās, vēritātis, f. truth (24)

vērō (*adv.*) indeed; but indeed (20)

vertō, vertere, vertī, versus turn (31)

  āvertō, āvertere, āvertī, āversus turn away, remove (31)

  convertō, convertere, convertī, conversus
  or
convertor, convertī, —, conversus sum turn around, change, convert (31)

  revertor, revertī, —, reversus sum return (31)

vērus, -a, -um true (4)

vespertīnus, -a, -um (of) evening (29)

vester, vestra, vestrum your, yours (*pl.*) (9)

vestīgium, vestīgiī, n. footstep (9)

vestiō, vestīre, vestīvī (vestiī), vestītus clothe (21)

vestis, vestis, vestium, f. garment; clothing (31)

vetō, vetāre, vetuī (vetāvī), vetitus (vetātus) forbid (30)

vetus (gen., veteris) old, ancient; former (17)

via, viae, f. way, road, street (5)

vīcīnus, -a, -um neighboring (30)
vīcīnus, vīcīnī, m. neighbor (30)

victor, victōris, m. conqueror, victor (31)

victōria, victōriae, f. victory (7)

videō, vidēre, vīdī, vīsus see, realize (9)

videor, vidērī, —, vīsus sum be seen; seem (+ inf.) (12)

vinciō, vincīre, vīnxī, vīnctus bind (33)

vincō, vincere, vīcī, victus overcome, conquer (32)
dēvincō, dēvincere, dēvīcī, dēvictus overcome thoroughly, conquer thoroughly (32)

vinculum, vinculī, n. bond, chain (10)

vīnum, vīnī, n. wine (3)

vir, virī, m. man, husband (3)

virgō, virginis, f. virgin (14)

virtūs, virtūtis, f. excellence, virtue; power, strength; pl., miracles (27)

vīsibilis, vīsibile tangible, visible (17)

vīsiō, vīsiōnis, f. vision (E31)

vīta, vītae, f. life (1)

vītis, vītis, vītium, f. vine, grapevine (23)

vitium, vitiī, n. fault, sin, vice (3)

vituperō, vituperāre, vituperāvī, vituperātus scold, censure (E30)

vīvificō, vīvificāre, vīvificāvī, vīvificātus bring to life, make live (17)

vīvō, vīvere, vīxī, vīctus live (12)

vīvus, -a, -um living, alive (4)

vocō, vocāre, vocāvī, vocātus call, invite (5)
ēvocō, ēvocāre, ēvocāvī, ēvocātus call forth (5)
invocō, invocāre, invocāvī, invocātus call upon, invoke (5)

volō, velle, voluī, — want, wish, be willing (17)

voluntās, voluntātis, f. will (14)

vōtum, vōtī, n. vow; prayer (7)

vōx, vōcis, f. sound, voice (27)

vulnerō, vulnerāre, vulnerāvī, vulnerātus wound (19)

vultus, vultūs, m. face [i.e., countenance] (16)

English-Latin Vocabulary

This is a selection of vocabulary sufficient to translate the English-Latin sentences found in each unit.

able, be possum, posse, potuī, —
about dē (*prep.* + *abl.*)
according to secundum (*prep.* + *acc.*)
Adam Adam, Adae, m.
adhere to inhaereō, inhaerēre, inhaesī, inhaesus (+ *dat.*)
after (*subord. conj.*) postquam; *abl. abs.*
aid adjuvō, adjuvāre, adjūvī, adjūtus; succurrō, succurrere, succurrī, succursus
alive vīvus, -a, -um
all cūnctus, -a, -um; ūniversus, -a, -um; omnis, -e
allowed, be *use impers. 3 s. pass. of* permittere (+ *pers. dat. & inf.*)
alone (*adv.*) sōlum
also etiam
although quamquam, etsī, licet (+ *ind. or subj.*); *abl. abs.*; cum (+ *subj.*)
always semper
and et
angel angelus, angelī, m.
announce nūntiō, nūntiāre, nūntiāvī, nūntiātus; annūntiō, annūntiāre, annūntiāvī, annūntiātus
apostle apostolus, apostolī, m.
arrest teneō, tenēre, tenuī, tentus

arrive adveniō, advenīre, advēnī, adventus
as *use pred. acc.*
as soon as ubi; simul ac (atque) (+ *ind.*)
ascend ascendō, ascendere, ascendī, ascēnsus
ashamed, be cōnfundor, cōnfundī, —, cōnfūsus sum
ask rogō, rogāre, rogāvī, rogātus
assembly ecclēsia, ecclēsiae, f.
at ad (*prep.* + *acc.*)
at the same time simul
Athens Athēnae, Athēnārum, f.
await exspectō, exspectāre, exspectāvī, exspectātus
baptize baptizō, baptizāre, baptizāvī, baptizātus
be sum, esse, fuī, futūrus
beat verberō, verberāre, verberāvī, verberātus
because quia, quod, quoniam; *abl. abs.*
become fīō; fierī, —, factus sum
before (*prep.*) ante (*prep.* + *acc.*)
before (*subord. conj.*) antequam, priusquam (+ *ind. or subj.*)
begin incipiō, incipere, incēpī, inceptus; perfect-system tenses: —, —, coepī, coeptus
beginning prīncipium, prīncipiī, n.
believe (in) crēdō, crēdere, crēdidī, crēditus

beseech dēprecor, dēprecārī, —,
dēprecātus sum; rogō, rogāre,
rogāvī, rogātus; poscō, poscere,
poposcī, —

betray trādō, trādere, trādidī,
trāditus

bid jubeō, jubēre, jussī, jussus

bind vinciō, vincīre, vīnxī, vīnctus

bishop episcopus, episcopī, m.

blame culpa, culpae, f.

bless benedīcō, benedīcere,
benedīxī, benedictus

blessed beātus, -a, -um; benedictus, -a, -um

blood sanguis, sanguinis, m.

body corpus, corporis, n.

book liber, librī, m.

both . . and et . . et

boy puer, puerī, m.

bread pānis, pānis, pānium, m.

break frangō, frangere, frēgī, frāctus; cōnfringō, cōnfringere,
cōnfrēgī, cōnfrāctus

breathe spīrō, spīrāre, spīrāvī,
spīrātus

bring ferō, ferre, tulī, lātus

bring forward prōferō, prōferre,
prōtulī, prōlātus

brother frāter, frātris, m.

bury sepeliō, sepelīre, sepelīvī
(sepeliī), sepultus

but sed

buy emō, emere, ēmī, ēmptus

by ā (ab, abs) (*prep.* + *abl.*); *abl.*
case alone

call vocō, vocāre, vocāvī, vocātus;
pass. of dīcō 'be called'

call upon invocō, invocāre,
invocāvī, invocātus

can possum, posse, potuī, —

canticle canticum, canticī, n.

cantor cantor, cantōris, m.

care cūra, cūrae, f.

cast out ējiciō, ējicere, ējēcī,
ējectus

cease dēsinō, dēsinere, dēsiī,
dēsitus

celebrate celebrō, celebrāre,
celebrāvī, celebrātus

chief prīnceps, prīncipis, m.

child nātus, nātī, m.; puer,
puerī, m.

choose legō, legere, lēgī, lēctus;
ēligō, ēligere, ēlēgī, ēlēctus

chosen ēlēctus, -a, -um

Christ Chrīstus, Chrīstī, m.

Christian Chrīstiānus, -a, -um

church ecclēsia, ecclēsiae, f.

city cīvitās, cīvitātis, f.; urbs,
urbis, urbium, f.

clean mundus, -a, -um

clemency clēmentia, clēmentiae, f.

climb subeō, subīre, subiī, subitus; scandō, scandere, scandī,
scānsus

come veniō, venīre, vēnī, ventus

coming adventus, adventūs, m.

command praeceptum, praeceptī, n.

commandment mandātum,
mandātī, n.

concern cūra, cūrae, f.

confound cōnfundō, cōnfundere,
cōnfūdī, cōnfūsus

conquer vincō, vincere, vīcī, victus; dēvincō, dēvincere, dēvīcī,
dēvictus

consecrate sacrō, sacrāre, sacrāvī,
sacrātus; cōnsecrō, cōnsecrāre,
cōnsecrāvī, cōnsecrātus

consider habeō, habēre, habuī,
habitus

consider worthy dīgnor, dīgnārī,
—, dīgnātus sum

console sōlor, sōlārī, —, sōlātus
sum; cōnsōlor, cōnsōlārī, —,
cōnsōlātus sum

continue perseverō, perseverāre,
perseverāvī, perseverātus

contrite contrītus, -a, -um
cross crux, crucis, f.
crowd turba, turbae, f.
crown corōnō, corōnāre, corōnāvī, corōnātus
cup calix, calicis, m.
cure cūrō, cūrāre, cūrāvī, cūrātus
dare audeō, audēre; —, ausus sum
darkness tenebrae, tenebrārum, f.
daughter fīlia, fīliae, f.
deacon diāconus, diāconī, m.
dead mortuus, -a, -um
death mors, mortis, mortium, f.
defend dēfendō, dēfendere, dēfendī, dēfēnsus
devout dēvōtus, -a, -um
die morior, morī, —, mortuus sum (*fut. act. part.*, moritūrus, -a, -um)
difficult difficilis, difficile
dinner, eat cēnō, cēnāre, cēnāvī, cēnātus; cēnam mandūcāre
disciple discipulus, disciplī, m.
do faciō, facere, fēcī, factus
do not (command) nōlī/nōlīte (+ *inf.*)
drag away dētrahō, dētrahere, dētrāxī, dētrāctus
draw near appropinquō, appropinquāre, appropinquāvī, appropinquātus
drink pōtus, pōtūs, m.
earth terra, terrae, f.
eat mandūcō, mandūcāre, mandūcāvī, mandūcātus
elder major; senior
elect ēlēctus, -a, -um
end fīniō, fīnīre, fīnīvī (fīniī), fīnītus
enemy inimīcus, inimīcī, m.; hostēs, hostium, m.
enough satis
enter intrō, intrāre, intrāvī, intrātus
eternal aeternus, -a, -um

evil malus, -a, -um
evil spirit daemonium, daemoniī, n.
express exprimō, exprimere, expressī, expressus
faith fidēs, fideī, f.
faithful fidēlis, -e
fall cadō, cadere, cecidī, cāsus
fall forward prōcidō, procidere, procidī, —
family famīlia, famīliae, f.
father pater, patris, m.
fault culpa, culpae, f.
fear timeō, timēre, timuī, —
field ager, agrī, m.
find inveniō, invenīre, invēnī, inventus
finger digitus, digitī, m.
first prīmus, -a, -um
flee fugiō, fugere, fūgī, fugitus
flock grex, gregis, m.
follow sequor, sequī, —, secūtus sum
food cibus, cibī, m.
for nam (*coord. conj.*); *dat. case alone*; (= in/on behalf of) prō (*prep. + abl.*)
for the purpose of ad (*prep. + acc.*); in (*prep. + acc.*)
for the sake of causā (+ *preceding gen.*)
forbid vetō, vetāre, vetuī (vetāvī), vetitus (vetātus)
force cōgō, cōgere, coēgī, coāctus
forefathers antīquī, antīquōrum, m.
forever in aeternum
free līberō, līberāre, līberāvī, līberātus
friend amīcus, amīcī, m.
from *abl. of separation*; (*away*) ā (ab, abs) (*prep. + abl.*); (*out of*) ē (ex) (*prep. + abl.*)
Galilaean Galilaeus, -a, -um
Galilee Galilaea, Galilaeae, f.

gift dōnum, dōnī, n.
give dō, dare, dedī, datus; dōnō,
dōnāre, dōnāvī, dōnātus
give back reddō, reddere, reddidī,
redditus
give thanks to grātiās agere
(+ dat.)
glory glōria, glōriae, f.
go eō, īre, īvī (iī), itus; vādō,
vādere, —, —
go around circu(m)eō, circu(m)-
īre, circu(m)īvī (circu(m)iī),
circu(m)itus
go away abeō, abīre, abīvī (abiī),
abitus
go in ineō, inīre, inīvī (iniī), initus
go out exeō, exīre, exīvī (exiī),
exitus
God Deus, Deī, m.
gold aurum, aurī, n.
good bonus, -a, -um
Gospel Evangelium, Evangeliī, n.
grace grātia, grātiae, f.
grant dōnō, dōnāre, dōnāvī,
dōnātus
grapevine vītis, vītis, vītium, f.
greater major, majus
greatest maximus, -a, -um
guard custōdiō, custōdīre, custōdiī, custōdītus
hand manus, manūs, f.
happy beātus, -a, -um; fēlīx (gen.,
fēlīcis)
hatred odium, odiī, n.
have dat. of the possessor with
sum; habeō, habēre, habuī,
habitus
he use is, ea, id
heal sānō, sānāre, sānāvī, sānātus
hear audiō, audīre, audīvī (audiī),
audītus
heart cor, cordis, cordium, n.
heaven caelum, caelī, n.
help (noun) ops, opis, f.

help (verb) adjuvō, adjuvāre,
adjūvī, adjūtus
here hīc; ecce
high altus, -a, -um
holy sacer, sacra, sacrum; sānctus,
-a, -um
honor honor, honōris, m.
hope (noun) spēs, speī, f.
hope (verb) spērō, spērāre, spērāvī,
spērātus
hour hōra, hōrae, f.
house domus, domī, f.
how quōmodo
human hūmānus, -a, -um
human being homō, hominis, m.
humanity hūmānitās, hūmānitātis, f.
hungry, be ēsuriō, ēsurīre, ēsurīvī
(ēsuriī), ēsuritus
I ego, meī (pron.)
if sī
in in (prep. + abl.)
in behalf of prō (prep. + abl.)
in order that ut (+ subj.)
in the presence of cōram (prep. +
abl.)
incense incēnsum, incēnsī, n.
indulgence venia, veniae, f.
innocence innocentia, innocentiae, f.
instruct moneō, monēre, monuī,
monitus; īnstruō, īnstruere,
īnstrūxī, īnstrūctus; praecipiō,
praecipere, praecēpī, praeceptus
into in (prep. + acc.)
Jesus Jēsūs (see Unit 7)
Jerusalem, in Hierosolymīs
Jew Jūdaeus, -a, -um
John Jōannēs, Jōannis, m.
joy gaudium, gaudiī, n.
joyful laetus, -a, -um
Judea Jūdaea, Jūdaeae, f.
judge jūdicō, jūdicāre, jūdicāvī, jūdicātus; exīstimō, exīstimāre,
exīstimāvī, exīstimātus

justice jūstitia, jūstitiae, f.
kindly benīgnus, -a, -um
king rēx, rēgis, m.
kingdom rēgnum, rēgnī, n.
know, get to nōscō, nōscere
know beforehand praenōscō, praenōscere, praenōvī, praenōtus
know, know how sciō, scīre, scīvī,
scītus
lamb agnus, agnī, m.
lead dūcō, dūcere, dūxī, ductus
lead into indūcō, indūcere, indūxī,
inductus
Levite Lēvīta (Lēvītēs), Lēvītae, m.
life vīta, vītae, f.
light lūmen, lūminis, n.
like similis, -e; pār (*gen.*, paris)
living vīvus, -a, -um
lord dominus, dominī, m.
love (*noun*) dīlēctiō, dīlēctiōnis, f.
love (*verb*) dīligō, dīligere, dīlēxī,
dīlēctus; amō, amāre, amāvī,
amātus
Luke Lūcās, Lūcae, m.
Magi magī, magōrum, m.
make faciō, facere, fēcī, factus;
efficiō, efficere, effēcī, effectus;
pass.: fīō; fierī, —, factus sum
man vir, virī, m.
many multus, -a, -um
martyr martyr, martyris, m.
Mary Marīa, Marīae, f.
master dominus, dominī, m.;
magister, magistrī, m.
meet up with occurrō, occurrere,
occurrī, occursus (+ *dat.*)
mercy misericordia, misericordiae, f.
mind mēns, mentis, mentium, f.
mindful memor (*gen.*, memoris)
minister minister, ministrī, m.
ministry ministerium, ministeriī, n.
more important *see* greater

mother māter, mātris, f.
mountain mōns, montis, montium, m.
multitude turba, turbae, f.; multitūdō, multitūdinis, f.; numerus,
numerī, m.
must *use passive periphrastic*
my meus, -a, -um
name nōmen, nōminis, n.
nature nātūra, nātūrae, f.
nearest proximus, -a, -um
necessary, it is necesse est; oportet, oportēre, oportuit, —
neighbor proximus, -a, -um
nevertheless tamen
new novus, -a, -um
night nox, noctis, noctium, f.
no nūllus, -a, -um
not nōn; nē
obey oboediō, oboedīre, oboedīvī
(oboediī), oboedītus
odor odor, odōris, m.
of *gen. case alone*
offering oblātiō, oblātiōnis, f.
on in (*prep.* + *abl.*)
one another invicem
only ūnigenitus, -a, -um
or aut
ought dēbeō, dēbēre, dēbuī, dēbitus; *passive periphrastic*
our noster, nostra, nostrum
Paul Paulus, Paulī, m.
peace pāx, pācis, f.
people populus, populī, m.
permit permittō, permittere,
permīsī, permissus
permitted, it is licet, licēre, licuit
(licitum est)
Peter Petrus, Petrī, m.
please placeō, placēre, placuī,
placitus
pleasing (to) grātus, -a, -um
(+ *dat.*)
poor pauper (*gen.*, pauperis)

pope pāpa, pāpae, m.
power potentia, potentiae, f.
praise laudō, laudāre, laudāvī, laudātus
pray ōrō, ōrāre, ōrāvī, ōrātus; precor, precārī, —, precātus sum
prayer ōrātiō, ōrātiōnis, f.
preach praedicō, praedicāre, praedicāvī, praedicātus
preach the Gospel evangelizō, evangelizāre, evangelizāvī, evangelizātus
precept praeceptum, praeceptī, n.
precious pretiōsus, -a, -um
prepare parō, parāre, parāvī, parātus; praeparō, praeparāre, praeparāvī, praeparātus
priest sacerdōs, sacerdōtis, m.
prince prīnceps, prīncipis, m.
psalm psalmus, psalmī, m.
purification pūrgātiō, pūrgātiōnis, f.
put mittō, mittere, mīsī, missus; pōnō, pōnere, posuī, positus
put to flight fugō, fugāre, fugāvī, fugātus
receive capiō, capere, cēpī, captus; accipiō, accipere, accēpī, acceptus
redeem redimō, redimere, redēmī, redēmptus
redeemer redēmptor, redēmptōris, m.
refresh reficiō, reficere, refēcī, refectus
regard respiciō, respicere, respexī, respectus
rejoice exsultō, exsultāre, exsultāvī, exsultātus; gaudeō, gaudēre; —, gāvīsus sum; laetor, laetārī, —, laetātus sum
remain maneō, manēre, mānsī, mānsus; permaneō, permanēre, permānsī, permānsus
resurrection resurrēctiō, resurrēctiōnis, f.

return regredior, regredī, —, regressus sum; revertor, revertī, —, reversus sum
reveal revēlō, revēlāre, revēlāvī, revēlātus
rich dīves (gen., dīvitis)
right hand dextera, dexterae, f.
rightly meritō (adv.)
Roman Rōmānus, -a, -um
Rome Rōma, Rōmae, f.
ruin ruīna, ruīnae, f.
rule rēgnō, rēgnāre, rēgnāvī, rēgnātus; regō, regere, rēxī, rēctus
Sabbath sabbatum, sabbatī, n.
sacrifice sacrificium, sacrificiī, n.
sad maestus, -a, -um
safe salvus, -a, -um
save servō, servāre, servāvī, servātus; facere + salvus, -a, -um
saving salūtifer, -a, -um
savior salvātor, salvātōris, m.
say dīcō, dīcere, dīxī, dictus
say . . not negō, negāre, negāvī, negātus
scripture scrīptūra, scrīptūrae, f.
see videō, vidēre, vīdī, vīsus
seek petō, petere, petīvī (petiī), petītus; quaerō, quaerere, quaesīvī, quaesītus; requīrō, requīrere, requīsīvī, requīsītus
seem videor, vidērī, —, vīsus sum
-self ipse, ipsa, ipsum
send mittō, mittere, mīsī, missus
servant famulus, famulī, m.; servus, servī, m.
serve serviō, servīre, servīvī (serviī), servītus (+ dat.)
sharer particeps, participis, m. & f.
shepherd pāstor, pāstōris, m.
show mōnstrō, mōnstrāre, mōnstrāvī, mōnstrātus; ostendō, ostendere, ostendī, ostentus (ostēnsus)
sick īnfirmus, -a, -um; male habentēs

side latus, lateris, n.
signify sīgnificō, sīgnificāre, sīgnificāvī, sīgnificātus
silence silentium, silentiī, n.
silent, be taceō, tacēre, tacuī, tacitus
sin peccātum, peccātī, n.
since cum (+ *subj.*); *abl. abs.*
sing cantō, cantāre, cantāvī, cantātus
sit (down) sedeō, sedēre, sēdī, sessus
sky caelum, caelī, n.
so ita; tam; sīc
so great tantus, -a, -um
soldier mīles, mīlitis, m.
some (*pron.*) aliquis, aliquid
some . . others aliī . . aliī
son fīlius, fīliī, m.
soon jam
sorrow dolor, dolōris, m.
sorrowful dolōrōsus, -a, -um
spare parcō, parcere, pepercī (parsī), parsus
speak loquor, loquī, —, locūtus sum
spirit spīritus, spīritūs, m.
sprinkle spargō, spargere, sparsī, sparsus; aspergō, aspergere, aspersī, aspersus
stand stō, stāre, stetī, status
stand at astō, astāre, astitī, —
stand by astō, astāre, astitī, —
star stēlla, stēllae, f.
still adhūc
strengthen firmō, firmāre, firmāvī, firmātus; cōnfirmō, cōnfirmāre, cōnfirmāvī, cōnfirmātus
stretch out extendō, extendere, extendī, extentus (extēnsus)
suddenly subitō
supper cēna, cēnae, f.
sustain sustineō, sustinēre, sustinuī, sustentus
sweet suāvis, -e

take capiō, capere, cēpī, captus; sūmō, sūmere, sūmpsī, sūmptus
take pity (on) misereor, miserērī, —, misertus sum
take up assūmō, assūmere, assūmpsī, assūmptus
teach doceō, docēre, docuī, doctus
teacher doctor, doctōris, m.; magister, magistrī, m.
teaching doctrīna, doctrīnae, f.
tell dīcō, dīcere, dīxī, dictus
temple templum, templī, n.
that (*subord. conj.*) quia, quod, quoniam; ut (*introducing result clause*); nē (*introducing affirmative fear clause*)
that . . not ut (*introducing negative fear clause*)
then tunc
think putō, putāre, putāvī, putātus; cōgitō, cōgitāre, cōgitāvī, cōgitātus
third tertius, -a, -um
this hic, haec, hoc; is, ea, id; iste, ista, istud
three trēs, tria
throne thronus, thronī, m.
through per (*prep.* + *acc.*)
time tempus, temporis, n.
to ad (*prep.* + *acc.*); *dat. case alone*
today hodiē
tongue lingua, linguae, f.
too much nimis
track down persequor, persequī, —, persecūtus sum
train fōrmō, fōrmāre, fōrmāvī, fōrmātus
true vērus, -a, -um
try cōnor, cōnārī, —, cōnātus sum
twelve duodecim
unceasing assiduus, -a, -um
unclean immundus, -a, -um
unfailing indēficiēns (*gen.*, indēficientis)

universe ūniversum, ūniversī, n.
used to *imperfect tense*
victory victōria, victōriae, f.
voice vōx, vōcis, f.
want volō, velle, voluī, —
watch respiciō, respicere, respexī,
    respectus; observō, observāre,
    observāvī, observātus
water aqua, aquae, f.
way modus, modī, m.
well bene
weep lacrimor, lacrimārī, —, lacrī
    mātus sum
what? (*interrog. adj.*) quī, quae,
    quod
when cum (+ *ind.*); quandō
where ubi
which (*interrog. adj.*) quī, quae,
    quod
which (*interrog. pron.*) *use* quid
while dōnec; dum
who quī, quae, quod
whoever quīcumque, quaecum-
    que, quodcumque
whole, the tōtus, -a, -um;
    ūniversus, -a, -um
why quārē

wicked impius, -a, -um; malus,
    -a, -um
wine vīnum, vīnī, n.
wipe out dēleō, dēlēre, dēlēvī,
    dēlētus
wisdom sapientia, sapientiae, f.
wish volō, velle, voluī, —
with cum (*prep.* + *abl.*); *abl. case
    alone*
without sine (*prep.* + *abl.*)
woman mulier, mulieris, f.
wood lignum, lignī, n.
worthy dīgnus, -a, -um (+ *abl.*)
word verbum, verbī, n.
work operō, operāre, operāvī, ope-
    rātus; operor, operārī, —, ope-
    rātus sum; labōrō, labōrāre,
    labōrāvī, labōrātus
work together cooperor, cooperārī,
    —, cooperātus sum
world mundus, mundī, m.
worship adōrō, adōrāre, adōrāvī,
    adōrātus
wretched miser, -a, -um
write scrībō, scrībere, scrīpsī,
    scrīptus
your, yours (*sing.*) tuus, -a, -um

Index

Reading passages are indexed under the headings "Readings" and "Further Readings."

The Hidden Churches in Rome

by Tim O'Donnell